Social research: principles and procedures

Social research:
principles and procedures

Edited by
John Bynner and Keith M. Stribley
at The Open University

Published by
Longman in association with
The Open University Press

Longman Group Limited London

*Associated companies, branches and representatives
throughout the world*

*Published in the United States of America
by Longman Inc., New York*

Selection and editorial material
copyright© The Open University 1978.

First published 1979

British Library Cataloguing in Publication Data

Social research.
   1. Social sciences – Methodology
   I. Bynner, John Morgan   II. Stribley, Keith M
   300'.7'2   H61   78-40423

ISBN 0-582-29501-7

Printed in Great Britain by Richard Clay (The Chaucer Press) Ltd, Bungay, Suffolk

Contents

Acknowledgements

We are grateful to the following for permission to reproduce copyright material:

Aldine Publishing Co., for an extract from *The Logic of Science in Sociology* by Walter Wallace, and *The Logic of Social Inquiry* by Scott Greer; The American Marketing Association for an extract from 'Interviewer Bias Once More Revisited' by H. W. Boyd and R. Westfall from *Journal of Marketing Research* 1970 Vol 7; The American Psychological Association and the authors for an extract from 'Reforms as Experiments' by D. T. Campbell from *American Psychologist* No. 4 © 1969 by the American Psychological Association, reprinted by permission, an extract from 'Human Use of Human Subjects' by Herbert C. Kelman from *Psychological Bulletin* Vol 67 No. 1 © 1967 by the American Psychological Association, reprinted by permission, and an extract from 'Construct Validity in Psychological Tests' by L. J. Cronbach and P. E. Meehl from *Psychological Bulletin* Vol 52 © 1955 by the American Psychological Association, reprinted by permission; The American Sociological Association and the authors for an extract from 'Some Statistical Problems in Research Design' by Leslie Kish from *American Sociological Review* Vol 24 pp. 328–338 1959, and an extract from 'Problems of Inference and Proof in Participant Observation' by Howard S. Becker from *American Sociological Review* Vol 23 pp. 652–660, 1958; American Statistical Association for an extract from 'Data Dredging Procedures in Survey Analysis' by H. C. Selvin and A. Stuart from *The American Statistician* Vol 20 1966; Basic Books Inc., for an extract from Chapter 2 of *The Logic of Survey Analysis* by Morris Rosenberg Foreword © 1968 by Basic Books Inc., Publishers, New York; Heinemann Educational Books Ltd., and Basic Books Inc., for an extract from *Survey Methods in Social Investigation* 2nd Edition by C. A. Moser and G. Kalton pp. 318–341 © C. A. Moser and G. J. Kalton 1958, 1971, Basic Books Inc., Publishers, New York, and *Questionnaire Design and Attitude Measurement* by A. N. Oppenheim pp. 227–248 © 1966 by A. N. Oppenheim, Basic Books Inc., Publishers, New York; The Journal of Philosophy for an extract from 'Concept and Theory Formation in the Social Sciences' by the late Alfred Schutz pp. 259–272 from *Journal of Philosophy* Vol II No. 9 April 29th 1954; McCutchan Publishing Corporation for an extract from 'Generalised Regression Analysis' by D. J. Amick and H. J. Walberg pp. 8–34 and 52 from *Introductory Multivariate Analysis* by Daneil J. Amick and Herbert J. Walberg. Berkeley: McCutchan Publishing Corporation 1975. Reprinted by permission of the Publisher; Oxford University Press for an extract from 'Attitude Measurement: Use of co-efficient Alpha with Cluster or Factor Analysis' by A. MacKennell from *Sociology 4 1970,* published by Oxford University Press; Routledge and Kegan Paul Ltd., and Cornel University Press for an extract from *Explanation and Understanding* by G. H. Von Wright pp. 169–173 Copyright © 1971 by Cornell University. Used by permission of the Publisher, Cornell University Press, Routledge and Kegan Paul Ltd., and Sir Karl Popper for an extract from *The Poverty of Historicism* by K. R. Popper pp. 130–143. First published by Routledge and Kegan Paul, London 1957, and Basic Books, New York 1964; also Harper Torch Books 1977; The Royal Statistical Society and the author, W. A. Belson for an extract from 'A Comparison of the Check-List and the Open Response Questioning Systems' pp. 120–132 by W. A. Belson and J. A. Duncan from *Applied Statistics* J.R. Statist. Soc., Series C, Vol II Part 2 (1962); Sage Publications Inc., and the author, Jacqueline P. Wiseman for an extract from 'The Research Web' by Jacqueline P. Wiseman from *Urban Life and Culture* Vol 3, No. 3 (October 1974) pp. 317–329 by permission of the Publisher, Sage Publications Inc; The Society for Applied Anthropology, and the author, William F. Whyte for an extract from 'How Do You Know If The Informant is Telling The Truth?' by the late J. P. Dean and W. F. Whyte from *Human Organisation* Vol 17 pp. 36–38 1958 reproduced by permission of the Society for Applied Anthropology; The Society for the Study of Social Problems and the authors for an extract from 'A Note on the Uses of Official Statistics' by John I. Kitsuse and A. V. Cicourel pp. 131–139 from *Social Problems* Vol II: 2 (Fall 1963); The University of Chicago Press and the author, Morris Zelditch for an extract from 'Some Methodological Problems of Field Studies' by Morris Zelditch pp. 566–567 from *American Journal of Sociology* Vol 67 1962; The University of North Carolina Press and the author, Norman K. Denzin, for an extract from *The Logic of Naturalistic Inquiry* by Norman K. Denzin pp. 166–169, 181–182 Reprinted from *Social Forces* Vol 50, December 1971 © The University of North Carolina Press; the author, Professor Arthur J. Vidich for an extract from 'Problems in the Publication of Field Studies' by H. S. Becker pp. 267–284 from *Reflections on Community Studies* by A. J. Vidich, J. Bensman and M. R. Stein, 1964.

Editors' acknowledgements

We wish to thank all those who have contributed towards the preparation of this reader but particularly the following.

The members of the Open University *Research Methods in Education and the Social Sciences* course team whose suggestions and comments on the various readings considered for inclusion were especially helpful. They were: Michael Wilson, Bob Peacock, John Bibby, Martyn Hammersley, Jeff Evans, Peter Coxhead, Martin Bulmer, Paul Atkinson, Desmond Nuttall and Cathie Marsh.

John Taylor of the Open University Publishing Department who advised on the preparation of the manuscript.

Our secretaries, Cathy Bayntun and Betty Gregory, merit special thanks for assistance that was as valuable as it was varied.

General introduction

Research methodology in social science is a topic of never-ending fascination. As the subjects of our studies are active, thinking, 'actors' with the full complement of motives, intentions and purposes, how can we find explanations of what they do and make precise predictions of what they are likely to do next as the natural scientist has been able to do with such consummate success in his study of natural phenomena? This question takes us to the core of the continuing debate in social science. How can we formulate a rigorous strategy for investigating social phenomena and how can we implement it? The mode of explanation we adopt, and the medium by which we ensure reliability, validity and generalizability of the models we construct, constitute the principles and procedures of social enquiry. In this book we shall see how different writers contribute to our understanding of them.

Three major themes underlie the selection of readings. The first is concerned with the variety of research methods currently in use in social science which relate to major differences in 'style' of research approach or methodology. Three such styles can be usefully identified, differing from each other both in relation to the mode of explanation they chose to employ and the importance they attach to particular methodological problems. The first of these styles may be described as 'interpretative', i.e. relying for explanation on the interpretations people themselves put on the reasons lying behind their actions. It is perhaps best symbolized by the school of research known as ethnography, which emphasizes naturalistic observation of phenomena in the field and seeks insights into social behaviour gained from data which are as unadulterated as possible by the procedures the researcher employs and the preconceptions he brings with him. Issues that concern him particularly are the accuracy of the information he collects, the problem of the role he has to adopt in collecting it and the generalizability of his findings outside the particular research setting. In sharp contrast to ethnography, we have the 'experimental' style of research in which the emphasis is on rigorous *testing* of hypotheses. Most widely employed by psychologists among social scientists, the experimental style takes segments of behaviour away from the 'natural habitat' into the controlled conditions of the psychological laboratory.

By manipulating one or other features of the experimental situation, the experimenter is able to observe changes in behaviour, which are then interpreted in terms of his predetermined hypotheses. Valid interpretation of experimental results depends on reliable and valid measurement of all the variables included and control of as many extraneous influences as possible that might vitiate the results. But of increasing concern to experimenters in recent years has been the cost of this scientific rigour to the generalizability of the results. Experiments are artificially contrived examples of social behaviour and there is no certainty that what occurs in them will occur under natural conditions as well. There is also the issue of where the boundary should be drawn between what is and is not permissible in developing a science of human behaviour. Are deception and even the infliction of pain illegitimate means to justify a scientific end under any circumstances, or is it simply a matter of the degree to which they are used that should cause concern?

Despite the problems inherent in experimental research, which rule it out from a wide field of social investigation, it does nevertheless provide a model for the logic of scientific enquiry which no social researcher can completely disregard. Our third style of enquiry, survey investigation, acknowledges this with its emphasis on reliability in data collection, and statistical control of variables using multivariate methods of data analysis in place of the physical controls of the laboratory. Again as a reaction to the major weakness of experiments, the prime concern of survey researchers is with the generalizability of results, both with respect to the population which the survey attempts to describe and with respect to the range of variables that it encompasses in a single investigation. Thus sample design and the procedures of data collection and measurement continue to absorb the attentions of survey researchers, and a great body of methodological literature concerned with these issues exists. The survey therefore can be seen to fall somewhere in between the two extremes of ethnographic investigation and laboratory experiment, sometimes mirroring the latter in the attempt to assess causes, e.g. 'quasi experiments', and the former where there is often an emphasis on extended exploratory and pilot work before the main survey.

But it would be wrong to see the three styles of research reflected in this reader as occupying discrete regions of a continuum. In reality the particular techniques researchers use cross the boundaries between them and in so far as the distinction between styles is worth making it is more to illuminate the emphasis that different researchers place on particular methodological problems.

Variety of method is the first major organizing principle for this book; the second is originality of approach. Throughout the history of social science a number of seminal contributions to methodology have been made by some outstanding writers. Identifying such contributions for a book as short as this one is clearly a highly subjective matter, but few people would probably deny that such people as Kish, Campbell, Cronbach, Zelditch and Becker deserve a place in any book that hopes to display methodological advances.

The third organizing principle for this book is one of clarity of exposition. Social science teaching abounds with text books on methodology, some of which have become classics of their kind. It would seem a serious omission in a book of readings to ignore such contributions to the literature, many of which are as important in the way they illuminate complex topics as those produced as articles for journals. Accordingly, in each section of the book, we have included at least one major extract from a methodology text.

The book is organized in a number of sections which parallel the Open University course, *Research Methods in Education and the Social Sciences,* for which it has been produced. This course presents research methods in terms of the stages of a typical experimental research programme – design, data collection, data analysis – which, particularly in the case of ethnography, are artificial distinctions. Consequently at times a particular reading may span several parts of the book. The first section displays some of the philosophical underpinnings of the different methodological styles and is followed by a lengthy section dealing with a number of salient issues in research design. The section following looks at data collection methods, considering particularly the problem of systematic bias in the data collected and ways in which researchers may attempt to reduce it. The book then moves to a section on measurement in which the central issues of reliability, validity and scale construction are taken up, and then on to a section on data analysis, which deals with some of the central issues in analysing both qualitative and quantitative data. Besides techniques of analysis the section also looks in some detail at the whole problem of inferring cause and effect from data and the writing up of research.

The language of social research

Introduction

In this section we introduce some of the basic terminology of social research and look at its epistemological foundations. The first reading by Wallace presents a useful model of the scientific process in which most of the key terms appear and introduces some of the principal actors on the research stage; theorist, research director, interviewer, sampling expert, statistician, etc. An important theme is also introduced: the distinction in the development of theory between 'discovery' and 'testing'. More of a historical perspective is presented in the next reading, from Von Wright, who usefully outlines the two major traditions of sociological enquiry, positivism, which looks to natural science as the only true model; and idealism of the kind espoused by Max Weber, who emphasized the notion of *'Verstehen'* or 'empathic understanding', as the distinctive feature of the human or social sciences.

These two traditions lay the foundation for one of the main distinctions in methodologies that we present in this book, the ethnographic as opposed to the experimental. The exploration is taken a stage further with Popper's classic discussion in *Poverty of Historicism* which, in line with the positivist tradition described by Von Wright, argues for the unity of all scientific method. Popper reduces all scientific reasoning to one basic principle, *falsificationism*. A scientific proposition is one that is capable of being disproved, and science advances as falsified propositions fall away through rigorous tests, leaving a core of theory which it has not yet been possible to disprove. To Popper the source of such propositions/hypotheses is of little significance; it is the creative element in the process of science which is unanalysable. To those working in the more idealistic or interpretative tradition, however, the source of social science concepts and the hypotheses expressing their relations is of crucial importance; for to them the theories of social phenomena are relatively worthless unless rooted within the meaning systems of the actors to whom they relate. In a rather difficult but powerful article, Alfred Schutz (Reading 4), argues this case, in no way contradicting Popper's demand for scientific rigour in the development of theory, but parting company with him in his belief that there are no rules to guide the origins of this theory.

Schutz's position is summed up through his conception of the 'homunculus', an idealized type of individual representing a culture/social group, typical with respect to intentions and purposes of the group members, and therefore recognizable to them. It is the job of the social scientist to build his higher level abstractions/explanatory concepts from his conceptions of the interactions of such homunculi, firmly rooted in the culture which they themselves have constructed.

Schutz's argument is brought down to earth by the introduction, reproduced here, to a lengthy article on methodology by Denzin (Reading 5). Denzin argues for a 'naturalistic behaviourism' which, following Schutz's suggestions, remains firmly based in the concepts of everyday life but uses the full tool-kit of the empirical investigator to develop theory. Unlike many such researchers, Denzin's concern here is with the origins of theory as well as with the methods by which it is tested. Thus he welcomes the full battery of quantitative or non-quantitative techniques which may be appropriate to particular problems in the social sciences. As he puts it in a footnote, 'It is the use to which the method is put and the degree of rigour under which it is employed that determines its usefulness. The quantitatively orientated researcher, then, can also share the naturalistic perspective.' Denzin's article seems an appropriate point to begin an examination of writings on the various stages of the social scientific process itself. He brings a refreshing openness of approach to the whole subject, advocating in effect both the rigour, which is the cornerstone of Popper's arguments, with the grounding of social science theory advocated by Schutz.

An overview of elements in the scientific process

Walter Wallace

The scientific process may be described as involving five principal information components whose transformations into one another are controlled by six principal sets of methods, in the general manner shown in Fig. 1.1 [. . .] In brief translation, Fig. 1.1 indicates the following ideas:

Individual observations are highly specific and essentially unique items of information whose synthesis into the more general form denoted by empirical generalizations is accomplished by measurement, sample summarization and parameter estimation. Empirical generalizations, in turn, are items of information that can be synthesized into a theory via concept formation, proposition formation and proposition arrangement. A theory, the most general type of information, is transformable into new hypotheses through the method of logical deduction. An empirical hypothesis is an information item that becomes transformed into new observations via interpretation of the hypothesis into observables, instrumentation, scaling and sampling. These new observations are transformable into new empirical generalizations (again, via measurement, sample summarization and parameter estimation), and the hypothesis that occasioned their construction may then be tested for conformity to them. Such tests may result in a new informational outcome: namely, a decision to accept or reject the truth of the tested hypothesis. Finally, it is inferred that the latter gives confirmation, modification or rejection of the theory[1].

Before going any further in detailing the meaning of Fig. 1.1 and of the translation above, I must emphasize that the processes described there occur (1) sometimes quickly, sometimes slowly; (2) sometimes with a very high degree of formalization and rigor, sometimes quite informally, unself-consciously and intuitively; (3) sometimes through the interaction of several scientists in distinct roles (of, say, 'theorist', 'research director', 'interviewer', 'methodologist', 'sampling expert',

Walter Wallace, 'An overview of elements in the scientific process', from *The Logic of Science in Sociology*. Chicago: Aldine-Atherton, 1971, Introduction, pp. 16–25.
*Superior numerals apply to Notes at end of Reading.

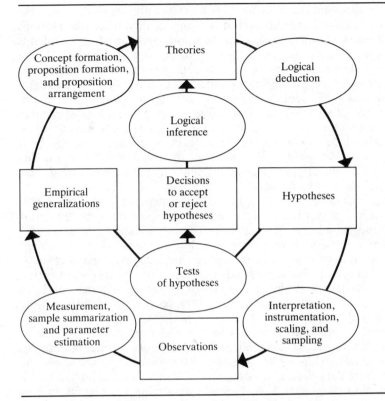

Fig. 1.1 The principal informational components (rectangles), methodological controls (ovals) and information transformations (arrows) of the scientific process.

'statistician', etc.), sometimes through the efforts of a single scientist; and (4) sometimes only in the scientist's imagination, sometimes in actual fact. In other words, although Fig. 1.1 [is] intended to be [a] *systematic* rendering of science as a field of socially organized human endeavor, it is not intended to be inflexible. The task I have chosen is to set forth the principal common elements – the themes – on which a very large number of variations can be, and are, developed by different scientists. It is not my principal aim here to analyze these many possible and actual variations; I wish only to state their underlying themes. Still, it seems useful to discuss briefly the types of variation mentioned above (particularly the last type), if only to defend the claim that my analysis of themes is flexible enough to incorporate, by implication, the analysis of variations as well.

Each scientific subprocess (for example, that of transforming one information component into another, and that of applying a given methodological control) almost always involves a series of preliminary *trials*. Sometimes these trials are wholly imaginary; that is, the scientist manipulates images in his mind of objects not present to his senses. He may think, 'If I had this sort of instrument, then these observations might be obtained; these generalizations and this theory and this hypothesis might be generated, etc.'; or perhaps, 'If I had a different theory, then I might entertain a different hypothesis – one that would conform better to existing empirical generalizations.' When these imaginary trials, sometimes running several times through the entire sequence of scientific transformations, seem to be accomplished all in one instant (and when, of course, these imaginary trials turn out, when actualized, to be correct and fruitful), the scientist's performance is said to be 'insightful'. It is here, in making imaginary trials, that 'intuition', 'intelligent speculation,' and 'heuristic devices' find their special usefulness in science.

For maximum social acceptance as statements of truth by the scientific community, trials must not be left to imagination alone; they must become actual fact. The actualization of scientific processes (for example, actually constructing a desired instrument) usually brings about a reduction in speed and an increase in the rigor and formalization with which trials are carried out, because it subjects the entire trial process to the constraints and intransigences of the material world. An increase in the role specialization of the scientists who carry out the trials is also likely to result.

It is important to note that in the trial process just referred to (whether imaginary or actualized), directions of influence opposite to those shown in Fig. 1.1 are often taken temporarily[2]. For example, the first formulation of a hypothesis deduced from a theory may be ambiguous, imprecise, logically faulty, untestable or otherwise unsatisfactory, and it may undergo several revisions before a satisfactory formulation is constructed. In this process, not only will the deduced hypothesis change, but the originating theory may also be modified as the implications of each trial formulation reveal more about the theory itself.

Similarly (to move further around Fig. 1.1), the process of transforming a hypothesis into observations may involve several interpretation trials, several scaling trials (in which new scales may be invented and alternative scales selected) and several sampling trials. In each trial (at this point in the scientific process, trials are often called 'pretests' or 'pilot studies'), new observations are at least imagined and often actually made; and from them the investigator judges not only how relevant to his hypothesis the final observations and empirical generalizations are likely to be, but how appropriate his hypothesis is, given the observations and generalizations he can make. He may also judge how appropriate his methods are, given the information he is seeking to transform. Thus, the invention and trial of a new scaling, or instrumentation, or sampling, or interpretation technique may result in the deduction of new hypotheses rather than the reverse process shown in Fig. 1.1.

Despite these retrograde effects that may be seen for every information transformation indicated in Fig. 1.1, the dominant processual directions remain as shown there. When counterdirections are taken, they are best described as background preparations and repairs prior to a new advance. Thus, the invention of a new instrument for taking observations may occasion the deduction of new hypotheses, so that when new observations are actually and formally taken with the new instrument, they will be scientifically interpretable (that is, transformable into empirical generalizations that will be comparable with hypotheses, etc.) rather than mere extra-scientific curiosities. Similarly, a particular formulation of a theoretically-deduced hypothesis may react on its parent theory or on the method of logical deduction, and the theory may react on its supporting empirical generalizations, decisions and on the rules of logical induction; so that when the next step is actually taken (that is, when observations are made, via interpretation of the hypothesis, scaling, instrumentation and sampling), it will rest on newly-examined and firm ground.

But as C. Wright Mills implied, such careful background preparation does not always occur, and in practice any element in the scientific process may vary widely in the degree of its formalization and integration with other elements. Mills argued specifically that the relationship of theorizing to other phases in the scientific process can be so tenuous that theory becomes distorted and enslaved by 'the fetishism of the Concept'. Similarly, he claimed, the relationship of research methods to hypotheses, observations and empirical generalizations can be so rigid that empirical research becomes distorted by 'the methodological inhibition'.[3] It may be added that the distinction between researches that 'explore' given phenomena and researches that 'test' specific hypotheses is another manifestation of the same variability in degree of formalization and integration; 'exploratory' studies, precisely because they probe new substantive or methodological areas, may rest on still unformalized and unintegrated theoretical, hypothetical and methodological arguments. Understanding a published report of such a study often depends on inferring the theory that 'must have' undergirded the study, or on guessing the empirical generalizations, or hypotheses, or observations, or tests, etc., that the researcher 'must have' had in mind. 'Hypothesis-testing' studies, however, are likely to have more explicit, more formalized and more thoroughly integrated foundations in all elements of the scientific process.[4]

Finally, in this description of elements in the scientific process, it seems useful to note that sociologists (and other scientists, as well) often refer simply to 'theory' (or 'theory construction') and 'empirical research' as the two major constituents of science. What is the relation of these familiar terms to the more detailed elements just outlined?

Fig. 1.2 is designed to answer this question by suggesting that the left half of Fig. 1.2 represents what seems to be meant by the inductive construction of theory from, and understanding of, observations;

Constructing theory;
understanding what
is observed;
inductive methods

Applying theory;
knowing what
to observe;
deductive methods

Theorizing;
logic methods

Doing
empirical research;
research methods

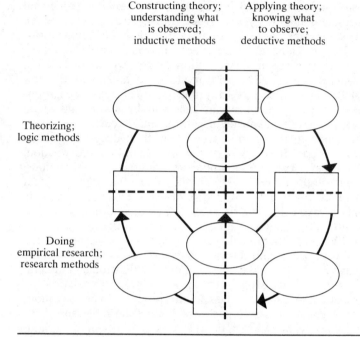

Fig. 1.2 Classification of the principal components, controls and transformations of the scientific process according to some conventional terms.

whereas the right half represents what seems to be meant by the deductive application of theory to observations and the knowledge of observations.[5] Similarly, the top half of Fig. 1.1 represents what is often referred to as theorizing, via the use of inductive and deductive logic as method; whereas the bottom half represents what is often meant by doing empirical research, with the aid of what are called 'research methods'. The manifold interrelations between these segments of the scientific process should be clear from Fig. 1.1, which also suggests that the process may be as readily divided along many other lines.[6]

It will be noted in Fig. 1.2, however, that all five information components, and two of the methodological control sets, are shown in marginal positions. The marginality of information components is meant to signify their ability to be transformed into each other, under the indicated controls, and thus to play at least dual roles in the scientific process. Of special importance is the transformational line up the middle. This line represents the closely related claims that tests of congruence between hypotheses and empirical generalizations depend on the deductive as well as the inductive side of scientific work and are as essential to constructing as to applying theory; that decisions to accept or reject hypotheses form an indispensable bridge between constructing and applying theory and also between theorizing and doing empirical research; and that the logical inference controlling the incorporation of such decisions into theory is marginal between constructing and applying theory. By pointing out these marginalities, I mean to emphasize the paramount importance of this series of methodological controls and information components, wherein 'concrete' observations made on the world and 'abstract' theories made within the mind are brought together in their most intimate confrontation, with inevitably profound consequences for both.

Notes

1. Compare Bergmann's similar, but more abbreviated, formula: 'The three pillars on which the house of science is built are observation, induction and deduction' (1957:31). For other capsule descriptions of the scientific process, see Popper (1961:111), Bohm (1961:4,5), Kaplan (1964:9–10), Stinchcombe (1968:15–18), Blalock (1969:8) and Greer (1969:4).
2. I am indebted to Richard J. Hill for pointing this out to me; the 'temporarily' and the 'trial' ideas are my own interpretations, however.
3. Mills dubbed these two distortions 'grand theory' and 'abstracted empiricism' (1959:25–75). Glaser and Strauss also derisively contrast 'logicodeductive theory, which . . . was merely thought up on the basis of *a priori* assumption and a touch of common sense, peppered with a few old theoretical speculations made by the erudite', with 'grounded' theory – theory generated 'from data systematically obtained from social research' (1967:29,2).
4. Diana Crane (1972) suggests that exploratory studies, and the variant of the scientific process that they represent, are typical of an early stage of growth in a scientific discipline (Kuhn's 'preparadigm' period, 1964), whereas hypothesis-testing studies are typical of a more mature ('paradigm-based') stage.
5. I use 'application' in its scientific, rather than in its engineering, sense.
6. For a more detailed discussion of some interdependencies based on the 'theory-versus-research' distinction, see Robert K. Merton, 'The Bearing of Sociological Theory on Empirical Research,' and 'The Bearing of Empirical Research on Sociological Theory' (1957:85–117). Figure 1.1 also embraces the factors that Kuhn indicates are meant by his term 'paradigm'. Kuhn says: 'By choosing [the term] paradigm I mean to suggest that some accepted examples of actual scientific practise – examples which include law, theory, application, and instrumentation together – provide models from which spring particular coherent traditions of scientific research' (1964:10); although at one point (1964:77) Kuhn identifies 'theory' alone with 'paradigm'.

References

Bergmann, G. (1957) *Philosophy of Science*. Madison, Wisconsin: The University of Wisconsin Press.

Blalock, H. M. Jr. (1969) *Theory Construction*. Englewood Cliff, New Jersey: Prentice-Hall.

Bohm, D. (1961) *Causality and Chance in Modern Physics*. New York: Harper Torchbook.

Crane, D. (1972) *Invisible Colleges and Social Circles: a sociological interpretation of scientific growth*. Chicago: University of Chicago Press.

Glaser, B. G. and Strauss, A. L. (1967) *The Discovery of Grounded Theory*. Chicago: Aldine Publishing Co.

Greer, S. (1969) *The Logic of Social Inquiry*. Chicago: Aldine Publishing Co.

Kaplan, A. (1964) *The Conduct of Inquiry*. San Francisco: Chandler Publishing Company.

Kuhn, T. S. (1964) *The Structure of Scientific Revolutions*. Phoenix: University of Chicago Press.

Merton, R. K. (1957) *Social Theory and Social Structure*. Glencoe, Illinois: The Free Press.

Mills, C. W. (1959) *The Sociological Imagination*. New York: Oxford University Press.

Popper, K. R. (1961) *The Logic of Scientific Discovery*. New York: Science Editions.

Stinchcombe, A. L. (1968) *Constructing Social Theories*. New York: Harcourt, Brace and World.

Two traditions

G. H. Von Wright

Scientific inquiry, seen in a very broad perspective, may be said to present two main aspects. One is the ascertaining and discovery of facts, the other the construction of hypotheses and theories. These two aspects of scientific activity are sometimes termed *descriptive* and *theoretical* science.

Theory-building can be said to serve two main purposes. One is to *predict* the occurrence of events or outcomes of experiments, and thus to anticipate new facts. The other is to *explain,* or to make intelligible facts which have already been recorded.

These classifications are useful for the purposes of a first approximation, but they must not be taken too rigidly. The discovery and description of facts cannot always be conceptually separated from a theory about them and is often an important step towards an understanding of their nature.[1] Prediction and explanation again are sometimes regarded as basically identical processes of scientific thinking – differing only in the time perspective, so to speak.[2] Prediction looks forward from what is to what will come, explanation usually looks back from what is to what went before. But, it is argued, the terms of the predictive and the explicative relations are similar, and so is the relation linking them. The former are some facts, the latter is a law. This view of prediction and explanation, however, may be challenged.[3] To challenge it is to question the role of general laws in scientific explanation and to raise the problem of whether theory-building is intrinsically the same endeavor in the natural sciences and in the humanistic and social disciplines.

Some of the problems concerning the interrelation of the various concepts just mentioned – description, explanation, prediction and theory – may usefully be considered in the light of intellectual history.

Two main traditions can be distinguished in the history of ideas, differing as to the conditions an explanation has to satisfy in order to be scientifically respectable. The one tradition is sometimes called *aris-*

G. H. Von Wright, 'Two traditions', from *Explanation and Understanding*. London: Routledge and Kegan Paul, 1971, Ch. 1, pp. 1–7 and 169–73.

totelian, the other *galilean.* The names suggest that the first has very ancient roots in the intellectual history of man, while the second is of relatively recent origin. There is some truth in this, but it should be taken with a grain of salt. What I here call the galilean tradition has an ancestry going back beyond Aristotle to Plato. One should also beware of thinking that the aristotelian tradition today represents merely the fading survival of obsolete elements from which science is gradually becoming 'liberated'.

As to their views of scientific explanation, the contrast between the two traditions is usually characterized as causal *versus* teleological explanation. The first type of explanation is also called mechanistic, the second finalistic. The galilean tradition in science runs parallel with the advance of the causal-mechanistic point of view in man's efforts to explain and predict phenomena, the aristotelian tradition with his efforts to make facts teleologically or finalistically understandable. [. . .]

The great awakening or revolution in the natural sciences during the late Renaissance and the Baroque era was to a certain extent paralleled in the nineteenth century in the systematic study of man, his history, languages, *mores* and social institutions. The work of Ranke and Mommsen in historiography, Wilhelm von Humboldt, Rasmus Rask, Jacob Grimm in linguistics and philology, Tylor in social anthropology, is comparable to the achievements, two or three centuries earlier, of Copernicus and Kepler in astronomy, Galileo and Newton in physics, or Vesalius and Harvey in anatomy and physiology.

Since natural science was already established on the intellectual stage, and the humanistic studies with a scientific claim were newcomers, it was but natural that one of the chief issues of nineteenth-century methodology and philosophy of science concerned the relationship between these two main branches of empirical inquiry. The principal stands on this issue can be linked with the two main traditions in methodological thinking we have distinguished.

One stand is the philosophy of science most typically represented by Auguste Comte and John Stuart Mill. It is usually called *positivism.* The name was coined by Comte, but used with due caution it is also appropriate for the position of Mill[4] and for an entire intellectual tradition extending from Comte and Mill not only down to the present day but also upward in the stream of time to Hume and the philosophy of the Enlightenment.

One of the tenets of positivism[5] is *methodological monism,* or the idea of the unity of scientific method amidst the diversity of subject matter of scientific investigation.[6] A second tenet is the view that the exact natural sciences, in particular mathematical physics, set a methodological ideal or standard which measures the degree of development and perfection of all the other sciences, including the humanities.[7] A third tenet, finally, is a characteristic view of scientific explanation.[8] Such explanation is, in a broad sense, 'causal'.[9] It consists, more specifically, in the subsumption of individual cases under hypothetically assumed general laws of nature, including 'human nature'.[10] The attitude towards finalistic explanations, i.e. towards attempts to account for facts in terms of intentions, goals, purposes, is either to reject them as unscientific or to try to show that they can, when duly purified of 'animist' or 'vitalist' remains, be transformed into causal explanations.[11]

Through its emphasis on unity of method, on the mathematical ideal-type of a science, and on the importance of general laws to explanation, positivism is linked with that longer and more ramified tradition in the history of ideas which I have here called galilean.

Another stand on the question of the relationship between the sciences of nature and of man was a reaction against positivism. The antipositivist philosophy of science which became prominent towards the end of the nineteenth century is a much more diversified and heterogenous trend than positivism. The name 'idealism' which is sometimes used to characterize it is appropriate only for some facets of this trend. A better name for it seems to me to be *hermeneutics*. Representatives of this type of thought included some eminent German philosophers, historians and social scientists. Perhaps the best known of them are Droysen, Dilthey, Simmel and Max Weber. Windelband and Rickert of the neo-kantian Baden School are related to them. The Italian Croce and eminent British philosopher of history and art Collingwood may be said to belong to the idealist wing of this anti-positivist trend in methodology.

All these thinkers reject the methodological monism of positivism and refuse to view the pattern set by the exact natural sciences as the sole and supreme ideal for a rational understanding of reality. Many of them emphasize a contrast between those sciences which, like physics or chemistry or physiology, aim at generalizations about reproducible and predictable phenomena, and those which, like history, want to grasp the individual and unique features of their objects. Windelband coined the label 'nomothetic' for sciences which search for laws, and 'ideographic' for the descriptive study of individuality.[12]

The antipositivists also attacked the positivist view of explanation. The German historian-philosopher Droysen appears to have been the first to introduce a methodological dichotomy which has had great influence. He coined for it the names *explanation* and *understanding,* in German *Erklären* and *Verstehen.*[13] The aim of the natural sciences, he said, is to explain; the aim of history is to understand the phenomena which fall within its domain. These methodological ideas were then worked out to systematic fulness by Wilhelm Dilthey.[14] For the entire domain of the understanding method he used the name *Geisteswissenschaften.* There is no good equivalent in English, but it should be mentioned that the word was originally coined for the purpose of translating into German the English term 'moral science'.

Ordinary usage does not make a sharp distinction between the words 'explain' and 'understand'. Practically every explanation, be it causal or teleological or of some other kind, can be said to further our understanding of things. But 'understanding' also has a psychological ring which 'explanation' has not. This psychological feature was emphasized by several of the nineteenth-century antipositivist methodologists, perhaps most forcefully by Simmel, who thought that understanding as a method characteristic of the humanities is a form of *empathy* (in German *Einfühlung*) or re-creation in the mind of the scholar of the mental atmosphere the thoughts and feelings and motivations, of the objects of his study.[15]

It is not only through this psychological twist, however, that understanding may be differentiated from explanation. Understanding is also connected with *intentionality* in a way explanation is not. One understands the aims and purposes of an agent, the meaning of a sign or symbol, and the significance of a social institution or religous rite. This intentionalistic or, as one could perhaps also call it, semantic dimension of understanding has come to play a prominent role in more recent methodological discussion.

If one accepts a fundamental methodological cleavage between the natural sciences and the historical *Geisteswissenschaften*, the question will immediately arise of where the social and behavioral sciences stand. These sciences were born largely under the influence of a cross pressure of positivist and antipositivist tendencies in the last century. It is therefore not surprising that they should have become a battleground for the two opposed trends in the philosophy of scientific method. The application of mathematical methods to political economy and other forms of social study was an inheritance of the eighteenth-century Enlightenment which found favor with nineteenth-century positivists. Comte himself coined the name 'sociology' for the scientific study of human society. Of the two great sociologists of the turn of the century, Emile Durkheim was essentially a positivist as far as his methodology is concerned,[16] while in Max Weber a positivist coloring is combined with emphasis on teleology ('*zweckrationales Handeln*') and empathic understanding ('*verstehende Soziologie*').[17]

Notes

1. Nearly all 'revolutions' in science testify to the inseparability of the discovery of new facts from the invention of a new theory to explain them – and also to the close interrelation of the description of facts and the formation of concepts. See, for example, the account given in Kuhn (1962), p. 56 and *passim*, of the discovery of oxygen and the overthrow of the phlogiston theory of combustion.
2. Cf. Popper (1935), Sect. 12; Hempel (1942), Sect. 4; Caws (1965), Sect. 13.

3. The thesis of 'the structural identity of explanation and prediction' has been criticized by several recent writers. The discussion received decisive impetus from Scheffler (1957) and Hanson (1959). The pros and cons of the thesis are skillfully dissected in Hempel (1965), Sect. 2.4. For a defense of the thesis see also Angel (1967).
4. Cf. Mill (1865) and the references to Comte and positivism in Mill (1843), especially in Bk. VI.
5. There are different ways of characterizing 'positivism'. One characterization links positivism with a phenomenalist or sensualist theory of knowledge, and modern positivism with a verificationist theory of meaning. Another characterization links it with a 'scientistic' and 'technological' view of knowledge and its uses. Mill is more of a positivist in the first sense than is Comte. Comte's positivism is above all a philosophy of science. (See Comte 1830, 'Avertissement de l'Auteur.') His ultimate ambition was to be a champion of the 'positive', scientific spirit in the study of social phenomena. (Comte 1830, Leçon I, Sect. 6.) With this he combined a firm belief in the usefulness of scientific knowledge for social reform. [. . . .]
6. Comte (1830), 'Avertissement', Leçon I, Sect. 10. [. . . .]
7. Comte (1830), Leçon I, Sect. 6 (on the notion of a 'physique sociale') and Leçon II, Sect. 11.
8. Mill (1843), Bk. III, Ch. xii; Comte (1830), Leçon I, Sects. 4 and 24. [. . . .]
9. Mill (1843), Bk. III, Ch. xii, Sect. 1: 'An individual fact is said to be explained, by pointing out its cause, that is, by stating the law or laws of causation, of which its production is an instance.' Comte repudiated the search for 'causes'. He associated it with the 'pre-positivist', metaphysical stage in the development of science. In positivist science the role of causes is taken over by general laws. Cf. Comte (1830), Leçon I, Sect. 4, and Comte (1844), Pt. I, Sect. 3.
10. Mill (1843), Bk. VI. Ch. iii, Sect. 2. [. . . .]
11. Cf. Comte (1844), Pt. I, Sect. 6. [. . . .]
12. Windelband (1894).
13. Droysen (1858). [. . . .]
14. Dilthey (1883); (1894); (1900); (1910). [. . . .]
15. Simmel (1892), particularly Ch. I, and Simmel (1918).
16. The methodological standpoint of Durkheim is best studied in Durkheim (1893) and (1894). His positivist attitude notwithstanding, some of Durkheim's chief ideas, for example those concerning the 'représentations collectives' of the social consciousness, could be profitably reinterpreted, I think, in the terms of a hermeneutic methodology of understanding.
17. On Weber's position see in particular Weber (1913) and Weber (1921), Pt. I, Ch. i.

References

Angel, R. B. (1967) 'Explanation and prediction: a plea for reason', *Philosophy of Science,* **34.**
Caws, P. (1965) *The Philosophy of Science.* Princeton, New Jersey: D. Von Nostrand.
Comte, A. (1830) *Cours de Philosophie Positive.*
Comte, A. (1844) *Discours sur L'esprit Positif.*
Dilthey, W. (1833) *Einleitung in die Geisteswissenschaften.*
Dilthey, W. (1894) *Ideen über eine beschreibende und zergliedernde Psychologie.*
Dilthey, W. (1900) *Die Entstehung der Hermeneutik.*
Dilthey, W. (1910) *Der Aufbau der geschichtlichen Welt in den Geisteswissenschaften.*
Droysen, J. G. (1858) *Grundriss der Historik.*
Durkheim, E. (1893) *De la Division du Travail Social.*
Durkheim, E. (1894) *Les Règles de la Méthode Sociologique.*
Hanson, N. R. (1959) 'On the symmetry of explanation and prediction', *The Philosophical Review,* **68.**

Hempel, C. G. (1942) 'The function of general laws in history', *The Journal of Philosophy*, **39**.

Hempel, C. G. (1965) 'Aspects of scientific explanation', in Hempel, C. G., *Aspects of Scientific Explanation and other Essays in the Philosophy of Science*. New York: The Free Press.

Kuhn, T. S. (1962) *The Structure of Scientific Revolutions*. Chicago: University of Chicago Press.

Mill, J. S. (1843) *A System of Logic*. London: John W. Parker.

Mill, J. S. (1865) 'Auguste Comte and positivism', *Westminster Review*.

Popper, K. (1935) *Logik der Forschung*. Vienna: Julius Springer.

Scheffler, I. (1957) 'Explanation, prediction and abstraction', *The British Journal for the Philosophy of Science*, **7**.

Simmel, G. (1892) *Die Probleme der Geschichtsphilosophie*. Leipzig: Duncker & Humblot.

Simmel, G. (1918) *Von Wesen des historischen Verstehens*. Berlin: E. S. Mittler & Sohn.

Weber, M. (1913) 'Über einige Kategorien der verstehenden Soziologie', *Logos*, **4**.

Weber, M. (1921) *Wirtschaft und Gesellschaft, Grundriss der verstehenden Soziologie*. 4th edn, Tübingen: J. C. B. Mohr.

Windelband, W. (1894) 'Geschichte und Naturwissenschaft', reprinted in *Präludien*. 3rd edn, Tübingen: J. C. B. Mohr.

The unity of method

K. R. Popper

I [have] suggested that deductive methods are widely used and important – more so than Mill, for example, ever thought. This suggestion will now be further elaborated, in order to throw some light on the dispute between naturalism and anti-naturalism. I am going to propose a doctrine of the unity of method; that is to say, the view that all theoretical or generalizing sciences make use of the same method, whether they are natural sciences or social sciences. At the same time, some of these doctrines of historicism which I have not yet sufficiently examined will be touched upon, such as the problems of Generalization; of Essentialism; of the role played by Intuitive Understanding; of the Inexactitude of Prediction; of Complexity; and of the application of Quantitative Methods.

I do not intend to assert that there are no differences whatever between the methods of the theoretical sciences of nature and of society; such differences clearly exist, even between the various natural sciences themselves, as well as between the various social sciences. (Compare, for example, the analysis of competitive markets and of Romance languages.) But I agree with Comte and Mill – and with many others, such as C. Menger – that the methods in the two fields are fundamentally the same (though the methods I have in mind may differ from those they had in mind). The methods always consist in offering deductive causal explanations, and in testing them (by way of predictions). This has sometimes been called the hypothetical–deductive method,[1] or more often the method of hypothesis, for it does not achieve absolute certainty for any of the scientific statements which it tests; rather, these statements always retain the character of tentative hypotheses, even though their character of tentativeness may cease to be obvious after they have passed a great number of severe tests.

Because of their tentative or provisional character, hypotheses were considered, by most students of method, as *provisional in the sense that they have ultimately to be replaced by proved theories* (or at least by theories which can be proved to be 'highly probable', in the sense of

K. R. Popper, The unity of method, from *The Poverty of Historicism*. London: Routledge and Kegan Paul, 1957, Ch. 4, pp. 130–43.

some calculus of probabilities). I believe that this view is mistaken and that it leads to a host of entirely unnecessary difficulties. But this problem[2] is of comparatively little moment here. What is important is to realize that in science we are always concerned with explanations, predictions, and tests, and that the method of testing hypotheses is always the same. From the hypothesis to be tested – for example, a universal law – together with some other statements which for this purpose are not considered as problematic – for example, some initial conditions – we deduce some prognosis. We then confront this prognosis, whenever possible, with the results of experimental or other observations. Agreement with them is taken as corroboration of the hypothesis, though not as final proof; clear disagreement is considered as refutation or falsification.

According to this analysis, there is no great difference between explanation, prediction and testing. The difference is not one of logical structure, but rather one of emphasis; it depends on *what we consider to be our problem* and what we do not so consider. If it is not our problem to find a prognosis, while we take it to be our problem to find the initial conditions or some of the universal laws (or both) from which we may deduce a *given* 'prognosis', then we are looking for an *explanation* (and the given 'prognosis' becomes our 'explicandum'). If we consider the laws and initial conditions as given (rather than as to be found) and use them merely for deducing the prognosis, in order to get thereby some new information, then we are trying to make a *prediction*. (This is a case in which we *apply* our scientific results.) And if we consider one of the premises, i.e. either a universal law or an initial condition, as problematic, and the prognosis as something to be compared with the results of experience, then we speak of a *test* of the problematic premise.

The result of tests is the *selection* of hypotheses which have stood up to tests, or the *elimination* of those hypotheses which have not stood up to them, and which are therefore rejected. It is important to realize the consequences of this view. They are these: all tests can be interpreted as attempts to weed out false theories – to find the weak points of a theory in order to reject it if it is falsified by the test. This view is sometimes considered paradoxical; our aim, it is said, is to establish theories, not to eliminate false ones. But just because it is our aim to establish theories as well as we can, we must test them as severely as we can; that is, we must try to find fault with them, we must try to falsify them. Only if we cannot falsify them in spite of our best efforts can we say that they have stood up to severe tests. This is the reason why the discovery of instances which confirm a theory means very little if we have not tried, and failed, to discover refutations. For if we are uncritical we shall always find what we want: we shall look for, and find, confirmations, and we shall look away from, and not see, whatever might be dangerous to our pet theories. In this way it is only easy to obtain what appears to be overwhelming evidence in favour of a theory which, if approached critically, would have been refuted. In order to make the method of selection by elimination work, and to ensure that only the fittest theories survive, their struggle for life must be made severe for them.

This, in outline, is the method of all sciences which are backed by experience. But what about the method by which we *obtain* our theories or hypotheses? What about *inductive generalizations,* and the way in which we proceed from observation to theory? To this question I shall give two answers. (*a*) I do not believe that we ever make inductive generalizations in the sense that we start with observations and try to derive our theories from them. I believe that the prejudice that we proceed in this way is a kind of optical illusion, and that at no stage of scientific development do we begin without something in the nature of a theory, such as a hypothesis, or a prejudice, or a problem – often a technological one – which in some way *guides* our observations, and helps us to select from the innumerable objects of observation those which may be of interest.[3] But if this is so, then the method of elimination – which is nothing but that of trial and error – can always be applied. However, I do not think that it is necessary for our present discussion to insist upon this point. For we can say (*b*) that it is irrelevant from the point of view of science whether we have obtained our theories by jumping to unwarranted conclusions or merely by stumbling over them (that is, by 'intuition'), or else by some inductive procedure. The question, 'How did you first *find* your theory?' relates, as it were, to an entirely private matter, as opposed to the question, 'How did you *test* your theory?' which alone is scientifically relevant. And the method of testing described here is fertile; it leads to new observations, and to a mutual give and take between theory and observation.

Now all this, I believe, is not only true for the natural but also for the social sciences. And in the social sciences it is even more obvious than in the natural sciences that we cannot see and observe our objects before we have thought about them. For most of the objects of social science, if not all of them, are abstract objects; they are *theoretical* constructions. (Even 'the war' or 'the army' are abstract concepts, strange as this may sound to some. What is concrete is the many who are killed; or the men and women in uniform, etc.) These objects, these theoretical constructions used to interpret our experience, are the result of constructing certain *models* (especially of institutions), in order to explain certain experiences – a familiar theoretical method in the natural sciences (where we construct our models of atoms, molecules, solids, liquids, etc.). It is part of the method of explanation by way of reduction, or deduction from hypotheses. Very often we are unaware of the fact that we are operating with hypotheses or theories, and we therefore mistake our theoretical models for concrete things. This is a kind of mistake which is only too common.[4] [. . .]

The unity of the methods of the natural and social sciences may be illustrated and defended by an analysis of two passages from Professor Hayek's *Scientism and the Study of Society.*[5]

In the first of these passages, Professor Hayek writes:

The physicist who wishes to understand the problems of the social sciences with the help of an analogy from his own field would have to imagine a world in which he knew by direct observation the inside of the atoms and had neither the possibility of making experiments with lumps of matter nor the opportunity to observe more than the interactions of a comparatively few atoms during a limited period. From his knowledge of the different kinds of atoms he could build up models of all the various ways in which they could combine into larger units and make these models more and more closely reproduce all the features of the few instances in which he was able to observe more complex phenomena. But the laws of the macrocosm which he could derive from his knowledge of the microcosm would always remain 'deductive'; they would, because of his limited knowledge of the data of the complex situation, scarcely even enable him to predict the precise outcome of a particular situation; and he could never verify them by controlled experiment — although they might be disproved *by the observation of events which according to his theory are impossible.*

I admit that the first sentence of this passage points to certain differences between social and physical science. But the rest of the passage, I believe, speaks for a complete *unity of method.* For if, as I do not doubt, this is a correct description of the method of social science, then it shows that it differs only from such interpretations of the method of natural science as we have already rejected. I have in mind, more especially, the 'inductivist' interpretation which holds that in the natural sciences we proceed systematically from observation to theory by some method of generalization, and that we can 'verify', or perhaps even prove, our theories by some method of induction. I have been advocating a very different view here – an interpretation of scientific method as deductive, hypothetical, selective by way of falsification, etc. And this description of the method of natural science agrees perfectly with Professor Hayek's description of the method of social science. (I have every reason to believe that my interpretation of the methods of science was not influenced by any knowledge of the methods of the social sciences; for when I developed it first, I had only the natural sciences in mind,[6] and I knew next to nothing about the social sciences.)

But even the differences alluded to in the first sentence of the quotation are not so great as may appear at first sight. It is undoubtedly true that we have a more direct knowledge of the 'inside of the human atom' than we have of physical atoms; but this knowledge is intuitive. In other words, we certainly use our knowledge of ourselves in order to frame *hypotheses* about some other people, or about all people. But these hypotheses must be tested, they must be submitted to the method of selection by elimination. (Intuition prevents some people from even imagining that anybody could possibly dislike chocolate.) The physicist, it is true, is not helped by such direct observation when he frames his hypotheses about atoms; nevertheless, he quite often uses some kind of sympathetic imagination or intuition which may easily make him feel that he is intimately acquainted with even the 'inside of the atoms' – with even their whims and prejudices. But this intuition is his private affair. Science is interested only in the hypotheses which his intuitions may have inspired, and then only if these are rich in consequences, and if they can be properly tested.

These few remarks may also indicate the way in which the historicist doctrine should be criticized – that is to say, the doctrine that social science must use the method of intuitive understanding.

In the second passage, Professor Hayek, speaking of social phenomena, says:

. . . *our knowledge of the principle by which these phenomena are produced will rarely if ever enable us to predict the precise result of any* concrete *situation. While we can explain the principle on which certain phenomena are produced and can from this knowledge* exclude the possibility *of certain results, e.g. of certain events occuring together, our knowledge will in a sense be only negative, i.e. it will merely enable us to preclude certain results but not enable us to narrow the range of possibilities sufficiently so that only one remains.*

This passage, far from describing a situation peculiar to the social sciences, perfectly describes the character of natural laws which, indeed, can never do more than *exclude certain possibilities*. ('You cannot carry water in a sieve'.) More especially the statement that we shall not, as a rule, be able 'to predict the precise result of any *concrete* situation' opens up the problem of the inexactitude of prediction. I contend that precisely the same may be said of the concrete physical world. In general it is only by the use of artificial experimental isolation that we can predict physical events. (The solar system is an exceptional case – one of natural, not of artificial isolation; once its isolation is destroyed by the intrusion of a foreign body of sufficient size, all our forecasts are liable to break down.) We are very far from being able to predict, even in physics, the precise results of a *concrete* situation, such as a thunderstorm, or a fire.

A very brief remark may be added here on the problem of complexity. There is no doubt that the analysis of any concrete social situation is made extremely difficult by its complexity. But the same holds for any concrete physical situation.[7] The widely held prejudice that social situations are more complex than physical ones seems to arise from two sources. One of them is that we are liable to compare what should not be compared; I mean on the one hand concrete social situations and on the other hand artificially insulated experimental physical situations. (The latter might be compared, rather, with an artificially insulated social situation – such as a prison, or an experimental community.) The other source is the old belief that the description of a social situation should involve the mental and perhaps even physical states of everybody concerned (or perhaps that it should even be reducible to them). But this belief is not justified; it is much less justified even than the impossible demand that the description of a concrete chemical reaction should involve that of the atomic and sub-atomic states of all the elementary particles involved (although chemistry may indeed be reducible to physics). The belief also shows traces of the popular view that social entities such as institutions or associations are concrete natural entities such as crowds of men, rather than abstract models constructed to interpret certain selected abstract relations between individuals.

But in fact, there are good reasons, not only for the belief that social science is less complicated than physics, but also for the belief that concrete social situations are in general less complicated than concrete physical situations. For in most social situations, if not in all, there is an element of *rationality*. Admittedly, human beings hardly ever act quite rationally (i.e. as they would if they could make the optimal use of all available information for the attainment of whatever ends they may have), but they act, none the less, more or less rationally; and this makes it possible to construct comparatively simple models of their actions and inter-actions, and to use these models as approximations.

The last point seems to me, indeed, to indicate a considerable difference between the natural and the social sciences – perhaps *the most important difference in their methods*, since the other important differences, i.e. specific difficulties in conducting experiments and in applying quantitative methods (see below), are differences of degree rather than of kind. I refer to the possibility of adopting, in the social sciences, what may be called the method of logical or rational construction, or perhaps the 'zero method'.[8] By this I mean the method of constructing a model on the assumption of complete rationality (and perhaps also on the assumption of the possession of complete information) on the part of all the individuals concerned, and of estimating the deviation of the actual behaviour of people from the model behaviour, using the latter as a kind of zero co-ordinate.[9] An example of this method is the comparison between actual behaviour (under the influence of, say, traditional prejudice, etc.) and model behaviour to be expected on the basis of the 'pure logic of choice', as described by the equations of economics. Marschak's interesting 'Money Illusion', for example, may be interpreted in this way.[10] An attempt at applying the zero method to a different field may be found in P. Sargant Florence's comparison between the 'logic of large-scale operation' in industry and the 'illogic of actual operation'.[11] [. . .]

In concluding, I have to mention what I consider to be the other main difference between the methods of some of the theoretical sciences of nature and of society. I mean the specific difficulties connected with the application of quantitative methods, and especially methods of measurement.[12] Some of these difficulties can be, and have been, overcome by the application of statistical methods, for example in demand analysis. And they *have to be overcome* if, for example, some of the equations of mathematical economics are to provide a basis even of merely qualitative applications; for without such measurement we should often not know whether or not some counteracting influences exceeded an effect calculated in merely qualitative terms. Thus merely qualitative considerations may well be deceptive at times; just as deceptive, to quote Professor Frisch, 'as to say that when a man tries to row a boat forward, the boat will be driven backward because of the pressure exerted by his feet'.[13] But it cannot be doubted that there are some fundamental difficulties here. In physics, for example, the parameters of our equations can, in principle, be reduced to a small number of natural constants – a reduction which has been successfully carried out in many important cases. This is not so in economics; here the parameters are themselves in the most important cases quickly changing variables.[14] This clearly reduces the significance, interpretability and testability of our measurements.

Notes and references

1. See V. Craft (1925), *Die Grundformen der wissenscaftlichen Methoden.*
2. See my *Logic of Scientific Discovery,* London, Hutchinson, on which the present section is based, especially the doctrine of tests by way of deduction ('deductivism') and of the redundancy of any further 'induction', since theories always retain their hypothetical character ('hypotheticism'), and the doctrine that scientific tests are genuine attempts to falsify theories ('eliminationism'); see also the discussion of testability and falsifiability.

    The opposition here pointed out, between *deductivism* and *inductivism,* corresponds in some respects to the classical distinction between *rationalism* and *empiricism*: Descartes was a deductivist, since he conceived all sciences as deductive systems, while the English empiricists, from Bacon on, all conceived the sciences as collecting observations from which generalizations are obtained by induction.

    But Descartes believed that the principles, the premises of the deductive systems, must be secure and self-evident – 'clear and distinct'. They are based upon the insight of reason. (They are synthetic and *a priori* valid, in Kantian language.) As opposed to this, I conceive them as tentative conjectures, or hypotheses.

    These hypotheses, I contend, must be refutable in principle: it is here that I deviate from the two greatest modern deductivists, Henri Poincaré and Pierre Duhem.

    Poincaré and Duhem both recognized the impossibility of conceiving the theories of physics as inductive generalizations. They realized that the observational measurements which form the alleged starting point for the generalizations are, on the contrary, *interpretations in the light of theories*. And they rejected not only inductivism, but also the rationalistic belief in synthetic *a priori* valid principles or axioms. Poincaré interpreted them as analytically true, as definitions; Duhem interpreted them as instruments (as did Cardinal Bellarmino and Bishop Berkeley), as means for the ordering of the experimental laws – the experimental laws which, he thought, were obtained by induction. Theories thus cannot contain either true or false information: they are nothing but instruments, since they can only be convenient or inconvenient, economical or uneconomical; supple and subtle, or else creaking and crude. (Thus, Duhem says, following Berkeley, there cannot be logical reasons why two or more theories which contradict one another should not all be accepted.) I fully agree with both these great authors in rejecting inductivism as well as the belief in the synthetic *a priori* validity of physical theories. But I cannot accept their view that it is impossible to submit theoretical systems to empirical tests. Some of them are testable, I think; that is, refutable in principle; and they are therefore synthetic (rather than analytic); *empirical* (rather than *a priori*); and *informative* (rather than purely instrumental). As to Duhem's famous criticism of crucial experiments, he only shows that crucial experiments can never *prove* or establish a theory; but he nowhere shows that crucial experiments cannot *refute* a theory. Admittedly, Duhem is right when he says that we can test only huge and complex theoretical systems rather than isolated hypotheses; but if we test two such systems which differ in one hypothesis only, and if we can design experiments which refute the first system while leaving the second very well corroborated, then we may be on reasonably safe ground if we attribute the failure of the first system to that hypothesis in which it differs from the other.

3. For a surprising example of the way in which even botanical observations are guided by theory (and in which they may be even influenced by prejudice) see O. Frankel (1941), 'Cytology and taxonomy of Hebe, etc.', in *Nature*, **147,**117.

4. With this and the following paragraph, cp. F. A. von Hayek, 'Scientism and the study of society', parts I and II, *Economica*, vols. ix and x, where methodological collectivism is criticized and where methodological individualism is discussed in detail.

5. For the two passages see *Economica*, vol. ix, 289 f. (italics mine).

6. Cp. *Erkenntnis*, III, p. 426 f., and my *Logik der Forschung* (1934), whose sub-title may be translated: 'On the epistemology of the natural sciences'.

7. A somewhat similar argument can be found in C. Menger (1893 and 1933), *Collected Works*, vol. II. London School of Economics and Political Science, pp. 259–60.

8. See the 'null hypothesis' discussed in J. Marschak, 'Money illusion and demand analysis', in *The Review of Economic Statistics*, vol. XXV, p. 40 – the method described here seems partly to coincide with what has been called by Professor Hayek, following C. Menger, the 'compositive' method.

9. Even here it may be said, perhaps, that the use of rational or 'logical' models in the social sciences, or of the 'zero method', has some vague parallel in the natural sciences, especially in thermodynamics and in biology (the construction of mechanical models, and of physiological models of processes and of organs). (Cp. also the use of variational methods.)

10. See J. Marschak, *op. cit.*

11. See Sargant Florence (1933). *The Logic of Industrial Organisations*. London: Kegan Paul.

12. These difficulties are discussed by Professor Hayek, *op. cit.*, p. 290 f.

13. See *Econometrica*, I (1933), 1 f.

14 See Lionel Robbins, in *Economica*, vol. v, especially p. 351.

Concept and theory formation in the social sciences

Alfred Schutz

I shall here concentrate on Nagel's criticism of the claim made by Weber and his school that the social sciences seek to 'understand' social phenomena in terms of 'meaningful' categories of human experience and that, therefore, the 'causal–functional' approach of the natural sciences is not applicable in social inquiry. This school, as Nagel sees it, maintains that all socially significant human behavior is an expression of motivated psychic states, that in consequence the social scientist cannot be satisfied with viewing social processes simply as concatenations of 'externally related' events, and that the establishment of correlations or even of universal relations of concomitance cannot be his ultimate goal. On the contrary, he must construct 'ideal types' or 'models of motivations' in terms of which he seeks to 'understand' overt social behavior by imputing springs of action to the actors involved in it. If I understand Nagel's criticism correctly, he maintains:

1. That these springs of action are not accessible to sensory observation. It follows and has frequently been stated that the social scientist must imaginatively identify himself with the participants and view the situation which they face as the actors themselves view it. Surely, however, we need not undergo other men's psychic experiences in order to know that they have them or in order to predict their overt behavior.

2. That the imputation of emotions, attitudes and purposes as an explanation of overt behavior is a twofold hypothesis: it assumes that the agents participating in some social phenomenon are in certain psychological states; and it assumes also definite relations of concomitance between such states, and between such states and overt behavior. Yet none of the psychological states which we imagine the subjects of our study to possess may in reality be theirs, and even if our imputations should be correct none of the overt actions which allegedly issue from those states may appear to us understandable or reasonable.

Extract from Alfred Schutz, 'Concept and theory formation in the social sciences', *Journal of Philosophy*, **51**, 1954, 257–73.

3. That we do not 'understand' the nature and operations of human motives and their issuance in overt behavior more adequately than the 'external' causal relations. If by meaningful explanation we assert merely that a particular action is an instance of a pattern of behavior which human beings exhibit under a variety of circumstances and that, since some of the relevant circumstances are realized in the given situation, a person can be expected to manifest a certain form of that pattern, then there is no sharp gulf separating such explanations from those involving merely 'external' knowledge of causal connections. It is possible to gain knowledge of the actions of men on the evidence supplied by their overt behavior just as it is possible to discover and know the atomic constitution of water on the evidence supplied by the physical and chemical behavior of that substance. Hence the rejection of a purely 'objective' or 'behavioristic' social science by the proponents of 'meaningful connections' as the goal of social sciences is unwarranted.

Since I shall have to disagree with Nagel's and Hempel's findings on several questions of a fundamental nature, I might be permitted to start with a brief summary of the no less important points on which I find myself happily in full agreement with them. I agree with Nagel that all empirical knowledge involves discovery through processes of controlled inference, and that it must be stateable in propositional form and capable of being verified by anyone who is prepared to make the effort to do so through observation – although I do not believe, as Nagel does, that this observation has to be sensory in the precise meaning of this term. Moreover, I agree with him that 'theory' means in all empirical sciences the explicit formulation of determinate relations between a set of variables in terms of which a fairly extensive class of empirically ascertainable regularities can be explained. Furthermore, I agree wholeheartedly with his statement that neither the fact that these regularities have in the social sciences a rather narrowly restricted universality, nor the fact that they permit prediction only to a rather limited extent, constitutes a basic difference between the social and the natural sciences, since many branches of the latter show the same features. As I shall try to show later on, it seems to me that Nagel misunderstands Weber's postulate of subjective interpretation. Nevertheless, he is right in stating that a method which would require that the individual scientific observer identify himself with the social agent observed in order to understand the motives of the latter, or a method which would refer the selection of the facts observed and their interpretation to the private value system of the particular observer, would merely lead to an uncontrollable private and subjective image in the mind of this particular student of human affairs, but never to a scientific theory. But I do not know of any social scientist of stature who ever advocated such a concept of subjectivity as that criticized by Nagel. Most certainly that was not the position of Weber.

I also think that our authors are prevented from grasping the point of vital concern to social scientists by their basic philosophy of sensationalistic empiricism or logical positivism, which identifies experience with sensory observation and which assumes that the only alternative to controllable and, therefore, objective sensory observation is that of subjective and, therefore, uncontrollable and unverifiable introspection. This is certainly not the place to renew the age-old controversy relating to the hidden presuppositions and implied metaphysical assumptions of this basic philosophy. On the other hand, in order to account for my own position, I should have to treat at length certain principles of phenomenology. Instead of doing so, I propose to defend a few rather simple propositions:

1. The primary goal of the social sciences is to obtain organized knowledge of social reality. By the term 'social reality' I wish to be understood the sum total of objects and occurrences within the social cultural world as experienced by the common-sense thinking of men living their daily lives among their fellow-men, connected with them in manifold relations of interaction. It is the world of cultural objects and social institutions into which we all are born, within which we have to find our bearings, and with which we have to come to terms. From the outset, we, the actors on the social scene, experience the world we live in as a world both of nature and of culture, not as a private but as an intersubjective one, that is, as a world common to all of us, either actually given or potentially accessible to everyone; and this involves intercommunication and language.

2. All forms of naturalism and logical empiricism simply take for granted this social reality, which is the proper object of the social sciences. Intersubjectivity, interaction, intercommunication and language are simply presupposed as the unclarified foundation of these theories. They assume, as it were, that the social scientist has already solved his fundamental problem, before scientific inquiry starts. To be sure, Dewey emphasized, with a clarity worthy of this eminent philosopher, that all inquiry starts and ends within the social cultural matrix; to be sure, Nagel is fully aware of the fact that science and its self-correcting process is a social enterprise. But the postulate of describing and explaining human behavior in terms of controllable sensory observation stops short before the description and explanation of the process by which scientist B controls and verifies the observational findings of scientist A and the conclusions drawn by him. In order to do so, B has to know what A has observed, what the goal of his inquiry is, why he thought the observed fact worthy of being observed, i.e. relevant to the scientific problem at hand, etc. The knowledge is commonly called understanding. The explanation of how such a mutual understanding of human beings might occur is apparently left to the social scientist. But whatever his explanation might be, one thing is sure, namely, that such an intersubjective understanding between scientist B and scientist A occurs neither by scientist B's observations

of scientist A's overt behavior, nor by introspection performed by B, nor by identification of B with Λ. To translate this argument into the language dear to logical positivism, this means, as Kaufman (1944, p. 126), has shown, that so-called protocol propositions about the physical world are of an entirely different kind than protocol propositions about the psycho-physical world.

   3. The identification of experience with sensory observation in general and of the experience of overt action in particular (and that is what Nagel proposes) excludes several dimensions of social reality from all possible inquiry.

(a) Even an ideally refined behaviorism can, as has been pointed out for instance by Mead (1934), merely explain the behavior of the observed, not of the observing behaviorist.

(b) The same overt behavior (say a tribal pageant as it can be captured by the movie camera) may have an entirely different meaning to the performers. What interests the social scientist is merely whether it is a war dance, a barter trade, the reception of a friendly ambassador or something else of this sort.

(c) Moreover, the concept of human action in terms of common-sense thinking and of the social sciences includes what may be called 'negative actions', i.e. intentional refraining from acting (Weber, 1964, p. 88), which, of course, escapes sensory observation. Not to sell certain merchandise at a given price is doubtless as economic an action as to sell it.

(d) Furthermore, as Thomas has shown (1951, p. 81), social reality contains elements of beliefs and convictions which are real because they are so defined by the participants and which escape sensory observation. To the inhabitants of Salem in the seventeenth century, witchcraft was not a delusion but an element of their social reality and is as such open to investigation by the social scientists.

(e) Finally, and this is the most important point, the postulate of sensory observation of overt human behavior takes as a model a particular and relatively small sector of the social world, namely, situations in which the acting individual is given to the observer in what is commonly called a face-to-face relationship. But there are many other dimensions of the social world in which situations of this kind do not prevail. If we put a letter in the mailbox we assume that anonymous fellow-men, called postmen, will perform a series of manipulations, unknown and unobservable to us, with the effect that the addressee, possibly also unknown to us, will receive the message and react in a way which also escapes our sensory observation; and the result of all this is that we receive the book we have ordered. Or if I read an editorial stating that France fears the rearmament of Germany, I know perfectly well what this statement means without knowing the editorialist and even without knowing a Frenchman or a German, let alone without observing their overt behavior.

In terms of common-sense thinking in everyday life men have knowledge of these various dimensions of the social world in which they live. To be sure, this knowledge is not only fragmentary since it is restricted principally to certain sectors of this world, it is also frequently inconsistent in itself and shows all degrees of clarity and distinctness from full insight or 'knowledge-about', as James (1890, p. 221) called it, through 'knowledge of acquaintance' or mere familiarity, to blind belief in things just taken for granted. In this respect there are considerable differences from individual to individual and from social group to social group. Yet, in spite of all these inadequancies, common-sense knowledge of everyday life is sufficient for coming to terms with fellow-men, cultural objects, social institutions – in brief, with social reality. This is so, because the world (the natural and the social one) is from the outset an intersubjective world and because, as shall be pointed out later on, our knowledge of it is in various ways socialized. Moreover, the social world is experienced from the outset as a meaningful one. The Other's body is not experienced as an organism but as a fellow-man, its overt behavior not as an occurrence in the space-time of the outer world, but as our fellow-man's action. We normally 'know' what the Other does, for what reason he does it, why he does it at this particular time and in these particular circumstances. That means that we experience our fellow-man's action in terms of his motives and goals. And in the same way, we experience cultural objects in terms of the human action of which they are the result. A tool, for example, is not experienced as a thing in the outer world (which of course it is also) but in terms of the purpose for which it was designed by more or less anonymous fellow-men and its possible use by others.

The fact that in common-sense thinking we take for granted our actual or potential knowledge of the meaning of human actions and their products, is, I suggest, precisely what social scientists want to express if they speak of understanding or *Verstehen* as a technique of dealing with human affairs. *Verstehen* is, thus, primarily not a method used by the social scientist, but the particular experiential form in which common-sense thinking takes cognizance of the social cultural world. It has nothing to do with introspection; it is a result of processes of learning or acculturation in the same way as the common-sense experience of the so-called natural world. *Verstehen* is, moreover, by no means a private affair of the observer which cannot be controlled by the experiences of other observers. It is controllable at least to the same extent to which the private sensory perceptions of an individual are controllable by any other individual under certain conditions. You have just to think of the discussion by a trial jury of whether the defendant has shown 'pre-meditated malice' or 'intent' in killing a person, whether he was capable of knowing the consequences of his deed, etc. Here we even have certain 'rules of procedure' furnished by the 'rules of evidence' in the juridical sense and a kind of verification of the findings resulting from processes of *Verstehen* by the Appellate Court, etc. Moreover, predictions based on *Verstehen* are continuously made in common-sense thinking with high success. There is more than a fair chance that a duly stamped and addressed letter put in a New York mailbox will reach the addressee in Chicago.

Nevertheless, both defenders and critics of the process of *Verstehen* maintain, and with good reason, that *Verstehen* is 'subjective'. Unfortunately, however, this term is used by each party in a different sense. The critics of understanding call it subjective, because they hold that understanding the motives of another man's action depends upon the private, uncontrollable and unverifiable intuition of the observer or refers to his private value system. The social scientists, such as Weber, however, call *Verstehen* subjective because its goal is to find out what the actor 'means' in his action, in contrast to the meaning which this action has for the actor's partner or a neutral observer. This is the origin of Weber's famous postulate of subjective interpretation, of which more will have to be said in what follows. The whole discussion suffers from the failure to distinguish clearly between *Verstehen* (a) as the experiential form of common-sense knowledge of human affairs, (b) as an epistemological problem, and (c) as a method peculiar to the social sciences.

So far we have concentrated on *Verstehen* as the way in which common-sense thinking finds its bearing within the social world and comes to terms with it. As to the epistemological question: 'How is such understanding or *Verstehen* possible?' Alluding to a statement Kant made in another context, I suggest that it is a 'scandal of philosophy' that so far a satisfactory solution to the problem of our knowledge of other minds and, in connection therewith, of the intersubjectivity of our experience of the natural as well as the socio-cultural world has not been found and that, until rather recent times, this problem has even escaped the attention of philosophers. But the solution of this most difficult problem of philosophical interpretation is one of the first things taken for granted in our common-sense thinking and practically solved without any difficulty in each of our everyday actions. And since human beings are born of mothers and not concocted in retorts, the experience of the existence of other human beings and of the meaning of their actions is certainly the first and most original empirical observation man makes.

On the other hand, philosophers as different as James, Bergson, Dewey, Husserl and Whitehead agree that the common-sense knowledge of everyday life is the unquestioned but always questionable background within which inquiry starts and within which alone it can be carried out. It is this *Lebenswelt*, as Husserl calls it, within which, according to him, all scientific and even logical concepts originate; it is the social matrix within which, according to Dewey, unclarified situations emerge, which have to be transformed by the process of inquiry into warranted assertibility; and Whitehead has pointed out that it is the aim of science to produce a theory which agrees with experience by explaining the thought objects constructed by common sense through the mental constructs or thought objects of science. For all these thinkers agree that any knowledge of the world, in common-sense thinking as well as in science, involves mental constructs, syntheses, generalizations, formalizations, idealizations, specific to the respective level of thought organization. The concept of Nature, for instance, with which the natural sciences have to deal is, as Husserl has shown, an idealizing abstraction from the *Lebenswelt*, an abstraction which, on principle and of course legitmately, excludes persons with their personal life and all objects of culture which originate as such in practical human activity. Exactly this layer of the *Lebenswelt*, however, from which the natural sciences have to abstract, is the social reality which the social sciences have to investigate.

This insight sheds a light on certain methodological problems peculiar to the social sciences. To begin with, it appears that the assumption that the strict adoption of the principles of concept and theory formation prevailing in the natural sciences will lead to reliable knowledge of social reality is inconsistent in itself. If a theory can be developed on such principles, say in the form of an ideally refined behaviorism – and it is certainly possible to imagine this – then it will not tell us anything about social reality as experienced by men in everyday life. As Nagel himself admits, it will be highly abstract, and its concepts will apparently be remote from the obvious and familiar traits found in any society. On the other hand, a theory which aims at explaining social reality has to develop particular devices foreign to the natural sciences in order to agree with the common-sense experience of the social world. This is indeed what all theoretical sciences of human affairs – economics, sociology, the sciences of law, linguistics, cultural anthropology, etc. – have done.

This state of affairs is founded on the fact that there is an essential difference in the structure of the thought objects or mental constructs formed by the social sciences and those formed by the natural sciences. It is up to the natural scientist and to him alone to define, in accordance with the procedural rules of his science, his observational field, and to determine the facts, data and events within it which are relevant for his problem or scientific purpose at hand. Neither are those facts and events pre-selected, nor is the observational field pre-interpreted. The world of nature, as explored by the natural scientists, does not 'mean' anything to molecules, atoms and electrons. But the observational field of the social scientist – social reality – has a specific meaning and relevance structure for the human beings living, acting and thinking within it. By a series of common-sense constructs they have pre-selected and pre-interpreted this world which they experience as the reality of their daily lives. It is these thought objects of theirs which determine their behavior by motivating it. The thought objects constructed by the social scientists, in order to grasp this social reality, have to be founded upon the thought objects constructed by the common-sense thinking of men, living their daily life within their social world.

Thus, the constructs of the social sciences are, so to speak, constructs of the second degree, that is, constructs of the constructs made by the actors on the social scene, whose behavior the social scientist has to observe and to explain in accordance with the procedural rules of his science.

Thus, the exploration of the general principles according to which man in daily life organizes his experiences, and especially those of the social world, is the first task of the methodology of the social sciences. This is not the place to outline the procedures of a phenomenological analysis of the so-called natural attitude by which this can be done. We shall briefly mention only a few problems involved.

The world, as has been shown by Husserl, is from the outset experienced in the pre-scientific thinking of everyday life in the mode of typicality. The unique objects and events given to us in a unique aspect are unique within a horizon of typical familiarity and pre-acquaintanceship. There are mountains, trees, animals, dogs – in particular Irish setters and among them my Irish setter, Rover. Now I may look at Rover either as this unique individual, my irreplaceable friend and comrade or just as a typical example of 'Irish setter', 'dog', 'mammal', 'animals', 'organism' or 'object of the outer world'. Starting from here, it can be shown that whether I do one or the other, and also which traits or qualities of a given object or event I consider as individually unique and which as typical, depends upon my actual interest and the system of relevances involved – briefly, upon my practical or theoretical 'problem at hand'. This 'problem at hand', in turn, originates in the circumstances within which I find myself at any moment of my daily life and which I propose to call my biographically determined situation. Thus, typification depends upon my problem at hand for the definition and solution of which the type has been formed. It can be further shown that at least one aspect of the biographically and situationally determined systems of interests and relevances is subjectively experienced in the thinking of everyday life as systems of motives for action, of choices to be made, of projects to be carried out, of goals to be reached. It is this insight of the actor into the dependencies of the motives and goals of his actions upon his biographically determined situation which social scientists have in view when speaking of the subjective meaning which the actor 'bestows upon' or 'connects with' his action. This implies that, strictly speaking, the actor and he alone knows what he does, why he does it, and when and where his action starts and ends.

But the world of everyday life is from the outset also a social cultural world in which I am interrelated in manifold ways of interaction with fellow-men known to me in varying degrees of intimacy and anonymity. To a certain extent, sufficient for many practical purposes, I understand their behavior, if I understand their motives, goals, choices and plans originating in *their* biographically determined circumstances. Yet only in particular situations, and then only fragmentarily, can I experience the Others' motives, goals, etc. – briefly, the subjective meanings they bestow upon their actions, in their uniqueness. I can, however, experience them in their typicality. In order to do so I construct typical patterns of the actors' motives and ends, even of their attitudes and personalities, of which their actual conduct is just an instance or example. These typified patterns of the Others' behavior become in turn motives of my own actions, and this leads to the phenomenon of self-typification well known to social scientists under various names.

Here, I submit, in the common-sense thinking of everyday life, is the origin of the so-called constructive or ideal types, a concept which as a tool of the social sciences has been analysed by Hempel in such a lucid way. But at least at the common-sense level the formation of these types involves neither intuition nor a theory, if we understand these terms in the sense of Hempel's statements (1952). As we shall see, there are also other kinds of ideal or constructive types, those formed by the social scientist, which are of a quite different structure and indeed involve theory. But Hempel has not distinguished between the two.

Next we have to consider that the common-sense knowledge of everyday life is from the outset socialized in many respects.

It is first, structurally socialized, since it is based on the fundamental idealization that if I were to change places with my fellow-man I would experience the same sector of the world in substantially the same perspectives as he does, our particular biographical circumstances becoming for all practical purposes at hand irrelevant. I propose to call this idealization that of the reciprocity of perspectives.

It is, second, genetically socialized, because the greater part of our knowledge, as to its content and the particuar forms of typification under which it is organized, is socially derived and this in socially approved terms.

It is, third, socialized in the sense of social distribution of knowledge, each individual knowing merely a sector of the world and common knowledge of the same sector varying individually as to its degree of distinctness, clarity, acquaintanceship or mere belief.

These principles of socialization of common-sense knowledge, and especially that of the social distribution of knowledge, explain at least partially what the social scientist has in mind in speaking of the functional structural approach to studies of human affairs. The concept of functionalism – at least in the modern social sciences – is not derived from the biological concept of the functioning of an organism, as Nagel holds. It refers to the socially distributed constructs of patterns of typical motives, goals, attitudes, personalities, which are supposed to be invariant and are then interpreted as the function or structure of the social system itself. The more these interlocked behavior patterns are standardized and institutionalized, that is, the more their typicality is socially approved by laws, folkways, mores and habits, the greater is their usefulness in common-sense and scientific thinking as a scheme of interpretation of human behavior.

These are, very roughly, the outlines of a few major features of the constructs involved in common-sense experience of the intersubjective world in daily life, which is called *Verstehen*. As explained before, they are the first level constructs upon which the second level constructs of the social sciences have to be erected. But here a major problem emerges. On the one hand, it has been shown that the constructs on the first level, the common-sense constructs, refer to subjective elements, namely the *Verstehen* of the actor's action from his, the actor's, point of view. Consequently, if the social sciences aim indeed at explaining social reality, then the scientific constructs on the second level, too, must include a reference to the subjective meaning an action has for the actor. This is, I think, what Weber understood by his famous postulate of subjective interpretation, which has, indeed, been observed so far in the theory formation of all social sciences. The postulate of subjective interpretation has to be understood in the sense that all scientific explanations of the social world *can*, and for certain purposes *must*, refer to the subjective meaning of the actions of human beings from which social reality originates.

On the other hand, I agreed with Nagel's statement that the social sciences, like all empirical sciences, have to be objective in the sense that their propositions are subjected to controlled verification and must not refer to private uncontrollable experience.

How is it possible to reconcile these seemingly contradictory principals? Indeed, the most serious question which the methodology of the social sciences has to answer is: How is it possible to form objective concepts and an objectively verifiable theory of subjective meaning-structures? The basic insight that the concepts formed by the social scientist are constructs of the constructs formed in common-sense thinking by the actors on the social scene offers an answer. The scientific constructs formed on the second level, in accordance with the procedural rules valid for all empirical sciences, are objective ideal typical constructs and, as such, of a different kind from those developed on the first level of common-sense thinking which they have to supersede. They are theoretical systems embodying testable general hypotheses in the sense of Hempel's definition. This device has been used by social scientists concerned with theory long before this concept was formulated by Weber and developed by his school.

Before describing a few features of these scientific constructs, let us briefly consider the particular attitude of the theoretical social scientist to the social world, in contradistinction to that of the actor on the social scene. The theoretical scientist – qua scientist, not qua human being (which he is, too) – is not involved in the observed situation, which is to him not of practical but merely of cognitive interest. The system or relevances governing common-sense interpretation in daily life originates in the biographical situation of the observer. By making up his mind to become a scientist, the social scientist has replaced his personal biographical situation by what I shall call, following Kaufmann (1944, pp. 52, 251), a scientific situation. The problems with which he has to deal might be quite unproblematic for the human being within the world and vice versa. Any scientific problem is determined by the actual state of the respective science, and its solution has to be achieved in accordance with the procedural rules governing this science, which among other things warrant the control and verification of the solution offered. The scientific problem, once established, alone determines what is relevant for the scientist as well as the conceptual frame of reference to be used by him. This and nothing else, it seems to me, is what Weber means when he postulates the objectivity of the social sciences, their detachment from the value patterns which govern or might govern the behavior of the actors on the social scene.

How does the social scientist proceed? He observes certain facts and events within social reality which refer to human action and he constructs typical behavior or course-of-action patterns from what he has observed. Thereupon he coordinates to these typical course-of-action patterns models of an ideal actor or actors, whom he imagines as being gifted with consciousness. Yet it is consciousness restricted so as to contain nothing but the elements relevant to the performing of the course-of-action patterns observed. He thus ascribes to this fictitious consciousness a set of typical notions, purposes, goals, which are assumed to be invariant in the specious consciousness of the imaginary actor-model. This homunculus or puppet is supposed to be interrelated in interaction patterns to other homunculi or puppets constructed in a similar way. Among these homunculi with which the social scientist populates his model of the social world of everyday life, sets of motives, goals, roles – in general, systems of relevances – are distributed in such a way as the scientific problems under scrutiny require. Yet – and this is the main point – these constructs are by no means arbitrary. They are subject to the postulate of logical consistency and to the postulate of adequacy. The latter means that each term in such a scientific model of human action must be constructed in such way that a human act performed within the real world by an individual actor as indicated by the typical construct would be understandable to the actor himself as well as to his fellow-men in terms of common-sense interpretation of everyday life. Compliance with the postulate of logical consistency warrants the objective validity of the thought objects constructed by the social scientist; compliance with the postulate of adequacy warrants their compatibility with the constructs of everyday life.

As the next step, the circumstances within which such a model operates may be varied, that is, the situation which the homunculi have to meet may be imagined as changed, but not the set of motives and relevances assumed to be the sole content of their consciousness. I may, for example, construct a model of a producer acting under conditions of unregulated competition, and another of a producer acting under cartel restrictions, and then compare the output of the same commodity of the same firm in the two models (Machlup, 1952, p. 9). In this way, it is possible to predict how such a puppet or system of puppets might behave under certain conditions and to discover certain 'determinate relations between a set of variables, in terms of which . . . empirically ascertainable regularities . . . can be explained'. This, however, is Nagel's definition of a theory. It can easily be seen that each step involved in the construction and use of the scientific model can be verified by empirical observation, provided that we do not restrict this term to sensory perceptions of objects and events in the outer world but include the experimental form, by which common-sense thinking in everyday life understands human actions and their outcome in terms of their underlying motives and goals.

References

Hempel, C. G. (1952) 'Symposium: problems of concept and theory formation in the social sciences', *Science, Language and Human Rights*. University of Pennsylvania Press, vol. 1, pp. 65–86.
James, W. (1890) *Principles of Psychology*. 2 vols., Henry Holt.
Kaufmann, F. (1944) *Methodology of the Social Sciences*. Humanities Press.
Machlup, F. (1952) *The Economics of Seller's Competition*. Johns Hopkins University Press.
Mead, G. H. (1934) *Mind, Self and Society*. University of Chicago Press.
Thomas, W. I. (1951) *Social Behaviour and Personality*. E. H. Volkart (ed.) Social Science Research.
Weber, M. (1964) *The Theory of Social and Economic Organization*. Collier-Macmillan.

The logic of naturalistic inquiry

Norman K. Denzin

Existing formulations of naturalism as a distinct approach to empirical inquiry in the social sciences suffer from several overriding flaws. On the one hand, naturalistic theorists and practitioners have seldom been in agreement on what they mean by the method. For some (Catton, 1966), it is seen as rigorous positivism. For others (Matza, 1969), it is viewed as humanism in disguise. For still others (Barker, 1968; Hutt and Hutt, 1970; Willems and Rausch, 1969; Wright, 1967), it is compared to ecological psychology and/or ethology – a bare kind of behaviorism that studies people in their natural habitats. Here the naturalist, like the ethologist, makes little effort to record, probe and study such social-psychological processes as attitudes and definitions of the situation. There are those (Lofland, 1971) who view naturalism as a deep commitment to collect rich, often atheoretical ethnographic specimens of human behavior.

These statements also suffer from a failure to specify the empirical phenomena to which the method is directed (e.g., if one observes behavior, what kinds of behavior?). Nor has there been any systematic attention given to such traditional and perduring methodological problems as measurement, sampling, validity, reliability and causal analysis. The basic unit of naturalistic analysis has never been clarified and the role of the naturalistic observer in his studies remains clouded. This conceptual diversity has led many to take a sceptical, if not irreverent, view of the naturalistic approach, viewing it as soft science or journalism.

Perhaps the basic deficiency of prior naturalistic formulations has been the absence of a more general theoretical perspective that would integrate all phases of the sociological act. With few exceptions the dominant scientific paradigm has been imported from physics, chemistry or biology.[1]

In this article I offer a view of naturalism that takes as its point of departure the social behaviorism of Mead (1934; 1938) and the sym-

Extract from Norman K. Denzin, 'The logic of naturalistic inquiry', *Social Forces*, 1971, **50**, 166–82.

bolic interactionism of Blumer (1969). I call this version of the research act *naturalistic behaviorism* and mean by the term the studied commitment to actively enter the worlds of native people and to render those worlds understandable from the standpoint of a theory that is grounded in the *behaviors, languages, definitions, attitudes* and *feelings* of those studied. Naturalistic behaviorism attempts a wedding of the covert, private features of the social act with its public, behaviorally observable counterparts. It thus works back and forth between word and deed, definition and act. Naturalistic behaviorism aims for viable social theory, it takes rich ethnographic descriptions only as a point of departure. This version of behaviorism recognizes that humans have social selves and as such act in ways that reflect their unfolding definitions of the situation. The naturalist is thus obliged to enter people's minds, if only through retrospective accounts of past actions (see Campbell's 1969 suggestions for such studies).

The basic unit of analysis for naturalistic behaviorism becomes the *joint act*, whether this is a dinner party, a socializing relationship, crowd behavior, nations at war or conduct in small groups. Naturalistic behaviorism places the sociological observer squarely in the center of the research act. It recognizes the observer for what he or she is and takes note of the fact that all sociological work somehow reflects the unique stance of the investigator. It assumes that all studies begin in some fashion from a problem, or set of problems, deeply troubling to the sociologist; whether this be the character of alienation, the social-ization of one's own children or an attempt to understand how mental hospitals create mental illness. Sound, viable and exciting sociology begins with biographically troubling issues and culminates in an attempt to offer public answers to what was initially personal and private (see Mills, 1959). The naturalistic behaviorist thus stands over and against the broader sociological community and takes himself or herself seriously. In this sense the sociologist becomes both object and subject in his studies. His reflections on self and other and his conduct in interactive sequences become central pieces of data. Introspection, then, is basic to naturalism (see Cooley, 1926). The naturalist employs any and all sociological methods, whether these be secondary analyses of quantitative data, limited surveys, unobtrusive measures, partici-pant observation, document analysis or life-history constructions. He will admit into his analyses any and all data that are ethically allowable. He works with statistical, quantitative accounts of people and their actions, if such accounts render more understandable the behavior in question. While taking a skeptical stance toward those research protocols that dictate how one approaches the empirical world, the naturalist is committed to *sophisticated rigor*. Which is to say he is committed to making his data and explanatory schemes as public and replicable as possible. Thus he details in careful fashion the nature of his sampling framework, triangulates his observations and continually assesses the empirical grounding of his causal propositions. Naturalism is grounded in the study of behavioral acts. It focuses on the timing, sequencing and consequences of such acts, whether these are symbolic utterances, covert conversations with self or overt behaviors.[2]

A programmatic statement of the naturalistic method is in order if sociologists of the interactionist and micro-behaviorist persuasion are to bring their theories in closer touch with the empirical social world. Accordingly special attention will be given to how the naturalistic observer: (1) samples from ongoing social organizations; (2) employs naturalistic indicators; (3) assesses these indicators by the usual canons of reliability, repeatability and validity; (4) selects and distinguishes for careful analysis representative, illustrative and negative cases; (5) develops processual, explanatory models of the unfolding joint act; (6) records and analyzes his own behavior. [. . .]

The Thrust of Naturalism

As a field strategy naturalism implies a profound respect for the character of the empirical world. It demands that the investigator take his theories and methods to that world. As such he collects *behavior specimens*.[3] That is, he attempts to reproduce in a rich and detailed fashion the experiences, thoughts and languages of those he studies. Such specimens will reflect the actual temporal sequence of the behavior under analysis and they will show how each interactant influenced and was influenced by all others in the behavioral situation. These specimens are then examined by the analyst from multiple perspectives. He compares how the persons in question organized and justified their actions and places these explanations over and against his emergent sociological scheme (see Campbell, 1969; Stauss and Glaser, 1970). Which is to say he grounds his theory in the behaviors of those studied. The naturalist resists schemes and models which over-simplify the complexity of everyday life. He asks whether such conventional sociological variables as age, sex, race, education and religion are seen as relevant by those he studies. He attempts to penetrate their worlds of experience to determine what forces they see shaping and influencing their behavior. Yet he understands that there will be an inevitable tension between his analytic schemes and the interpretative models of those studied (see Becker, 1970). The sociological model is general, abstract and relativistic. The everyday model is personal and nongeneralizing. He attempts, then, to impose order on the social world and to reduce as much as possible the distance between his *outsider imposed* concepts and those employed by the native person.[4]

As a consequence sampling strategies are fitted to the temporal, ritual, moral and sentimental features of the social worlds under examination. Measurement strategies are couched around naturalistic indicators. While he may have occasion to use more formalized interview techniques, the observer prefers to take as central indicators behaviors routinely engaged in by his subjects. He moves from sensitizing concepts to the immediate world of social experience and permits that world to shape and modify his conceptual framework. In this way he moves continually between the realm of more general social theory and the worlds of native people. Such an approach recognizes that social phenomena, while displaying regularities, vary by time, place and circumstance. The observer, then, looks for repeatable regularities (see Kaplan, 1964: 127–8). He uses ritual patterns of dress and body-spacing as indicators of self-image. He takes special languages, codes and dialects as indicators of group boundaries. He studies his subject's prized social objects as indicators of prestige, dignity and esteem hierarchies. He studies moments of interrogation and derogation as indicators of socialization strategies. He attempts to enter his subject's closed worlds of interaction so as to examine the character of private, versus public acts and attitudes.

His theories are constructed on the basis of such observations. In building up a theory the naturalistic observer respects and takes seriously those he studies. Indeed he cultivates close relationships. Hoping to be taken seriously by the subject, he recognizes that alert, observant participants know more than he ever will about the realities under investigation (see Blumer, 1969: 41). Such persons serve as natural resources and checks on the emerging theory. Acting as a panel of judges, they collectively and singly evaluate and help reconstruct valid and viable theories of their social worlds (see for example the work of Alan G. Sutter, 1966, on righteous dope fiends). Native persons serve, too, as methodological consultants and field guides. While this feature of the informant has been repeatedly noted in the fieldwork literature (see for example Back, 1960; Becker *et al.,* 1961; Dalton, 1964; Lofland, 1971; Strauss and Glaser, 1970; Whyte, 1955), it must be stressed again. Often the observer finds himself in a situation where the phenomena he wishes to observe (1) occur at a low frequency, or (2) are not amenable to investigative procedures used in the past. In such situations the native person can often produce records of past occurrences of the phenomena in question, thus broadening the sociologist's data base. The observer can then check his hunches against the 'native's' interpretations.

On other occasions the native can coach the observer on new field techniques, suggesting important modifications in existing research strategy. In the early phases of my field study on two-, three-, and four-year-old children I wished to gather data on the self-concept and intended to employ a version of the 'Who Am I?', Twenty-Statements Test. Such data, if gathered, would have permitted comparisons with previous studies on older age-groups. I subsequently approached the head preschool instructor in the setting where I was working and sought her counsel. She suggested that I modify the question by telling the children that I was writing a book about the school, wanted a page about each of them, and what would they like to write on their page. I then asked the children 'What should I say about you? If someone asked me who you were, what would you want me to say?' This modification of the standard research procedure proved highly successful and permitted me to approach the children on a more familiar footing.

It is important to stress that equal weight cannot be given all native informants. Their perspectives and ability to aid the observer vary by their position in the social organization under study (e.g., isolate, leader, oldhand, marginal, etc.). Their motives for aiding the observer shape the character of their information (e.g., attempts to win his favor, etc.). There exists, then, a hierarchy of credibility among informants (see Becker, 1967). The naturalist seeks to employ multiple native informants. His task is one of threading and weaving their diverse and often contradictory reports into an accurate picture. Which means he may eventually have to discredit or drop one or more of his informants because their information fails to stand up under close scrunity.

Naturalism places severe strain on the observer – emotional, physical and ethical. It obligates him or her to take seriously their own introspections and reflections on the social process, as that process is recorded, perceived and acted towards. This methodology immediately opens for sociological analysis all of one's daily actions and conversations as sources of data on the self and the joint act. Recording one's behavior permits the observer to be both objective and subjective. He can note that he made a specific act at a specific time and place in the company of a certain set of others. But simultaneously he can probe the subjective features of the act by noting what his thoughts were at the time he acted. In such observations the sociologist is forced to stand outside his own conduct and view it as a third party. He treats himself as an object, like any other object in the interaction process. But by probing his own motives and inclinations and by discussing them with his fellows he can reconstruct the covert dialogues with self that produced the behavior just observed. In this way the sociologist uses himself and his interactive others as native audiences in the construction of social theory.

Notes

1. The major exceptions here are Becker (1970), Lofland (1971), and Schatzman and Strauss (1973).
2. It is relevant here to distinguish types of quantitative approaches. On the one hand there are those sociologists Mills (1959) and Blumer (1969) term naive positivists or abstracted empiricists. Here scientific protocol stands in the way of careful, close-up studies of social life. My introduction of the phrase 'sophisticated rigor' is intended to describe any and all sociologists who employ multiple methods, seek out diverse data sources and attempt to develop behaviorally grounded theories of their subject's

behavior. Such scholars may, as did Lieberson (1970), give greater weight to quantitative indicators but still employ ingenious, unobtrusive indicators (e.g. bilingual listings in the yellow pages of telephone books) with first-hand observations and retrospective accounts. They may, as Stark (1972), reanalyze existing survey data (in this case surveys of the police), collect historical documents, make on-the-spot participant observations (observing police riots) and conduct intensive interviews. Here the analyst moves back and forth between quantitative and qualitative observations as he builds theory. Such is found in Suttles (1968) only to a lesser degree where unobtrusive, nonreactive observations were gathered on the distribution of persons of diverse ethnic background in public places (parks, buses, etc.). These observations were then built into Suttles' emerging theory that was largely qualitative in nature. I am suggesting that there is nothing inherent in a method, or a perspective, that renders that approach useless – or unacceptable. It is the use to which the method is put, and the degree of rigor under which it is employed that determines its usefulness. The quantitatively oriented researcher, then, can also share the naturalistic perspective.

3. The notion of behavior specimen is taken from the extensive work of Barker and Wright, and Barker's (1968) more recent theoretical formulations on ecological psychology.

4. 'Native person' is introduced here as a generic term which covers all people studied by the sociologist. They may be experimental subjects, interviewees, friends, colleagues and neighbors.

References

Back, K. W. (1960) 'The well-informed informant', pp. 179–87 in Richard N. Adams and Jack D. Preiss (eds), *Human Organization Research*. Homewood, Illinois: Dorsey.

Barker, Roger G. (1968) *Ecological Psychology*. Stanford: Stanford University Press.

Becker, H. S. (1967) 'Whose side are we on?', *Social Problems*, **14**(Winter), 239–48.

Becker, H. S. (1970) *Sociological Work*. Chicago: Aldine.

Becker, H. S., Geer, B., Hughes, E. C. and Strauss, A. L. (1961) *Boys in White*. Chicago: University of Chicago Press.

Blumer, H. (1969) *Symbolic Interactionism*. Englewood Cliffs: Prentice-Hall.

Campbell, D. T. (1969) 'A phenomenology of the other one: corrigible, hypothetical, and critical', pp. 41–69 in Theodore Mischel (ed.), *Human Action: Conceptual and Empirical Issues*. New York: Academic Press.

Catton, W. R., Jr. (1966) *From Animistic to Naturalistic Sociology*. New York: McGraw-Hill.

Cooley, C. H. (1926) 'The roots of social knowledge', *American Journal of Sociology*, **32** (July), 59–79.

Dalton, M. (1964) 'Preconceptions and methods in men who manage', pp. 50–95 in Phillip E. Hammond (ed.), *Sociologists at Work*. New York: Basic Books.

Hutt, S. J. and Hutt, C. (1970) *Direct Observation and Measurement of Behavior*. Springfield, Illinois: Thomas.

Kaplan, A. (1964) *The Conduct of Inquiry*. San Francisco: Chandler.

Lieberson, S. (1970) *Language and Ethnic Relations in Canada*. New York: Wiley.

Lofland, J. (1971) *Analyzing Social Settings*. Belmont, California: Wadsworth.

Matza, D. (1969) *Becoming Deviant*. Englewood Cliffs: Prentice-Hall.

Mead, G. H. (1934) *Mind, Self and Society*. Chicago: University of Chicago Press.

Mead, G. H. (1938) *The Philosophy of the Act*. Chicago: University of Chicago Press.

Mills, C. W. (1959) *The Sociological Imagination*. New York: Oxford University Press.

Schatzman, L. and Strauss, A. (1973), *Field Research: Strategies for a Natural Sociology*. Englewood Cliffs: Prentice-Hall.

Stark, Rodney (1972) *Police Riots*, Belmont, California: Wadsworth.

Strauss, A. and Glaser, B. G. (1970) *Anguish: A Case Study of a Dying Trajectory.* San Francisco: Sociology Press.

Suttles, G. D. (1968) *The Social Order of the Slum.* Chicago: University of Chicago Press.

Sutter, A. G. (1966) 'The world of the righteous dope fiend', *Issues in Criminology,* **2,** 177–222.

Whyte, W. F. (1955) *Street Corner Society.* 2nd edn, Chicago: University of Chicago Press.

Willems, E. P. and Rausch, H. L. (eds.) (1969) *Naturalistic Viewpoints in Psychological Research.* New York: Holt, Rinehart & Winston.

Wright, H. F. (1967) *Recording and Analyzing Child Behavior.* New York: Harper & Row.

Research design

Introduction

The articles here are concerned with the strategy of social enquiry: the sequence of decisions that have to be taken in any piece of research. We start with the origins of research problems themselves. In the first Reading, Greer locates these in the areas of social policy, social philosophy and substantive discipline-based theory. Traditionally, researchers have often used official statistics as the source of their insights into such social phenomena as suicide and crime. In their important article Kitsuse and Cicourel challenge the validity of this approach, maintaining that such statistics say more about the ways in which societies categorize individuals than they do about the behaviour of interest. They argue for studies directed specifically at the organizational processes by which 'social facts' are established. We then turn to empirical research itself, in Kish's classic statement of design issues (including the use of statistical testing) under the three headings of experiments, surveys and 'investigations'. Experiments give the investigator the opportunity to make strong causal inferences because of his ability to control relevant variables; surveys on the other hand, though weak in the control aspect, have the great advantage of representativeness with respect to a specified population; investigations capitalize on natural settings, thus avoiding the artificiality of experiments and the standard interviews in the typical social survey. To Kish the 'true' experiment is one in which the effects of extraneous variables are controlled by random allocation of groups (experimental and control) to treatments. Such random allocation is rarely possible in naturally occurring social situations of the kind that follow new policy implementation; hence the need for research strategy, which can lead to strong causal inferences without it. Campbell tackles this problem in his seminal examination of social reforms in terms of quasi-experimental designs. He sets out the defining characteristics of the two types of validity which apply to experimental designs – 'internal' and 'external'. Drawing on a number of examples, he then considers various ways in which both types of validity can be improved (especially the former) in the absence of randomized allocation to groups. You may find some of the technical discussion in the article, particularly that concerned with regression/discontinuity designs, a little difficult. This need not concern you, as the main point of the article is to stress the distinction between what amounts to 'testimonial' evaluation, the commonest and most useless method for evaluating the effects of social reforms, and true experimental evaluation, perhaps the rarest.

The articles so far take as axiomatic the need to specify research objectives, before data are actually collected. In the reading by Wiseman, we see an entirely different approach where design, data collection and data analysis all evolve as the research process unfolds. This is the classic ethnographic strategy, in which the researcher remains as receptive as possible to his field experience, not closing his options by specifying hypotheses and particular types of data to be collected in order to test them before clarifying in his own mind what form the hypotheses should take. Though much of this kind of work is highly systematic and concerned with such central concerns of all scientists as the reliability and validity of data, it does appear to exclude certain kinds of quantitative research. This position, though advocated by many field researchers, is disputed in the final article. In another classic of its kind, Zelditch identifies three types of research problems for which different types of data collection method are appropriate. To obtain frequency distributions of certain kinds of behaviour, enumeration and sampling may be appropriate; for incidents and life histories participant observation is the appropriate method; and to identify institutionalized norms and statuses, interviewing of informants is the method to use. Zelditch's article adds up to a plea to field researchers to use the *appropriate* method for a particular research problem.

On the selection of problems

Scott Greer

Science as intellectual innovation of a specific kind represents finding and solving problems. And the nature of the problem, the way it is posed, determines the kind of solution possible; problem selection is a major part of social inquiry. Curiously enough, there is little real agreement on 'problematics'; indeed, the question is muted in the literature of social science methodology. Yet it is very important to distinguish between the kinds of problematic situations that give rise to inquiry, for their fruits vary consistently.

Let us begin with the scientist as an actor within a setting, for both actor and setting are necessary to produce a problematic situation. The setting is one in which those aspects that concern the actor are not fully defined. (It is important to remember that only some aspects of a situation are of any concern to any one actor.) Some aspects are presumed to be clearly known, but others are indeterminate – unknown. The actor faces first a problem of intellectual definition.

Resolution of the problematic situation may come about in many ways. These include religion ('trust in God') and other styles of rejecting the problem, from fatalism to suppression of the disturbing unknown. More specifically, resolution may come about in rationalistic ways, by taking thought and subsuming the problematic situation under general regularities already known, or inventing new kinds of regularities that may not have been propounded before.

These resolutions, rational though they are, need not be scientific. The intellectual history of mankind is littered with the pseudosciences, from astrology to palmistry. And historically theological explanations have been an important form of rationalism; they explain the given instant of mystery through assumptions about the ultimate purposes of God or the gods in history and the world. To be scientific, the resolution of the problem must follow the research cycle; to be adequately scientific it must follow rather rigorously certain rules that will be discussed later. But prior to the resolution, the question: where do the problems of social science come from?

Scott Greer, 'On the selection of problems', from *The Logic of Social Inquiry,* Chicago: Aldine Publishing Company, 1961, Ch. 1, pp. 8–14.

There seem to be at least three broad classes of problematic situations that give rise to social inquiry. Each grows out of change and resulting conflict, and each remains important in contemporary research in the social sciences. They may be grouped under three labels: policy problems; problems of social philosophy; and problems intrinsic to developing scientific disciplines.

The policy problem was the first sort to be attacked empirically, for its resolution must be in empirically testable terms. It is the problem of everyday life in the society, a problem of practical urgency. Its salience is clear in the general concern with social and clinical problems and the industries (social welfare, psychiatry) that have emerged to deal with them. Much of the public acceptance of the social sciences today comes from the average citizen's concern with poverty, race relations, mental illness and crime.

Such problems are always defined by the *values* of the society. Growing out of value conflict, they represent efforts to reformulate the world and bring it closer to what is desired. At an extreme, policy problems represent the impulse symbolized in a speech from a play by Dennis Johnston: 'I will take this world between my two hands and batter it into the symbol of my heart's desire.' Such a problematic situation evokes no need for general knowledge, other than that which allows us to intervene with confidence in the stream of things, diverting it in directions we prefer.

Policy problems emerge from the discrepancy between the ideal and the actual and signal overt conflict between them. This may be conflict within the group, as in our present concern with the rights and duties of Negro citizens in the United States; it may be conflict between the values of the group and the nature of the environment, as in the gap between the rising aspirations of the new nations and their economic poverty; it may be conflict between groups, as in the tension between the two major thermonuclear powers in the world today. In any case, it is a dramatic difference between what the actor believes desirable and what he thinks exists that triggers the policy problem.

It is in such terms that it must be solved. The goal is to move actuality, as seen by the problem-definer, toward his ideal state of things. Negroes achieve rights and duties acceptable to the working consensus; the rate of economic activity rises at the same speed as rising aspirations; Russia and the United States achieve a *détente*. The focus of social inquiry into policy problems is upon clues to manipulation and action.

But note carefully that the policy problem is an abstraction from a very complex social situation. There are, after all, many other striking and intriguing aspects of minority–majority relations, of the specific ways of life among Negroes and whites or the change of simple into urban societies, that are ignored by those concerned with policy problems. For them, the world is seen in a perspective that reduces things to a means-end schema: What do we do in order to achieve what we want? This is social science as the handmaiden of policy.

The second source of problems for social science is in the philosophy of history, or more broadly social philosophy. Here we find intellectual problems of great scope, many as old as the history of human thought. In the most general terms, new elements, unknown in their implications, must be fitted into the given context of the culture, reconciled with the known. Such problems grow out of the effort to integrate, in one map of the world, newly discovered regions and continents of knowledge and/or belief.

Such problems originate in the conflict between an ideology, a *weltanschaung* and new experiences. What was the meaning of Copernican cosmology for the Judeo-Christian world view? What was the meaning of the newly discovered 'savages' of the western hemisphere for urban European man? Later, what was the meaning of Marx's historical determinism for liberal capitalist societies? Such questions are broad and ultimately beyond the grasp of social science, yet they stimulate social inquiry. The concern with primitive societies led to anthropology, the comparative science of societies; concern with Marxism led scholars to compare seriously the different social classes in their relations with the larger society. In short, the questions generated by philosophers and intellectuals, generalists and dilettantes, are fertile sources for social inquiry. (And too, some social scientists have been intellectuals, and some philosophers.)

The aim of such inquiry is, finally, a recreation of intellectual order, an integrated world view. The new knowledge and belief interacts with the older frame of reference; both are changed in the process and much is rejected. The intellectual map of the world is left different. Today no serious thinker concerned with society could ignore the relationship between the organization of economic production and reward and the political (and ideological) life of a society. Nor could he ignore the results of comparative anthropology, which turned the 'noble savage' and 'the war of each against all' into myths, but in the process greatly broadened our knowledge of the possible forms human life may take.

The focus of such inquiry is, then, upon ways of integrating new phenomena, new ideas, with an older frame of reference. It is an operation in which we abstract from the welter of history and the array of social forms what appear to be massive tendencies, radical innovations in thought and act, as well as the assumed nature of the world before these occurred. In this kind of inquiry there is a tendency toward a conservative bias, for the pre-existing situation is taken as causal and the novel ideas and facts are seen as deriving from it. If, however, the abstract picture of the earlier situation is incorrect (as it often is), the definition of the new may be grossly deformed. Those who interpret the Soviet regime in Russia as a continuation of Tsarist absolutism may purchase a grain of truth at the price of a carload of illusion. (Indeed, one might understand more about Tsarism through studying the Soviets – the data are nearer at hand.)

The third origin of problems in the social sciences is in the emerging questions raised by previously accumulated propositions. These are questions intrinsic to the discipline; that may have significance for policy or social philosophy, but that is not their significance for the scientist. The plotting of 'learning curves' may be useful to the teacher, but the research psychologist is concerned with the general theory of learning. Such problems, requiring previously formalized theories, come later in the development of a science than policy problems (which may reflect the vocabulary of the folk culture and the assumptions of causation prevalent in everyday life) or problems of social philosophy (which may rest upon unsystematic and unproven beliefs about history and the nature of society).

Thus the scientific problems are generic to an existing scientific community, or 'discipline'. They emerge from conflicts between existing theories, conflicts between theories and findings, hiatuses within the theoretical house, and gaps in empirical proof for accepted propositions. Their resolution must either increase the pragmatic scope of the propositions embodied in the science, its 'empirical bite', or increase the unity and power of propositions through expanding their theoretical significance. (It is, of course, an achievement to demonstrate that propositions do not have the relevance to the experienced world they are believed to have, for the elimination of error is a necessary condition for truth.)

The solution to a problem of this sort requires focusing upon theory, evidence, and the rules by which each enters into the argument. Thus the scientist working at problems generic to his discipline tries to extend the theoretical structure in the light of new data which he has created through observation, and he tries to extend the meaning of the empirical known by new theory which he has created to accommodate the facts. Such problem-solving may result in rigorous, controlled tests: at an extreme, the 'crucial experiment' in which opposing interpretations allow one to focus observation on a given situation in which one or the other must be falsified.

One such crucial experiment was that in which Sherif demonstrated the power of repetition to create norms, or regularities in definitions of situations. Using the 'autokinetic phenomenon', exposing subjects in a dark room to an unmoving point of light that appears to move, he found that individuals in isolation will develop strongly patterned but individually varying definitions of how the (unmoving) light moves; and that when individuals can communicate about the phenomenon, they develop strong group patterns – consensus concerning the distance the (still unmoving) light moves. By eliminating the 'objective facts' he could demonstrate the tendency of the individual to stabilize phenomena in patterns, and the tendency of groups to organize individual interpretations in patterns. The alternative hypothesis of random projection was clearly disproved.[1]

Such research has only the most indirect relevance for policy problems. Its relevance to the problems of social philosophy requires considerable added information and interpretation. But for the discipline of social psychology, it may fairly be called a 'crucial experiment'. In the process of generalizing and interpreting the findings for other kinds of individual and group situations, however, its empirical limits emerge: at that point, conflicting evidence leads to conflicting theory and a new 'crucial experiment' is possible.

The crucial experiment is relatively rare in social inquiry. More common is the pilot inquiry, the descriptive study, the application of some theory to new data, the collection of new evidence for new hypotheses developed from older notions. In each case the problem-solver, the scientist, is abstracting from the complexity of experience (including speculation) and formulating a problem that may be irrelevant to both policy and philosophy of history. For this reason, those who are not aware of his disciplinary tradition and the sometimes long and torturous lines of intellectual descent may condemn his work as trivial. And studying how far people think an unmoving light moves can easily sound like a trick or a trivial hobby; but we must remember that a monk studying the blossoms of sweet peas contributed a great deal to our knowledge of genetics. The danger is that of misplacing the grounds for significance. Problems that seem wholly internal to a social science may, in the long run, be of most significance for both policy and philosophy; their solutions may revolutionize our general conceptions of the constraints and possibilities of human action.

Note and reference

1. M. Sherif describes his famous experiment in 'Group influences upon the formation of norms and attitudes', in *Readings in Social Psychology,* T. M. Newcomb and E. L. Hartley (eds), 1947, Holt.

A note on the uses of official statistics

John I. Kitsuse and Aaron V. Cicourel

Current theoretical and research formulations in the sociology of deviance are cast within the general framework of social and cultural differentiation, deviance and social control. In contrast to the earlier moralistic conceptions of the 'pathologies', the focus of description and analysis has shifted from the vagaries of morbid behavior to the patterning effects of the social–cultural environment on forms of deviant conduct. These forms of deviation are conceived as social products of the organization of groups, social structures and institutions.

Three major lines of inquiry have developed within this general framework. One development has been the problem of explaining the rates of various forms of deviation among various segments of the population. The research devoted to this problem has produced a large body of literature in which individual, group and areal (e.g. census tracts, regions, states, etc.) characteristics are correlated with rates of deviation. Durkheim's pioneer study of suicide is a classic example of this sociological interest. Merton's more general theory of social structure and anomie[1] may be cited as the most widely circulated statement of this problem.

The second line of investigation has been directed to the question of how individuals come to engage in various types of deviant behavior. From the theoretical standpoint, this question has been posed by the fact that although an aggregate of individuals may be exposed to the 'same' sociogenic factors associated with deviant behavior, some individuals become deviant while others do not. Research into this problem has led some sociologists into the field of actuarial statistics and others to social and depth psychology to investigate differences in individual 'adaptation' to the social–cultural environment. The search for the etiology of deviant behavior in individual differences has reintroduced the notion of 'pathology', in the garb of 'emotionally disturbed', 'psychopathic personality', 'weak ego-structure', and other psychological concepts, which has created an hiatus between

sociological and social psychological approaches. Sutherland's differential association theory[2] represents a counterformulation which
attempts to account for the etiology of deviant behavior within the
general framework of 'normal' learning processes.

A third line of inquiry has been concerned with the developmental
processes of 'behavior systems'. Theory and research on this aspect of
deviant behavior focuses on the relation between the social differentiation of the deviant, the organization of deviant activity and the
individual's conception of himself as deviant. Studies of the professional thief, convicts, prostitutes, alcoholics, hoboes, drug addicts,
carnival men and others describe and analyze the deviant sub-culture
and its patterning effects on the interaction between deviant and
others. The work of Lemert[3] presents a systematic theoretical and
empirical integration of this interest in the sociology of deviance.

Although the three lines of investigation share a common interest in
the organizational 'sources' of deviant behavior, a theoretical integration between them has not been achieved. This is particularly apparent
in the theoretical and methodological difficulties posed by the problem
of relating the rates of deviant behavior to the distribution of
'sociogenic' factors within the social structure. These difficulties may
be stated in the form of two questions: (1) How is 'deviant behavior' to
be defined sociologically, and (2) what are the relevant rates of deviant
behavior which constitute the 'facts to be explained'? We shall propose
that these difficulties arise as a consequence of the failure to distinguish between the social conduct which produces a *unit* of behavior
(the behavior-producing processes) and organizational activity which
produces a unit in the rate of *deviant* behavior (the rate-producing
processes).[4] The failure to make this distinction has led sociologists to
direct their theoretical and empirical investigations to the behavior-
producing processes on the implicit assumption that the rates of
deviant behavior may be explained by them. We shall discuss some of
the consequences of this distinction for theory and research in the
sociology of deviance by examining the problems of the 'appropriateness' and 'reliability' of official statistics.[5]

I

The following statement by Merton is a pertinent and instructive point
of departure for a discussion of the questions raised above:

Our primary aim is to discover how some social structures exert a
definite pressure upon certain persons in the society to engage in
non-conforming rather than conforming conduct. *If we can locate
groups peculiarly subject to such pressures, we would expect to find
fairly high rates of deviant behavior in those groups, not because the
human beings comprising them are compounded of distinctive biological tendencies but because they are responding normally to the social*

situation in which they find themselves. Our perspective is sociological. We look at variations in the rates *of deviant behavior, not at its incidence.* [6]

The central hypothesis that Merton derives from his theory is that 'aberrant behavior may be regarded as a symptom of dissociation between culturally prescribed aspirations and socially structured avenues for realizing these aspirations'.[7] The test of this general hypothesis, he suggests, would be to compare the variations in the rates of aberrant behavior among populations occupying different positions within the social structure. The question arises: What are the units of behavior which are to be tabulated to compile these rates of aberrant behavior?

Merton answers this question by discussing the kinds of rates which are 'inappropriate', but he is less explicit about what may be considered 'appropriate' data for sociological research. Discussing the relevance of his theory for research on juvenile delinquency, Merton presents two arguments against the use of 'official' rates of deviant behavior. He asks:

. . . to what extent and for which purposes is it feasible to make use of existing data in the study of deviant behavior? By existing data I mean the data which the machinery of society makes available — census data, delinquency rates as recorded in official or unofficial sources, data on the income distribution of an area, on the state of housing in an area, and the like . . .

There is little in the history of how statistical series on the incidence of juvenile delinquency came to be collected that shows them to be the result of efforts to identify either the sources or the contexts of juvenile delinquency. These are social bookkeeping data. And it would be a happy coincidence if some of them turned out to be in a form relevant for research.

From the sociological standpoint, 'juvenile delinquency' and what it encompasses is a form of deviant behavior for which the epidemiological data, as it were, may not be at hand. You may have to go out and collect your own appropriately organized data rather than to take those which are ready-made by governmental agencies. [8]

Our interpretation of this statement is that for the purposes of sociological research, official statistics may use categories which are unsuitable for the classification of deviant behavior. At best such statistics classify the 'same' forms of deviant behavior in different categories and 'different' forms in the same categories. Thus, the 'sources or the contexts' of the behavior are obscured.

Merton also argues against the use of official statistics on quite different grounds. He states that such data are 'unreliable' because 'successive layers of error intervene between the actual event and the recorded event, between the actual rates of deviant behavior and the records of deviant behavior.'[9] In this statement, the argument is that the statistics are unreliable because some individuals who manifest deviant behavior are apprehended, classified and duly recorded while others are not. It is assumed that if the acts of all such individuals were called to the attention of the official agencies they would be defined as deviant and so classified and recorded. In referring to the 'unreliability' of the statistics in this sense, however, Merton appears to suspend his 'sociologically relevant' definition of deviant behavior and implicitly invokes the definitions applied by the agencies which have compiled the statistics. That is, the 'unreliability' is viewed as a technical and organizational problem, not a matter of differences concerning the definition of deviant behavior.

Thus, Merton argues against the use of official statistics on two separate grounds. On the one hand, official statistics are not appropriately organized for sociological research because they are not collected by the application of a 'sociologically relevant' definition of deviant behavior. On the other hand, he implies that official statistics *could* be used if 'successive layers of error' did not make them 'unreliable'. But if the statistics are inappropriate for sociological research on the first ground, would they not be inappropriate regardless of their 'unreliability'?

It is evident, however, that 'inappropriate' or not, sociologists, including Merton himself,[10] do make use of the official statistics after a few conventional words of caution concerning the 'unreliability' of such statistics. The 'social bookkeeping data' are, after all, considered to bear some, if unknown, relation to the 'actual' rates of deviant behavior that interest sociologists. But granted that there are practical reasons for the use of official statistics, are there any theoretical grounds which justify their use, or is this large body of data useless for research in the sociology of deviance? This question directs us to examine more closely the theoretical and methodological bases of the two arguments against their use.

II

The objection to the official statistics because they are 'inappropriate' is, as indicated above, on definitional grounds. The argument is that insofar as the definitions of deviant behavior incorporated in the official statistics are not 'sociologically relevant', such statistics are *in principle* 'inappropriate' for sociological research. What then is a sociologically relevant definition of deviant behavior and what are to be considered 'appropriately organized data' for sociological research?[11]

We suggest that the question of the theoretical significance of the official statistics can be re-phrased by shifting the focus of investigation from the processes by which *certain forms of behavior* are socially and culturally generated to the processes by which *rates of deviant behavior* are produced. Merton states that his primary aim is to explain the former processes, and he proposes to look at variations in the rates of deviant behavior as indices of the processes. Implicit in this proposal is the assumption that an explanation of the behavior-producing processes is also an explanation of the rate-producing processes. This assumption leads Merton to consider the correspondence between the forms of behavior which his theory is designed to explain and their distribution in the social structure as reflected in some set of statistics, including those commonly used official statistics 'which are ready-made by governmental agencies'.

Let us propose, however, the following: Our primary aim is to explain the *rates of deviant behavior*. So stated, the question which orients the investigation is not how individuals are motivated to engage in behavior defined by the sociologist as 'deviant'. Rather, the definition and content of deviant behavior are viewed as problematic, and the focus of inquiry shifts from the forms of behavior (modes of individual adaptation in Merton's terminology) to the 'societal reactions' which define various forms of behavior as deviant.[12] In contrast to Merton's formulation which focuses on forms of behavior as dependent variables (with structural pressures conceived to be the independent variables), we propose here to view the rates of deviant behavior as dependent variables. Thus, the explanation of rates of deviant behavior would be concerned specifically with the processes of rate construction.

The problem of the definition of 'deviant behavior' is directly related to the shift in focus proposed here. The theoretical conception which guides us is that the *rates of deviant behavior* are produced by *the actions taken by persons in the social system* which define, classify and record certain behaviors as deviant.[13] If a given form of behavior is not interpreted as deviant by such persons it would not appear as a unit in whatever set of rates we may attempt to explain (e.g. the statistics of local social welfare agencies, 'crimes known to the police', Uniform Crime Reports, court records, etc.). The persons who define and activate the rate-producing processes may range from the neighborhood 'busybody' to officials of law enforcement agencies.[14] From this point of view, *deviant behavior* is behavior which is organizationally defined, processed and treated as 'strange', 'abnormal', 'theft', 'delinquent', etc. by the personnel in the social system which has produced the rate. By these definitions, a sociological theory of deviance would focus on three interrelated problems of explanation: (1) How different forms of behavior come to be defined as deviant by various groups or organizations in the society, (2) how individuals manifesting such behaviors are organizationally processed to produce rates of deviant behavior among various segments of the population, and (3) how acts which are officially or unofficially defined as deviant are generated by such conditions as family organization, role inconsistencies or situational 'pressures'.

What are the consequences of these definitions for the question regarding the relevance of official statistics for sociological research? First, the focus on the processes by which rates are produced allows us to consider any set of statistics, 'official' as well as 'unofficial', to be relevant. The question of whether or not the statistics are 'appropriately organized' is not one which is determined by reference to the correspondence between the sociologist's definition of deviant behavior and the organizational criteria used to compile the statistics. Rather the categories which organize a given set of statistics are taken as given – the 'cultural definitions', to use Merton's term, of deviant behavior are *par excellence* the relevant definitions for research. The specification of the definitions explicitly or implicitly stated in the statistical categories is viewed as an empirical problem. Thus, the question to be asked is not about the 'appropriateness' of the statistics, but about the definitions incorporated in the categories applied by the personnel of the rate-producing social system to identify, classify and record behavior as deviant.

Second, a unit in a given rate of deviant behavior is not defined in terms of a given form of behavior or a 'syndrome' of behavior. The behaviors which result in the classification of individuals in a given deviant category are *not necessarily* similar, i.e. the 'objective' manifestation of the 'same' forms of behavior may result in the classification of some individuals as deviant but not others. For example, with reference to the rates of delinquency reported by the police department, we would ask: What are the criteria that the police personnel use to identify and process a youth as 'incorrigible', 'sex offender', 'vandal', etc.? The criteria of such categories are vague enough to include a wide range of behaviors which in turn may be produced by various 'sources and contexts' within the social structure.[15]

Third, the definition of deviant behavior as behavior which is organizationally processed as deviant provides a different perspective on the problem of the 'unreliability' of the official statistics. Insofar as we are primarily concerned with explaining rates rather than the forms of deviant behavior, such statistics may be accepted as a record of the number of those who have been differentiated as variously deviant at different levels of social control and treatment. The 'successive layers of error' which may result from the failure of control agencies to record all instances of certain forms of behavior, or from the exclusion of cases from one set of statistics that are included in another, do not render such statistics 'unreliable', unless they are assigned self-evident status. By the definition of deviance proposed here, such cases are not among those processed as deviant by the organizations which have produced the statistics and thus are not officially deviant. To reject these statistics as 'unreliable' because they fail to record the 'actual' rate of deviant behavior assumes that certain behavior is always deviant independent of social actions which define it as deviant.

Fourth, the conception of rates of deviant behavior as the product of the socially organized activities of social structures provides a method of specifying the 'relevant structure' to be investigated. The rates are constructed from the statistics compiled by specifiable organizations, and those rates must be explained in terms of the deviant-processing activities of those organizations. Thus, rates can be viewed as indices of organizational processes rather than as indices of the incidence of certain forms of behavior. For example, variations in the rates of deviant behavior among a given group (e.g., Negroes) as reflected in the statistics of different organizations may be a product of the differing definitions of deviant behavior used by those organizations, differences in the processing of deviant behavior, differences in the ideological, political and other organizational conditions which affect the rate-making processes.

III

We wish now to discuss briefly some recent work[16] concerning adult and juvenile criminal acts which lends support to the thesis presented above. Let us assume that an ideal system of law-enforcement would lead to the apprehension of all persons who have committed criminal acts as defined by the statutes, and adjudicated in the manner prescribed by those statutes. In the ideal case, there would be little room for administrative interpretation and discretion. The adjudication process would proceed on the basis of evidence deemed legally admissible and the use of the adversary system to convict those who are guilty and exonerate those against whom there is insufficient evidence.[17] Criminologists have long recognized that the practiced and enforced system of criminal law, at all levels of the process, does not fulfill this ideal conception of criminal justice strictly governed by the definitions and prescriptions of statutes. Therefore, criminal statistics clearly cannot be assumed to reflect a system of criminal justice functioning as ideally conceived, and 'labels assigned convicted defendants' are not to be viewed as 'the statutory equivalents of their actual conduct'.[18]

What such statistics do reflect, however, are the specifically organizational contingencies which condition the application of specific statutes to actual conduct through the interpretations, decisions and actions of law enforcement personnel. The decisions and discretionary actions of persons who administer criminal justice have been documented by the American Bar Foundation study cited above. That study and other research[19] indicates the following:

1. There is considerable ambiguity in defining the nature of criminal conduct within the limits defined by the statutes. Categories of criminal conduct are the product of actual practices within these limits, and the decisions which must be made to provide the basis for choosing the laws which will receive the greatest attention.

2. The discretion allowed within the administration of criminal justice means that admissible evidence may give way to the
   prosecutor's power to determine whether or not to proceed, even
   in cases where there is adequate evidence to prosecute. The judge,
   as well as the police or the victim, also has discretion (e.g. sentencing), and some discretion is also extended to correctional institutions.
3. Most persons charged with criminal conduct plead guilty (from 80
   to 90 per cent, according to the references cited by Newman) and
   jury trials are rare. Thus, the adversary aspect of the law is not
   always practiced because many of the lower income offenders
   cannot afford lawyers and often distrust public defenders. Criminal justice depends upon a large number of guilty pleas. Many of
   these cases would be acquitted if there were more trials.
4. Statistics are affected by such 'accommodations in the conviction
   process'. Some offenders are excluded because they are not
   processed even though known to be guilty (e.g. drug addicts,
   prostitutes and gamblers are often hired by the police or coerced
   by them to help apprehend other offenders), and the practice of
   re-labeling offenses and reducing sentences because of insufficient
   evidence, 'deals', and tricks (e.g. telling the defendant or his
   lawyer that because the offender 'seems like a decent person' the
   charge will be reduced from a felony to a misdemeanor, when in
   fact the prosecution finds there is insufficient evidence for either
   charge). These accommodations may occur at the time of arrest, or
   during prior or subsequent investigation of crimes, filing of complaints, adjudication, sentencing and post-sentencing relations with
   authorities, and so on.

The significance of the American Bar Foundation study goes beyond
the documentation of the usual complaints about inadequate recording, inflated recording and the like. More importantly, it underlines the
way criminal statistics fail to reflect the decisions made and discretion
used by law-enforcement personnel and administrators, and the general accommodations that can and do occur. An offender's record,
then, may never reflect the ambiguous decisions, administrative
discretions or accommodations of law enforcement personnel; a statistical account may thus seriously distort an offender's past activities.

The administration of justice *vis-à-vis* juveniles is even more discretionary than for adults due to the philosophy of the juvenile court
law. The juvenile offender is not officially viewed as a criminal, but
rather as an adolescent who is 'mis-directed', 'disturbed', from a 'poor
environment', and the like. The legal concept of an adversary system is
notably absent. The philosophy, however, is differentially interpreted,
with police more likely to view juveniles as adult criminals, while
probation officers and some judges view the offender within the
intended meaning of the law. The early work of Paul Tappan on

juvenile court practices[20] shows how a juvenile court judge, on the counsel of a social worker or other 'treatment oriented' personnel, may dispose of a case in a manner which negates all previous characterizations of the offender by police, probation officer, school officials and the like. The report of the more recent California Special Study Commission on Juvenile Justice[21] alludes vaguely to and in some passages flatly states that many variations of organizational procedures and interpretations by personnel differentially influence the administration of juvenile justice in California. The use of existing stereotypes and imputations of social characteristics to juvenile defendants by law enforcement personnel routinely introduce nonlegal criteria and actions into the organizational procedures of the legal process and significantly influences the realization of judicial objectives.[22]

We wish to state explicitly that the interpretation of official statistics proposed here *does not* imply that the forms of behavior which the sociologist might define and categorize as deviant (e.g. Merton's modes of adaptation) have no factual basis or theoretical importance. Nor do we wish to imply that the question of how behaviors so defined are produced by the social structure is not a sociologically relevant question. The implication of our interpretation is rather that *with respect to the problem of rates of deviant behavior* the theoretical question is: what forms of behavior are organizationally defined as deviant, and how are they classified, recorded and treated by persons in the society?

In our discussion, we have taken the view that official statistics, reflecting as they do the variety of organizational contingencies in the process by which deviants are differentiated from nondeviants, are sociologically relevant data. An individual who is processed as 'convicted', for example, is sociologically differentiable from one who is 'known to the police' as criminal – the former may legally be incarcerated, incapacitated and socially ostracized, while the latter remains 'free'. The fact that both may have 'objectively' committed the same crime is of theoretical and empirical significance, but it does not alter the sociological difference between them. The *pattern* of such 'errors' is among the facts that a sociological theory of deviance must explain, for they are indications of the organizationally defined processes by which individuals are differentiated as deviant.

Indeed, in modern societies where bureaucratically organized agencies are increasingly invested with social control functions, the activities of such agencies are centrally important 'sources and contexts' which generate as well as maintain definitions of deviance and produce populations of deviants. Thus, rates of deviance constructed by the use of statistics routinely issued by these agencies are social facts *par excellence*. A further implication of this view is that if the sociologist is interested in how forms of *deviant* behavior are produced by social structures, the forms that must be explained are those which not only are defined as deviant by members of such structures but those which also activate the unofficial and/or 'official' processes of social control. By directing attention to such processes, the behavior-producing and rate-producing processes may be investigated and compared within a single framework.

Notes and references

1. Robert K. Merton (1957) *Social Theory and Social Structure*. Revised, Glencoe: The Free Press, Ch. 4.
2. Edwin H. Sutherland and Donald R. Cressey (1956) *Principles of Criminology*. 5th edn, New York: Macmillan, Ch. 4.
3. Edwin M. Lemert (1951) *Social Pathology*. New York: McGraw-Hill, esp. Chs 1–4. See also, Sutherland and Cressey, *op. cit.*, Chs 12–13.
4. The conception of the 'rate-producing' processes as socially organized activities is taken from work by Harold Garfinkel, and is primarily an application of what he has termed the 'praxeological rule'. See Harold Garfinkel, 'Some sociological concepts and methods for psychiatrists', *Psychiatric Research Reports*, 6 (Oct. 1956), 181–95; Harold Garfinkel and Harry Brickman, 'A Study of the Composition of the Clinic Patient Population of the Outpatient Department of the U.C.L.A. Neuro-psychiatric Institute', unpublished manuscript.
5. For a discussion of these problems, see Sophia M. Robison (1936) *Can Delinquency Be Measured?* New York: Columbia University Press. See also Sutherland and Cressey, *op. cit.*, Ch. 2.
6. Robert K. Merton, *op. cit.*, p. 147. Merton's comments on the theory of social structure and anomie may be found in Chapter 5 of that volume, and in 'Social conformity, deviation, and opportunity structures: a comment on the contributions of Dubin and Cloward', *American Sociological Review*, 24 (April 1959), 177–89; See also his remarks in *New Perspectives for Research on Juvenile Delinquency*, H. Witmer and R. Kotinsky (eds) U.S. Government Printing Office, 1956.
7. *Social Theory and Social Structure, op. cit.*, p. 134.
8. *New Perspectives for Research in Juvenile Delinquency, op. cit.*, p. 32.
9. *Ibid.*, p. 31.
10. For example '. . . crude (and not necessarily reliable) crime statistics suggest . . .' etc., *Social Theory and Social Structure, op. cit.*, p. 147. In a more extensive comment on the limitations imposed on research by the use of official statistics, Merton states: 'Its decisive limitation derives from a circumstance which regularly confronts sociologists seeking to devise measures of theoretical concepts by drawing upon an array of social data which *happen* to be recorded in the statistical series established by agencies of the society – namely, the circumstance that these data of social bookkeeping which happen to be on hand are not necessarily the data which best measure the concept. . . . Pragmatic considerations of this sort are of course no suitable alternative to theoretically derived indicators of the concept.' p. 165.
11. Merton proposes to define deviant behavior in terms of the 'acceptance' or 'rejection' of cultural goals and/or institutionalized means. Interpreting the two terms literally, a given form of behavior (adaptation) is to be considered deviant if it is oriented by some cultural goals (to be specified by the sociologists) and/or the institutionalized means (also to be specified) which govern conduct with respect to those goals. By this definition, appropriately organized data would require that behaviors be classified in the typology of 'modes of individual adaptation'. But what are the operational criteria by which 'acceptance' or 'rejection' of cultural goals and institutionalized means are to be inferred from observed behavior? How, for example, is the sociologist to distinguish between behavior which indicates 'con-

formity' from 'over-conformity' (which presumably would be classified as 'ritualism'), or 'retreatism' from 'innovation'? Unless a set of rules for the classification of behavior as deviant can be derived from the theory, rates of deviant behavior cannot be constructed to test its validity.

12. For a discussion of the concept of 'societal reaction' see Edwin M. Lemert, *op. cit.*, Ch. 4.
13. For a preliminary research application of this formulation, see John I. Kitsuse, 'Societal reaction to deviant behavior: problems of theory and method', *Social Problems,* **9** (Winter 1962), 247–56.
14. We recognize, or course, that many individuals may be labeled 'strange', 'crooks', 'crazy', etc. and ostracized by members of a community, yet be unknown to the police or any other official agency. Insofar as such individuals are labeled and treated as deviants, they constitute a population which must be explained in any theory of deviance. In this paper, however, we are primarily concerned with the theoretical relevance of official statistics for the study of deviance.
15. In any empirical investigation of such criteria, it is necessary to distinguish between the formal (official) interpretive rules (as defined by a manual of procedures, constitution and the like) which are to be employed by the personnel of the organizations in question, and the unofficial rules used by the personnel in their deviant-processing activities, e.g. differential treatment on the basis of social class, race, ethnicity or varying conceptions of 'deviant' behavior.
16. The material in this section is taken from an unpublished paper by Cicourel entitled 'Social Class, Family Structure and the Administration of Juvenile Justice', and is based on a study of the social organization of juvenile justice in two Southern California communities with populations of approximately 100,000 each.
17. See Donald J. Newman, 'The effects of accommodations in justice administration on criminal statistics', *Sociology and Social Research,* **46** (Jan. 1962), 144–55; *Administration of Criminal Justice,* Chicago: American Bar Foundation, 1955, unpublished.
18. Newman, 'The Effects of Accommodations. . .', *op. cit.,* pp. 145–6.
19. See *ibid.,* pp. 146–51, and the references cited.
20. *Juvenile Delinquency.* New York: McGraw-Hill, 1949.
21. Report of the *Governor's Special Study Commission on Juvenile Justice,* Parts I and II, Sacramento: California State Printing Office, 1960.
22. To illustrate how organizational procedures and imputations can affect official statistics, we refer to a preliminary finding by Cicourel (cited in footnote 17) which shows that one of two communities studied (Community A) has both a slightly larger population and a higher adult crime rate. Yet this community had (as of November, 1962) 3,200 current cases of juveniles suspected or confirmed to be offenders. Community B, on the other hand, had approximately 8,000 current suspected or confirmed juvenile cases. Community A has two juvenile officers on its staff, while Community B has five juvenile officers.

Some statistical problems in research design

Leslie Kish

Statistical inference is an important aspect of scientific inference. The statistical consultant spends much of his time in the borderland between statistics and the other aspects, philosophical and substantive, of the scientific search for explanation. This marginal life is rich both in direct experience and in discussions of fundamentals; these have stimulated my concern with the problems treated here.

I intend to touch on several problems dealing with the interplay of statistics with the more general problems of scientific inference. We can spare elaborate introductions because these problems are well known. Why then discuss them here at all? We do so because, first, they are problems about which there is a great deal of misunderstanding, evident in current research; and, second, they are *statistical* problems on which there is broad agreement among research statisticians – and on which these statisticians generally disagree with much in the current practice of research scientists.[1]

Several problems will be considered briefly, hence incompletely. The aim of this paper is not a profound analysis, but a clear elementary treatment of several related problems. The notes contain references to more thorough treatments. Moreover, these are not *all* the problems in this area, nor even necessarily the most important ones; the reader may find that his favorite, his most annoying problem, has been omitted. The problems selected are a group with a common core, they arise frequently, yet they are widely misunderstood.

Statistical tests of survey data

That correlation does not prove causation is hardly news. Perhaps the wittiest statements on this point are in George Bernard Shaw's preface to *The Doctor's Dilemma*, in the sections on 'Statistical Illusions', 'The Surprises of Attention and Neglect', 'Stealing Credit from Civilization' and 'Biometrika'. (These attack, alas, the practice of vaccination.) The

From *American Sociological Review*, 1959, **24**, 328–38.

excellent introductory textbook by Yule and Kendall[2] deals in three separate chapters with the problems of advancing from correlation to causation. Searching for causal factors among survey data is an old, useful sport; and the attempts to separate true explanatory variables from extraneous and 'spurious' correlations have taxed scientists since antiquity and will undoubtedly continue to do so. Neyman and Simon[3] show that beyond common sense, there are some technical skills involved in tracking down spurious correlations. Econometricians and geneticists have developed great interest and skill in the problems of separating the explanatory variables.[4]

The researcher designates the explanatory variables on the basis of substantive scientific theories. He recognizes the evidence of other *sources of variation* and he needs to separate these from the explanatory variables. Sorting all sources of variation into four classes seems to me a useful simplification. Furthermore, no confusion need result from talking about sorting and testing 'variables', instead of 'sources of variation'.

1. The *explanatory* variables, sometimes called the 'experimental' variables, are the objects of the research. They are the variables among which the researcher wishes to find and to measure some specified relationships. They include both the 'dependent' and the 'independent' variables, that is, the 'predictand' and 'predictor' variables.[5] With respect to the aims of the research all other variables, of which there are three classes, are extraneous.
2. There are extraneous variables which are *controlled*. The control may be exercised in either or both the selection and the estimation procedures.
3. There may exist extraneous uncontrolled variables which are *confounded* with the Class 1 variables.
4. There are extraneous uncontrolled variables which are treated as *randomized* errors. In 'ideal' experiments (discussed below) they are actually randomized; in surveys and investigations they are only assumed to be randomized. Randomization may be regarded as a substitute for experimental control or as a form of control.

The aim of efficient design both in experiments and in surveys is to place as many of the extraneous variables as is feasible into the second class. The aim of randomization in experiments is to place all of the third class into the fourth class; in the 'ideal' experiment there are no variables in the third class. And it is the aim of controls of various kinds in surveys to separate variables of the third class from those of the first class; these controls may involve the use of repeated cross-tabulations, regression, standardization, matching of units and so on.

The function of statistical 'tests of significance' is to test the effects found among the Class 1 variables against the effects of the variables of Class 4. An 'ideal' experiment here denotes an experiment for which this can be done through randomization without any possible confusion with Class 3 variables. (The difficulties of reaching this 'ideal' arc discussed below.) In survey results, Class 3 variables are confounded with those of Class 1; the statistical tests actually contrast the effects of the random variables of Class 4 against the explanatory variables of Class 1 confounded with unknown effects of Class 3 variables. In both the ideal experiment and in surveys the statistical tests serve to separate the effects of the random errors of Class 4 from the effects of other variables. These, in surveys, are a mixture of explanatory and confounded variables; their separation poses severe problems for logic and for scientific methods; statistics is only one of the tools in this endeavor. The scientist must make many decisions as to which variables are extraneous to his objectives, which should and can be controlled, and what methods of control he should use. He must decide where and how to introduce statistical tests of hypotheses into the analysis.

As a simple example, suppose that from a probability sample survey of adults of the United States we find that the level of political interest is higher in urban than in rural areas. A test of significance will show whether or not the difference in the 'levels' is large enough, compared with the sampling error of the difference, to be considered 'significant'. Better still, the confidence interval of the difference will disclose the limits within which we can expect the 'true' population value of the difference to lie.[6] If families had been sent to urban and rural areas respectively, after the randomization of a true experiment, then the sampling error would measure the effects of Class 4 variables against the effects of urban *versus* rural residence on political interest; the difference in levels beyond sampling errors could be ascribed (with specified probability) to the effects of urban *versus* rural residence.

Actually, however, residences are not assigned at random. Hence, in survey results, Class 3 variables may account for some of the difference. If the test of significance rejects the null hypothesis of no difference, *several* hypotheses remain in addition to that of a simple relationship between urban *versus* rural residence and political interest. Could differences in income, in occupation or in family life cycle account for the difference in the levels? The analyst may try to remove (for example, through cross-tabulation, regression, standardization) the effects due to such variables, which are extraneous to his expressed interest; then he computes the difference, between the urban and rural residents, of the levels of interest now free of several confounding variables. This can be followed by a proper test of significance – or, preferably, by some other form of statistical inference, such as a statement of confidence intervals.

Of course, other variables of Class 3 may remain to confound the measured relationship between residence and political interest. The separation of Class 1 from Class 3 variables should be determined in accord with the nature of the hypothesis with which the researcher is concerned; finding and measuring the effects of confounding variables of Class 3 tax the ingenuity of research scientists. But this separation is beyond the functions and capacities of the statistical tests, the tests of null hypotheses. Their function is not explanation; they cannot point to causation. Their function is to ask: 'Is there anything in the data that *needs* explaining?' – and to answer this question with a certain probability.

Agreement on these ideas can eliminate certain confusion, exemplified by Selvin in a recent article:

Statistical tests are unsatisfactory in nonexperimental research for two fundamental reasons: it is almost impossible to design studies that meet the conditions for using the tests, and the situations in which the tests are employed make it difficult to draw correct inferences. The basic difficulty in design is that sociologists are unable to randomize their uncontrolled variables, so that the difference between 'experimental' and 'control' groups (or their analogs in nonexperimental situations) are a mixture of the effects of the variable being studied and the uncontrolled variables or correlated biases. Since there is no way of knowing, in general, the sizes of these correlated biases and their directions, there is no point in asking for the probability that the observed differences could have been produced by random errors. The place for significance tests is after all relevant correlated biases have been controlled. . . . In design and in interpretation, in principle and in practice, tests of statistical significance are inapplicable in nonexperimental research.[7]

Now it is true that in survey results the explanatory variables of Class 1 are confounded with variables of Class 3; but it does not follow that tests of significance should not be used to separate the random variables of Class 4. Insofar as the effects found 'are a mixture of the effects of the variable being studied and the uncontrolled variables'; insofar as 'there is no way of knowing, in general, the sizes' and directions of these uncontrolled variables, Selvin's logic and advice should lead not only to the rejection of statistical tests; it should lead one to refrain altogether from using survey results for the purposes of finding explanatory variables. *In this sense,* not only tests of significance but any comparisons, any scientific inquiry based on surveys, any scientific inquiry other than an 'ideal' experiment, is 'inapplicable'. That advice is most unrealistic. In the (unlikely) event of its being followed, it would sterilize social research – and other nonexperimental research as well.

Actually, much research – in the social, biological, and physical sciences – must be based on nonexperimental methods. In such cases the rejection of the null hypothesis leads to several alternate hypotheses that may explain the discovered relationships. It is the duty of scientists to search, with painstaking effort and with ingenuity, for bases on which to decide among these hypotheses.

As for Selvin's advice to refrain from making tests of significance until 'after all relevant' uncontrolled variables have been controlled –

this seems rather farfetched to scientists engaged in empirical work who consider themselves lucky if they can explain 25 or 50 per cent of the total variance. The control of all relevant variables is a goal seldom even approached in practice. To postpone to that distant goal all statistical tests illustrates that often 'the perfect is the enemy of the good'.[8]

Experiments, surveys and other investigations

Until now, the theory of sample surveys has been developed chiefly to provide descriptive statistics – especially estimates of means, proportions and totals. On the other hand, experimental designs have been used primarily to find explanatory variables in the analytical search of data. In many fields, however, including the social sciences, survey data must be used frequently as the analytical tools in the search for explanatory variables. Furthermore, in some research situations, neither experiments nor sample surveys are practical, and other investigations are utilized.

By 'experiments' I mean here 'ideal' experiments in which all the extraneous variables have been randomized. By 'surveys' (or 'sample surveys'), I mean probability samples in which all members of a defined population have a known positive probability of selection into the sample. By 'investigations' (or 'other investigations'), I mean the collection of data – perhaps with care, and even with considerable control – without either the randomization of experiments or the probability sampling of surveys. The differences among experiments, surveys and investigations are not the consequences of statistical techniques; they result from different methods for introducing the variables and for selecting the population elements (subjects). These problems are ably treated in recent articles by Wold and Campbell.[9]

In considering the larger ends of any scientific research, only part of the total means required for inference can be brought under objective and firm control; another part must be left to more or less vague and subjective – however skillful – judgment. The scientist seeks to maximize the first part, and thus to minimize the second. In assessing the ends, the costs and the feasible means, he makes a strategic choice of methods. He is faced with the three basic problems of scientific research: measurement, representation and control. We ignore here the important but vast problems of measurement and deal with representation and control.

Experiments are strong on control through randomization; but they are weak on representation (and sometimes on the 'naturalism' of measurement). Surveys are strong on representation, but they are often weak on control. Investigations are weak on control and often on representation; their use is due frequently to convenience or low cost and sometimes to the need for measurements in 'natural settings'.

Experiments have three chief advantages:

1. Through randomization of extraneous variables the confounding variables (Class 3) are eliminated.
2. Control over the introduction and variation of the 'predictor' variables clarifies the *direction* of causation from 'predictor' to 'predictand' variables. In contrast, in the correlations of many surveys this direction is not clear – for example, between some behaviors and correlated attitudes.
3. The modern design of experiments allows for great flexibility, efficiency and powerful statistical manipulation, whereas the analytical use of survey data presents special statistical problems.[10]

The advantages of the experimental method are so well known that we need not dwell on them here. It is the scientific method *par excellence* – when feasible. In many situations experiments are not feasible and this is often the case in the social sciences, but it is a mistake to use this situation to separate the social from the physical and biological sciences. Such situations also occur frequently in the physical sciences (in meteorology, astronomy, geology), the biological sciences, medicine and elsewhere.

The experimental method also has some shortcomings. First, it is often difficult to choose the 'control' variables so as to exclude *all* the confounding extraneous variables; that is, it may be difficult or impossible to design an 'ideal' experiment. Consider the following examples: The problem of finding a proper control for testing the effects of the Salk polio vaccine led to the use of an adequate 'placebo'. The Hawthorne experiment demonstrated that the design of a proposed 'treatment *versus* control' may turn out to be largely a test of *any* treatment *versus lack* of treatment.[11] Many of the initial successes reported about mental therapy, which later turn into vain hopes, may be due to the hopeful effects of *any* new treatment in contrast with the background of neglect. Shaw, in 'The Surprises of Attention and Neglect', writes: 'Not until attention has been effectually substituted for neglect as a general rule, will the statistics begin to show the merits of the particular methods of attention adopted.'

There is an old joke about the man who drank too much on four different occasions, respectively, of scotch and soda, bourbon and soda, rum and soda and wine and soda. Because he suffered painful effects on all four occasions, he ascribed, with scientific logic, the common effect to the common cause: 'I'll never touch soda again!' Now, to a man (say, from Outer Space) ignorant of the common alcoholic content of the four 'treatments' and of the relative physiological effects of alcohol and carbonated water, the subject is not fit for joking, but for further scientific investigation.

Thus, the advantages of experiments over surveys in permitting better control are only relative, not absolute.[12] The design of proper experimental controls is not automatic; it is an art requiring scientific knowledge, foresight in planning the experiment, and hindsight in interpreting the results. Nevertheless, the distinction in control between experiments and surveys is real and considerable; and to emphasize this distinction we refer to 'ideal' experiments in which the control of the random variables is complete.

Second, it is generally difficult to design experiments so as to represent a specified important population. In fact, the questions of sampling, of making the experimental results representative of a specified population, have been largely ignored in experimental design until recently. Both in theory and in practice, experimental research has often neglected the basic truth that causal systems, the distributions of relations – like the distributions of characteristics – exist only within specified universes. The distributions of relationships, as of characteristics, exist only within the framework of specific populations. Probability distributions, like all mathematical models, are abstract systems; their application to the physical world must include the specification of the populations. For example, it is generally accepted that the statement of a value for mean income has meaning only with reference to a specified population; but this is not generally and clearly recognized in the case of regression of assets on income and occupation. Similarly, the *statistical* inferences derived from the experimental testing of several treatments are restricted to the population(s) included in the experimental design.[13] The clarification of the population sampling aspects of experiments is now being tackled vigorously by Wilk and Kempthorne and by Cornfield and Tukey.[14]

Third, for many research aims, especially in the social sciences, contriving the desired 'natural setting' for the measurements is not feasible in experimental design. Hence, what social experiments give sometimes are clear answers to questions, the meanings of which are vague. That is, the artificially contrived experimental variables *may* have but a tenuous relationship to the variables the researcher would like to investigate.

The second and third weaknesses of experiments point to the advantages of surveys. Not only do probability samples permit clear statistical inferences to defined populations, but the measurements can often be made in the 'natural settings' of actual populations. Thus in practical research situations the experimental method, like the survey method, has its distinct problems and drawbacks as well as its advantages. In practice one generally cannot solve simultaneously all of the problems of measurement, representation and control; rather, one must choose and compromise. In any specific situation one method may be better or more practical than the other; but there is no over-all superiority in all situations for either method. Understanding the advantages and weaknesses of both methods should lead to better choices.

In social research, in preference to both surveys and experiments, frequently some design of controlled investigation is chosen – for reasons of cost or of feasibility or to preserve the 'natural setting' of the measurements. Ingenious adaptations of experimental designs have been contrived for these controlled investigations. The statistical framework and analysis of experimental designs are used, but not the randomization of true experiments. These designs are aimed to provide flexibility, efficiency and, especially, some control over the extraneous variables. They have often been used to improve considerably research with controlled investigations.

These designs are sometimes called 'natural experiments'. For the sake of clarity, however, it is important to keep clear the distinctions among the methods and to reserve the word 'experiment' for designs in which the uncontrolled variables are randomized. This principle is stated clearly by Fisher,[15] and is accepted often in scientific research. Confusion is caused by the use of terms like 'ex post facto experiments' to describe surveys or designs of controlled investigations. Sample surveys and controlled investigations have their own justifications, their own virtues; they are not just second-class experiments. I deplore the borrowing of the prestige word 'experiment', when it cloaks the use of other methods.

Experiments, surveys and investigations can all be improved by efforts to overcome their weaknesses. Because the chief weakness of surveys is their low degree of control, researchers should be alert to the collection and use of auxiliary information as controls against confounding variables. They also should take greater advantage of changes introduced into their world by measuring the effects of such changes. They should utilize more often efficient and useful statistics instead of making tabular presentation their only tool.

On the other hand, experiments and controlled investigations can often be improved by efforts to specify their populations more clearly and to make the results more representative of the population. Often more should be done to broaden the area of inference to more important populations. Thus, in many situations the deliberate attempts of the researcher to make his sample more 'homogeneous' are misplaced; and if common sense will not dispel the error, reading Fisher may.[16] When he understands this, the researcher can view the population base of his research in terms of efficiency – in terms of costs and variances. He can often avoid basing his research on a comparison of one sampling unit for each 'treatment'. If he cannot obtain a proper sample of the entire population, frequently he can secure, say, four units for each treatment, or a score for each.[17]

Suppose, for example, that thorough research on one city and one rural county discloses higher levels of political interest in the former. It is presumptuous (although common practice) to present this result as evidence that urban people in *general* show a higher level. (Unfortunately, I am not beating a dead horse; this nag is pawing daily in the garden of social science.) However, very likely there is a great deal of variation in political interest among different cities, as well as among rural counties; the results of the research will depend heavily on which city and which county the researcher picked as 'typical'. The research would have a broader base if a city and a rural county would have been chosen in each of, say, four different situations – as different as possible (as to region, income, industry, for example); or better still in twenty different situations. A further improvement would result if the stratification and selection of sampling units followed a scientific sample design.

Using more sampling units and spreading them over the breadth of variation in the population has several advantages. First, some measure of the variability of the observed effect may be obtained. From a probability sample, statistical inference to the population can be made. Second, the base of the inference is broadened, as the effect is observed over a variety of situations. Beyond this lies the combination of results from researches over several distinct cultures and periods. Finally, with proper design, the effects of several potentially confounding factors can be tested.

These points are brought out by Keylfitz in an excellent example of controlled investigation (which also uses sampling effectively): 'Census enumeration data were used to answer for French farm families of the Province of Quebec the question: Are farm families smaller near cities than far from cities, other things being equal? The sample of 1,056 families was arranged in a 2^6 factorial design which not only controlled 15 extraneous variables (income, education, etc.) but incidentally measured the effect of 5 of these on family size. A significant effect of distance from cities was found, from which is inferred a geographical dimension for the currents of social change.'[18] The mean numbers of children per family were found to be 9.5 near and 10.8 far from cities; the difference of 1.3 children has a standard error of 0.28.

Some misuses of statistical tests

Of the many kinds of current misuses this discussion is confined to a few of the most common. There is irony in the circumstance that these are committed usually by the more statistically inclined investigators; they are avoided in research presented in terms of qualitative statements or of simple descriptions.

First, there is 'hunting with a shot-gun' for significant differences. Statistical tests are designed for distinguishing results at a predetermined level of improbability (say at $P = 0.05$) under a specified null hypothesis of random events. A rigorous theory for dealing with individual experiments has been developed by Fisher, the Pearsons, Neyman, Wold and others. However, the researcher often faces more complicated situations, especially in the analysis of survey results; he is often searching for interesting relationships among a vast number of data. The keen-eyed researcher hunting through the results of one thousand random tosses of perfect coins would discover and display about fifty 'significant' results (at the $P = 0.05$ level).[19] Perhaps the problem has become more acute now that high-speed computers allow hundreds of significance tests to be made. There is no easy answer to this problem. We must be constantly aware of the nature of tests of null hypotheses in searching survey data for interesting results. After finding a result improbable under the null hypothesis the researcher must not accept blindly the hypothesis of 'significance' due to a presumed cause. Among the several alternative hypotheses is that of having discovered an improbable random event through sheer diligence. Remedy can be found sometimes by a reformulation of the statistical aims of the research so as to fit the available tests. Unfortunately, the classic statistical tests give clear answers only to some simple decision problems; often these bear but faint resemblance to the complex problems faced by the scientist. In response to these needs the mathematical statisticians are beginning to provide some new statistical tests. Among the most useful are the new 'multiple comparison' and 'multiple range' tests of Tukey, Duncan, Scheffé,[20] and others. With a greater variety of statistical statements available, it will become easier to choose one without doing great violence either to them or to the research aims.

Second, statistical 'significance' is often confused with and substituted for substantive significance. There are instances of research results presented in terms of probability values of statistical significance' alone, without noting the magnitude and importance of the relationships found. These attempts to use the probability levels of significance tests as measures of the strengths of relationships are very common and very mistaken. The function of statistical tests is merely to answer: Is the variation great enough for us to place some confidence in the result; or, contrarily, may the latter be merely a happenstance of the specific sample on which the test was made? This question is interesting, but it is surely *secondary*, auxiliary, to the main question: Does the result show a relationship which is of substantive interest because of its nature and its magnitude? Better still: Is the result consistent with an assumed relationship of substantive interest?

The results of statistical 'tests of significance' are functions not only of the magnitude of the relationships studied but also of the numbers of sampling units used (and the efficiency of design). In small samples significant, that is, meaningful, results may fail to appear 'statistically significant'. But if the sample is large enough the most insignificant relationships will appear 'statistically significant'.

Significance should stand for meaning and refer to substantive matter. The statistical tests merely answer the question: Is there a big enough relationship here which *needs* explanation (and is not merely chance fluctuation)? The word *significance* should be attached to another question, a substantive question: Is there a relationship here *worth* explaining (because it is important and meaningful)? As a remedial step I would recommend that statisticians discard the phrase 'test of significance', perhaps in favor of the somewhat longer but proper phrase 'test against the null hypothesis' or the abbreviation 'TANH'.

Yates, after praising Fisher's classic *Statistical Methods*, makes the following observations on the use of 'tests of significance':

Second, and more important, it has caused scientific research workers to pay undue attention to the results of the tests of significance they perform on data, particularly data derived from experiments, and too little to the estimates of the magnitude of the effects they are investigating.

Nevertheless the occasions, even in research work, in which quantitative data are collected solely with the object of proving or disproving a given hypothesis are relatively rare. Usually quantitative estimates and fiducial limits are required. Tests of significance are preliminary or ancillary.

The emphasis on tests of significance, and the consideration of the results of each experiment in isolation, have had the unfortunate consequence that scientific workers have often regarded the execution of a test of significance on an experiment as the ultimate objective. Results are significant or not significant and this is the end of it.[21]

For presenting research results statistical estimation is more frequently appropriate than tests of significance. The estimates should be provided with some measure of sampling variability. For this purpose confidence intervals are used most widely. In large samples, statements of the standard errors provide useful guides to action. These problems need further development by theoretical statisticians.[22]

The responsibility for the current fashions should be shared by the authors of statistical textbooks and ultimately by the mathematical statisticians. As Tukey puts it:

Statistical methods should be tailored to the real needs of the user. *In a number of cases, statisticians have led themselves astray by choosing a problem which they could solve exactly but which was far from the needs of their clients. . . . The broadest class of such cases comes from the choice of significance procedures rather than confidence procedures. It is often much easier to be 'exact' about significance procedures than about confidence procedures. By considering only the most null 'null hypothesis' many inconvenient possibilities can be avoided.*[23]

Third, the tests of null hypotheses of *zero* differences, of no relationships, are frequently weak, perhaps trivial statements of the researcher's aims. In place of the test of zero difference (the nullest of null hypotheses), the researcher should often substitute, say, a test for a difference of a specific size based on some specified model. Better still, in many cases, instead of the tests of significance it would be more to the point to measure the magnitudes of the relationships, attaching proper statements of their sampling variation. The magnitudes of relationships cannot be measured in terms of levels of significance; they can be measured in terms of the difference of two means, or of the proportion of the total variance 'explained', of coefficients of correlations and of regressions, of measures of association, and so on. These views are shared by many, perhaps most, consulting statisticians – although they have not published full statements of their philosophy. Savage expresses himself forcefully: 'Null hypotheses of no difference are usually known to be false before the data are collected; when they are, their rejection or acceptance simply reflects the size of the sample and the power of the test, and is not a contribution to science.'[24]

Too much of social research is planned and presented in terms of the mere existence of some relationship, such as: individuals high on variate x are also high on variate y. The *exploratory* stage of research may be well served by statements of this order. But these statements are relatively weak and can serve *only* in the primitive stages of research. Contrary to a common misconception, the more advanced stages of research should be phrased in terms of the quantitative aspects of the relationships. Again, to quote Tukey:

There are normal sequences of growth in immediate ends. *One natural sequence of immediate ends follows the sequence: (1) Description, (2) Significance statements, (3) Estimation, (4) Confidence statement, (5) Evaluation. . . . There are, of course, other normal sequences of immediate ends, leading mainly through various decision procedures, which are appropriate to development research and to operations research, just as the sequence we have just discussed is appropriate to basic research.*[25]

At one extreme, then, we may find that the contrast between two 'treatments' of a labor force results in a difference in productivity of 5 per cent. This difference may appear 'statistically significant' in a sample of, say, 1,000 cases. It may also mean a difference of millions of dollars to the company. However, it 'explains' only about 1 per cent of the total variance in productivity. At the other extreme is the far-away land of completely determinate behavior, where every action and attitude is explainable, with nothing left to chance for explanation.

The aims of most basic research in the social sciences, it seems to me, should be somewhere between the two extremes; but too much of it is presented at the first extreme, at the primitive level. This is a matter of over-all strategy for an entire area of any science. It is difficult to make this judgment off-hand regarding any specific piece of research of this kind: the status of research throughout the entire area should be considered. But the superabundance of research aimed at this primitive level seems to imply that the over-all strategy of research errs in this respect. The construction of scientific theories to cover broader fields – the persistent aim of science – is based on the synthesis of the separate research results in those fields. A coherent synthesis cannot be forged from a collection of relationships of unknown strengths and magnitudes. The necessary conditions for a synthesis include an *evaluation* of the results available in the field, a coherent interrelating of the *magnitudes* found in those results, and the construction of models based on those magnitudes.

Notes and references

1. Cf. R. A. Fisher (1953) *The Design of Experiments.* 6th edn, London: Oliver and Boyd, pp. 1–2: 'The statistician cannot evade the responsibility for understanding the processes he applies or recommends. My immediate point is that the questions involved can be disassociated from all that is strictly technical in the statistician's craft, and *when so detached,* are questions only of the right use of human reasoning powers, with which all intelligent people, who hope to be intelligible, are equally concerned, and on which the statistician, as such, speaks with no special authority. The statistician cannot excuse himself from the duty of getting his head clear on the principles of scientific inference, but equally no other thinking man can avoid a like obligation.'
2. G. Undy Yule and M. G. Kendall (1937) *An Introduction to the Theory of Statistics.* 11th edn, London: Griffin, Chs 4, 15 and 16.
3. Jerzy Neyman (1952) *Lectures and Conferences on Mathematical Statistics and Probability.* Washington, D.C.: Graduate School of Department of Agriculture, pp. 143-54; Herbert A. Simon (1954) 'Spurious correlation: a causal interpretation', *Journal of the American Statistical Association,* **49** (Sept.), 467-79; also in his *Models of Man,* New York: Wiley, 1956.
4. See the excellent and readable article, Herman Wold (1956) 'Causal inference from observational data', *Journal of the Royal Statistical Society (A),* **119** (Part 1, Jan.), 28–61. Also the two-part technical article, M. G. Kendall (1951) 'Regression, structure and functional relationship', *Biometrika,* **38** (June), 12–25; and **39** (June 1952), 96–108. The interesting methods of 'path coefficients' in genetics have been developed by Wright for inferring causal factors from regression coefficients. See, in Oscar Kempthorne *et al.* (1954) *Statistics and Mathematics in Biology.* Ames, Iowa: The Iowa State College Press; Sewall Wright, 'The interpretation of multi-variate systems', Ch. 2; and John W. Tukey, 'Causation, regression and path analysis', Ch. 3. Also C. C. Li (1956) 'The concept of path coefficient and its impact on population genetics', *Biometrics,* **12** (June), 190–209. I do not know whether these methods can be of wide service in current social science research in the presence of numerous factors, of large unexplained variances, and of doubtful directions of causation.
5. Kendall points out that these latter terms are preferable. See his paper cited in note 4, and M. G. Kendall and W. R. Buckland (1957) *A Dictionary of Statistical Terms,* prepared for the International Statistical Institute with assistance of UNESCO, London: Oliver and Boyd. I have also tried to follow in 4 below his distinction of 'variate' for random variables from 'variables' for the usual (non-random) variable.
6. The sampling error measures the chance fluctuation in the difference of levels due to the sampling operations. The computation of the sampling error must take proper account of the actual sample design, and not blindly follow the standard simple random formulas. See Leslie Kish (1957) 'Confidence intervals for complex samples', *American Sociological Review,* **22** (April), 154–65.
7. Hanan C. Selvin (1957) 'A critique of tests of significance in survey research', *American Sociological Review,* **22** (Oct.) 527. In a criticism of this article, McGinnis shows that the separation of explanatory from extraneous variables depends on the type of hypothesis at which the research is aimed. Robert McGinnis (1958) 'Randomization and inference in sociological research', *American Sociological Review,* **23** (Aug.), 408–14.

8. Selvin performs a service in pointing to several common mistakes: (a) The mechanical use of 'significance tests' can lead to false conclusions. (b) Statistical 'significance' should not be confused with substantive importance. (c) The probability levels of the common statistical tests are not appropriate to the practice of 'hunting' for a few differences among a mass of results. However, Selvin gives poor advice on what to do about these mistakes; particularly when, in his central thesis, he reiterates that 'tests of significance are inapplicable in nonexperimental research', and that 'the tests are applicable only when all relevant variables have been controlled'. I hope that the benefits of his warnings outweigh the damages of his confusion.

   I noticed three misleading references in the article. (a) In the paper which Selvin appears to use as supporting him, Wold (*op. cit.,* p. 39) specifically disagrees with Selvin's central thesis, stating that 'The need for testing the statistical inference is no less than when dealing with experimental data, but with observational data other approaches come to the foreground.' (b) In discussing problems caused by complex sample designs, Selvin writes that 'Such errors are easy enough to discover and remedy' (p. 520), referring to Kish (*op. cit.*). On the contrary, my article pointed out the seriousness of the problem and the difficulties in dealing with it. (c) 'Correlated biases' is a poor term for the confounded uncontrolled variables and it is not true that the term is so used in literature. Specifically, the reference to Cochran is misleading, since he is dealing there only with errors of measurement which may be correlated with the 'true' value. See William G. Cochran (1953) *Sampling Techniques.* New York: Wiley, p. 305.

9. Wold, *op. cit.*; Donald T. Campbell (1957) 'Factors relevant to the validity of experiments in social settings', *Psychological Bulletin,* **54** (July), 296–312.

10. Kish, *op. cit.*

11. F. J. Roethlisberger and W. J. Dickson (1939) *Management and the Worker.* Cambridge: Harvard University Press. Troubles with experimental controls misled even the great Pavlov into believing *temporarily* that he had proof of the inheritance of an acquired ability to learn: 'In an informal statement made at the time of the Thirteenth International Physiological Congress, Boston, August, 1929, Pavlov explained that in checking up these experiments it was found that the apparent improvement in the ability to learn, on the part of successive generations of mice, was really due to an improvement in the ability to teach, on the part of the experimenter.' From B. G. Greenberg (1929) *The Story of Evolution.* New York: Garden City, p. 327.

12. Jerome Cornfield (1954) 'Statistical relationships and proof in medicine', *American Statistician,* **8** (Dec.), 19–21.

13. McGinnis, *op. cit.,* p. 412, points out that usually 'it is not true that one can uncover "general" relationships by examining some arbitrarily selected population. . . . There is no such thing as a completely general relationship which is independent of population, time, and space. The extent to which a relationship is constant among different populations is an empirical question which can be resolved only by examining different populations at different times in different places.'

14. Martin B. Wilk and Oscar Kempthorne (1956) 'Some aspects of the analysis of factorial experiment in a completely randomized design', *Annals of Mathematical Statistics,* **27** (Dec.) 950–85; and (1956) 'Fixed, mixed and random models', *Journal of the American Statistical Association,* **50** (Dec.), 1144–67; Jerome Cornfield and John W. Tukey (1956) 'Average values of mean squares in factorials', *Annals of Mathematical Statistics,* **27** (Dec.), 907–49.

15. Fisher, *op. cit.,* pp. 17–20. 'Controlled investigation' may not be the best term for these designs. 'Controlled observations' might do, but 'observation' has more fundamental meanings.

16. *Ibid.,* pp. 99–100. Fisher says: 'We have seen that the factorial arrangement possesses two advantages over experiments involving only single factors: (i) Greater *efficiency,* in that these factors are evaluated with the same precision by means of a quarter of the number of observations that would otherwise be necessary; and (ii) Greater *comprehensiveness* in that, in addition to the 4 effects of single factors, their 11 possible interactions are evaluated. There is a third advantage which, while less

obvious than the former two, has an important bearing upon the utility of the experimental results in their practical application. This is that any conclusion, such as that it is advantageous to increase the quantity of a given ingredient, has a wider inductive basis when inferred from an experiment in which the quantities of other ingredients have been varied, than it would have from any amount of experimentation, in which these had been kept strictly constant. The exact standardization of experimental conditions, which is often thoughtlessly advocated as a panacea, always carried with it the real disadvantage that a highly standardized experiment supplies direct information only in respect of the narrow range of conditions achieved by standardization. Standardization, therefore, weakens rather than strengthens our ground for inferring a like result, when, as is invariably the case in practice, these conditions are somewhat varied.'

17. For simplicity the following illustration is a simple contrast between two values of the 'explanatory' variable, but the point is more general; and this aspect is similar whether for true experiments or controlled observations. Incidentally, it is poor strategy to 'solve' the problem of representation by obtaining a good sample, or complete census, of some small or artificial population. A poor sample of the United States or of Chicago *usually* has more over-all value than the best sample of freshman English classes at X University.

18. Nathan Keyfitz (1953) 'A factorial arrangement of comparisons of family size', *American Journal of Sociology,* **53** (Mar.) 470.

19. William H. Sewell (1952) 'Infant training and the personality of the child', *American Journal of Sociology,* **53** (Sept.) 150–9. Sewell points to an interesting example: 'On the basis of the results of this study, the general null hypothesis that the personality adjustments and traits of children who have undergone varying training experiences do not differ significantly cannot be rejected. Of the 460 chi-square tests, only 18 were significant at or beyond the 5 per cent level. Of these, 11 were in the expected direction and 7 were in the opposite direction from that expected on the basis of psychoanalytic writings. . . . Certainly, the results of this study cast serious doubts on the validity of the psychoanalytic claims regarding the importance of the infant disciplines and on the efficacy of prescriptions based on them' (pp. 158–9). Note that by chance alone one would expect 23 'significant' differences at the 5 per cent level. A 'hunter' would report either the 11 or the 18 and not the hundreds of 'misses'.

20. John W. Tukey (1949) 'Comparing individual means in the analysis of variance', *Biometrics,* **5** (June), 99–114; David B. Duncan (1955) 'Multiple range and multiple *F* tests', *Biometrics,* **11** (Mar.), 1–42; Henry Scheffé (1953), 'A method for judging all contrasts in the analysis of variance', *Biometrika,* **40** (June), 87–104.

21. Frank Yates (1951) 'The influence of *Statistical Methods for Research Workers* on the development of the science of statistics', *Journal of the American Statistical Association,* **46** (Mar.), 32–3.

22. D. R. Cox (1958) 'Some problems connected with statistical inference', *Annals of Mathematical Statistics,* **29** (June), 357-72.

23. John W. Tukey (1954) 'Unsolved problems of experimental statistics', *Journal of the American Statistical Association,* **49** (Dec.), 710. See also D. R. Cox, *op. cit.,* and David B. Duncan, *op. cit.*

24. Richard J. Savage (1957) 'Nonparametric statistics', *Journal of the American Statistical Association,* **52** (Sept.) 332–3.

25. Tukey, *op. cit.,* pp. 712–13.

Reforms as experiments

Donald T. Campbell

The United States and other modern nations should be ready for an experimental approach to social reform, an approach in which we try out new programs designed to cure specific social problems, in which we learn whether or not these programs are effective, and in which we retain, imitate, modify or discard them on the basis of apparent effectiveness on the multiple imperfect criteria available. Our readiness for this stage is indicated by the inclusion of specific provisions for program evaluation in the first wave of the 'Great Society' legislation, and by the current congressional proposals for establishing 'social indicators' and socially relevant 'data banks'. So long have we had good intentions in this regard that many may feel we are already at this stage, that we already are continuing or discontinuing programs on the basis of assessed effectiveness. It is a theme of this article that this is not at all so, that most ameliorative programs end up with *no* interpretable evaluation (Etzioni, 1968; Hyman & Wright, 1967; Schwartz, 1961). We must look hard at the sources of this condition, and design ways of overcoming the difficulties. This article is a preliminary effort in this regard.

Many of the difficulties lie in the intransigencies of the research setting and in the presence of recurrent seductive pitfalls of interpretation. The bulk of this article will be devoted to these problems. But the few available solutions turn out to depend upon correct administrative decisions in the initiation and execution of the program. These decisions are made in a political arena, and involve political jeopardies that are often sufficient to explain the lack of hard-headed evaluation of effects. Removing reform administrators from the political spotlight seems both highly unlikely, and undesirable even if it were possible. What is instead essential is that the social scientist research advisor understand the political realities of the situation, and that he aid by helping create a public demand for hard-headed evaluation, by contributing to those political inventions that reduce the liability of honest evaluation, and by educating future administrators to the problems and possibilities.

From *American Psychologist*, 1969, **24**, 409–29.

For this reason, there is also an attempt in this article to consider the political setting of program evaluation, and to offer suggestions as to political postures that might further a truly experimental approach to social reform. Although such considerations will be distributed as a minor theme throughout this article, it seems convenient to begin with some general points of this political nature.

Political vulnerability from knowing outcomes

It is one of the most characteristic aspects of the present situation that *specific reforms are advocated as though they were certain to be success-ful.* For this reason, knowing outcomes has immediate political impli-cations. Given the inherent difficulty of making significant improve-ments by the means usually provided and given the discrepancy be-tween promise and possibility, most administrators wisely prefer to limit the evaluations to those the outcomes of which they can control, particularly insofar as published outcomes or press releases are con-cerned. Ambiguity, lack of truly comparable comparison bases, and lack of concrete evidence all work to increase the administrator's control over what gets said, or at least to reduce the bite of criticism in the case of actual failure. There is safety under the cloak of ignorance. Over and above this tie-in of advocacy and administration, there is another source of vulnerability in that the facts relevant to experimen-tal program evaluation are also available to argue the general effi-ciency and honesty of administrators. The public availability of such facts reduces the privacy and security of at least some administrators.

Even where there are ideological commitments to a hard-headed evaluation of organizational efficiency, or to a scientific organization of society, these two jeopardies lead to the failure to evaluate organiza-tional experiments realistically. If the political and administrative sys-tem has committed itself in advance to the correctness and efficacy of its reforms, it cannot tolerate learning of failure. To be truly scientific we must be able to experiment. We must be able to advocate without that excess of commitment that blinds us to reality testing.

This predicament, abetted by public apathy and by deliberate cor-ruption, may prove in the long run to permanently preclude a truly experimental approach to social amelioration. But our needs and our hopes for a better society demand we make the effort. There are a few signs of hope. In the United States we have been able to achieve cost-of-living and unemployment indices that, however imperfect, have embarrassed the administrations that published them. We are able to conduct censuses that reduce the number of representatives a state has in Congress. These are grounds for optimism, although the corrupt tardiness of state governments in following their own constitu-tions in revising legislative districts illustrates the problem.

One simple shift in political posture which would reduce the problem is the shift from the advocacy of a specific reform to the advocacy of the seriousness of the problem, and hence to the advocacy of persistence in alternative reform efforts should the first one fail. The political stance would become: 'This is a serious problem. We propose to initiate Policy A on an experimental basis. If after five years there has been no significant improvement, we will shift to Policy B.' By making explicit that a given problem solution was only one of several that the administrator or party could in good conscience advocate, and by having ready a plausible alternative, the administrator could afford honest evaluation of outcomes. Negative results, a failure of the first program, would not jeopardize his job, for his job would be to keep after the problem until something was found that worked.

Coupled with this should be a general moratorium on ad hominum evaluative research, that is, on research designed to evaluate specific administrators rather than alternative policies. If we worry about the invasion-of-privacy problem in the data banks and social indicators of the future (e.g., Sawyer & Schechter, 1968), the touchiest point is the privacy of administrators. If we threaten this, the measurement system will surely be sabotaged in the innumerable ways possible. While this may sound unduly pessimistic, the recurrent anecdotes of administrators attempting to squelch unwanted research findings convince me of its accuracy. But we should be able to evaluate those alternative policies that a given administrator has the option of implementing.

Field experiments and quasi-experimental designs

In efforts to extend the logic of laboratory experimentation into the 'field', and into settings not fully experimental, an inventory of threats to experimental validity has been assembled, in terms of which some 15 or 20 experimental and quasi-experimental designs have been evaluated (Campbell, 1957, 1963; Campbell & Stanley, 1963). In the present article only three or four designs will be examined, and therefore not all of the validity threats will be relevant, but it will provide useful background to look briefly at them all. Following are nine threats to internal validity.[1]

1. *History:* events, other than the experimental treatment, occurring between pretest and posttest and thus providing alternate explanations of effects.
2. *Maturation:* processes within the respondents or observed social units producing changes as a function of the passage of time per se, such as growth, fatigue, secular trends, etc.
3. *Instability:* unreliability of measures, fluctuations in sampling persons or components, autonomous instability of repeated or 'equivalent' measures. (This is the only threat to which statistical tests of significance are relevant.)

4. *Testing:* the effect of taking a test upon the scores of a second testing. The effect of publication of a social indicator upon subsequent readings of that indicator.
5. *Instrumentation:* in which changes in the calibration of a measuring instrument or changes in the observers or scores used may produce changes in the obtained measurements.
6. *Regression artifacts:* pseudo-shifts occurring when persons or treatment units have been selected upon the basis of their extreme scores.
7. *Selection:* biases resulting from differential recruitment of comparison groups, producing different mean levels on the measure of effects.
8. *Experimental mortality:* the differential loss of respondents from comparison groups.
9. *Selection—maturation interaction:* selection biases resulting in differential rates of 'maturation' or autonomous change.

If a change or difference occurs, these are rival explanations that could be used to explain away an effect and thus to deny that in this specific experiment any genuine effect of the experimental treatment had been demonstrated. These are faults that true experiments avoid, primarily through the use of randomization and control groups. In the approach here advocated, this checklist is used to evaluate specific quasi-experimental designs. This is evaluation, not rejection, for it often turns out that for a specific design in a specific setting the threat is implausible, or that there are supplementary data that can help rule it out even where randomization is impossible. The general ethic, here advocated for public administrators as well as social scientists, is to use the very best method possible, aiming at 'true experiments' with random control groups. But where randomized treatments are not possible, a self-critical use of quasi-experimental designs is advocated. We must do the best we can with what is available to us.

Our posture *vis-à-vis* perfectionist critics from laboratory experimentation is more militant than this: the only threats to validity that we will allow to invalidate an experiment are those that admit of the status of empirical laws more dependable and more plausible than the law involving the treatment. The mere possibility of some alternative explanation is not enough – it is only the *plausible* rival hypotheses that are invalidating. *Vis-à-vis* correlational studies and common-sense descriptive studies, on the other hand, our stance is one of greater conservatism. For example, because of the specific methodological trap of regression artifacts, the sociological tradition of 'ex post facto' designs (Chapin, 1947; Greenwood, 1945) is totally rejected (Campbell & Stanley, 1963, pp. 240–1; 1966, pp. 70–1).

Threats to external validity, which follow, cover the validity problems involved in interpreting experimental results, the threats to valid generalization of the results to other settings, to other versions of the treatment, or to other measures of the effect:[2]

1. *Interaction effects of testing:* the effect of a pretest in increasing or decreasing the respondent's sensitivity or responsiveness to the experimental variable, thus making the results obtained for a pretested population unrepresentative of the effects of the experimental variable for the unpretested universe from which the experimental respondents were selected.
2. *Interaction of selection and experimental treatment:* unrepresentative responsiveness of the treated population.
3. *Reactive effects of experimental arrangements:* 'artificiality'; conditions making the experimental setting atypical of conditions of regular application of the treatment: 'Hawthorne effects'.
4. *Multiple-treatment interference:* where multiple treatments are jointly applied, effects atypical of the separate application of the treatments.
5. *Irrelevant responsiveness of measures:* all measures are complex, and all include irrelevant components that may produce apparent effects.
6. *Irrelevant replicability of treatments:* treatments are complex, and replications of them may fail to include those components actually responsible for the effects.

These threats apply equally to true experiments and quasi-experiments. They are particularly relevant to applied experimentation. In the cumulative history of our methodology, this class of threats was first noted as a critique of true experiments involving pretests (Schanck & Goodman, 1939; Solomon, 1949). Such experiments provided a sound basis for generalizing to other *pretested* populations, but the reactions of unpretested populations to the treatment might well be quite different. As a result, there has been an advocacy of true experimental designs obviating the pretest (Campbell, 1957; Schanck & Goodman, 1939; Solomon, 1949) and a search for non-reactive measures (Webb, Campbell, Schwartz & Sechrest, 1966).

These threats to validity will serve as a background against which we will discuss several research designs particularly appropriate for evaluating specific programs of social amelioration. These are the 'interrupted time-series design', the 'control series design', 'regression discontinuity design' and various 'true experiments'. The order is from a weak but generally available design to stronger ones that require more administrative foresight and determination.

Interrupted time-series design

By and large, when a political unit initiates a reform it is put into effect across the board, with the total unit being affected. In this setting the only comparison base is the record of previous years. The usual mode of utilization is a casual version of a very weak quasi-experimental design, the one-group pretest–posttest design.

A convenient illustration comes from the 1955 Connecticut crackdown on speeding, which Sociologist H. Laurence Ross and I have been analyzing as a methodological illustration (Campbell & Ross, 1968; Glass, 1968; Ross & Campbell, 1968). After a record high of traffic fatalities in 1955, Governor Abraham Ribicoff instituted an unprecedentedly severe crackdown on speeding. At the end of a year of such enforcement there had been but 284 traffic deaths as compared with 324 the year before. In announcing this the Governor stated, 'With the saving of 40 lives in 1956, a reduction of 12.3 per cent from the 1955 motor vehicle death toll, we can say that the program is definitely worthwhile.' These results are graphed in Fig. 9.1, with a deliberate effort to make them look impressive.

In what follows, while we in the end decide that the crackdown had some beneficial effects, we criticize Ribicoff's interpretation of his results, from the point of view of the social scientist's proper standards of evidence. Were the now Senator Ribicoff not the man of stature that he is, this would be most unpolitic, because we could be alienating one of the strongest proponents of social experimentation in our nation. Given his character, however, we may feel sure that he shares our interests both in a progressive program of experimental social

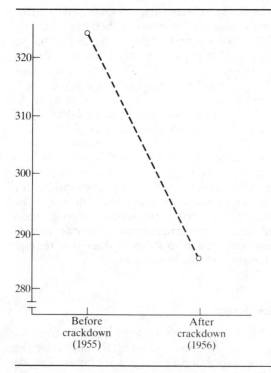

Fig. 9.1 Connecticut traffic fatalities.

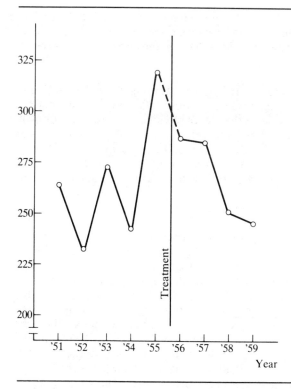

Fig. 9.2 Connecticut traffic fatalities. (Same data as in Fig. 9.1, presented as part of an extended time series.)

amelioration, and in making the most hard-headed evaluation possible of these experiments. Indeed, it was his integrity in using every available means at his disposal as Governor to make sure that the unpopular speeding crackdown was indeed enforced that make these data worth examining at all. But the potentials of this one illustration and our political temptation to substitute for it a less touchy one, point to the political problems that must be faced in experimenting with social reform.

Keeping Fig. 9.1 and Ribicoff's statement in mind, let us look at the same data presented as a part of an extended time series in Fig. 9.2 and go over the relevant threats to internal validity. First, *History*. Both presentations fail to control for the effects of other potential change agents. For instance, 1956 might have been a particularly dry year, with fewer accidents due to rain or snow. Or there might have been a dramatic increase in use of seat belts, or other safety features. The advocated strategy in quasi-experimentation is not to throw up one's hands and refuse to use the evidence because of this lack of control, but rather to generate by informed criticism appropriate to this specific setting as many *plausible* rival hypotheses as possible, and then to do the supplementary research, as into weather records and safetybelt sales, for example, which would reflect on these rival hypotheses.

Maturation

This is a term coming from criticisms of training studies of children. Applied here to the simple pretest–posttest data of Fig. 9.1, it could be the plausible rival hypothesis that death rates were steadily going down year after year (as indeed they are, relative to miles driven or population of automobiles). Here the extended time series has a strong methodological advantage, and rules out this threat to validity. The general trend is inconsistently up prior to the crackdown, and steadily down thereafter.

Instability

Seemingly implicit in the public pronouncement was the assumption that all of the change from 1955 to 1956 was due to the crackdown. There was no recognition of the fact that all time series are unstable even when no treatments are being applied. The degree of this normal instability is the crucial issue, and one of the main advantages of the extended time series is that it samples this instability. The great pretreatment instability now makes the treatment effect look relatively trivial. The 1955–56 shift is less than the gains of both 1954–55 and 1952–53. It is the largest drop in the series, but it exceeds the drops of 1951–52, 1953–54 and 1957–58 by trivial amounts. Thus the unexplained instabilities of the series are such as to make the 1955–56 drop understandable as more of the same. On the other hand, it is noteworthy that after the crackdown there are no year-to-year gains, and in this respect the character of the time series seems definitely to have changed.

The threat of instability is the only threat to which tests of significance are relevant. Box and Tiao (1965) have an elegant Bayesian model for the interrupted time series. Applied by Glass (1968) to our monthly data, with seasonal trends removed, it shows a statistically significant downward shift in the series after the crackdown. But as we shall see, an alternative explanation of at least part of this significant effect exists.

Regression

In true experiments the treatment is applied independently of the prior state of the units. In natural experiments exposure to treatment is often a cosymptom of the treated group's condition. The treatment is apt to be an *effect* rather than, or in addition to being, a cause. Psychotherapy is such a cosymptom treatment, as is any other in which the treated group is self-selected or assigned on the basis of need. These all present special problems of interpretation, of which the present illustration provides one type.

The selection–regression plausible rival hypothesis works this way: Given that the fatality rate has some degree of unreliability, then a subsample selected for its extremity in 1955 would on the average, merely as a reflection of that unreliability, be less extreme in 1956. Has there been selection for extremity in applying this treatment? Probably yes. Of all Connecticut fatality years, the most likely time for a crackdown would be after an exceptionally high year. If the time series showed instability, the subsequent year would on the average be less, *purely as a function of that instability*. Regression artifacts are probably the most recurrent form of self-deception in the experimental social reform literature. It is hard to make them intuitively obvious. Let us try again. Take any time series with variability, including one generated of pure error. Move along it as in a time dimension. Pick a point that is the 'highest so far'. Look then at the next point. On the average this next point will be lower, or nearer the general trend.

In our present setting the most striking shift in the whole series is the upward shift just prior to the crackdown. It is highly probable that this caused the crackdown, rather than, or in addition to, the crackdown causing the 1956 drop. At least part of the 1956 drop is an artifact of the 1955 extremity. While in principle the degree of expected regression can be computed from the autocorrelation of the series, we lack here an extended-enough body of data to do this with any confidence.

Advice to administrators who want to do genuine reality-testing must include attention to this problem, and it will be a very hard problem to surmount. The most general advice would be to work on chronic problems of a persistent urgency or extremity, rather than reacting to momentary extremes. The administrator should look at the pretreatment time series to judge whether or not instability plus momentary extremity will explain away his program gains. If it will, he should schedule the treatment for a year or two later, so that his decision is more independent of the one year's extremity. (The selection biases remaining under such a procedure need further examination.)

In giving advice to the *experimental* administrator, one is also inevitably giving advice to those *trapped* administrators whose political predicament requires a favorable outcome whether valid or not. To such trapped administrators the advice is pick the very worst year, and the very worst social unit. If there is inherent instability, there is nowhere to go but up, for the average case at least.

Two other threats to internal validity need discussion in regard to this design. By *testing* we typically have in mind the condition under which a test of attitude, ability or personality is itself a change agent, persuading, informing, practicing, or otherwise setting processes of change in action. No artificially introduced testing procedures are involved here. However, for the simple before-and-after design of Fig. 9.1, if the pretest were the first data collection of its kind ever publicized, this publicity in itself might produce a reduction in traffic deaths which would have taken place even without a speeding crackdown. Many traffic safety programs assume this. The longer time-series evidence reassures us on this only to the extent that we can assume that the figures had been published each year with equivalent emphasis.[3]

Instrumentation changes
These are not a likely flaw in this instance, but would be if recording practices and institutional responsibility had shifted simultaneously with the crackdown. Probably in a case like this it is better to use raw frequencies rather than indices whose correction parameters are subject to periodic revision. Thus per capita rates are subject to periodic jumps as new census figures become available correcting old extrapolations. Analogously, a change in the miles per gallon assumed in estimating traffic mileage for mileage-based mortality rates might explain a shift. Such biases can of course work to disguise a true effect. Almost certainly, Ribicoff's crackdown reduced traffic speed (Campbell & Ross, 1968). Such a decrease in speed increases the miles per gallon actually obtained, producing a concomitant drop in the estimate of miles driven, which would appear as an inflation of the estimate of mileage-based traffic fatalities if the same fixed approximation to actual miles per gallon were used, as it undoubtedly would be.

The 'new broom' that introduces abrupt changes of policy is apt to reform the record keeping too, and thus confound reform treatments with instrumentation change. The ideal experimental administrator will, if possible, avoid doing this. He will prefer to keep comparable a partially imperfect measuring system rather than lose comparability altogether. The politics of the situation do not always make this possible, however. Consider, as an experimental reform, Orlando Wilson's reorganization of the police system in Chicago. Fig. 9.3 shows his impact on petty larceny in Chicago – a striking *increase!* Wilson, of course, called this shot in advance, one aspect of his reform being a reform in the bookkeeping. (Note in the pre-Wilson records the suspicious absence of the expected upward secular trend.) In this situation Wilson had no choice. Had he left the record keeping as it was, for the purposes of better experimental design, his resentful patrolmen would have clobbered him with a crime wave by deliberately starting to record the many complaints that had not been getting into the books.[4]

Those who advocate the use of archival measures as social indicators (Bauer, 1966; Gross, 1966, 1967; Kaysen, 1967; Webb *et al.,* 1966) must face up not only to their high degree of chaotic error and systematic bias, but also to the politically motivated changes in record keeping that will follow upon their public use as social indicators (Etzioni & Lehman, 1967). Not all measures are equally susceptible. In Fig. 9.4, Orlando Wilson's effect on homicides seems negligible one way or the other.

Of the threats to external validity, the one most relevant to social experimentation is *Irrelevant Responsiveness of Measures.* This seems

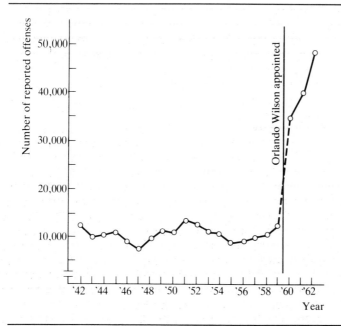

Fig. 9.3 Number of reported larcenies under $50 in Chicago, Illinois, from 1942 to 1962. (Data from *Uniform Crime Reports for the United States,* 1942–62.)

best discussed in terms of the problem of generalizing from indicator to indicator or in terms of the imperfect validity of all measures that is only to be overcome by the use of multiple measures of independent imperfection (Campbell & Fiske, 1959; Webb *et al.,* 1966).

For treatments on any given problem within any given governmental or business subunit, there will usually be something of a governmental monopoly on reform. Even though different divisions may optimally be trying different reforms, within each division there will usually be only one reform on a given problem going on at a time. But for measures of effect this need not and should not be the case. The administrative machinery should itself make multiple measures of potential benefits and of unwanted side effects. In addition, the loyal opposition should be allowed to add still other indicators, with the political process and adversary argument challenging both validity and relative importance, with social science methodologists testifying for both parties, and with the basic records kept public and under bipartisan audit (as are voting records under optimal conditions). This competitive scrutiny is indeed the main source of objectivity in sciences (Polanyi, 1966, 1967; Popper, 1963) and epitomizes an ideal of democratic practice in both judicial and legislative procedures.

The next few figures return again to the Connecticut crackdown on speeding and look to some other measures of effect. They are relevant

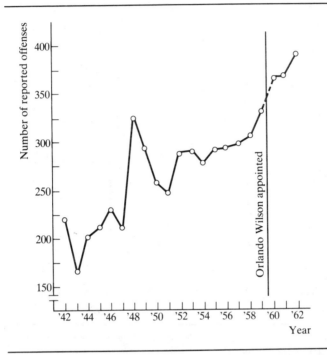

Fig. 9.4 Number of reported murders and non-negligent manslaughters in Chicago, Illinois, from 1942 to 1962. (Data from *Uniform Crime Reports for the United States, 1942–62*.)

to the confirming that there was indeed a crackdown, and to the issue of side effects. They also provide the methodological comfort of assuring us that in some cases the interrupted time-series design can provide clear-cut evidence of effect. Figure 9.5 shows the jump in suspensions of licenses for speeding – evidence that severe punishment was abruptly instituted. Again a note to experimental administrators: with this weak design, *it is only abrupt and decisive changes that we have any chance of evaluating*. A gradually introduced reform will be indistinguishable from the background of secular change, from the net effect of the innumerable change agents continually impinging.

We would want intermediate evidence that traffic speed was modified. A sampling each year of a few hundred five-minute highway movies (random as to location and time) could have provided this at a moderate cost, but they were not collected. Of the public records available, perhaps the data of Fig. 9.6, showing a reduction in speeding violations, indicate a reduction in traffic speed. But the effects on the legal system were complex, and in part undesirable. Driving with a suspended license markedly increased (Fig. 9.7), at least in the biased sample of those arrested. Presumably because of the harshness of the punishment if guilty, judges may have become more lenient (Fig. 9.8)

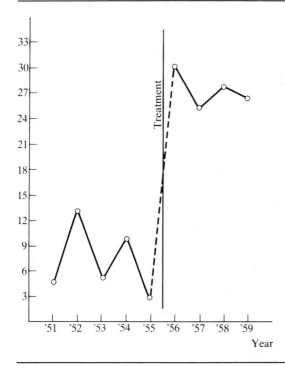

Fig. 9.5 Suspensions of licenses for speeding, as a percentage of all suspensions.

although this effect is of marginal significance.

The relevance of indicators for the social problems we wish to cure must be kept continually in focus. The social indicators approach will tend to make the indicators themselves the goal of social action, rather than the social problems they but imperfectly indicate. There are apt to be tendencies to legislate changes in the indicators per se rather than changes in the social problems.

To illustrate the problem of the irrelevant responsiveness of measures, Fig. 9.9 shows a result of the 1900 change in divorce law in Germany. In a recent reanalysis of the data with the Box and Tiao (1965) statistic, Glass (Glass, Tiao, & Maguire, 1969) has found the change highly significant, in contrast to earlier statistical analyses (Rheinstein, 1959; Wolf, Lüke, & Hax, 1959). But Rheinstein's emphasis would still be relevant: This indicator change indicates no likely improvement in marital harmony, or even in marital stability. Rather than reducing them, the legal change has made the divorce rate a less valid indicator of marital discord and separation than it had been earlier (see also Etzioni & Lehman, 1967).

Control series design

The interrupted time-series design as discussed so far is available for

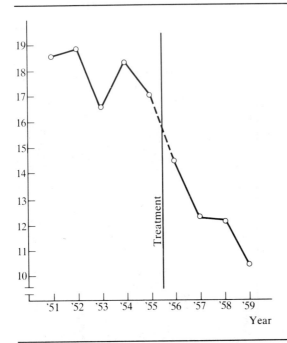

Fig. 9.6 Speeding violations as a percentage of all traffic violations.

those settings in which no control group is possible, in which the total governmental unit has received the experimental treatment, the social reform measure. In the general program of quasi-experimental design, we argue the great advantage of untreated comparison groups even where these cannot be assigned at random. The most common of such designs is the non-equivalent control-group pretest–posttest design, in which for each of two natural groups, one of which receives the treatment, a pretest and posttest measure is taken. If the traditional mistaken practice is avoided of matching on pretest scores (with resultant regression artifacts), this design provides a useful control over those aspects of history, maturation, and test-retest effects shared by both groups. But it does not control for the plausible rival hypothesis of *selection – maturation interaction* – that is, the hypothesis that the selection differences in the natural agregations involve not only differences in mean level, but differences in maturation rate.

This point can be illustrated in terms of the traditional quasi-experimental design problem of the effects of Latin on English vocabulary (Campbell, 1963). In the hypothetical data of Fig. 9.10(b), two alternative interpretations remain open. Latin may have had effect, for those taking Latin gained more than those not. But, on the other hand, those students taking Latin may have a greater annual rate of vocabulary growth that would manifest itself whether or not they

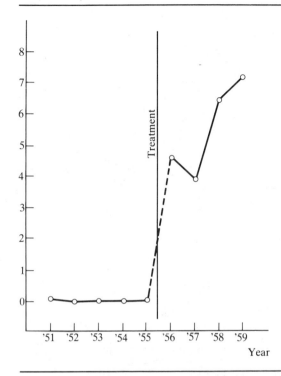

Fig. 9.7 Arrested while driving with a suspended license, as a percentage of suspensions.

took Latin. Extending this common design into two time series provides relevant evidence, as comparison of the two alternative outcomes of Fig. 9.10(c) and 9.10(d) shows. Thus approaching quasi-experimental design from either improving the non-equivalent control-group design or from improving the interrupted time-series design, we arrive at the control series design. Fig. 9.11 shows this for the Connecticut speeding crackdown, adding evidence from the fatality rates of neighboring states. Here the data are presented as population-based fatality rates so as to make the two series of comparable magnitude.

The control series design of Fig. 9.11 shows that downward trends were available in the other states for 1955–56 as due to history and maturation, that is, due to shared secular trends, weather, automotive safety features, etc. But the data also show a general trend for Connecticut to rise relatively closer to the other states prior to 1955, and to steadily drop more rapidly than other states from 1956 on. Glass (1968) has used our monthly data for Connecticut and the control states to generate a monthly difference score, and this too shows a significant shift in trend in the Box and Tiao (1965) statistic. Impressed particularly by the 1957, 1958, and 1959 trend, we are willing to

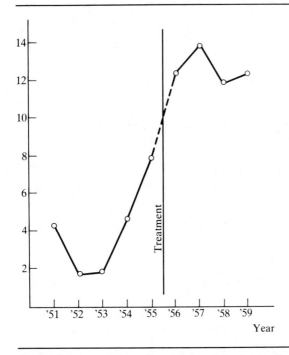

Fig. 9.8 Percentage of speeding violations judged not guilty.

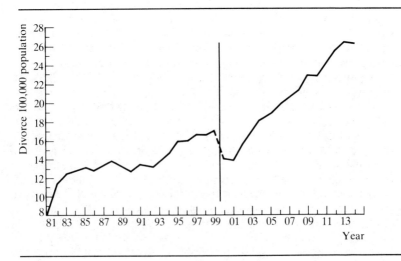

Fig. 9.9 Divorce rate for German Empire, 1881–1914.

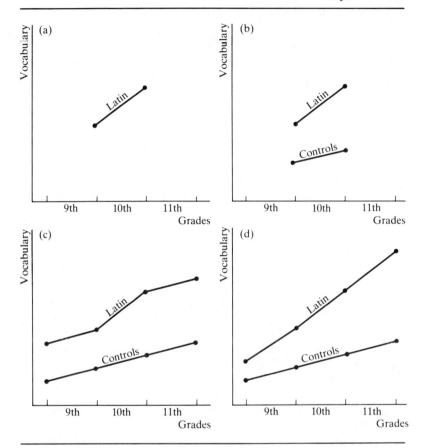

Fig. 9.10 Forms of quasi-experimental analysis for the effect of specific course work, including control series design.

conclude that the crackdown had some effect, over and above the undeniable pseudo-effects of regression (Campbell & Ross, 1968).

The advantages of the control series design point to the advantages for social experimentation of a social system allowing subunit diversity. Our ability to estimate the effects of the speeding crackdown, Rose's (1952) and Stieber's(1949) ability to estimate the effects on strikes of compulsory arbitration laws, and Simon's (1966) ability to estimate the price elasticity of liquor were made possible because the changes were not being put into effect in all states simultaneously, because they were matters of state legislation rather than national. I do not want to appear to justify on these grounds the wasteful and unjust diversity of laws and enforcement practices from state to state. But I would strongly advocate that social engineers make use of this diversity while it remains available, and plan cooperatively their changes in

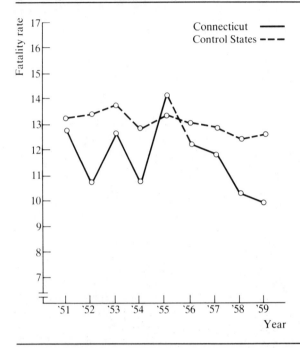

Fig. 9.11 Control series design comparing Connecticut fatalities with those of four comparable states.

administrative policy and in record keeping so as to provide optimal experimental inference. More important is the recommendation that, for those aspects of social reform handled by the central government, a purposeful diversity of implementation be envisaged so that experimental and control groups be available for analysis. Properly planned, these can approach true experiments, better than the casual and ad hoc comparison groups now available. But without such fundamental planning, uniform central control can reduce the present possibilities of reality testing, that is of true social experimentation. In the same spirit, decentralization of decision making, both within large government and within private monopolies, can provide a useful competition for both efficiency and innovation, reflected in a multiplicity of indicators.

Regression discontinuity design

We shift now to social ameliorations that are in short supply, and that therefore cannot be given to all individuals. Such scarcity is inevitable under many circumstances, and can make possible an evaluation of effects that would otherwise be impossible. Consider the heroic Salk poliomyelitis vaccine trials in which some children were given the vaccine while others were given an inert saline placebo injection – and in which many more of these placebo controls would die than would have if they had been given the vaccine. Creation of these placebo controls would have been morally, psychologically and socially impossible had there been enough vaccine for all. As it was, due to the scarcity, most children that year had to go without the vaccine anyway. The creation of experimental and control groups was the highly moral allocation of that scarcity so as to enable us to learn the true efficacy of the supposed good. The usual medical practice of introducing new cures on a so-called trial basis in general medical practice makes evaluation impossible by confounding prior status with treatment, that is, giving the drug to the most needy or most hopeless. It has the further social bias of giving the supposed benefit to those most assiduous in keeping their medical needs in the attention of the medical profession, that is, the upper and upper-middle classes. The political stance furthering social experimentation here is the recognition of randomization as the most democratic and moral means of allocating scarce resources (and scarce hazardous duties), plus the moral imperative to further utilize the randomization so that society may indeed learn true value of the supposed boon. This is the ideology that makes possible 'true experiments' in a large class of social reforms.

But if randomization is not politically feasible or morally justifiable in a given setting, there is a powerful quasi-experimental design available that allows the scarce good to be given to the most needy or the most deserving. This is the regression discontinuity design. All it requires is strict and orderly attention to the priority dimension. The design originated through an advocacy of a tie-breaking experiment to measure the effects of receiving a fellowship (Thistlethwaite & Campbell, 1960), and it seems easiest to explain it in that light. Consider as in Fig. 9.12, pre-award ability-and-merit dimension, which would have some relation to later success in life (finishing college, earnings 10 years later, etc.). Those higher on the premeasure are most deserving and receive the award. They do better in later life, but does the award have an effect? It is normally impossible to say because they would have done better in later life anyway. Full randomization of the award was impossible given the stated intention to reward merit and ability. But it might be possible to take a narrow band of ability at the cutting point, to regard all of these persons as tied, and to assign half of them to awards, half to no awards, by means of a tie-breaking randomization.

The tie-breaking rationale is still worth doing, but in considering that design it became obvious that, if the regression of premeasure on later effects were reasonably orderly, one should be able to extrapolate to the results of the tie-breaking experiment by plotting the regression of posttest on pretest separately for those in the award and non-award regions. If there is no significant difference for these at the decision-

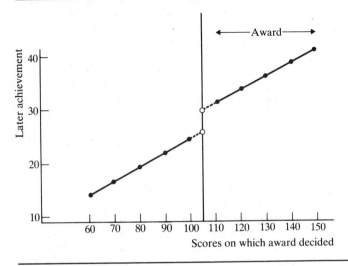

Fig. 9.12 Tie-breaking experiment and regression discontinuity analysis.

point intercept, then the tie-breaking experiment should show no difference. In cases where the tie breakers would show an effect, there should be an abrupt discontinuity in the regression line. Such a discontinuity cannot be explained away by the normal regression of the posttest on pretest, for this normal regression, as extensively sampled within the nonaward area and within the award area, provides no such expectation.

Figure 9.12 presents, in terms of column means, an instance in which higher pretest scores would have led to higher posttest scores even without the treatment, and in which there is in addition a substantial treatment effect. Figure 9.13 shows a series of paired outcomes, those on the left to be interpreted as no effect, those in the center and on the right as effect. Note some particular cases. In instances of granting opportunity on the basis of merit, like Fig. 9.13(a) and (b) (and Fig. 9.12), neglect of the background regression of pretest on posttest leads to optimistic pseudo-effects: in Fig. 9.13(a), those receiving the award do no better in later life, though not really because of the award. But in social ameliorative efforts, the setting is more apt to be like Fig. 9.13(d) and (e), where neglect of the background regression is apt to make the program look deleterious if no effect, or ineffective if there is a real effect.

The design will of course work just as well or better if the award dimension and the decision base, the pretest measure, are unrelated to the posttest dimension, if it is irrelevant or unfair, as instanced in Fig. 9.13(g), (h) and (i). In such cases the decision base is the functional equivalent of randomization. Negative background relationships are obviously possible, as in Fig. 9.13(j), (k) and (l). In Fig. 9.13, (m), (n) and (o) are included to emphasize that it is a jump in intercept at the cutting point that shows effect, and that differences in slope without differences at the cutting point are not acceptable as evidences of effect. This becomes more obvious if we remember that in cases like (m), a tie-breaking randomization experiment would have shown no difference. Curvilinear background relationships, as in Fig. 9.13(p), (q) and (r), will provide added obstacles to clear inference in many instances, where sampling error could make Fig. 9.13(p) look like 9.13(b).

As further illustration, Fig. 9.14 provides computer-simulated data, showing individual observations and fitted regression lines, in a fuller version of the no-effect outcome of Fig. 9.13(a). Figure 9.15 shows an outcome with effect. These have been generated by assigning to each individual a weighted normal random number as a 'true score', to which is added a weighted independent 'error' to generate the 'pretest'. The 'true score' plus another independent 'error' produces the 'posttest' in no-effect cases such as Fig.9.14. In treatment-effect simulations, as in Fig. 9.15, there are added into the posttest 'effects points' for all 'treated' cases, that is, those above the cutting point on the pretest score.

This design could be used in a number of settings. Consider Job Training Corps applicants, in larger number than the program can accommodate, with eligibility determined by need. The setting would be as in Fig. 9.13(d) and (e). The base-line decision dimension could be per capita family income, with those at below the cutoff getting training. The outcome dimension could be the amount of withholding tax withheld two years later, or the percentage drawing unemployment insurance, these follow-up figures being provided from the National Data Bank in response to categorized social security numbers fed in, without individual anonymity being breached, without any real invasion of privacy – for it is the program that is being examined, via regularities of aggregates of persons. While the plotted points could be named, there is no need that they be named. In a classic field experiment on tax compliance, Richard Schwartz and the Bureau of Internal Revenue have managed to put together sets of personally identified interviews and tax-return data so that statistical analyses such as these can be done, without the separate custodians of either interview or tax returns learning the corresponding data for specific persons (Schwartz & Orleans, 1967; see also Schwartz & Skolnick, 1963). Manniche and Hayes (1957) have spelled out how a broker can be used in a two-staged matching of doubly coded data. Kaysen (1967) and Sawyer and Schechter (1968) have wise discussions of the more general problem.

What is required of the administrator of a scarce ameliorative commodity to use this design? Most essential is a sharp cutoff point on a decision-criterion dimension, on which several other qualitatively similar analytic cutoffs can be made both above and below the award

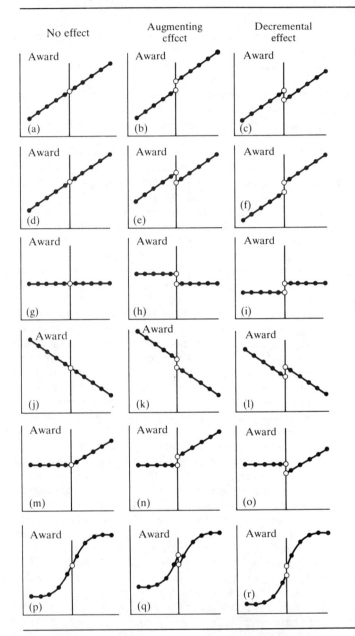

Fig. 9.13 Illustrative outcomes of regression discontinuity analyses.

cut. Let me explain this better by explaining why National Merit scholarships were unable to use the design for their actual fellowship decision (although it has been used for their Certificate of Merit). In their operation, diverse committees make small numbers of award decisions by considering a group of candidates and then picking from them the N best to which to award the N fellowships allocated them. This provides one cutting point on an unspecified pooled decision base, but fails to provide analogous potential cutting points above and below. What could be done is for each committee to collectively rank its group of 20 or so candidates. The top N would then receive the award. Pooling cases across committees, cases could be classified according to number of ranks above and below the cutting point, these other ranks being analogous to the award-nonaward cutting point as far as regression onto posttreatment measures was concerned. Such group ranking would be costly of committee time. An equally good procedure, if committees agreed, would be to have each member, after

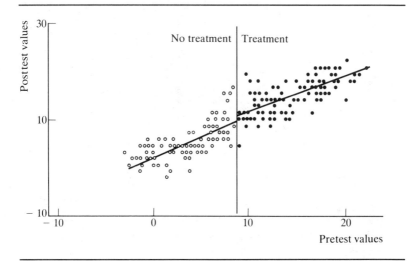

Fig. 9.14 Regression discontinuity design: No effect.

full discussion and freedom to revise, give each candidate a grade, A+, A, A−, B+, B, etc. and to award the fellowships to the N candidates averaging best on these ratings, with no revisions allowed after the averaging process. These ranking or rating units, even if not comparable from committee to committee in range of talent, in number of persons ranked, or in cutting point, could be pooled without bias as far as a regression discontinuity is concerned, for that range of units above and below the cutting point in which all committees were represented.

It is the dimensionality and sharpness of the decision criterion that is at issue, not its components or validity. The ratings could be based upon nepotism, whimsey, and superstition and still serve. As has been stated, if the decision criterion is utterly invalid we approach the pure randomness of a true experiment. Thus the weakness of subjective committee decisions is not their subjectivity, but the fact that they provide only the one cutting point on their net subjective dimension. Even in the form of average ratings the recommended procedures probably represent some slight increase in committee work load. But this could be justified to the decision committees by the fact that through refusals, etc. it cannot be known at the time of the committee meeting the exact number to whom the fellowship can be offered. Other costs at the planning time are likewise minimal. The primary additional burden is in keeping as good records on the nonawardees as on the awardees. Thus at a low cost, an experimental administrator can lay the groundwork for later scientific follow-ups, the budgets for which need not yet be in sight.

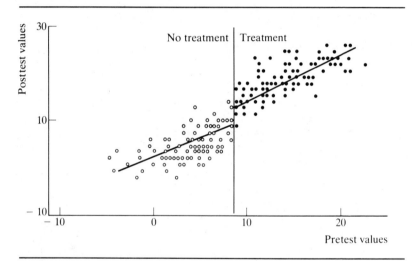

Fig. 9.15 Regression discontinuity design: Genuine effect.

Our present situation is more apt to be one where our pretreatment measures, aptitude measures, reference ratings, etc. can be combined via multiple correlation into an index that correlates highly but not perfectly with the award decision. For this dimension there is a fuzzy cutoff point. Can the design be used in this case? Probably not. Figure 9.16 shows the pseudo-effect possible if the award decision contributes any valid variance to the quantified pretest evidence, as it usually will. The award regression rides above the nonaward regression just because of that valid variance in this simulated case, there being no true award effect at all. (In simulating this case, the award decision has been based upon a composite of true score plus an independent award error.) Figure 9.17 shows a fuzzy cutting point plus a genuine award effect.[5] The recommendation to the administrator is clear: aim for a sharp cutting point on a quantified decision criterion. If there are complex rules for eligibility, only one of which is quantified, seek out

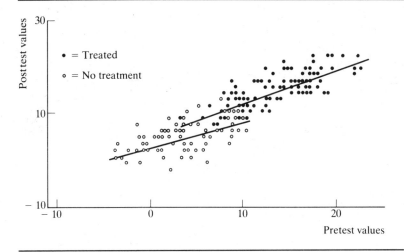

Fig. 9.16 Regression discontinuity design: Fuzzy cutting point, pseudo treatment effect only.

for follow-up that subset of persons for whom the quantitative dimension was determinate. If political patronage necessitates some decisions inconsistent with a sharp cutoff, record these cases under the heading 'qualitative decision rule' and keep them out of your experimental analysis.

Almost all of our ameliorative programs designed for the disadvantaged could be studied via this design, and so too some major governmental actions affecting the lives of citizens in ways we do not think of as experimental. For example, for a considerable period, quantitative test scores have been used to call up for military service or reject as unfit at the lower ability range. If these cutting points, test scores, names, and social security numbers have been recorded for a number of steps both above and below the cutting point, we could make elegant studies of the effect of military service on later withholding taxes, mortality, number of dependents, etc. Unfortunately for this purpose, the nobly experimental 'Operation 100,000' (Office of the Secretary of Defense, 1967) is fuzzing up this cutting point, but there are several years of earlier Vietnam experience all ready for analysis.

This illustration points to one of the threats to external validity of this design, or of the tie-breaking experiment. The effect of the treatment has only been studied for that narrow range of talent near the cutting point, and generalization of the effects of military service, for example, from this low ability level to the careers of the most able would be hazardous in the extreme. But in the draft laws and the requirements of the military services there may be other sharp cutting points on a quantitative criterion that could also be used. For example, those over 6 feet 6 inches are excluded from service. Imagine a five-

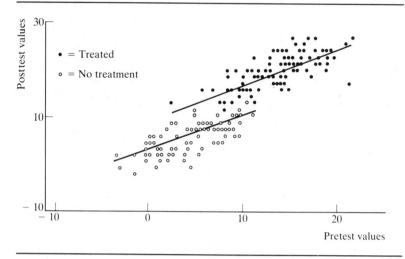

Fig. 9.17 Regression discontinuity design: Fuzzy cutting point, with real treatment plus pseudo treatment effects.

year-later follow-up of draftees grouped by inch in the 6 feet 1 inch to 6 feet 5 inches range, and a group of their counterparts who would have been drafted except for their heights, 6 feet 6 inches to 6 feet 10 inches. (The fact that the other grounds of deferment might not have been examined by the draft board would be a problem here, but probably not insurmountable.) That we should not expect height in this range to have any relation to later-life variables is not at all a weakness of this design, and if we have indeed a subpopulation for which there is a sharp numerical cutting point, an internally valid measure of effects would result. Deferment under the present system is an unquantified committee decision. But just as the sense of justice of United States soldiers was quantified through paired comparisons of cases into an acceptable Demobilization Points system at the end of World War II (Guttman, 1946; Stouffer, 1949), so a quantified composite index of deferment priority could be achieved and applied as uniform justice across the nation, providing another numerical cutting point.

In addition to the National Data Bank type of indicators, there will be occasions in which new data collections as by interview or question-naire are needed. For these there is the special problem of uneven cooperation that would be classified as instrumentation error. In our traditional mode of thinking, completeness of description is valued more highly than comparability. Thus if, in a fellowship study, a follow-up mailed out from the fellowship office would bring a higher return from past winners, this might seem desirable even if the nonawardees' rate of response was much lower. From the point of view of quasi-experimentation, however, it would be better to use an independent survey agency and a disguised purpose, achieving equally low response rates from both awardees and nonawardees, and avoiding a regression discontinuity in cooperation rate that might be misinterpreted as a discontinuity in more important effects.

Randomized control group experiments

Experiments with randomization tend to be limited to the laboratory and agricultural experiment station. But this certainly need not be so. The randomization unit may be persons, families, precincts or larger administrative units. For statistical purposes the randomization units should be numerous, and hence ideally small. But for reasons of external validity, including reactive arrangements, the randomization units should be selected on the basis of the units of administrative access. Where policies are administered through individual client contacts, randomization at the person level may be often inconspicuously achieved, with the clients unaware that different ones of them are getting different treatments. But for most social reforms, larger administrative units will be involved, such as classrooms, schools, cities, counties or states. We need to develop the political postures and ideologies that make randomization at these levels possible.

'Pilot project' is a useful term already in our political vocabulary. It designates a trial program that, if it works, will be spread to other areas. By modifying actual practice in this regard, without going outside of the popular understanding of the term, a valuable experimental ideology could be developed. How are areas selected for pilot projects? If the public worries about this, it probably assumes a lobbying process in which the greater needs of some areas are only one consideration, political power and expediency being others. Without violating the public tolerance or intent, one could probably devise a system in which the usual lobbying decided upon the areas eligible for a formal public lottery that would make final choices between matched pairs. Such decision procedures as the drawing of lots have had a justly esteemed position since time immemorial (e.g. Aubert, 1959). At the present time, record keeping for pilot projects tends to be limited to the experimental group only. In the experimental ideology, comparable data would be collected on designated controls. (There are of course exceptions, as in the heroic Public Health Service fluoridation experiments, in which the teeth of Oak Park children were examined year after year as controls for the Evanston experimentals [Blayney & Hill, 1967].)

Another general political stance making possible experimental social amelioration is that of *staged innovation*. Even though by intent a new reform is to be put into effect in all units, the logistics of the situation usually dictate that simultaneous introduction is not possible. What results is a haphazard sequence of convenience. Under the program of staged innovation, the introduction of the program would be deliberately spread out, and those units selected to be first and last would be randomly assigned (perhaps randomization from matched pairs), so that during the transition period the first recipients could be analyzed as experimental units, the last recipients as controls. A third ideology making possible true experiments has alrady been discussed: randomization as the democratic means of allocating scarce resources.

This article will not give true experimentation equal space with quasi-experimentation only because excellent discussions of, and statistical consultation on, true experimentation are readily available. True experiments should almost always be preferred to quasi-experiments where both are available. Only occasionally are the threats to external validity so much greater for the true experiment that one would prefer a quasi-experiment. The uneven allocation of space here should not be read as indicating otherwise.

More advice for trapped administrators

But the competition is not really between the fairly interpretable quasi-experiments here reviewed and 'true' experiments. Both stand together as rare excellencies in contrast with a morass of obfuscation and self-deception. Both to emphasize this contrast, and again as guidelines for the benefit of those trapped administrators whose political predicament will not allow the risk of failure, some of these alternatives should be mentioned.

Grateful testimonials

Human courtesy and gratitude being what it is, the most dependable means of assuring a favorable evaluation is to use voluntary testimonials from those who have had the treatment. If the spontaneously produced testimonials are in short supply, these should be solicited from the recipients with whom the program is still in contact. The rosy glow resulting is analogous to the professor's impression of his teaching success when it is based solely upon the comments of those students who come up and talk with him after class. In many programs, as in psychotherapy, the recipient, as well as the agency, has devoted much time and effort to the program and it is dissonance reducing for himself, as well as common courtesy to his therapist, to report improvement. These grateful testimonials can come in the language of letters and conversation, or be framed as answers to multiple-item 'tests' in which a recurrent theme of 'I am sick,' 'I am well', 'I am happy', 'I am sad' recurs. Probably the testimonials will be more favorable as: (*a*) the more the evaluative meaning of the response measure is clear to the recipient – it is completely clear in most personality, adjustment, morale and attitude tests; (*b*) the more directly the recipient is identified by name with his answer; (*c*) the more the recipient gives the answer directly to the therapist or agent of reform; (*d*) the more the agent will continue to be influential in the recipient's life in the future; (*e*) the more the answers deal with feelings and evaluations rather than with verifiable facts; and (*f*) the more the recipients participating in the evaluation are a small and self-selected or agent-selected subset of all recipients. Properly designed, the grateful testimonial method can involve pretests as well as posttests, and randomized control groups as well as experimentals, for there are usually no placebo treatments, and the recipients know when they have had the boon.

Confounding selection and treatment
Another dependable tactic bound to give favorable outcomes is to confound selection and treatment, so that in the published comparison those receiving the treatment are also the more able and well placed. The often-cited evidence of the dollar value of a college education is of this nature – all careful studies show that most of the effect, and of the superior effect of superior colleges, is explainable in terms of superior talents and family connections, rather than in terms of what is learned or even the prestige of the degree. Matching techniques and statistical partialings generally undermatch and do not fully control for the selection differences – they introduce regression artifacts confusable as treatment effects.

There are two types of situations that must be distinguished. First, there are those treatments that are given to the most promising, treatments like a college education which are regularly given to those who need it least. For these, the later concomitants of the grounds of selection operate in the same direction as the treatment: those most likely to achieve anyway get into the college most likely to produce later achievement. For these settings, the trapped administrator should use the pooled mean of all those treated, comparing it with the mean of all untreated, although in this setting almost any comparison an administrator might hit upon would be biased in his favor.

At the other end of the talent continuum are those remedial treatments given to those who need it most. Here the later concomitants of the grounds of selection are poorer success. In the Job Training Corps example, casual comparisons of the later unemployment rate of those who received the training with those who did not are in general biased against showing an advantage to the training. Here the trapped administrator must be careful to seek out those few special comparisons biasing selection in his favor. For training programs such as Operation Head Start and tutoring programs, a useful solution is to compare the later sucess of those who completed the training program with those who were invited but never showed plus those who came a few times and dropped out. By regarding only those who complete the program as 'trained' and using the others as controls, one is selecting for conscientiousness, stable and supporting family backgrounds, enjoyment of the training activity, ability, determination to get ahead in the world – all factors promising well for future achievement even if the remedial program is valueless. To apply this tactic effectively in the Job Training Corps, one might have to eliminate from the so-called control group all those who quit the training program because they had found a job – but this would seem a reasonable practice and would not blemish the reception of a glowing progress report.

These are but two more samples of well-tried modes of analysis for the trapped administrator who cannot afford an honest evaluation of the social reform he directs. They remind us again that we must help create a political climate that demands more rigorous and less self-deceptive reality testing. We must provide political stances that permit true experiments, or good quasi-experiments. Of the several suggestions toward this end that are contained in this article, the most important is probably the initial theme: Administrators and parties must advocate the importance of the problem rather than the importance of the answer. They must advocate experimental sequences of reforms, rather than one certain cure-all, advocating Reform A with Alternative B available to try next should an honest evaluation of A prove it worthless or harmful.

Multiple replication in enactment

Too many social scientists expect single experiments to settle issues once and for all. This may be a mistaken generalization from the history of great crucial experiments in physics and chemistry. In actuality the significant experiments in the physical sciences are replicated thousands of times, not only in deliberate replication efforts, but also as inevitable incidentals in successive experimentation and in utilizations of those many measurement devices (such as the galvanometer) that in their own operation embody the principles of classic experiments. Because we social scientists have less ability to achieve 'experimental isolation', because we have good reason to expect our treatment effects to interact significantly with a wide variety of social factors many of which we have not yet mapped, we have much greater needs for replication experiments than do the physical sciences.

The implications are clear. We should not only do hard-headed reality testing in the initial pilot testing and choosing of which reform to make general law; but once it has been decided that the reform is to be adopted as standard practice in all administrative units, we should experimentally evaluate it in each of its implementations (Campbell, 1967).

Conclusions

Trapped administrators have so committed themselves in advance to the efficacy of the reform that they cannot afford honest evaluation. For them, favorably biased analyses are recommended, including capitalizing on regression, grateful testimonials and confounding selection and treatment. *Experimental administrators* have justified the reform on the basis of the importance of the problem, not the certainty of their answer, and are committed to going on to other potential solutions if the one first tried fails. They are therefore not threatened by a hard-headed analysis of the reform. For such, proper administrative decisions can lay the base for useful experimental or quasi-experimental analyses. Through the ideology of allocating scarce resources by lottery, through the use of staged innovation, and through the pilot project, true experiments with randomly assigned control groups can be achieved. If the reform must be introduced across the board, the interrupted time-series design is available. If there are similar units under independent administration, a control series design adds strength. If a scarce boon must be given to the most needy or to the most deserving, quantifying this need or merit makes possible the regression discontinuity analysis.

Notes

1. This list has been expanded from the major previous presentations by the addition of *Instability* (but see Campbell, 1968; Campbell & Ross, 1968). This has been done in reaction to the sociological discussion of the use of tests of significance in nonexperimental or quasi-experimental research (e.g. Selvin, 1957; and as reviewed by Galtung, 1967, pp. 358–89). On the one hand, I join with the critics in criticizing the exaggerated status of 'statistically significant differences' in establishing convictions of validity. Statistical tests are relevant to at best 1 out of 15 or so threats to validity. On the other hand, I join with those who defend their use in situations where randomization has not been employed. Even in those situations, it is relevant to say or to deny, 'This is a trivial difference. It is of the order that would have occurred frequently *had* these measures been assigned to these classes solely by chance.' Tests of significance, making use of random reassignments of the actual scores, are particularly useful in communicating this point.
2. This list has been lengthened from previous presentations to make more salient Threats 5 and 6 which are particularly relevant to social experimentation. Discussion in previous presentations (Campbell, 1957, pp. 309–10; Campbell & Stanley, 1963, pp. 203–4) had covered these points, but they had not been included in the check-list.
3. No doubt the public and press shared the Governor's special alarm over the 1955 death toll. This differential reaction could be seen as a negative feedback servosystem in which the dampening effect was proportional to the degree of upward deviation from the prior trend. Insofar as such alarm reduces traffic fatalities, it adds a negative component to the autocorrelation, increasing the regression effect. This component should probably be regarded as a rival cause or treatment rather than as artifact. (The regression effect is less as the positive autocorrelation is higher, and will be present to

some degree insofar as this correlation is less than positive unity . Negative correlation in a time series would represent regression beyond the mean, in a way not quite analogous to negative correlation across persons. For an autocorrelation of Lag 1, high negative correlation would be represented by a series that oscillated maximally from one extreme to the other.)

4. Wilson's inconsistency in utilization of records and the political problem of relevant records are ably documented in Kamisar (1964). Etzioni (1968) reports that in New York City in 1965 a crime wave was proclaimed that turned out to be due to an unpublicized improvement in record keeping.

5. There are some subtle statistical clues that might distinguish these two instances if one had enough cases. There should be increased pooled column variance in the mixed columns for a true effects case. If the data are arbitrarily treated as though there had been a sharp cutting point located in the middle of the overlap area, then there should be no discontinuity in the no-effect case, and some discontinuity in the case of a real effect, albeit an underestimated discontinuity, since there are untreated cases above the cutting point and treated ones below, dampening the apparent effect. The degree of such dampening should be estimable, and correctable, perhaps by iterative procedures. But these are hopes for the future.

References

Aubert, V. (1959) 'Chance in social affairs', *Inquiry*, **2**, 1–24.
Bauer, R. M. (1966) *Social indicators*. Cambridge, Mass.: M.I.T. Press.
Blayney, J. R. and Hill, I. N. (1967) 'Fluorine and dental caries', *The Journal of the American Dental Association* (Special Issue), **74**, 233–302.
Box, G. E. P. and Tiao, G. C. (1965) 'A change in level of non-stationary time series', *Biometrika*, **52**, 181–92.
Campbell, D. T. (1957) Factors relevant to the validity of experiments in social settings', *Psychological Bulletin*, **54**, 297–312.
Campbell, D. T. (1963) 'From description to experimentation: interpreting trends as quasi-experiments', in C. W. Harris (ed.), *Problems in Measuring Change*. Madison: University of Wisconsin Press.
Campbell, D. T. (1967) 'Administrative experimentation, institutional records, and nonreactive measures', in J. C. Stanley (ed.), *Improving Experimental Design and Statistical Analysis*. Chicago: Rand McNally.
Campbell, D. T. (1968) 'Quasi-experimental design', in D. L. Sills (ed.), *International Encyclopedia of the Social Sciences*. New York: Macmillan and Free Press, Vol. 5, 259–63.
Campbell, D. T. and Fiske, D. W. (1959) 'Convergent and discriminant validation by the multitrait-multimethod matrix', *Psychological Bulletin*, **56**, 81–105.
Campbell, D. T. and Ross, H. L. (1968) 'The Connecticut crackdown on speeding: Time-series data in quasi-experimental analysis', *Law and Society Review* 3(1), 33–53.
Campbell, D. T. and Stanley, J. C. (1963) 'Experimental and quasi-experimental designs for research on teaching', in N. L. Gage (ed.), *Handbook of Research on Teaching*. Chicago: Rand McNally. (Reprinted as *Experimental and Quasi-experimental Design for Research*. Chicago: Rand McNally, 1966.)
Chapin, F. S. (1947) *Experimental Design in Sociological Research*, New York: Harper.
Etzioni, A. (1968) ' "Shortcuts" to social change?', *The Public Interest*, **12**, 40–51.
Etzioni, A. and Lehman, E. W. (1967) 'Some dangers in "valid" social measurement', *Annals of the American Academy of Political and Social Science*, **373**, 1–15.
Galtung, J. (1967) *Theory and Methods of Social Research*. Oslo: Universitetsforloget; London: Allen & Unwin; New York: Columbia University Press.
Glass, G. V. (1968) 'Analysis of data on the Connecticut speeding crackdown as a time-series quasi-experiment', *Law and Society Review*, 3(1), 55–76.

Glass, G. V., Tiao, G. C. and Maguire, T. O. (1969) 'Analysis of data on the 1900 revision of the German divorce laws as a quasi-experiment', *Law and Society Review*.

Greenwood, E. (1945) *Experimental Sociology: a study in method*. New York: King's Crown Press.

Gross, B. M. (1966) *The State of the Nation: social system accounting*. London: Tavistock Publications. (Also in R. M. Bauer (1966) *Social Indicators*. Cambridge, Mass.: M.I.T. Press.)

Gross, B. M. (ed.) (1967) 'Social goals and indicators', *Annals of the American Academy of Political and Social Science*, **371**, Part 1 (May) i–iii and 1–177; Part 2 (Sept.) i–iii and 1–218.

Guttman, L. (1946) 'An approach for quantifying paired comparisons and rank order', *Annals of Mathematical Statistics*, **17**, 144–63.

Hyman, H. H. and Wright, C. R. (1967) 'Evaluating social action programs', in P. F. Lazarsfeld, W. H. Sewell, & H. L. Wilensky (eds), *The Uses of Sociology*. New York: Basic Books.

Kamisar, Y. (1964) 'The tactics of police-persecution oriented critics of the courts', *Cornell Law Quarterly*, **49**, 458–71.

Kaysen, C. (1967) 'Data banks and dossiers', *The Public Interest*, **7**, 52–60.

Manniche, E. and Hayes, D. P. (1957) 'Respondent anonymity and data matching', *Public Opinion Quarterly*, **21**(3), 384–88.

Office of the Secretary of Defense (1967) Assistant Secretary of Defense (Manpower). Guidance paper: Project One Hundred Thousand. Washington, D.C., March 31 (Multilith).

Polanyi, M. (1966) 'A society of explorers', in, *The Tacit Dimension*. New York: Doubleday, Ch. 3.

Polanyi, M. (1967) 'The growth of science in society', *Minerva*, **5**, 533–45.

Popper, K. R. (1963) *Conjectures and Refutations*. London: Routledge and Kegan Paul; New York: Basic Books.

Rheinstein, M. (1959) 'Divorce and the law in Germany: A review', *American Journal of Sociology*, **65**, 489–98.

Rose, A. M. (1952) 'Needed research on the mediation of labor disputes', *Personnel Psychology*, **5**, 187–200.

Ross, H. L. and Campbell, D. T. (1968) 'The Connecticut speed crackdown: a study of the effects of legal change', in H. L. Ross (ed), *Perspectives on the Social Order: readings in sociology*. New York: McGraw-Hill.

Sawyer, J. and Schechter, H. (1968) 'Computers, privacy, and the National Data Center: The responsibility of social scientists', *American Psychologist*, **23**, 810–18.

Schanck, R. L. and Goodman, C. (1939) 'Reactions to propaganda on both sides of a controversial issue', *Public Opinion Quarterly*, **3**, 107–12.

Schwartz, R. D. (1961) 'Field experimentation in sociological research', *Journal of Legal Education*, **13**, 401–10.

Schwartz, R. D. and Orleans, S. (1967) 'On legal sanctions', *University of Chicago Law Review*, **34**, 274–300.

Schwartz, R. D., & Skolnick, J. H. (1963) 'Televised communication and income tax compliance', in L. Arons & M. May (eds.), *Television and Human Behavior*. New York: Appleton-Century-Crofts.

Selvin, H. (1957) 'A critique of tests of significance in survey research', *American Sociological Review*, **22**, 519–27.

Simon, J. L. (1966) 'The price elasticity of liquor in the U.S. and a simple method of determination', *Econometrica*, **34**, 193–205.

Solomon, R. W. (1949) 'An extension of control group design', *Psychological Bulletin*, **46**, 137–50.

Stieber, J. W. (1949) *Ten Years of the Minnesota Labor Relations Act*. Minneapolis: Industrial Relations Center, University of Minnesota.

Stouffer, S. A. (1949) 'The point system for redeployment and discharge', in S. A. Stouffer *et al.*, *The American Soldier. Vol. 2, Combat and its aftermath*. Princeton: Princeton University Press.

Suchman, E. A. (1967) *Evaluative Research: principles and practice in public service and social action programs.* New York: Russell Sage.

Sween, J. and Campbell, D. T. (1965) A study of the effect of proximally auto-correlated error on tests of significance for the interrupted time-series quasi-experimental design'. (Multilith.)

Thistlethwaite, D. L. and Campbell, D. T. (1960) 'Regression-discontinuity analysis: an alternative to the ex post facto experiment', *Journal of Educational Psychology,* **51,** 309–17.

Walker, H. M. and Lev, J. (1953) *Statistical Inference.* New York: Holt.

Webb, E. J., Campbell, D. T., Schwartz, R. D. and Sechrest, L. B. (1966) *Unobtrusive Measures: nonreactive research in the social sciences.* Chicago: Rand McNally.

Wolf, E., Lüke, G. and Hax, H. (1959) *Scheidung und Scheidungsrecht: Grundfrägen der Ehescheidung in Deutschland.* Tübigen: J. C. B. Mohr.

The research web

Jacqueline P. Wiseman

The qualitative researcher is not unlike the detective in the classic murder mystery. Starting with a few clues, the detective questions persons connected with the case, develops hunches, questions further on the basis of those hunches, begins to see a picture of 'what happened' start to emerge, looks for evidence pro and con, elaborating or modifying that picture – until finally the unknown is known. The murderer is caught; what was once a mystery is now understandable. The facts have been 'organized' in a way to accommodate – with as few contradictions as possible – the largest amount of empirical data.

This constant interplay of data gathering and analysis is at the heart of qualitative research. It is therefore difficult indeed to discuss coding, processing, analysis and writing without also discussing planning and data gathering, for in no other approach is the interrelatedness of all portions of the research act quite so obvious. For me, with the possible exception of the early planning stages, all aspects of the research act are going on almost simultaneously. Early fragments of analysis and of conceptual insights make their appearance both in the organization or coding of material and in the most current decisions I make about what field material to gather in the future.

Taking the analogy of the murder mystery one step further, qualitative research is like a detective story that starts out with no suspects. Thus the outcome is quite open. This is in contrast to survey research, for example, in which the elements to be investigated are thought already to be known – much as a murder in which the M.O. (method of operation) is familiar to police. The structure provided by the M.O. or hypotheses allows for a *pre-organized* investigation, just as it does in survey research with pre-coded answers and set questions. In the qualitative approach there is minimal originating organization. The method of data gathering (unstructured interviews or observations), as well as methods of actual handling data, reflect this. Thus in data gathering, topic and form are inextricably bound together because they develop together.

From *Urban Life and Culture*, 1974, **3**, 317–28.

Topic and form – early stages

Before going into the field, I write out a list of topics that I am interested in covering by depth interviewing, watching for, or otherwise obtaining information about. Naturally, these cannot be collected in any given order because the flow of life or the respondents' interests precludes this, but I do refer to the sheet from time to time to see if I have forgotten anything. (This is easier to do with depth interviewing than participant or non-participant observation.)

After some material has been gathered (say ten depth interviews or ten sets of observations), I sit down and read my notes in order to begin three separate but overlapping operations. First of all, I want to see what I am learning from the data:

1. In answer to my initial questions;
2. In raising questions I never thought to ask.

Following this review, I expand and revise my list of topics to investigate.

At the same time I am reviewing early findings to expand the list of topics for pursuit, I also begin to assemble lists of the kinds of things I am finding out within a given topic area. These eventually form the skeleton of the *codes* that will be used to organize sub-units of the data prior to analysis.

None of these operations is done mechanically because I also use this review and code-developing time to initiate analytic approaches to the data. For instance, I ask myself the following questions:

1. What sociological concepts does a piece of action or some depth interview material illustrate? (For example, the norm of reciprocity, or an instance of labeling.)
2. In what parallel areas of social life are these concepts in operation? (Examples might include 'treaties' among agents of social control, parents and children, or warring nations, or labeling as it occurs in alcoholism, mental illness, and deafness.) When a sociological phenomenon occurs for which no existing concept seems to apply, I create a name for it. (For instance, in *Stations of the Lost* [Wiseman, 1970: 223–6] 'social margin' refers to the differential margin for social errors we all have as a result of our past performances and reputation. Another instance from that study might be 'defining encounters' [xv], which refers to assessments people make of each other at their initial meeting.) I also review the literature for other instances of the same phenomenon. I try to think of the detailed ways a concept 'operates' in other settings or situations. This mental exercise alerts me to new and subtle things to watch for in my own study. Naturally, this expands the list of topics that must be covered in my continuing interviewing, as well as suggests the glimmerings of an analysis.

Topic and form – second wave

Interviewing continues with the new, expanded topics guide. About ten interviews or observations later a second review is instituted. In the meantime all the previous steps are being repeated, and another step is usually added – *early analytic decisions.*

Of primary concern at this stage is a decision concerning what data will become the major focus of the analysis, and what data shall be relegated to the position of 'background' or 'givens'. This is an *arbitrary decision* on the part of the researcher and an important one. For instance, one may do research on various theories of the cause of alcoholism, or one may do research taking these theories as given and asking how drinkers are treated as a result. Failure to make this type of organizational decision results in a study in which so much is in major focus that analysis is impossible.

Decisions in the area of focus and background also pave the way for consideration of the next major analytic decision – what Lofland (1971: 123–4) calls the general design, and Becker and Geer (1960: 276–7) refer to as the social system model. This is the major pattern of organization of the social world being presented. At the same time, it becomes the organizing scheme of the analysis. The grand model comes out of the data already gathered while simultaneously aiding in the collection and categorization of data yet to come. It allows me, the researcher, to encompass the entire situation under study as though I were high on a mountain looking down and seeing all the action going on at once – a stance similar to the omniscient approach in fiction. With the development of this broad perspective, the researcher can see the sub-parts of the action and how they interact; then he can gear his analysis to reflect this information as closely as possible. Usually, each section or chapter of a report represents one of these sub-parts.

In evolving this model, I usually write several outlines and accept *temporarily* the one that makes the most sense and seems to accommodate the most data. In *Stations of the Lost* (Wiseman, 1970), the 'loop' of institutions became my general design or model and each major institution a chapter in the monograph. One can mentally review some of the possible models utilized by other researchers. Note they involve time, settings and people:

1. Time order or careers model – probably the most useful and natural. Everything has a natural history – a beginning, a middle and end. (I am using a 'career of wife of alcoholic' as a model in my current research [Wiseman, 1974]. Thus, the presentation begins with the wife's first inkling that her husband's drinking may be 'compulsive', goes through her strategies of therapy, her life with him and finally how things turn out for both spouses years later.)
2. Cyclical – related to the above model, but in addition suggesting a constant renewal and replay of the phenomenon, often resulting in acceleration. This is probably used most often in studies of deviant

behavior, labeling, the development of secondary deviance and in similar phenomena.

3. Social types – a description of the various types of people that populate a setting and interact within it.
4. Social actions and interactions – descriptions, usually in comparison form, of behavioral variations on one social action theme. I used this approach in my article on time structuring by alcoholics within various social situations (Wiseman, 1972).
5. Social settings or scenes (behavior settings) – descriptions of the special culture and activities in these social subscenes.
6. The interrelationships of one or more of the above models probably accounts for most of the organizational schemes of qualitative data. In accomplishing this interrelationship, the decision must be made again as to which model is to dominate the organization of the analysis and which is to be contained within it. That is, if there is to be a model involving social types and social scenes, the researcher must decide whether the chapters will be based on each type of person, with the scenes they frequent being presented as background, or, whether, on the other hand, the scenes will provide major organizational focus and the people will be described within them.

Once this decision on the general design is made, the organization of the code book can follow this preliminary model and also offer a sort of elaborated guideline to the analysis-to-be.

Coding mechanics

At the same time that I am gathering material either in longhand or by tape recorder, it is being typed with two carbons. The two sets are for coding and cutting apart. Two are needed because sometimes the same statement or incident can be coded in more than one way. Sometimes it can be used in more than two ways. When this is the case, extra copies of the particular item can be made. One page is left intact so that I can refer back to statements and see them in context of the entire interview or scene, if desired.

A hired coder is instructed to read the typed material and code it according to the codes I have developed. Each 'piece of data' is marked off with a red line. It is then coded with the topic code (a number), and the sub-topic code (a letter). It is identified by the interview number and page so that it may be read in context any time. The coder eventually cuts these pieces of coded data apart and pastes them on 5 × 8 cards. I might mention that it is not always easy to decide where one codable piece ends and another begins, and sometimes rules must be developed to aid this decision. During this reading by the coder, the codes may be expanded or modified in consultation with the researcher.

It should be emphasized that despite the fact that the codes are quite detailed (possibly fifteen to twenty major topics each with ten to fifteen minor parts), I still consider this first coding to be 'gross' coding. I personally do a sub-code within each sub-division created by this first coding. This occurs as part of another step in analysis.

After quite a bit of field work is done, and there is a great deal of repeat material, I take off time to perform this preliminary analysis as it has come to me on the coded cards. At this point, I function as a sort of human IBM machine, doing more intricate sorting than a coder can be asked to do. I look at all the cards that are under one topic and sub-topic and I think of what such data mean not only as sociological concepts, but as constructs. By 'constructs' I mean various concepts found together in numerous combinations. Then I ask myself: What does this information mean:

(a)   In terms of the goals of my study?
(b)   In terms of the life of the people being studied?

At this stage, I am usually working on a large table or, more likely, the floor. Sub-sub sorts are neatly stacked in piles with a descriptive card attached to them by rubber band. These labeled card piles can now be boxed in order of their probable use.

This refined coding also alerts me to other possible research needs, such as citations from parallel studies, areas where more data is needed to fill in a gap in knowledge, material that might better be held for another part of the analysis, and data that does not seem to fit anywhere in my current master plan.

These latter 'orphan' data are put in either one of two possible places: as footnote material, or in an envelope marked 'miscellaneous'. This envelope is dumped out on the floor when it is full, and I sit down with the scraps of data that seemed to fit nowhere but which obviously are part of the social world I am studying. The job then is to see what can be done with them. For example, my chapter on 'benefactors and beneficiaries' in *Stations of the Lost* (Wiseman, 1970: 239–68) came out of such a reclamation project. (It is also possible that this data will not fit in anywhere and would best be saved for a separate paper rather than stuffed into the study merely to make immediate use of it.)

First draft

It is absolutely necessary that a first draft be started before data gathering is completed and coding too far along. The very effort of fleshing out the grand and the subsidiary topics alerts one to areas where specific types of data are inadequate, contradictory, confusing or absent.

Once there is a first draft, I like to offer it as a seminar or colloquium paper as often as possible and to a great variety of audiences. It is here that I get challenges, ideas and insights that greatly enhance the final analysis. Lacking a colloquium invitation, I also discuss findings with others – lay persons as well as professionals – and keep track of the questions they ask and the comments they make.

The first draft is always the hardest – even with the help of a master plan. Sometimes the smaller sections are difficult actually to organize. To overcome a writing block, I hit upon the idea of writing in 'takes' (half pages). For each take, I would put down one analytic point, plus a list of the coded evidence (by identification number) following it. Psychologically, the take eases the pain of analysis and writing. All that is demanded is one-half page of prose. This is less intimidating than planning to write full page after full page – the more orthodox approach. Takes can be written in any order so that one can methodically plow through many little stacks of data cards without worrying about organization for the time being.

The next step is to look at the analytic takes and see if an order of presentation suggests itself and to stack the takes in this order. The identification numbers of the data that will be presented as evidence for each analytic point on the takes are noted, and these coded data cards pulled, Xeroxed and affixed to the analytic take. Next I write an introduction and the necessary transition sentences. The result (with the aid of scissors and stapler) is a fairly painless first rough draft ready for editing, re-roughing and review. This draft represents something to work from and will, of course, be rewritten many times.

Meanwhile, back in the field

The writing of this initial draft usually alerts me to the need for further field work. Can I explain the differential arrest patterns on Skid Row if I do seasonal observations? How can I explain deviant cases – some men liking the Christian Missionaries; some women not minding if their husbands are alcoholics?

In addition to getting specialized data from the field on troublesome areas, I begin to puzzle about various problematic aspects of the study in my spare time; when driving, walking, doing routine tasks, and so on. I carry a notebook with me at all times for the moment when an analytic 'solution' occurs to me. These little insights, which come from more or less constant immersion in a problem for long periods, are often extremely valuable to the analysis.

It is also at this time that I check to see if degree and detail of the investigation are *consistent* from section to section. For instance, if I cover informal relationships in one setting, I try to cover them in all settings, or offer an explanation as to why I am not doing this.

At the same time, I am aided in the field by these initial analytic efforts that have sharpened the questions asked respondents and the behavior watched for in various settings.

Validity, reliability and significance

Concern for validity and reliability in qualitative data can be of great help in the development of analytic insights. The mandate is different from that used in survey research. In the qualitative study, I am trying to make valid sense out of the social world of the people I am studying; I am attempting to reconstruct *their* view of their world. The approach outlined below forces me to continue to try to find logic in a world that may seem illogical on an objective basis.

In judging the validity and usefulness of data, I follow several seat-of-the-pants rules that have evolved from my working with exploratory studies:

1. Assume, at least at first, that no one is lying.
2. If you must choose between an official's story and that of an individual (that is, institution vs. individual) – most likely the institution is not being totally honest.
3. There is nothing that happens or that people tell you about that 'doesn't make any sense'. It is part of their lives. They think it makes sense. It is up to you to make sociological sense of it. (This is how I made sense of the fact that men start to drink almost immediately after they had just taken the cure for alcoholism [Wiseman, 1970: 217–38].)
4. Assume that human beings may not be very smart in the decisions they make, but they do the very best they can. They are not pathological, neurotic or in any way irrational in their decisions. They do make mistakes of judgment, perception and logic, and can seem very stupid to an objective observer, but they are not the victims of personality or social forces compelling them to act – to my mind the least acceptable alternative explanations for human behavior.
5. There is usually nothing that people tell you or that you will see (if it is within the research topic) that is truly irrelevant to your study. It probably belongs under another code heading, and is either background or foreground.
6. There is no such thing as absolute truth. All the most objective researcher can report is his version of the actions and decisions of others and how they see their world. No one has the final word on this. Forcing myself to assume this perspective leaves the door open for many insights. I try to understand the logic, perceptions, judgments and decisions of my subjects in light of their often divergent definitions of the situation.

A consideration of the significance of a finding in qualitative research also sharpens the analysis. Instead of limiting myself to statistical significance or its equivalent (does it happen very frequently or merely idiosyncratically), I concern myself with the following questions:

1. Is it significant because it affects a great many people?
2. Is it significant because it illustrates or reveals something of a more general (and significant) nature about human behavior?

By subjecting data to this sort of test, very little data is lost; most is reconceptualized.

Drafts and decisions

As my field work winds down, the rough drafts of pieces, sections and chapters increase. All the data is coded and I go over the codes, subdividing them further, Xeroxing stacks and then picking the best examplars for analytic points. The analytic points written earlier are reviewed and perhaps modified in the light of newly-collected data.

I also look to see how the whole general design is hanging together. Are earlier parts contradicted by later data? How can I explain that? Do some parts substantiate each other or form a construct that I have overlooked?

If the people I am studying were to read my report – would they recognize their world in it? That is one of the final analytic as well as validating steps. One should be ready to handle the criticisms of those who actually live this life. The closer they think you come to describing it, the better you can feel about your data gathering, your organization and your analysis.

Peers, too, should again be asked to read chapters and comment. It is not too late at this point to go back into the field to clarify an area with additional data.

Final drafts consist of this weaving back and forth in the manuscript, investigating loose ends, trying to make things understandable, non-contradictory, a web of social explanation.

Letting go

One could keep on polishing forever, adding little points, embroidering on others. However, after about eight or ten drafts and numerous revisits to the field, I force myself to let it go. I have found a world that is much more complex than I ever imagined when I embarked on the project. Hopefully, my presentation will be a true reflection of life as it is lived there.

References

Becker, H. S. and B. Geer (1960) 'Participant observation: the analysis of qualitative field data', pp. 267–89, in R. N. Adams and J. J. Preiss (eds) *Human Organization Research*. Homewood, Ill.: Dorsey.

Lofland, J. (1971) *Analyzing Social Settings*. Belmont, Calif.: Wadsworth.

Wiseman, J. P. (1970) *Stations of the Lost*. Englewood Cliffs, N.J.: Prentice-Hall.

Wiseman, J. P. (1972) 'Sober time: the neglected variable in the recidivism of alcoholic persons'. Proceedings of the Second Annual Alcoholic Conference of the National Institute on Alcohol Abuse and Alcoholism; 165–84.

Wiseman, J. P. (1974) 'Wives of alcoholics: a study of deviance where the deviant is dominant'. San Francisco State University (unpublished).

Reading 11

Some methodological problems of field studies

Morris Zelditch Jr.

The original occasion for this paper was a reflection of the use of sample survey methods in the field: that is, the use of structured interview schedules, probability samples, etc. in what is usually thought of as a participant-observation study. There has been a spirited controversy between, on the one hand, those who have sharply criticized field workers for slipshod sampling, for failing to document assertions quantitatively and for apparently accepting impressionistic accounts – or accounts that the quantitatively minded could not distinguish from purely impressionistic accounts;[1] and, on the other hand, those who have, sometimes bitterly, been opposed to numbers, to samples, to questionnaires, often on the ground that they destroy the field workers' conception of a social system as an organic whole.[2]

Although there is a tendency among many young field workers to accent criticisms made from the quantitative point of view,[3] there is reason to believe that the issue itself has been stated falsely. In most cases field methods are discussed as if they were 'all of a piece'.[4] There is, in fact, a tendency to be either *for* or *against* quantification, as if it were an either/or issue. To some extent the battle lines correlate with a relative concern for 'hardness' versus 'depth and reality' of data. Quantitative data are often thought of as 'hard', and qualitative as 'real and deep'; thus if you prefer 'hard' data you are for quantification and if you prefer 'real deep' data you are for qualitative participant observation. What to do if you prefer data that are real, deep *and* hard is not immediately apparent.

A more fruitful approach to the issue must certainly recognize that a field study is not a single method gathering a single kind of information. This approach suggests several crucial questions: *What* kinds of methods and *what* kinds of information are relevant? How can the 'goodness' of different methods for different purposes be evaluated? Even incomplete and imperfect answers – which are all that we offer here – should be useful, at least in helping to restate the issue. They also pose, order and to some extent resolve other issues of field method

From *American Journal of Sociology*, 1962, **67**, 566–76.

so that in pursuing their implications this paper encompasses a good deal more than its original problem.

Three types of information

The simplest events are customarily described in statements predicting a single property of a single object at a particular time and in a particular place. From these descriptions one may build up more complex events in at least two ways. The first is by forming a configuration of many properties of the same object at the same time in the same place. This may be called an 'incident'. A more complex configuration but of the same type would be a sequence of incidents, that is, a 'history'.

A second way to build up more complex events is by repeating observations of a property over a number of units. Units here can be defined formally, requiring only a way of identifying events as identical. They can be members of a social system or repetitions of the same type of incident at different times or in different places (e.g. descriptions of five funerals). The result is a frequency distribution of some property.

From such information it is possible to deduce certain underlying properties of the system observed, some of which may be summarized as consequences of the 'culture' of S (S stands here for a social system under investigation). But at least some portion of this culture can be discovered not only by inference from what is observed but also from verbal reports by members of S – for example, accounts of its principal institutionalized norms and statuses. The rules reported, of course, are to some extent independent of the events actually observed; the norms actually followed may not be correctly reported, and deviance may be concealed. Nevertheless, information difficult to infer can be readily and accurately obtained from verbal reports. For example, it may take some time to infer that a member occupies a given status but this may readily be discovered by asking either him or other members of S.

We thus combine various types of information into three broad classes.

Type I: Incidents and histories. A log of events during a given period, a record of conversations heard, descriptions of a wedding, a funeral, an election, etc. Not only the actions observed, but the 'meanings', the explanations, etc. reported by the participants can be regarded as part of the 'incident' insofar as they are thought of as data rather than actual explanations.

Type II: Distributions and frequencies. Possessions of each member of S, number of members who have a given belief, number of times member m is observed talking to member n, etc.

Type III: Generally known rules and statuses.   Lists of statuses, lists of persons occupying them, informants' accounts of how rules of exogamy apply, how incest or descent are defined, how political leaders are supposed to be chosen, how political decisions are supposed to be made, etc.

This classification has nothing to do with what is *inferred* from data, despite the way the notion of reported rules and statuses was introduced. In particular, more complex configurations of norms, statuses, events which are 'explained' by inferring underlying themes or structures involve a level of inference outside the scope of this paper: the classification covers only information *directly* obtained from reports and observations. Moreover, this classification cuts across the distinction between what is observed by the investigator and what is reported to him. Although Type III consists only of reports, Types I and II include both observations by the investigator himself *and* reports of members of *S*, insofar as they are treated as data. Later we talk of an event as seen through the eyes of an informant, where the investigator trusts the informant as an accurate observer and thinks of the report as if it were his own observation. Now, however, interest is focused not on the facts of the report but rather on what the report reveals of the perceptions, the motivations, the world of meaning of the informant himself. The report, in this case, does not transmit observational data; it is, itself, the datum and so long as it tells what the person reporting thinks, the factual correctness of what he thinks is irrelevant. (This is sometimes phrased as making a distinction between *informants* and *respondents*, in the survey research sense.) Thus Type I includes both observations (what we see going on) and the statements of members telling what they understand the observed events to mean, which is regarded as part of the event. In a somewhat different way, Type II also includes both reports (e.g. an opinion poll) and observations (e.g. systematically repeated observations with constant coding categories).

Three types of method

It is possible to make a pure, logically clear classification of methods of obtaining information in the field, but for the present purpose this would be less useful than one that is, though less precise, rather closer to what a field worker actually does.

Two methods are usually thought of as characteristic of the investigator in the field. He invariably keeps a daily log of events and of relatively casual, informal continuous interviews, both of which go into his field notes. Almost invariably he also develops informants, that is, selected members of *S* who are willing and able to give him information about practices and rules in *S* and events he does not directly observe. (They may also supply him with diaries, autobiographies and their own personal feelings; i.e. they may also function as respondents.) Contrary to popular opinion, almost any well-trained field worker also keeps various forms of census materials, records of systematic observations, etc. including a basic listing of members of S, face-sheet data on them, and systematically repeated observations of certain recurrent events. Many field workers also collect documents; however, we will classify field methods into only three broad classes which we conceive of as primary. These are:

Type I. Participant-observation.   The field worker directly observes and also participates in the sense that he has durable social relations in S. He may or may not play an active part in events, or he may interview participants in events which may be considered part of the process of observation.

Type II. Informant-interviewing.   We prefer a more restricted definition of the informant than most field workers use, namely that he be called an 'informant' only where he is reporting information presumed factually correct about others rather than about himself; and his information about events is about events in their absence. Interviewing during the event itself is considered part of participant-observation.

Type III. Enumerations and samples.   This includes both surveys and direct, repeated, countable observations. Observation in this sense may entail minimal participation as compared with that implied in Type I.

This classification excludes documents on the ground that they represent resultants or combinations of primary methods. Many documents, for example, are essentially informant's accounts and are treated exactly as an informant's account is treated: subjected to the same kinds of internal and external comparisons, treated with the same suspicions and often, in the end, taken as evidence of what occurred at some time and place from which the investigator was absent. The fact that the account is written is hardly important. Many other documents are essentially enumerations; for example, personnel and cost-accounting records of a factory, membership rolls of a union, tax rolls of a community.

Two criteria of 'goodness'

Criteria according to which the 'goodness' of a procedure may be defined are:

1. *Informational adequacy,* meaning accuracy, precision and completeness of data.

2. *Efficiency,* meaning cost per added input of information.

It may appear arbitrary to exclude validity and reliability. Validity is excluded because it is, in a technical sense, a relation between an indicator and a concept, and similar problems arise whether one obtains information from an informant, a sample or from direct observation. Construed loosely, validity is often taken to mean 'response validity', accuracy of report, and this is caught up in the definition of informational adequacy. Construed more loosely yet, validity is sometimes taken as equivalent to 'real', 'deep' data, but this seems merely to beg the question. Reliability is relevant only tangentially; it is a separate problem that cuts across the issues of this paper.

Fundamental strategies

Certain combinations of method and type of information may be regarded as formal prototypes, in the sense that other combinations may be logically reduced to them. For example: Instead of a sample survey or enumeration, an informant is employed to list dwelling units, or to estimate incomes, or to tell who associates with whom or what each person believes with respect to some issue. The information is obtained from a single informant, but he is treated *as if he himself* had conducted a census or poll. More generally, in every case in which the information obtained is logically reducible to a distribution of the members of S with respect to the property a, the implied method of obtaining the information is also logically reducible to an enumeration. The enumeration may be either through direct observation (estimating the number of sheep each Navaho has by actually counting them; establishing the sociometric structure of the community by watching who interacts with whom), or through a questionnaire survey (determining household composition by questioning a member of each household, or administering a sociometric survey to a sample of the community). If an informant is used, it is presumed that he has himself performed the enumeration. We are not at the moment concerned with the validity of this assumption in specific instances but rather in observing that regardless of the actual way in which the information was obtained, the logical and formal character of the procedure is that of a census or survey.

Suppose an informant is asked to describe what went on at a community meeting which the observer is unable to attend; or a sample of respondents is asked to describe a sequence of events which occurred before the observer entered S. In either case his reports are used as substitutes for direct observation. Such evidence may, in fact, be examined critically to establish its accuracy – we begin by assuming the bias of the reports – but it is presumed that, having 'passed' the statements they become an objective account of what has occurred in the same sense that the investigator's own reports are treated as objective, once his biases have been taken into account. The informant, one usually says in this case, is the observer's observer; he differs in no way from the investigator himself. It follows that the prototype is direct observation by the observer himself.

The prototype so far is not only a formal model; it is also a 'best' method, efficiently yielding the most adequate information. In learning institutionalized rules and statuses it is doubtful that there is a formal prototype and all three methods yield adequate information. Here we may choose the *most efficient* method as defining our standard of procedure. To illustrate: We wish to study the political structure of the United States. We are told that the principal national political figure is called a 'president', and we wish to know who he is. We do not ordinarily think of sampling the population of the United States to obtain the answer; we regard it as sufficient to ask one well-informed member. This question is typical of a large class of questions asked by a field worker in the course of his research.

A second example: Any monograph on the Navaho reports that they are matrilineal and matrilocal. This statement may mean either of two things:

1. All Navaho are socially identified as members of a descent group defined through the mother's line, and all Navaho males move to the camp of their wife's family at marriage.
2. There exists a set of established rules according to which all Navaho are supposed to become socially identified as members of a descent group defined through the mother's line, and to move to the camp of their wife's family at marriage.

The truth of the first interpretation can be established only by an enumeration of the Navaho, or a sample sufficiently representative and sufficiently precise. It is readily falsified by exceptions, and in fact there *are* exceptions to both principles. But suppose among thirty Navaho informants at least one says that the Navaho are patrilineal and patrilocal. If this is intended to describe institutionalized norms as in (2) above, we are more likely to stop using the informant than we are to state that there are 'exceptions' in the sense of (1) above. We might sample a population to discover the motivation to conform to a rule, or the actual degree of conformity, but are less likely to do so to establish that the rule *exists,* if we confront institutionalized phenomena. This also constitutes a very large class of questions asked by the field worker.

Adequacy of informants for various problems in the field

It does not follow from the definition of a prototype method that no other form of obtaining information can suffice; all we intend is that it *does* suffice, and any other method is logically reducible to it. Further, comparison with the prototype is a criterion by which other forms can be evaluated. In considering the adequacy in some given instance of the use of an informant as the field worker's surrogate census, for example, we are interested primarily in whether he is likely to know enough, to recall enough and to report sufficiently precisely to yield the census that we ourselves would make. Comments below, incidentally, are to be taken as always prefixed with the phrase, 'by and large'. It is not possible to establish, at least yet, a firm rule which will cover every case.

The informant as a surrogate censustaker

A distinction must again be made between *what* information is obtained and how it is obtained. It is one thing to criticize a field worker for not obtaining a frequency distribution where it is required – for instance, for not sampling mothers who are weaning children in order to determine age at weaning – and another to criticize him for not obtaining it *directly* from the mothers. If the field worker reports that the average age at weaning is two years and the grounds for this is that he asked an informant, 'About when do they wean children around here?' it is not the fact that he asked an informant but that he asked the wrong question that should be criticized. He should have asked, 'How many mothers do you know who are now weaning children? How old are their children?'

The critical issue, therefore, is whether or not the informant can be assumed to have the information that the field worker requires, granting that he asks the proper questions. In many instances he does. In some cases he is an even better source than an enumerator; he either knows better or is less likely to falsify. Dean, for example, reports that workers who are ideologically pro-union, but also have mobility aspirations and are not well-integrated into their factory or local unions, are likely to report attending union meetings which they do not in fact attend.[5] She also shows that, when *respondent-reported* attendance is used as a measure of attendance, this tends spuriously to increase correlations of attendance at union meetings with attitudes toward unions in general, and to reduce correlations of attendance at union meetings with attitudes more specifically directed at the local union. The list of those actually attending was obtained by an observer, who, however, had sufficient rapport with officers of the local to obtain it from them.[6] Attendance, largely by 'regulars', was stable from meeting to meeting so that the officers could have reproduced it quite accurately.[7]

On the other hand, there are many instances in which an informant is *prima facie* unlikely to be adequate, although no general rule seems to identify these clearly for the investigator. The nature of the information – private versus public, more or less objective, more or less approved – is obviously relevant, yet is often no guide at all. Some private information, for example, is better obtained from informants, some from respondents. The social structure of *S*, particularly its degree of differentiation and complexity, is also obviously relevant. An informant must be in a position to know the information desired, and if *S* is highly differentiated and the informant confined to one part of it, he can hardly enumerate it. Probably in order to discover attitudes and opinions that are relatively private and heterogeneous in a structure that is relatively differentiated, direct enumeration or sampling should be used.

The informant as a 'representative respondent'

An 'average' of a distribution is sometimes obtained not by asking for an enumeration by the informant, nor even by asking a general question concerning what people typically do; sometimes it is obtained by treating the informant as if he were a 'representative respondent'. The informant's reports about himself – perhaps deeper, more detailed, 'richer', but nevertheless like those of a respondent in a survey rather than an informant in the technical sense – stand in place of a sample. Where a multivariate distribution is thought of, this person is treated as a 'quintessential' subject, 'typical' in many dimensions. Some field workers speak favorably of using informants in this way, and it is likely that even more of them actually do so.

Since, as yet, we have no really hard and fast rules to follow, it is possible that in some cases this is legitimate; but, by and large, it is the most suspect of ways of using informants. It is simply a bad way of sampling. The legitimate cases are probably of three types: first, as suggestive of leads to follow up; second, as illustration of a point to be made in a report that is verifiable on other grounds. But in this second case the proviso ought to be thought of as rather strict; it is not sufficient to 'have a feeling' that the point is true, to assume that it is verifiable on other grounds. The third case is perhaps the most legitimate, but is really a case of using informants to provide information about generally known rules: for example, using informants to collect 'typical' genealogies or kinship terms, the assumption being that his kin terms are much like those of others (which is not always true, of course) and his genealogy sufficiently 'rich' – this being the basis on which he was chosen – to exhibit a wide range of possibilities.

The informant as the observer's observer

The third common use of the informant is to report events not directly observed by the field worker. Here the investigator substitutes the observations of a member for his own observation. It is not simply interviewing that is involved here, because participant observation was defined earlier as including interviewing on the spot, in conjunction with direct observation. Thus, some of the most important uses of the informant – to provide the meaning and context of that which we are observing, to provide a running check on variability, etc. – are actually part of participant observation. It is the use of informants as if they were colleagues that we must now consider.

Such a procedure is not only legitimate but absolutely necessary to adequate investigation of any complex structure. In studying a social structure by participant observation there are two problems of bias that override all others, even the much belabored 'personal equation'. One results from the fact that a single observer cannot be everywhere at the same time, nor can he be 'everywhere' in time, for that matter – he has not been in *S* forever, and will not be there indefinitely – so that, inevitably, something happens that he has not seen, cannot see or will not see. The second results from the fact that there exist parts of the social structure into which he has not penetrated and probably will not, by virtue of the way he has defined himself to its members, because of limitations on the movement of those who sponsor him, etc. There has never been a participant-observer study in which the observer acquired full knowledge of all roles and statuses through his own direct observation, and for that matter there never will be such a study by a single observer. To have a team of observers is one possible solution; to have informants who stand in the relation of team members to the investigator is another. The virtue of the informant used in this way, is to increase the accessibility of *S* to the investigator.

Efficiency of sampling for various problems in the field

Sampling to obtain information about institutionalized norms and statuses

It has already been argued that a properly obtained probability sample gives adequate information about institutionalized norms and statuses but is not very efficient. Two things are implied: that such information is *general* information so that any member of *S* has the same information as any other; and that the truth of such information does not depend solely on the opinions of the respondents – the information is in some sense objective.

The first of these implications is equivalent to assuming that *S* is homogeneous with respect to the property *a*, so that a sample of one suffices to classify *S* with respect to it. It then becomes inefficient to continue sampling. The principal defect in such an argument is a practical one: By what criterion can one decide *S* is homogeneous with respect to *a* without sampling *S*? There are two such criteria, neither of which is wholly satisfactory. The first is to use substantive knowledge. We would expect in general that certain norms are invariably institutionalized, such as incest and exogamy, descent, inheritance, marriage procedures, patterns of exchange of goods, formal structure of labor markets, etc. We may assume a priori, for example, that a sample of two hundred Navaho is not required to discover that marriage in one's own clan is incestuous. But the pitfall for the unwary investigator is that he may stray beyond his substantive knowledge or apply it at the wrong time in the wrong place.

A second is to employ a loose form of sequential sampling. Suppose, for example, that we ask an informed male in S whom he may marry, or whom any male may marry. He answers, 'All who are A, but no one who is B.' We ask a second informant and discover again that he may marry all who are A, but no one who is B. We ask a third, a fourth, a fifth, and each tells us the same rule. We do not need to presume that the rule is actually obeyed; that is quite a different question. But we may certainly begin to believe that we have found an institutionalized norm. Conversely, the more variability we encounter, the more we must investigate further. The pitfall here is that we may be deceived by a homogeneous 'pocket' within which all members agree but which does not necessarily represent all structural parts of S. For this reason we try to choose representative informants, each from a different status group. This implies, however, that we are working outward from earlier applications of this dangerous principle; we have used some informants to tell us what statuses there are, thereafter choosing additional informants from the new statuses we have discovered.

The second implication – that in some sense the truth of the information obtained depends not on the opinions of respondents but on something else that is 'objective' in nature – simply paraphrases Durkheim: institutions are 'external' to given individuals, even though they exist only 'in' individuals; they have a life of their own, are *sui generis*. Illustrating with an extreme case: a 'belief' of S's religion can be described by an informant even where neither he nor any living member of S actually believes it, although if no member ever did believe it we might regard the information as trivial. In other words, this type of information does not refer to individuals living at a given time, but rather to culture as a distinct object of abstraction. It is this type of information that we mean by 'institutionalized norms and statuses'. It bears repeating at this point that if one Navaho informant told us the Navaho were patrilineal and patrilocal, we would be more likely to assume he was wrong than we would be to assume that the Navaho had, for the moment, changed their institutions.

Sampling to obtain information about incidents and histories
If we had the good fortune to have a report from every member of S about what happened in region R at time T, would it really be good fortune? Would we not distinguish between those in a position to observe the event and those not? Among those who had been in the region R itself, would we not also distinguish subregions which provided different vantage points from which to view the event? Among those viewing it from the same vantage point, would we not distinguish more or less credible witnesses? Enumeration or not, we would apply stringent internal and external comparisons to each report

in order to establish what truly occurred. Formally, of course, this describes a complex technique of stratification which, if carried out properly, would withstand any quantitative criticism. But if all the elements of decision as to what is 'truth' in such a case are considered, it is a moot point how important enumeration or random sampling is in the process.[8]

Informants with special information
Some things happen that relatively few people know about. A random sample is not a sensible way in which to obtain information about these events, although it is technically possible to define a universe U containing only those who do know and sample from U. A parallel case is the repetitive event in inaccessible parts of a social structure. A social structure is an organized system of relationships, one property of which is that certain parts of it are not readily observed by members located in other parts. There is a considerable amount of relatively esoteric information about S. It may be satisfactory from a formal point of view to regard S as consisting in many universes U_i, each of which is to be sampled for a different piece of information, but again the usefulness of such a conception is questionable, particularly if most U_i contain very few members.

Efficiency and adequacy of participant observation for various problems in the field

Ex post facto quantitative documentation
Because certain things are observed repeatedly, it sometimes occurs to the field worker to count these repetitions in his log as quantitative documentation of an assertion. In such cases, the information obtained should be subjected to any of the canons by which other quantitative data are evaluated; The care with which the universe is defined and the sense in which the sample is representative are particularly critical. With few exceptions, frequency statements made from field logs will *not* withstand such careful examination.

This sharp stricture applies only to ex post facto enumeration or sampling of field logs, and it is because it is ex post facto that the principal dangers arise. Events and persons represented in field logs will generally be sampled according to convenience rather than rules of probability sampling. The sample is unplanned, contains unknown biases. It is not so much random as haphazard, a distinction which is critical. When, after the fact, the observer attempts to correlate two classes of events in these notes very misleading results will be obtained. If we wish to correlate a and b it is characteristic of such samples that 'a' will be more frequently recorded than '*not-a*,' and '*a and b*' more frequently than '*not-a and b*' or '*a and not-b*'. As a general rule, only those data which the observer actually intended to enumerate should be treated as enumerable.

There are, of course, some valid enumerations contained in field notes. For example, a verbatim account kept of all meetings of some organization is a valid enumeration; a record kept, in some small rural community, of all members of it who come to the crossroads hamlet during a year is a valid enumeration. These will tend, however, to be intentional enumerations and not subject to the strictures applicable to ex post facto quantification. A much rarer exception will occur when, looking back through one's notes, one discovers that without particularly intending it, every member of the community studied has been enumerated with respect to the property *a*, or that almost all of them have. This is likely to be rare because field notes tend not to record those who do *not* have the property *a*, and, of all those omitted in the notes, one does not know how many are *not-a* and how many simply were not observed. If everyone, or almost everyone, can be accounted for as either *a* or *not-a*, then a frequency statement is validly made.[9] But, if such information were desired in the first place, participant observation would clearly be a most inefficient means of obtaining it.

Readily verbalized norms and statuses
It is not efficient to use participant observation to obtain generally known norms and statuses so long as these can be readily stated. It may take a good deal of observation to infer that which an informant can quickly tell you. Participant observation would in such cases be primarily to check what informants say, to get clues to further questions, etc. It is, of course, true that the concurrent interviewing involved in participant observation will provide the information – it is necessary to make sense out of the observations – but it comes in bits and pieces and is less readily checked for accuracy, completeness, consistency, etc.

Latent phenomena
Not all norms and statuses can be verbalized. Consequently, there remains a special province to which participant observation lays well-justified claims. But certain misleading implications should be avoided in admitting them. Because such phenomena may be described as 'latent' – as known to the observer but not to the members of *S* – it may be concluded that *all* latent phenomena are the province of participant observation. This does not follow. The term 'latent' is ambiguous; it has several distinct usages, some of which do not even share the core meaning of 'known to the observer, unknown to members'. Lazarsfeld, for example, refers to a dimension underlying a series of manifest items as a 'latent' attribute; it cannot be observed by anyone, and is inferred by the investigator from intercorrelations of observables. But the members of *S* may also make these inferences. (They infer that a series of statements classify the speaker as 'liberal', for example.) The most advanced techniques for searching out such latent phenomena are found in survey research and psychometrics, not in participant observation.

These are matters of inference, not of how data are directly obtained. The same is true of the discovery of 'latent functions'. Often the observer is aware of connections between events when the members of *S* are not, even though they are aware of the events themselves. But again, relations among events are not the special province of any one method; we look for such connections in *all* our data. In fact, owing to the paucity and non-comparability of units that often plague the analysis of field notes, it might be argued that participant observation is often incapable of detecting such connections. The great value of participant observation in detecting latent phenomena, then, is in those cases in which members of *S* are unaware of actually observable events, of some of the things they do, or some of the things that happen around them, which can be directly apprehended by the observer. Any other case requires inference and such inference should be made from *all* available data.

Summary and conclusion

Figure 11.1 offers a general summary.

With respect to the problem with which this paper originated the following conclusion may be drawn: Because we often treat different methods as concretely different types of study rather than as analytically different aspects of the same study, it is possible to attack a field study on the ground that it ought to be an enumeration and fails if it is not; and to defend it on the ground that it ought to be something *else* and succeeds only if it is. But, however we classify types of information in the future – and the classification suggested here is only tentative – they are not all of one type. True, a field report is unreliable if it gives us, after consulting a haphazard selection of informants or even a

Information types	Methods of obtaining information		
	Enumerations and samples	Participant observation	Interviewing informants
Frequency distributions	Prototype and best form	Usually inadequate and inefficient	Often, but not always, inadequate; if adequate it is efficient
Incidents, histories	Not adequate by itself; not efficient	Prototype and best form	Adequate with precautions, and efficient
Institutionalized norms and statuses	Adequate but inefficient	Adequate, but inefficient, except for unverbalized norms	Most efficient and hence best form

Fig. 11.1

carefully planned 'representative' selection, a statement such as, 'All members of *S* believe that . . .' or 'The average member of *S* believes that . . .' *and* (1) there is variance in the characteristic reported, (2) this variance is relevant to the problem reported *and* (3) the informants cannot be seriously thought of as equivalent to a team of pollsters, *or* (4) the investigator has reported what is, essentially, the 'average' beliefs of his *informants, as if they* were a representative, probability sample of respondents. But to demand that every piece of information be obtained by a probability sample is to commit the researcher to grossly inefficient procedure and to ignore fundamental differences among various kinds of information. The result is that we create false methodological issues, often suggest quite inappropriate research strategies to novices, and sometimes conceal real methodological issues which deserve more discussion in the literature – such as how to establish institutionalized norms given only questionnaire data. It should be no more satisfactorily rigorous to hear that everything is in some way a sample, and hence must be sampled, than to hear that everything is in some sense 'whole' and hence cannot be sampled.

Notes and references

1. See Harry Alpert (1952) 'Some observations on the sociology of sampling', *Social Forces*, **31**, 30–1; Robert C. Hanson (1958) 'Evidence and procedure characteristics of "reliable" propositions in social science', *American Journal of Sociology*, **63**, 357–63.
2. See W. L. Warner and P. Lunt (1941) *Social Life of a Modern Community*. New Haven, Conn.: Yale University Press, p. 55; Conrad Arensberg (1952) 'The community study method', *American Journal of Sociology*, **60**, 109–24; Howard Becker (1956) 'Field work among Scottish shepherds and German peasants', *Social Forces*, **35**, 10–15; Howard S. Becker and Blanche Geer (1957) 'Participant observation and interviewing; a comparison', *Human Organization*, **16**, 28–34; Solon Kimball (1955) 'Problems of studying American culture', *American Anthropologist*, **57**, 1131–42; and A. Vidich and J. Bensman (1954) 'The validity of field data', *Human Organization*, **13**, 20–7.
3. See particularly Oscar Lewis (1953) 'Controls and experiments in field work', in *Anthropology Today*. Chicago: University of Chicago Press, p. 455n.; also cf. Howard S. Becker (1958) 'Problems of inference and proof in participant observation', *American Sociological Review*, **23**, 652–60; Elizabeth Colson (1954) 'The intensive study of small sample communities', in R. F. Spencer (ed.), *Method and Perspective in Anthropology*. Minneapolis: University of Minnesota Press, pp. 43–59; Fred Eggan (1954) 'Social anthropology and the method of controlled comparison', *American Anthropologist*, **56**, 743–60; Harold E. Driver (1953) 'Statistics in anthropology', *American Anthropologist*, **55**, 42–59; Melville J. Herskovitz (1954) 'Some problems of method in ethnography', in R. F. Spencer (ed.), *op. cit.*, pp. 3–24; George Spindler and Walter Goldschmidt (1952) 'Experimental design in the study of culture change', *Southwestern Journal of Anthropology*, **8**, 68–83. And see the section 'Field methods and techniques', in *Human Organization*, esp. in its early years and its early editorials. Some quantification has been characteristic of 'field' monographs for a very long time; cf. Kroeber's *Zuni Kin and Clan* (1916). Such classics as *Middletown* and the *Yankee City* series are studded with tables.

4. A significant exception is a comment by M. Trow directed at Becker and Geer. Becker and Geer, comparing interviewing to participant observation, find participant observation the superior method and seem to imply that it is superior for all purposes. Trow insists that the issue is not correctly formulated, and that one might better ask: 'What kinds of problems are best studied through what kinds of methods; . . . how can the various methods at our disposal complement one another?' In their reply, Becker and Geer are more or less compelled to agree. See Becker and Geer (1957), 'Participant observation and interviewing: a comparison', *op. cit.;* Trow's 'Comment', *Human Organization,* **16,** 33–5; and Becker and Geer's (1958), 'Rejoinder', *Human Organization,* **17,** 39–40.

5. L. R. Dean (1958) 'Interaction, reported and observed: the case of one local union', *Human Organization,* **17,** 36–44.

6. *Ibid.,* p. 37n.

7. *Ibid.*

8. None of this applied to *repeated* events. If we are interested in comparing several repetitions of the same event, generalizing as to the course that is typical, care must be taken in sampling the events.

9. We may make a less stringent requirement of our notes, using what might be called 'incomplete' indicator spaces. Briefly, if we wish to classify all members of S with respect to the underlying property A, and behaviors $a, b, c, d . . .$, all indicate A, then it is sufficient for our purpose to have information on *at least one* of these indicators for each member of S. For some we might have only a, for some only b, etc. but we might have one among the indicators for all members, even though not the same one for all members; and thus be able to enumerate S adequately.

Data collection

Introduction

The grand strategy of research design gives away to the detailed tactics of data collection and analysis. It is at this point that the researcher puts his ideas to the test, and interaction with the subjects of his investigation begins. Such interaction may be at a premium to the ethnographer and a source of nothing but bias to the experimenter. On the other hand the ethnographer, though confident that he is getting valid insights into the meaning of a particular social action, may still be uncertain about the reliability of any one informant. The twin aims of improving the reliability and validity of data collected in any research mode have led to a great deal of work on the nature and size of all types of bias in data as a basis for finding the means either to reduce it or to accommodate it.

The first reading by Moser and Kalton, taken from their text book on survey methods, deals with the issue of prime concern to survey researchers, question design. They provide a useful review of the different types of question used in surveys and the types of bias likely to be associated with each. From their account some basic principles of question design become apparent but, in the last analysis, we have to see the wording of questions as almost as much of an art as a science. A specific example of the effects question format can have on responses in a survey is given by Belson and Duncan, which also provides an excellent example of methodological research. They set out to compare the effects in self-completion questionnaires of presenting questions requiring informants to recall such behaviours as newspaper reading, either in the 'open' or checklist form. They demonstrate striking differences in results from the two approaches, the latter providing much higher rates of recall. The conclusion is a simple one: in the absence of any additional means of validating informants' replies, researchers should avoid treating the two types of data as being equivalent, and when using interviewers should always provide precise instructions regarding prompting of answer categories.

Possible biases produced by question format and wording are only one issue in data collection, another relates to the means by which the data are elicited, i.e. biases associated with the use of interviewers. In the third Reading Boyd and Westfall provide a useful review of the research into this subject under the three headings, respondent selection (i.e. the problem of non-response) data collection biases, of which the Belson and Duncan research is an example, and research into interviewer selection, training and control. Their conclusion is a somewhat pessimistic one; despite the large number of studies carried out in the 1950s and 1960s on the types of bias that exist, little further research has been conducted to show the possible ways of reducing it. Consequently much of survey research continues to rely on hope, rather than hard evidence, that the distortions introduced into the data collected will not seriously damage the conclusions drawn.

The next reading raises a different kind of problem of particular importance in ethnographic field work, but also of some significance for interview surveys as well. This is the problem of bias introduced by the informant himself, who wittingly or unwittingly misleads researchers by failing to disclose true information about himself and his actions. Dean and Whyte use a useful analogy of the courtroom in considering the difficulties that exist here, and suggest four useful checks for the field worker to employ – implausibility of the account, unreliability of the informant, knowledge of the informant's mental set and comparison between informant's account and that of other informants. We see in this reading one of the important strengths of ethnographic research method, largely unavailable to the survey and experimental researcher: validation of informants' replies through the crosschecking that the field situation provides, together with an accumulating knowledge of informants' perceptions.

From the deception practised by informants we move to deception by the researcher often employed as in 'secret' observation to improve data quality. In Kelman's thought-provoking article the legitimacy of much experimental procedure which frequently sets out to mislead the subject is questioned, both from an ethical standpoint and because of the threats it presents to the validity of the results. The experimenter tries to disguise the true purposes of the experiment from the subject (frequently a student) and the subject, convinced of the experimenter's traditional duplicity, tries to behave in accordance with his speculations about what the experimenter is really trying to find out. Despite the pessimistic tone of much of the article, Kelman ends with a number of useful alternative strategies to deception for researchers.

Question wording

C. A. Moser and G. Kalton

The literature on the wording of questions is bewildering. Numerous papers have appeared showing the relative advantages of various specific questions, the danger of using a certain word or phrase, the sensitivity of answers to changes in wording and presentation; but it is exceedingly difficult to build out of them any general principles. We shall confine ourselves to some aspects of wording which are of general importance in social research surveys.

(a) *Questions that are insufficiently specific.* A common error is to ask a general question when an answer on a specific issue is wanted. If one is interested specifically in a canteen's meal prices and the quality of its service, the question 'Are you satisfied or dissatisfied with your canteen?' is unsatisfactory, since it fails to provide the respondent with the necessary frames of reference. As there are two distinct frames of reference of interest here, two questions are needed; perhaps: 'Are you satisfied or dissatisfied with the prices of meals in your canteen?' and 'Are you satisfied or dissatisfied with the service in your canteen?' Although these two questions now cover the topics required in a seemingly straightforward way, they still need to be pre-tested to check on their suitability for the particular situation. It may, for instance, be the case that the canteen serves special meals once a week at a higher cost and that, although generally satisfied with the canteen's prices, a respondent objects to the cost of the special meals; or he may be dissatisfied only with one particular aspect of the service. In cases like these he would have difficulty answering the questions. Such problems are brought to light by pre-testing and pilot work, the importance of which for question wording cannot be overrated.

In the above example the general question was faulted because it failed to specify the required frames of reference; but there are occasions when no required frame of reference is wanted, and then a

C. A. Moser and G. Kalton, 'Question wording', from *Survey Methods in Social Investigation*. London: Heinemann Educational Books, 1971, Ch. 13, pp. 318–31 and 340–41.

general question may be appropriate. However, even in this case, if the surveyor is to understand the answers properly he still needs to know the frames of reference chosen by the respondents; often this extra information can be discovered by asking the supplementary probe question 'Why?' after the general question.

Another way to make questions more specific is to frame them in terms of the respondent's personal experience rather than in general terms. An example comes from the penultimate chapter of Payne's (1951) book, in which he applied the principles outlined in his previous chapters to the question: 'Which do you prefer – dichotomous or open questions?' In this form the question has obvious defects; so it does in the other thirty-nine forms that Payne discusses, and dismisses, in turn. Only the forty-first attempt finds his favour: 'Which questions did you like best – those stating two answers to decide between, those stating more than two answers, or those leaving the answers for you to state?'

This is essentially a different question from the first: respondents are now asked to state a preference between question types in the context of immediate experience rather than to give a general opinion. All the answers will now refer to specific, well-defined issues.

(b) Simple language. In choosing the language for a questionnaire the population being studied should be kept in mind. The aim in question wording is to communicate with respondents as nearly as possible in their own language. A survey of the members of a particular profession, for instance, can usefully employ the profession's common technical terms; not only are such terms part of the informants' common language, but they also normally have a single precise meaning, unlike everyday terms, which particularly to professionals are often vague and ambiguous.

Technical terms and jargon are, however, obviously to be avoided in surveys of the general population. The hypothetical question quoted above included the word 'dichotomous', and such a word would not of course be used in practice. The use of the common word 'open' would equally have to be avoided, for its use in this technical sense is quite unfamiliar to the lay public. And obviously we would not ask a respondent whether his household is run on matriarchal lines, what he thinks about bilateral trading, amortization of the National Debt and fiscal policy.

Much less easy to recognize and reject are words which, though everyday usage to the university-trained survey expert, are far from common in ordinary conversation. Words like hypothetical, irrespective, aggravate, deprecate and hundreds more are in this category.

Question designers try to put themselves in the position of their typical, or rather their least educated, respondents, but they are not always the best judges of the simplicity and clarity of their own questions. The reactions of typical respondents – not only of their professional colleagues – should be sought (informally and in pre-tests) to ensure that the questions are comprehensible. Payne (1951) names a large number of words which analysis of American magazines has *shown* to be in common usage by writers; this does not necessarily mean that they are suitable for survey questions, but at least they are known to be much used. Gowers (1954) mentions many words which can often be replaced by simpler alternatives. The following are a few from his list:

Acquaint	Inform or tell
Assist	Help
Consider	Think
Initiate	Begin; start
Major	Important; chief; main; principal
Purchase	Buy
Require	Want; need
Reside	Live
State	Say
Sufficient	Enough
Terminate	End

With surveys of the general population, the first principles in wording are that questions should use the simplest words that will convey the exact meaning, and that the phrasing also should be as simple and informal as possible. It is more natural to ask: 'Do you think ... ?' than: 'Is it your opinion ... ?'; 'What is your attitude to ... ?' than: 'What is your attitude with regard to ... ?' In fact the more questions sound like ordinary conversation the smoother the interview will be. Of course, this should not be overdone. Bad grammar may be more common than good, but one would not advocate its deliberate use in survey questions. Nor are slang expressions advisable; as with technical jargon, not everyone uses the same expressions. It is not indeed enough to know that a word or phrase is commonly used; one must equally be sure that it is used in the same sense by all groups of respondents. Even words like 'dinner' and 'tea' have different meanings in different parts of the country. A simple case is the word 'book', which in some parts of the population is taken to include magazines. Hence the phrasing of the following question in a readership survey by Stuart (1952): 'During the past week roughly how many hours would you say you had spent reading *books* – I mean books not magazines or papers?'

Clarity can be still further ensured by remembering that a simple question is more readily understood than a long complex one. Payne (1951) has suggested that the more complex a question is, the more 'sensitive' to wording will it tend to be.

An instance of a question which is too complex for comfort occurred in the enquiry into Family Limitation conducted for the Royal Commission on Population and reported by Lewis-Faning (1949): 'Has it happened to you that over a long period of time, when you neither practised abstinence, nor used birth control, you did not conceive?

YES/NO.' This question is vague (what is 'a long period?'), too formal ('Has it happened to you . . . ?') and complex, because of its length and double negative.

There is a temptation to ask complex questions when the subject matter is inherently complicated, involving a variety of different facets. This, for example, would be the case in a housing survey in which one wanted to discover how many households comprised three-generation families, that is grandparents, parents and children. Once the term 'three-generation family' has been precisely defined (how about widowed grandparents, unmarried mothers, divorced or separated parents?), one might with ingenuity design a single question to obtain the information, but many respondents would certainly fail to understand it. Rather than rely on a single complex question, a series of simple questions should be asked, the number of such questions depending on the degree of simplicity required. Household composition is generally a complex subject and one for which several descriptive indices are required; the information is usually best obtained by using a 'household box' on the questionnaire in which the household members are listed together with their relevant characteristics, e.g. age, sex, marital status, working status and educational level. From these basic data the surveyor can determine for himself all the indices he requires for his analysis.

Another example of a complex subject is income, which is extremely difficult to determine accurately. Among the many aspects to be considered are: income before or after tax; income from subsidiary employment; state benefits; deduction for superannuation, etc.; expenses; and income from investments. The reader is referred to the Income Schedule of the Family Expenditure Survey to see the number of questions needed to measure income accurately (Kemsley, 1969).

Complex questions are typically long and complexity is certainly to be avoided; but this does not mean that the shortest questions are necessarily the best. There is some evidence indicating that the longer the interviewer speaks, the more the respondent will say in reply. An experiment on increasing the length of some questions in a health questionnaire is reported by Marquis (1969). The longer questions were formed from the short ones by adding superfluous remarks; in going through a list of symptoms, for example, the short version of one question was: 'Bad sore throats?' and the longer one was: 'Now a question about bad sore throats. We're looking for information about these. Have you had bad sore throats?' In checking on chronic conditions reported in answer to such questions with information obtained from the respondents' physicians, the replies to the longer versions were found to agree more closely with the physicians' reports, thus suggesting that they had greater validity.[1]

(c) Ambiguity.   Ambiguous questions are to be avoided at all costs. If an ambiguous word creeps in, different people will understand the question differently and will in effect be answering different questions.

The following example is taken from a university research survey: 'is your work made more difficult because you are expecting a baby?' The question was asked of all women in the survey, irrespective of whether they were expecting a baby or not. What, then, did a 'No' answer mean? Depending on the respondent, it might have meant 'No, I'm not expecting a baby' or 'No, my work is not made more difficult by the fact that I'm expecting a baby'.

Ambiguity also arises with double barrelled questions, such as the following question on public transport: 'Do you like travelling on trains and buses?' Respondents liking one and disliking the other would be in a dilemma in answering this question. Clearly it needs to be divided into two questions, each concerned with a single idea, in this case with a single mode of transport.

(d) Vague words.   Vague questions encourage vague answers. If people are asked whether they go to the cinema regularly or occasionally, the meaning of their answers will be vague. (This common choice of alternatives is strictly illogical; the word 'occasional' refers to frequency, the word 'regular' does not. However, this may be a case where logic can give way to common usage.) The meaning can easily be made more precise, as in the following question from the 1968 National Readership Survey: 'How often these days do you go to the cinema? Would it be nearer to – twice a week or more often; once a week; once a fortnight; once a month; three or four times a year; less often; or do you never go these days?'

Vague words and phrases like 'kind of', 'fairly', 'generally', 'often', 'many', 'much the same', 'on the whole' should be avoided, unless one is only seeking vague answers. If one asks 'What kind of house do you have?' without specifying a frame of reference, some people will answer that it is semi-detached, others that it is suburban, others that it is very pleasant, and so on.

A similar type of vagueness occurs in 'Why' questions. In answering the question: 'Why did you go to the cinema last night?' some respondents will say that they wanted to see that particular film, some that they did not want to stay at home, others that 'the wife suggested it', or that they hadn't been since last week. The word 'Why' in this question – as the phrase 'kind of' in the previous one – can mean so many different things that its use would produce a useless mixture of answers.[2] Lazarsfeld (1935) discusses the problems of the 'Why' question.

(e) Leading questions.   A leading question is one which, by its content, structure or wording, leads the respondent in the direction of a certain answer. The question form: 'You don't think . . . do you?' as obviously leads to a negative answer as the form: 'Should not something be done about . . . ?' leads to a positive one.

Equally, a question which suggests only some of the possible answers may lead in their direction. Take the question: 'Do you read any weekly newspapers, such as the *New Statesman* or *Punch*?' Respondents, especially if they are not sure of their correct or complete reply, may seek refuge in the answers named; either all or none of the alternatives should be stated.

There are numerous words that have been shown on occasion to have a 'leading' influence in survey questions (see Payne, 1951, and Cantril, 1944). The word 'involved' in a question like: 'Do you think that the Government should get involved in . . . ?' may have a sufficiently sinister ring to lead people in the negative direction. Similarly, the wording: 'Do you agree that the Government is right in staying out of . . . ?' invites a 'Yes' answer. The 'leading' nature of these examples is obvious, but more subtle leads can often creep unnoticed into survey questions.

In addition to 'leading words', there is the risk that the general context of a question, the content of those preceding it and the tone of the whole questionnaire or interview can lead the respondent in a given direction. An interesting argument related to this was provoked by an article by Kornhauser (1946–47) entitled 'Are polls fair to organised labour?'

An example nearer home was the 1954 ballot on attitudes to the (Football) Pool Betting Bill.[3] As a result of a debate in Parliament, the Pools Promoters' Association conducted a ballot among their clients. A statement by the Association arguing against the Bill was circulated with the football pool coupons in a certain week and each client was asked to vote for one of the following alternatives by placing a cross against it:

1. 'I agree with what you say in the statement which you sent me and I am against the Bill.'
2. 'In spite of what you say in the statement which you sent me I support the Bill.'

As many as 75 per cent of the votes were cast for (1), 7 per cent for (2) and 18 per cent of the clients did not vote. At the same time the Gallup Poll asked a sample of the population: 'At present football pool promoters do not have to publish accounts. A Bill is being introduced to make it compulsory for them to show each week where the money goes. Do you think that this is a good or bad thing?' Of the sample, 63 per cent said it was a good thing, 15 per cent that it was a bad thing, and 22 per cent expressed no opinion. Of those in the sample who filled in coupons, 66 per cent said it was a good thing.

That the two surveys produced such contradictory results must in part be attributed to the fact that the Pools Promoters' questions were printed on the weekly football coupon and were in no way secret or anonymous; for this reason alone, it is difficult to accept the results at face value. But this point apart, the differences between the two surveys in the context and wording of the questions could account for some of the differences in results. The alternatives proffered by the

Pools Promoters were preceded by a detailed and somewhat complicated statement on football pool finance, which stressed how the cost of complying with the Bill's requirements would affect the amount of money available for dividends. Finally, the phrase 'in spite of' in the second alternative suggests that this would be a rather irrational view. The Gallup question was set in a more neutral context, but here the phrase 'to show each week where the money goes' might be thought to carry a slight implication that this is a clear and obvious duty for a Pools Promoter.

There were, in this instance, several complicating features, and the difference in results cannot with certainty be attributed to the question forms. Yet the example is instructive in that it shows how differently the same issue can be presented. Some issues are so clear and well-understood that such differences would hardly affect results. But when an issue is complex and many-sided, when its implications are not widely or easily understood, then one must expect answers to be sensitive to the way it is presented.

(f) Presuming questions.   Questions should not, generally speaking, presume anything about the respondent. They should not imply that he necessarily possesses any knowledge or an opinion on the survey subject, or that he engages in the activity about which he is being asked. Questions like: 'How many cigarettes a day do you smoke?' or 'How did you vote in the last General Election?' are best asked only after a 'filter' question has revealed that the respondent does smoke cigarettes and did vote in the last election.

On occasion, however, one might deliberately depart from this procedure. Kinsey and others (1948) did not first ask respondents *whether* they had engaged in certain sexual practices, but went straight into questions about frequency and detail. Respondents were thus spared the embarrassment of admitting the experiences directly and were made to feel that these represented perfectly usual behaviour: thus they found themselves able to talk freely and give detailed answers. The case for such an approach is obvious, but one cannot ignore the possibility that it may discourage 'I never do' answers and thus cause an upward bias in the results.

(g) Hypothetical questions.   Questions of the 'Would you like to live in a flat?' type are of very limited value. Most people would like to try anything once, and an affirmative answer would have little value as a prediction of behaviour. It is another matter if one has first made sure that the person has experience of both flat and house dwelling. Equally, answers to the 'What would you do if . . . ?' kind of question, although perhaps a good reflection of wishful thinking or of what people feel to be right and proper, are unsafe pointers to future behaviour.

Yet prediction of future behaviour on the basis of survey questions plays, and must be expected to play, a central role in survey applications. Market researchers would like – and try – to predict how people will react to a proposed change in the price of a product, to an alteration to its quality or packaging; how many people are likely to buy cars, radios or television sets in a given period, and so on.[4] They may rely on straight questions (a Gallup Poll question in 1950 was: 'Supposing the price of (a certain newspaper) went up from 1d. to 1½d. would you change over to another paper where the price hadn't gone up?') but the answers are recognized to be imperfect guides to future behaviour. People are not good at predicting their behaviour in a hypothetical situation and the prediction has somehow to be taken out of their hands and made by the researcher himself – naturally on the basis of the information he has obtained.

Another kind of hypothetical question is 'Would you like a more frequent bus service?' or 'Would you like an increase in wages?' Such questions are unlikely to be of any value because the respondent is being asked if he would like something for nothing. It is hard to see how he could possibly say 'No'. If he did, it could only be because he has taken into account some hidden factors of his own, or because he has failed to understand the question.

(h) Personalized questions. It is often necessary to decide whether a question should be asked in a personalized form or not. This is well illustrated by the following questions which appeared, one after the other, in a schedule dealing with health matters (see David, 1952): 'Do you think it is a good idea to have everyone's chest regularly checked by X-ray?' and 'Have you ever had yours checked?' Some 96 per cent of the respondents answered 'Yes' to the first question, but only 54 per cent to the second. As the author suggested, the opinion given in answer to the first question 'is more a pious hope for some vague corporate decision than a considered aim involving personal action'.

(i) Embarrassing questions. Subjects which people do not like to discuss in public present a problem to the questionnaire designer. Respondents are often embarrassed to discuss private matters, to give low-prestige answers, and to admit to socially unacceptable behaviour and attitudes. If, for instance, questions on sexual behaviour, frequency of taking a bath, cheating in examinations or attitudes to Communism were asked in the usual way, many respondents would probably refuse to reply and others would distort their answers.[5] There are several ways of attempting to deal with this problem.

One method of reducing the threatening nature of a question is to express it in the third person; instead of asking the respondent for his views, he is asked about the views of others. An example from market research of an indirect question of this sort is given by Smith (1954): 'Some women who use this cleanser find a lot of faults with it. I wonder if you can guess what they are objecting to'.[6] The purpose of this wording was to make the housewives feel free to criticize the product. The aim of such questions is to obtain the respondent's own views, but he may of course answer the question asked, and give what he believes to be the views of others. For this reason it is often advisable to follow the indirect question by a direct one asking the respondent whether he holds the views he has described.

There are several other indirect methods which can be useful in dealing with embarrassing topics. The respondent can for instance be shown a drawing of two persons in a certain setting, with 'balloons' containing speech coming from their mouths, as in comic strips and cartoons. One person's balloon is left empty and the respondent is asked to put himself in the position of that person and to fill in the missing words. Another method is that of sentence completion; the respondent is given the start of a sentence and is asked to complete it, usually under time pressure to ensure spontaneity. Oppenheim (1966) describes the use of the following two examples of sentence completion in a study among psychiatric nurses in a mental hospital:

'I wish that doctors . . .'
'Patients who are incontinent . . .'

The different ways in which a group of student nurses and a group of nurses with twelve or more years of experience completed these sentences showed the difference of attitude and approach of the two groups. For a discussion of other projective techniques the reader is referred to the chapters on this subject in Oppenheim (1966) and Selltiz and others (1959).

Belson (1968) describes a study of a randomly derived sample of London teenage boys on the sensitive subject of stealing. A variety of procedures were employed in this study to make it easier for the boys to admit that they had stolen things. On arrival at the interviewing centre a boy chose a false name and, in order to preserve his anonymity, he was introduced under his false name to the interviewer, who knew him only by that name. After an extended initial phase, the interview proceeded to the card-sorting technique by which the information on stealing was to be obtained. The interviewer and the boy sat on either side of a table, with a screen in between so that they could not see each other. Through a slot in the screen the interviewer passed to the boy a card on which one type of stealing (e.g. 'I have stolen cigarettes') was recorded. The boy was asked to put the card in a box labelled 'Yes' if he had ever done what was recorded on it, and in a box labelled 'Never' if not. This was repeated for 44 kinds of theft. At the end of this sorting stage, the interviewer went through a procedure which tried to reduce the force of a boy's resistances, and to strengthen his feeling of willingness, to admitting thefts. Then the boy was asked to re-sort all the cards he had put in the 'Never' box. Finally he was asked for further details on each type of theft he had admitted. This detailed procedure elicited reports of many types of theft from many boys with, for example, 69 per cent of boys admitting 'I have stolen something from a shop' and 58 per cent 'I have stolen money' at least once in their lives.

Finally we should mention an ingenious recent development known as the randomized response technique. This was proposed by Warner (1965) and has been further developed by Abul-Ela and others (1967) and Greenberg and others (1969b). The basic idea of the technique is that the respondent chooses to answer one of two (or more, but we will restrict the discussion to two) statements, one of which is the sensitive statement under study. The choice is made by means of a random device provided by the surveyor, who therefore knows the probability of selection for each statement. The respondent employs the random device to choose one of the statements, and then answers 'Yes' or 'No' to the selected statement, without disclosing to the interviewer which statement he is answering. By this means the respondent maintains his privacy and this, it is hoped, leads him to give a truthful answer.

To see how the procedure works, let us look at the equation relating the proportion of respondents answering 'Yes' to whichever statement they have chosen, λ, to the proportion answering 'Yes' to the sensitive statement, π_2. The equation is

$$\lambda = P\pi_1 + (1 - P)\pi_2 \tag{12.1}$$

where P is the probability that the sensitive statement is chosen by the random device, and hence $(1 - P)$ is the probability that the other statement is chosen. The surveyor observes the value of λ for the sample and determines P by the way he forms the random device, but there still remain two unknowns (π_1 and π_2) in the equation so that it cannot be solved as it stands; another equation is needed. Warner obtained the additional equation by choosing two related statements of the form 'I have A' and 'I do not have A' where A is the sensitive factor; the additional equation is then $\pi_1 + \pi_2 = 1$, since one, and only one, of the statements must be true. Greenberg and others (1969b) extended the theory to unrelated questions, for which two situations can be distinguished: the first is where the proportion answering 'Yes' to the other statement, π_2, is known or can be estimated from external sources; the second is when π_2 needs to be estimated from the survey. The solution in the first case is straightforward, the known value of π_2 being substituted in (12.1); the second can be solved by dividing the survey into two samples, employing different random devices giving different values of P for the two samples.

Greenberg and others (1969a) describe an application of the randomized response technique in a survey of women aged 18–44 in North Carolina, designed to estimate abortion rates and the use of oral contraceptives. The two statements for the abortion enquiry were:

'1. I was pregnant at some time during the past 12 months and had an abortion which terminated the pregnancy.
2. I was born in the month of April.'

In this case the proportion answering 'Yes' to the second statement could be estimated from external data, from the distribution of months of births for live births in North Carolina between 1924 and 1950; the estimate so obtained was $\pi_2 = 0.0826$. The random device by which the respondent chose which question to answer was a box containing 35 red and 15 blue balls. She tipped the box to allow one of the balls to appear in a window; if a red ball appeared she answered the abortion question; if a blue ball, the other question. The probability of a respondent answering the abortion question was thus $P=35/50=0.7$, and of the other question $(1 -P)=15/50=0.0$. The values of π_2, P and $(1-P)$ can be substituted in equation (12.1) to give

$$\lambda=0.7\pi_1+(0.3\times0.0826)$$

from which, knowing λ from the sample, π_1 is easily calculated. In this case the value of π_1 was 0.0342, or 3.42 per cent of women having an abortion in the last year.

A price to be paid for the randomized response technique is that the sampling error of the estimate of π_1 is increased through the use of the random device. The approach is a sophisticated one and it may prove difficult to convince respondents that it is not a trick; Greenberg and others (1969a) report, however, that most of their respondents said they were satisfied that it was legitimate and did protect their privacy. There is also the danger that respondents may cheat by answering the inoffensive statement when they have selected the sensitive one. They may argue that, if the interviewer really cannot tell which statement they are responding to, their cheating cannot be detected; on the other hand, if the interviewer can tell, they do not want to respond to the sensitive statement. More research is needed on the applications of the technique before its usefulness can be firmly established.

(j) Questions on periodical behaviour.   An interesting choice arises in studying the frequency of periodical behaviour. The main choice of questions can be illustrated with reference to cinema-going:

(i) 'How often have you been to the cinema during the last fortnight (or any other period chosen)?'
(ii) 'How often do you go to the cinema on the average?'
(iii) 'When did you last go to the cinema?'

The first question covers a number of different possibilities corresponding to the period chosen, and answers will depend on the type of activity and on the extent to which one is willing to rely on the respondent's memory (see *(k)* below). In any case, the three question types might produce different results, and there is little evidence on which to choose between them. At first sight, (i) seems to be most specific, but many people's answers might simply be an estimate of their average cinema-going rather than the actual figure; i.e. if they normally go twice a fortnight, they may give this as an answer, although they went only once in the last fortnight. As a case in point, Belson

(1964) reports that an intensive interview follow-up enquiry of respondents to the National Readership Survey suggested that people frequently answered in terms of what publications they *usually* looked at, rather than what they had *actually* looked at, which was what was required. Of course the two answers will often be the same, and it is only when a difference arises that an answer in the wrong terms produces error.

Many survey questions involve this type of choice, e.g. questions on newspaper reading, radio listening, television watching and consumer purchases. It is a matter deserving further research.

(k) Questions involving memory. Most factual questions to some extent involve the respondent in recalling information. His degree of success in doing this accurately is thus a basic determinant of the quality of his response. With certain questions, such as 'Are you married, single or widowed?', there is no such problem, but with a large range of survey questions recalling information does present a problem, the severity of which depends on what is to be recalled. Two factors of primary importance in memory are the length of time since the event took place and the event's importance to the respondent; events the respondent considers insignificant are likely to be forgotten almost immediately and even the recollection of significant events decreases as time elapses. Moreover, for events not forgotten in their entirety, memory acts selectively, retaining some aspects and losing others, thus producing distorted images. For questions dealing with the past, serious attention must therefore be given to the respondents' abilities to recall the required information accurately, and to ways by which they can be helped to do so.

As an example of a memory problem, let us see how we might collect reasonably accurate information from housewives on when their present washing machines were purchased, a type of information often difficult to recollect. One approach would be to try to avoid reliance on memory by asking the housewives to consult records if they have them, perhaps a cheque-book stub for the date the payment cheque was made out, a hire-purchase agreement, a receipt or a guarantee certificate. Failing this, a housewife might be helped in placing the event by questions designed to provide a contextual framework, such as 'Was it before or after your holidays?', 'Was it before or after Christmas?', or 'Was it before or after the children returned to school?' In the stress of the interview situation, the respondent may be unable to recall the information without such assistance.

Another memory problem arises with questions asking respondents to provide a list, as would be the case for instance if they were asked which television programmes they had viewed yesterday, or which newspapers they had read or looked at in the preceding seven days; without help many respondents would be unable to give a complete list. A sensible way to aid recall in this case is to provide the respondent with a list of all television programmes transmitted yesterday (or a list of all newspapers), from which he can pick out the ones he had seen (or read, or looked at). In the National Readership Surveys, for example, respondents are asked about their readership of each publication from a complete list of every publication with which the surveys are concerned. With the interviewer they go through booklets containing the title blocks of the publications, and are asked about each one in turn. The use of the title blocks in these recall-aid booklets is an example of another useful device, visual aids, to assist recall.

With questions like the readership one, there are two types of memory error. The first is the 'recall loss', occurring when the respondent fails to report an activity in the recall period because he has forgotten about it, and this loss is likely to be more serious the longer the period. The second occurs when he reports an activity in the recall period when it actually took place outside that period; the tendency to report as occurring in the current period events which in fact occurred earlier has been termed the 'telescoping effect'. A greater telescoping effect for shorter recall periods has been suggested as part of the explanation for the commonly found effect of relatively greater reporting rates for short recall periods.

In panel studies, 'bounded' recalls can be used to deal with the telescoping effect. At the second and subsequent interviews, the respondent can be told of the activities he had reported previously and, if he reports an activity again, the interviewer can verify with him that he is not giving a duplicate report of the earlier activity. Neter and Waksberg (1965) used bounded and unbounded recalls to investigate the telescoping effect, in an experiment in which house-owners were interviewed about the number and size of jobs undertaken for alteration and repair of houses. They found that, for the number of jobs of 100 US dollars or more, with a one-month recall period the reporting at the unbounded recall was about 55 per cent higher than that at the bounded recall; with a three-month recall period, the unbounded recall rate was about 26 per cent higher. Both findings indicate substantial telescoping effects.

With serious memory errors having been demonstrated in many studies, it is natural to look for a procedure which does not rely heavily on an informant's ability to recall information. One obvious possibility is to persuade informants to keep diaries of the events of interest, as is done in the Family Expenditure and National Food Surveys. Diaries, however, have their own limitations. First, the amount of work asked of the respondent is much greater with the diary method, and this may make it difficult to gain the co-operation of the selected sample – the refusal rate may be high. Secondly, the diary method is likely to be more expensive, for interviewers will probably need to contact informants at least twice. One visit is needed to gain the informant's co-operation and to explain the recording procedure, and another is needed to collect the completed diaries. During the recording period other visits may be made to ensure that the instructions have been understood, to check that the data are being correctly recorded, and to maintain morale. The last visit serves not only for the collection of the diary, but also as an opportunity for the interviewer to edit the diary with the respondent; were it not for this editing, the last visit could perhaps be dispensed with, for the diaries could be returned by post.

Even with careful editing, however, the standard of informants' recording cannot be expected to reach that achieved by well-trained interviewers. Surveys of the general population contain people from a wide range of educational levels and with varying amounts of form-completing experience; it can be anticipated that some of them will fail to understand from one interview exactly what they are to do. In addition, others may lack the motivation to complete the diaries as accurately as is required. One particular way in which informants may deviate from instructions is by failing to record the events while they are fresh in their memories; the main strength of the diary approach is the avoidance of reliance on memory, but, if the informant does not keep the diary up-to-date, at least part of that strength is lost. Another source of error is that, although instructed not to change their habits as the result of their recording, some informants will do so; in consumer expenditure surveys, for instance, housewives keeping log-books of their purchases may become more aware of their shopping habits, and this may for example persuade them of the advantages of buying larger items of shopping in supermarkets. This is the panel conditioning effect.

These limitations of the diary method must be balanced against the memory errors involved in the recall method. The choice between the methods depends on the subject matter of the survey and, in particular, on the ability of respondents to recall accurately the necessary details of the information required. In situations where, even with assistance from the interviewer, informants are unable to recollect details accurately, the recall method is inappropriate and the diary method may be the only possible approach.

Notes

1. Another part of the experiment examined the effect of interviewer 'reinforcement', by which the interviewer encouraged the respondent reporting a chronic condition or symptom with a remark such as 'That's the kind of information we need'. Reinforcement was also found to reduce the mismatches with the physicians' reports; but, strangely, the combination of longer questions and reinforcement did not lower the mismatch rate, the effects of the two techniques apparently partially cancelling each other out.
2. There are exceptions to even this statement. The surveyor might want to see what type of reason each respondent produces when asked this question, what factors are uppermost in his mind.
3. Reported in *The Times,* 8 March 1954.
4. There is a sizeable literature on obtaining consumer buying intentions from surveys.

Three recent articles on this subject in the *Journal of the American Statistical Association* are those of Mueller (1963), Friend and Adams (1964) and Juster (1966).

5 Perhaps this risk can be overstated. On sexual behaviour, for example, the studies of Kinsey and others (1948, 1953), Schofield (1965a, 1965b), and others have been impressive.

6. Quoted by Selltiz and others (1959).

References

Abul-Ela, A.-L.A., Greenberg, B. G. and Horvitz, D. G. (1967) 'A multi-proportions randomized response model', *Journal of the American Statistical Association*, **62**, 990–1008.

Belson, W. A. (1964) 'Readership in Britain', *Business Review (Australia)*, **6**, 416–20.

Belson, W. A. (1968) 'The extent of stealing by London boys and some of its origins', *Advancement of Science*, **25**, 171–84.

Cantril, H. (ed.) (1944) *Gauging Public Opinion*, Princeton: Princeton University Press.

David, S. T. (1952) 'Public opinion concerning tuberculosis', *Tubercle (Journal of the British Tuberculosis Associations)*, **33**, 78–90.

Friend, I. and Adams, F. G. (1964) 'The predictive ability of consumer attitudes, stock prices, and non-attitudinal variables', *Journal of the American Statistical Association*, **59**, 987–1005.

Gowers, E. A. (1954), *The Complete Plain Words*. London: HMSO.

Greenberg, B. G., Abernathy, J. R. and Horvitz, D. G. (1969a) 'A method for estimating the incidence of abortion in an open population'. Paper read at the 37th Session of the International Statistical Institute, London.

Greenberg, B. G., Abul-Ela, A.-L. A., Simmons, W. R., and Horvitz, D. G. (1969b) 'The unrelated question randomized response model: theoretical framework', *Journal of the American Statistical Association*, **64**, 520–39.

Juster, F. T. (1966) 'Consumer buying intentions and purchase probability: an experiment in survey design', *Journal of the American Statistical Association*, **61**, 658–96.

Kemsley, W. F. F. (1969) *Family Expenditure Survey. Handbook on the sample, fieldwork and coding procedures*. London: HMSO.

Kinsey, A. C., Pomeroy, W. B. and Martin, C. E. (1948) *Sexual Behaviour in the Human Male*. Philadelphia: Saunders.

Kinsey, A. C., Pomeroy, W. B. and Martin C. E. (1953) *Sexual Behaviour in the Human Female*. Philadelphia: Saunders.

Kornhauser, A. (1946–7) 'Are public opinion polls fair to organized labour?' *Public Opinion Quarterly*, **10**, 484–500.

Lazarsfeld, P. F. (1935); 'The art of asking why', *National Marketing Review*, **1**, 26–38.

Lewis-Faning, E. (1949) 'Report on an enquiry into family limitation and its influence on human fertility during the past fifty years'. Royal Commission on Population. Papers Vol. 1. London: HMSO.

Marquis, K. H. (1969) 'An experimental study of the effects of reinforcement, question length, and reinterviews on reporting selected chronic conditions in household interviews'. Survey Research Center, Instititute for Social Research, University of Michigan.

Mueller, E. (1963) 'Ten years of consumer attitude surveys: their forecasting record', *Journal of the American Statistical Association*, **58**, 899–917.

Neter, J. and Waksberg, J. (1965). 'Response errors in collection of expenditures data by household interviews: an experimental study', US Department of Commerce, Bureau of Census, Technical Paper No. 11. Washington, D.C.: US Government Printing Office.

Oppenheim, A. N. (1966) *Questionnaire Design and Attitude Measurement*. London: Heinemann.

Payne, S. L. B. (1951) *The Art of Asking Questions* (Studies in Public Opinion No. 3). Princeton: Princeton University Press.

Schofield, M. (1965a) *The Sexual Behaviour of Young People*. London: Longmans (rev. edn 1968). Harmondsworth, Middlesex: Penguin Books.

Schofield, M. (1965b) *Sociological Aspects of Homosexuality: a comparative study of three types of homosexuals*. London: Longmans.

Selltiz, C., Jahoda, M., Deutsch, M. and Cook, S. W. (rev. edn 1959) *Research Methods in Social Relations*. New York: Holt, Rinehart and Winston; London: Methuen.

Smith, G. H, (1954) *Motivation Research in Advertising and Marketing*. New York: McGraw-Hill.

Stuart, A. (1952) 'Reading habits in three London boroughs', *Journal of Documentation*, **8**, 33–49.

Warner, S. L. (1965) 'Randomized response: a survey technique for eliminating evasive answer bias', *Journal of the American Statistical Association*, **60**, 63–9.

A comparison of the Check-List and the Open Response/ questioning systems

William Belson and Judith A. Duncan

Aims

The purpose of this enquiry was to compare the results of two different methods of getting information about certain of 'yesterday's' behaviour. One of the methods is the traditional check-list system followed by an 'All Others?' request; the other method is the open response system where it is up to the respondent to *volunteer* yesterday's behaviour. The behaviour with respect to which the comparison was made concerned (*a*) publications looked at 'yesterday' and (*b*) television programmes seen 'yesterday'.

Research practitioners are of course generally aware that the two methods *can* give different results under at least some conditions, but there is very little published and scientific documentation of the phenomenon. In this situation, it is understandable that there should be a certain amount of looseness – and in practice there is a lot of it – in the thinking that leads to the use of one method rather than the other. The present enquiry was undertaken as one of a series of checks on this particular issue. Clearly the topics involved in the present check (i.e. viewing and one form of reading) are limited in character and this must be kept in mind in considering the generality of such findings as emerge.

Methods

The two questionnaires
Two kinds of questionnaire were developed for the comparison, one of them on the check-list system and the other on the open response system. In the check-list questionnaire, various publications (daily, Sunday, weekly and monthly) were set out in the form of a list, with a space for endorsing them; there were sixteen in all. The list was not comprehensive and it was followed by a lined space requesting 'All Others'. In the open response questionnaire there was ample lined

From *Applied Statistics*, 1962, **11**, 120–32.

space for the entry of publications. In the two questionnaires the space for endorsement or writing was preceded by a question as nearly as possible the same for each. In the check-list questionnaire it read:

> *'Did you happen to look at any of the following newspapers or magazines or journals YESTERDAY. Put a tick (√) against each of them that you definitely looked at YESTERDAY. Put a cross (X) if you did NOT look at it YESTERDAY.'*

In the open response questionnaire the instruction read:

> *'Did you happen to look at any newspapers or magazines or journals YESTERDAY? This would include daily papers, Sunday papers, weeklies and any that come out monthly. Write down the name of each that you definitely looked at YESTERDAY.'*

Each questionnaire carried a second test of a similar kind, this one based on comparable questions about *television programmes* seen yesterday. Here again the check-list was followed by a request for 'All Others?'.

People taking part

The comparison was repeated four times with four separate groups of people. Each group was made up of between 200 and 300 people. For one of the groups, 'yesterday' was a Sunday and for each of the other three it was a week-day. The composition of each group was similar. The people in them were ordinary members of the public whose names had been drawn from electoral registers. Invitations had been sent to them to attend at a central 'hall' in order to watch and judge some new television programmes. Compared with the general population (Greater London) the four groups were somewhat under-represented in terms of the elderly, of the unskilled and of men. Full details of invitation system, percentage turn-out and of group composition are available.

Elicitation procedure

For each group, the procedure was the same. Every second person, in order of seating position in the hall, was given a check-list questionnaire. The rest were given an open response questionnaire. The purpose of this was to increase the likelihood that the two questionnaires would be completed by comparable sets of people. Beyond this, further matching took place (see details later). A test administrator controlled the completion of the questionnaires and special care was taken to see that the completion process was not stopped before respondents had written all they could. Personal details were available through another questionnaire completed in the course of the evening.

Matching the sub-groups

The device of alternating the two forms of questionnaire amongst the people taking part was meant to increase the likelihood that people completing the check-list questionnaire on the one hand and those completing the open response questionnaire on the other were closely comparable. In order to find out if this was in fact so, an analysis was made of the characteristics of each of the two sub-samples. This was in terms of age, sex, education, occupational level, whether or not respondent had children under 16, television ownership and cinema attendance. In one of the four groups taking part in the enquiry, a limited amount of matching was necessary. Otherwise there was a reasonable balance of characteristics between the sub-groups being compared (with respect to each of the four groups).

Terminology
Throughout the statement of results the term 'test items' will be used to refer to the items presented in the check-list questionnaire. They are 'test items' in the sense that the enquiry was intended to compare the yield on them *with* and *without* the use of the check-list.

Findings

Publications: the comparative yield on test items
Table 13.1 brings out differences in the degree to which test items (the publications named in the check-list) are endorsed when (*a*) they are offered in the form of a list and (*b*) when it is up to the respondent to think of them himself and write them down. The results for group 1 are presented separately from those of groups 2, 3 and 4 because the 'yesterday' about which group 1 was asked was a Sunday (so that Sunday papers had to be included), whilst the 'yesterday' for groups 2, 3 and 4 was in each case a week-day.

The device of offering test items in the form of a check-list produced an appreciably higher rate of claim that they were looked at 'yesterday'. This applied individually to each test item. In principle there is nothing surprising about this, but Table 13.1 serves to document the extent and the pervasiveness of the phenomenon in this situation. Table 13.3 compares the total number of items enumerated in the two systems. It gives this comparison for each of the four groups tested and, since the relative yield of the two systems is much the same in all of them, it serves to emphasize the stability of the check-list's tendency to give an appreciably higher yield.

A second feature of Table 13.1 is that there are sharp differences in the yield of check-list and open response systems in going from daily and Sunday papers on the one hand to weekly and monthly papers on the other. Thus, amongst the dailies, the average enumeration of test items when *no* check-list was used was 0.73 of the average enumeration when a check-list *was* used; for Sunday papers the ratio was 0.71 but for the weekly and monthly publications (combined) the ratio was only 0.25. In other words, in this particular enquiry the tendency of the

Table 13.1 Comparison of publications looked at 'yesterday' named using a Check-List system and using an Open Response system

Publications in the Check-List (test items)	Comparative percentage yield when 'yesterday' was a Sunday (Group 1)			Comparative percentage yield when 'yesterday' was a weekday (Groups 2, 3 & 4)		
	Check-List (CL)	Open Response (OR)	Recall* ratio (OR÷CL)	Check-List (CL)	Open Response (OR)	Recall* ratio (OR÷CL)
Number of cases:	99	110		448	415	
Daily						
Daily Mail				16	12	0.78
The Times				4	3	0.70
Daily Herald				9	5	0.54
Evening News				39	27	0.70
Daily Mirror				46	39	0.85
Star				21	12	0.56
Daily Telegraph				17	13	0.77
Average no. of these endorsed per person				1.52	1.12	0.73
Sunday						
News of the World	46	35	0.74			
Sunday Times	5	3	0.54			
Sunday Express	28	21	0.74			
Sunday Pictorial	42	34	0.79			
Sunday Dispatch	18	7	0.40			
People	26	23	0.87			
Empire News	6	1	0.15			
Average no. of these endorsed per person	1.72	1.23	0.71			
Weekly and Monthly						
Radio Times	41	5	0.13	38	7	0.17
John Bull	2	0	N.C.	5	1	0.31
Woman	12	8	0.67	20	10	0.47
Illustrated	2	0	N.C.	3	0	N.C.
Weekend	7	1	0.13	6	2	0.27
Readers Digest	5	2	0.36	7	3	0.39
Ideal Home	0	0	N.C.	3	†	0.17
Practical Householder	6	1	0.15	4	†	0.06
Practical Motorist	2	0	N.C.	4	0	N.C.
Average no. of these endorsed per person	0.78	0.17	0.22	0.90	0.23	0.25

*Based upon percentage figures before rounding.   N.C. No calculation.
†< 0.5 per cent.

check-list to give a higher yield of claims was much greater for weekly and monthly publications than it was for the daily and Sunday publications.

A third and seemingly allied indication of Table 13.1 is that even *within* any one sub-group of papers (e.g. dailies) there was an appreciable variation in the ratio of responses under the two systems: thus, the ratio for the *Daily Mirror* was 0.85 compared with the average of 0.73 for *all* the test-dailies, whilst ratios for the *Star* and the *Daily Herald* were 0.56 and 0.54 respectively.

A point of special interest in Table 13.1 is that the *Radio Times* appears to be subject to massive change (in the frequency with which it is said to be looked at) in going from the check-list to the open response system (38%: 7%). One can only suggest that in the absence of a check-list people take this publication for granted.

Publications: The comparative yields on the non-test items

In the questionnaire based on a check-list, that list was followed by a request for 'All Others'. Table 13.2 is concerned with the *effect* of the check-list upon the numerical yield of items (non-test items) under 'All Others'. It gives two separate examples of this effect. In *each* example, the figures on the *left*-hand side of the table give the relative yield of the check-list and the open response system *with respect to test items*; the figures on the *right*-hand side of the table give the same information with respect to '*All Other*' items (i.e. those enumerated through the 'All Others' space at the tail of the check-list).

It is clear enough from Table 13.2 that the effect of the check-list is to depress or dampen the enumeration of items under 'All Others'. Thus, for the test-dailies (second example, Table 13.2), the open response system produced only 0.73 of the volume of endorsements produced by the check-list system; but it gave 1.72 times as many with respect to the 'All Other' items. This reversed tendency applies also to the total yield of Sunday papers, of weeklies and of monthlies. Table 13.4, taken in conjunction with Table 13.1, makes it clear that the damping effect of the check-list on the mention of 'All Others' applies not only to the *total* yield of items but also to the frequency of mention of individual publications.

Television programmes: comparative yields

In the second part of the enquiry, the same sort of comparison was made with respect to television programmes. The results, which are given in Tables 13.5 to 13.8, were markedly similar to those applying to publications. First, and generally speaking, the 'test items' (programmes appearing in the check-list) got much higher mention when listed than when it was left to the respondent to volunteer them (Table 13.5). In fact, *all* the 'test items' got a higher yield when the check-list system was used (Table 13.6). Even so, there appear to be sharp differences, in going from one to another test item, in the degree to which the *listing* of them produces a higher yield. For example, the ratio of 'open' to 'check-list' is 0.21 for the play 'Mill on the Floss', 0.83 for 'I Love Lucy', 0.49 for the play 'Homecoming', 0.03 for Television

Table 13.2 Two examples of the apparent effect of the Check-List on the total number of papers volunteered (as seen) under 'All Others'

Main groups of publications	Test items appearing in Check-List			Items volunteered under 'All others'		
	Using Check-List (CL)	Using Open Response (OR)	Recall Ratio** (OR+CL)	Using Check-List (CL)	Using Open Response (OR)	Recall Ratio** (OR÷CL)
First example*						
('Yesterday' was a Sunday)						
All daily				†	0.06	N.C.
All Sunday	1.72	1.23	0.71	0.18	0.26	1.45
All weekly	0.65	0.15	0.22	0.21	0.20	0.94
All monthly	0.13	0.03	0.21	0.02	0.06	3.15
All specialist				0.05	0.13	2.52
All others				0.01	†	N.C.
ALL	2.50	1.41	0.56	0.47	0.71	1.59
Number of cases	*99*	*110*		*99*	*110*	
Second example‡						
('Yesterday' was a week-day)						
All daily	1.52	1.12	0.73	0.35	0.61	1.72
All Sunday				0.02	0.04	2.45
All weekly	0.72	0.19	0.27	0.19	0.35	1.82
All monthly	0.18	0.04	0.20	0.04	0.07	1.71
All specialist				0.09	0.12	1.36
All others				0.01	0.03	4.74
ALL	2.42	1.35	0.55	0.70	1.22	1.74
Number of cases	*448*	*415*		*448*	*415*	

*Using group 1 only.   ‡Using groups 2, 3, and 4 combined.
†None offered.   N.C. No calculation.   **Based on figures before rounding.

News (ITV) (See Table 13.6). Finally, the effect of the check-list was to depress, quite sharply, the number of items enumerated under 'All Others' (i.e. the non-test items – see Table 13.8). Moreover the depressing effect appears to apply to practically all the non-test items for which a sufficient number of cases was available for meaningful study. (See Tables 13.6 and 13.7).

The results for the fourth test group (see Table 13.6) raise a special issue. Five of the seven BBC programmes listed were trap items in the sense that they were not in fact broadcast the previous evening. These items got no mention in the open response questionnaire; they got a limited endorsement when offered in check-list form, suggesting a small inflating tendency when the check-list is used. (At the same time, however, it must be pointed out that the great majority of people were not misled by the trap in the check-list.)

Several additional features of Table 13.6 are worth comment. One is that the free recall of television news is markedly lower than check-list recall – more so than for any other programme (1%: 30% for ITV and 1%: 22% for BBC). Also very low in free recall (i.e. compared with check-list recall) come programmes with one or another of the following features: those where viewing seems likely to be incidental; where the programme is not established and has a hard-to-remember sort of name; where the programme has a shifting content or changing personnel and so lacks any familiar, stable character. At the other extreme are programmes which on other evidence rank as 'old favourites' or are definite in character or are well-established. Presumably there is nothing more subtle in these trends than a tendency to recall more readily the familiar programme or the programme vividly experienced (and *vice versa*) and to omit what is taken for granted (e.g. TV news). But the difference this can make is remarkable and, as we point out in the next section, it has important implications for research methods. It will be remembered that the same sort of thing as happened for TV news appeared to happen with the publication *Radio Times*.

Findings according to personal characteristics

The results were analysed by age, sex, occupational background and educational level. This was done to find out if the effects brought out for the sample as a whole were common or whether they tended to occur more in one section of the population than in another. This series of comparisons was made with respect to the relative yield of the two questionnaire systems.

Table 13.3 Publications looked at 'yesterday': percentage distribution of number of claims (for test items) yielded by the Check-List and Open Response systems

Number of publications (test items) endorsed or volunteered	Group 1		Group 2		Group 3		Group 4	
	Check-List	Open Response	Check-List	Open Response	Check-List	Open Response	Check-List	Open Response
None	8	20	5	22	11	19	9	22
1	16	34	24	40	20	44	20	34
2	32	34	26	27	22	25	27	30
3 or more	44	12	45	11	47	12	44	14
	100	100	100	100	100	100	100	100
Number of cases	99	110	148	140	142	135	158	140
Average* claims per person	2.50	1.41	2.39	1.31	2.51	1.30	2.42	1.42

*Based on percentages before rounding.

The findings relating to publications were somewhat different from those relating to TV programmes. For test items amongst *publications*, the relative yield of the two questionnaires (0.55 – see Table 13.2) was much the same in all the population sub-groups studied. For *television* test-items, however, the ratio of open response to check-list was slightly greater than the average for TV test items (0.41) in going to the younger people and to those with a higher level of education. Somewhat greater variability characterized the depressing effect of the check-list upon the responses to the 'All Other' question. This applies to publications and to programmes alike; the variation is related to sex and to education, but it follows no regular pattern.

These results must, however, be seen in perspective. They are but minor variations from a common pattern. The results from none of the

Table 13.4 Percentage frequency of mention of specific publications volunteered in the 'All Others' section of a Check-List compared with the frequency of their mention in Open Response

Papers not amongst test items (i.e. not listed in Check-List)	Check-List 'All Others' (CL)	Open Response (OR)	Recall Ratio* (OR÷CL)
Dailies			
('Yesterday' was a Weekday)			
News Chronicle	6	7	1.12
Daily Express	15	25	1.72
Daily Sketch	7	13	1.95
Evening Standard	5	10	1.94
All Others	3	5	1.99
Number of cases	*448*	*415*	
Sundays			
('Yesterday' was a Sunday)			
Sunday Graphic	12	9	0.75
Observer	5	11	2.16
Reynolds News	0	5	—
All Others	1	2	1.79
Number of cases	*99*	*110*	
Weekly and Monthly†			
TV Times	5	5	0.86
Woman's Illustrated	1	2	2.31
Woman's Own	4	6	1.39
Woman's Weekly	1	2	2.39
Woman's Realm	1	3	3.14
Woman's Day	2	2	0.76
She	1	1	1.38
All Others	9	20	2.15
Number of cases	*547*	*525*	

*Based on percentages before rounding.
†Combining one group where 'yesterday' was a Sunday, and three groups where 'yesterday' was a weekday.

sub-groups studied depart very much from the broad findings for the sample as a whole.

The meaningfulness of the difference in yield between the two systems
This series of comparisons was made by having the respondent write or tick his answers. Hence it is always feasible that the differences reported here arise out of special difficulties experienced by some people in writing down what they have in mind. That such a situation contributes to the differences cannot be ruled out. But the evidence is rather against it as a major explanatory factor.

(a) As far as publications are concerned, there are no meaningful differences in the amount of discrepancy between check-list and open response as we go from one educational sub-group to another. For television programmes, the association between discrepancy and educational level is of only a minor order.

(b) The depressing effect of the check-list upon what is given under 'All Others' cannot, when one considers the pattern of the evidence, be credited to poor writing ability.

(c) People completing the open response questionnaire had as much time for this (and more) than they wanted and in any case the phenomenon is apparent in the earlier part of the questionnaire as well as in the later part.

(d) The discrepancy is much more marked for some sorts of items than for others and this variation is consistent with well-established knowledge about patterns of forgetfulness (e.g. recalling the familiar but not the incidental or the new).

Table 13.5 TV programmes seen 'yesterday': percentage distribution of number of claims (for test items) yielded by the Check-List and Open Response systems

Number of programmes (test items)* endorsed or volunteered	Group 1		Group 2		Group 3		Group 4	
	Check-List	Open Response	Check-List	Open Response	Check-List	Open Response	Check-List	Open Response
None	42	59	44	52	39	63	43	68
1	17	23	9	14	12	12	13	18
2	15	13	11	20	7	16	14	10
3 or more	26	5	36	14	42	9	30	4
	100	100	100	100	100	100	100	100
Number of cases	99	110	148	140	142	135	158	140
Average per person†	1.37	0.63	1.97	1.05	2.08	0.71	1.60	0.49

*Test items are those appearing in the Check-List.
†Based on percentages before rounding.

These points do not close the matter, but they do serve to increase the likelihood that the phenomena described are considerably more than a mere by-product of semi-literacy.

The implications of the findings

The findings for publications and for television programmes are remarkably similar. To the extent that they may be generalized, they have some important implications at the methodological level.

1. The enquiry was not designed as a check on validity, but was simply comparative. But the sharp difference in the yields from the two systems makes it quite clear that at least one of them can be seriously in error when used to assess yesterday's behaviour in relation to publications and TV programmes. In the circumstances, validation of each of these methods becomes a pressing issue (i.e. the check-list and the open response systems).

2. Without waiting for any such validation, however, several things emerge from the mere comparison of the results from the two systems, the second of them being the more important. (a) On the evidence of this enquiry, the yields from the two systems cannot safely be combined or compared with respect to specific categories of behaviour (that is, either *within* a survey or from one survey to another): not only are their two yields at different levels, but their relative yields can vary sharply from one item to another. (b) If, in fact, we limit ourselves to the check-list system, we cannot regard as comparable the information from the check-list itself and from any 'All Others' question which may follow it: when the 'All Others' question is included, the yield from it is sharply depressed by the use of the check-list. (Apparently respondents feel that they have done enough after working through the check-list.)

3. These phenomena, as such, may well be recognized by many people. But that they should apply so sharply to activity as recent as yesterday's may not be as well known.

4. Points (2a) and (2b) – particularly (2b) – above appear to have special bearing on that intermediate type of survey in which *some* items are set in front of the respondent, and some are not. This may happen by intention of the research planner (e.g. to avoid creating boredom, to save time, etc.) or it may be the result of leaving to the interviewer the verbal implementation of a requirement to prompt *all* items. Under the pressures of interviewing, selective prompting all too easily occurs and develops. However, whatever lies behind a system of only *partial* prompting, it gives us a situation not unlike that described in (2b) (i.e. a check-list followed by a request for 'All Others'), or in (2a) (i.e. a combining of open and of check-list responses). In some surveys

involving this intermediate position, it may be that the interviewer is left to decide *where* to prompt and where *not* to. But just as in the case where the interviewer fails to obey instructions to prompt *all* items (and instead prompts only *some*), this situation raises the additional problem that we do not know if the final frequencies for different items rest equally upon the one or the other method (i.e. check-list; open response).

Finally, it seems desirable to put special emphasis upon our view that the findings reported here serve to open, rather than to close, an important issue. What we are left with is evidence of appreciable difference between two systems of getting information and, accordingly, a strong case for studying their respective validities.

Table 13.6 Percentage frequency of mention of specific TV programmes using a Check-List system and an Open Response System

Programmes tested in the Check-List (test items)	Check-List (CL)	Open Response (OR)	Recall Ratio* (OR÷CL)
Group 1			
Film Festival: Mill on the Floss	13	3	0.21
People ask Parliament	3	0	–
ITV I Love Lucy	13	11	0.83
Armchair Theatre: Homecoming	31	15	0.49
Oh 'Boy'	20	10	0.50
Brains Trust	3	1	0.33
Meeting Point	7	1	0.13
BBC What's my Line?	17	6	0.37
Saturday-night Theatre: Sulky Fire	13	9	0.69
Music for you	16	6	0.39
Average no. of these endorsed or			
*volunteered per person**	*1.37*	*0.63*	*0.46*
Number of cases	*99*	*110*	
Group 2			
Sheriff of Cochise	7	3	0.38
Right to Reply	4	1	0.18
Make up your Mind	18	8	0.45
ITV Murder Bag	24	11	0.47
Wagon Train	35	21	0.59
Free and Easy	20	9	0.47
The Randall Touch	8	6	0.71
Tonight	9	8	0.90
Starr and Company	5	4	0.76
Ask Me Another	7	4	0.53
BBC The Phil Silvers Show	5	4	0.91
Panorama	18	15	0.82
Picture Parade (Film Festival)	18	8	0.43
Relax with Michael Holliday	19	4	0.22

Table 13.6 (continued)

Programmes tested in the Check-List (test items)	Check-List (CL)	Open Response (OR)	Recall Ratio (OR÷CL)
*Average no. of these endorsed or volunteered per person**	*1.97*	*1.05*	*0.53*
Number of cases	*148*	*140*	

Group 3

Gliding	9	2	0.22
Tell the Truth	22	11	0.51
Emergency Ward 10	30	16	0.55
ITV Watch on the Ruhr	23	15	0.66
Summertime	12	1	0.06
The Verdict is Yours	23	4	0.20
Late Extra	8	1	0.09
Cricket (England v. N. Zealand)	8	1	0.10
BBC Documentary	12	1	0.06
BBC Emney's Interlude	11	1	0.07
Sid Caesar invites you	10	1	0.15
International Swimming	17	6	0.35
Television playwright	25	11	0.45
*Average no. of these endorsed or volunteered per person**	*2.08*	*0.71*	*0.34*
Number of cases	*142*	*135*	

Group 4

Melody Ranch	10	3	0.30
I've Got a Secret	12	7	0.56
Play of the week: A Month in the Country	18	15	0.82
ITV The Verdict is Yours	23	11	0.48
Roving Report	10	1	0.07
Armand and Michaela Denis: Wild Life in Kenya	21	9	0.44
Television News	30	1	0.03
Canadian TV Theatre: Three to Get Married†	1	0	–
BBC Documentary: No Tile to Life**†	3	0	–
BBC Emney's Interlude	10	1	0.13
Starr and Company†	1	0	–
Daphne Laureola – a play†	1	0	–
Lifeline: Silent Order†	0	0	–
Television News	22	1	0.04
Average no. of these endorsed or volunteered per person‡	*1.60*	*0.49*	*0.30*
Number of cases	*158*	*140*	

*Based on percentages before rounding.
**Instead a BBC documentary, 'A Port and Its People', was shown.
†Trap items, not in fact shown yesterday.   ‡Based on percentages before rounding.

Table 13.7 Percentage frequency of mention of specific programmes volunteered in the 'All Others' section of a Check-List compared with the frequency of their mention in Open Response

Group	Programmes not amongst test items (i.e. not appearing in Check-List)	Check-List 'All Others' (CL)	Open Response (OR)	Recall Ratio* (OR÷CL)
1	Highway Patrol (ITV)	4	16	4.05
	Sunday Night at the London Palladium (ITV)	11	28	2.54
	All Others	30	42	1.38
	Number of cases	*99*	*110*	
2	Cartoon: Popeye (ITV)	1	4	5.29
	News (ITV)	1	4	5.29
	News (BBC)	2	6	2.82
	Henry Hall Show (BBC)	0	4	–
	All Others	12	24	2.11
	Number of cases	*148*	*140*	
3	News, Sport, Weather (BBC)	1	5	3.68
	All Others	13	35	2.60
	Number of cases	*142*	*135*	
4	My Wife and I – Play (ITV)	0	8	–
	Perry Como Show (BBC)	4	11	2.86
	Documentary: On Safari (BBC)	4	6	1.29
	You are there (BBC)	2	5	2.68
	Sportsview (BBC)	6	5	0.95
	News – not specified (BBC/ITV)	0	17	–
	All Others	10	30	3.05
	Number of cases	*158*	*140*	

*Based on percentages before rounding.

Table 13.8 Four examples of the apparent effect of the Check-List on the total number of programmes volunteered (as seen) under 'All Others'

Origin of programme	Items appearing in Check-List (test items)			Items volunteered under 'All Others'		
	Check-List (CL)	Open Response (OR)	Recall Ratio† (OR÷CL)	Check-List (CL)	Open Response (OR)	Recall Ratio† (OR÷CL)
First Example (group 1)*						
BBC	0.57	0.24	0.42	0.08	0.11	1.35
ITV	0.31	0.39	0.48	0.21	0.52	2.44
Unidentified				0.16	0.24	1.46
All	1.38	0.63	0.46	0.45	0.87	1.90
Number of cases	99	110		99	110	
Second Example (group 2)*						
BBC	0.80	0.46	0.58	0.05	0.20	4.23
ITV	1.16	0.59	0.50	0.02	0.08	3.88
Unidentified				0.08	0.13	1.56
All	1.96	1.05	0.53	0.15	0.41	2.70
Number of cases	148	140		148	140	
Third Example (group 3)*						
BBC	0.82	0.21	0.25	0.04	0.11	2.63
ITV	1.26	0.50	0.40	0.01	0.04	2.63
Unidentified				0.09	0.25	2.75
All	2.08	0.71	0.34	0.14	0.40	2.70
Number of cases	142	135		142	135	
Fourth Example (group 4)*						
BBC	0.36	0.02	0.06	0.16	0.35	2.11
ITV	1.24	0.47	0.38	0.05	0.18	3.52
Unidentified				0.05	0.30	6.52
All	1.60	0.49	0.30	0.26	0.83	3.20
Number of cases	158	140		158	140	

*For group 1 'yesterday' was a Sunday; for groups 2, 3, and 4 it was a weekday.
†Based on figures before rounding.

Interviewer bias once more revisited

Harper W. Boyd Jr. and Ralph Westfall

In 1955, and again in 1964, we conducted an extensive search of the literature dealing with interviewer bias and summarized our findings in articles in the *Journal of Marketing* and in the *Journal of Marketing Research*.[5][6] The major conclusion of both investigations was that interviewers were a major source of error in marketing field studies and that little was known about the magnitude of such error under varying conditions or ways to minimize it. The 1964 study revealed progress in reducing errors in listing dwelling units, controlling the size and patterns of not-at-homes, and understanding the effects on data collection generated by race, caste, class, deference, age and sex. Despite such developments, it seemed clear in 1964 that little had been accomplished in dealing effectively with the overall problem.

What can we say about this subject today? Has any progress been made in reducing this major source of error? Has research been reported that provides us with important insights concerning the errors which occur because of the interface between respondents and interviewers under a variety of conditions? Do we know any more about how to select, train and control interviewers so as to reduce bias? This article describes the progress made since 1964 in providing answers to these and related questions.

Respondent selection

In nearly every study, no response is obtained from some part of the designated sample. Responses are not obtained from those who refuse to cooperate, who cannot be located and who are unsuitable for interview (such as the ill and the senile). It is usually assumed that those who do reply are representative of the entire group – including those not responding. That this is a dangerous assumption – particularly if the non-response group is large – has been demonstrated beyond doubt. Nevertheless, most studies have large non-response

From *Journal of Marketing Research*, 1970, **7**, 249–53.

groups even when special efforts are made to reduce them. Mayer's findings in 1964 in this regard are still the best available. He found that the completion rate on the first call in a national probability sample is about one-third and that this varies from 20 per cent in large metropolitan areas to 42 per cent in rural areas. If two call backs are attempted, then the percentage of completion rises to between 70 and 75 per cent.[21]

Deming's 1953 statement on the handling of this problem has not been improved upon [10]:

. . . the bias of nonresponse is probably so serious in many if not most surveys that the specification of the number of recalls, and the adjustment of the original size of the sample . . . to balance the bias of nonresponse against the variance . . . are an essential part of sample-design. . . .

There is no new information on the character of the not-at-home and refusal problems. We have known for quite some time that those who are 'not-at-home' (e.g. married women who work, and families with no children) differ from those who are at home, and that the rate of not-at-home calls varies by the time of the year, the day of the week, the time of the day and the city size.[17,22] Refusals tend to be concentrated among the high and low income groups.[22] It has been found that experienced interviewers have fewer 'not-at-homes' and refusals than do inexperienced interviewers.[12]

Dalenius suggested in 1961 that the probability of finding a person at home be assigned before an interviewing call is made. Given such information (obtained as a by-product of regular surveys) the interviewer could do a better job of scheduling her field work to reduce not-at-homes. Dalenius provided no data to indicate the success of this plan and no further comments on it have appeared in the literature, although it appears to have considerable merit. He also suggested that marketing research firms be paid on a graduated scale; for example, if the non-response rate were 15 per cent, 100 per cent of the originally quoted charge would be paid, versus 133 per cent if the non-response rate were less than 15 per cent. He reported that this plan generated relatively low non-response rates – 11 per cent in one survey and 7 per cent in another, but he gave no information as to its effect on cheating or on the reliability of the data obtained. There is no indication that this suggestion has been tried by others.[9]

Sudman *et al.* have reported that where the sampling plan calls for interviewing more than one household member and where the additional individuals are not at home, the use of self-administered questionnaires (presumably left by the interviewer after completing the interview with the member of the household who is at home) reduces the amount of interviewer time. This method, under certain conditions, provides a better indication of the respondent's real feelings than personal interviews, and the cost per completed interview is about half that of completing all interviews personally. Whether or not there is an interaction effect between the person already interviewed and the individual completing the self-administered questionnaire is not reported.[32]

Sudman also reported that telephoning for appointments before making a personal visit did *not* affect the cooperation rate (when compared to making no appointments by phone), but did reduce the interviewer time by 10 to 15 per cent. The use of the telephone to screen, locate and interview relatively unique populations (e.g. certain kinds of doctors) reduced interviewing costs substantially and, in some cases, also lowered the refusal rate.[30]

Twenty years ago Politz and Simmons described an imaginative method for treatment of non-response bias by weighting obtained responses to avoid the cost and time involved in callbacks.[23] No further tests of the validity or economy of the method have been published.

The best ways to handle the refusal bias continue to be improvement of interviewer selection, training and supervision, and increasing the respondent's motivation to cooperate. There appears to have been no follow-up on the work reported by Ferber and Hauck in 1964 which showed that an explanatory letter to respondents had a salutary effect on the response rate,[13] nor has any new method of respondent motivation been advanced.

Listing errors, which affect the sample selection process, continue to plague studies, particularly in lower income neighborhoods. Weiss reports new evidence in this regard:[32]

The central Harlem adult survey conducted in 1964, which encountered problems in the listing and location of housing units, as well as in contact, had an interview completion rate of only 63 per cent. Comparison with the 1960 census figures revealed that the uninterviewed were heavily concentrated in the lowest income category (under $3,000 a year).

Aside from this, there has been nothing new on 'listing and non-coverage' since 1958 when Kish and Hess reported that the use of city directories and the full enumeration of small rural segments reduced listing errors from about 10 per cent to 3 per cent.[18]

Collecting data

It has long been recognized that response errors are often quite sizeable – especially when attitudinal, open-end and dichotomous questions are used.[16,25] Recent research by Schyberger using planted respondents indicates that *even* where a relatively simple, straightforward, structured questionnaire, is used, interviewers 'showed a high number of deviations from instructed behavior'.[24] Belson found much the same. He concluded that 'on the evidence of tape recordings one-third of the interviewers deviated frequently and markedly from their instructions, sometimes failing to explain the key terms or to repeat them as required, sometimes leaving them out altogether, shortening questions, or failing to follow up certain ambiguous answers in the manner required'.[2] Dohrenwend has confirmed the large error problem encountered with open-end questions.[11]

It has typically been thought that in some interviewing situations, such as group interviews, a tape recorder was useful in reducing bias by recording both questions and answers verbatim. A recent study by Belson, however, raises doubt as to this conclusion; he found that tape recording increased the accuracy of reported responses from lower-class respondents, but reduced the accuracy of reported responses from middle- and upper-class respondents.[3]

Collins studied the recording behavior of the interviewers (i.e. the faithfulness with which a respondent's answer was recorded) from an idiosyncratic point of view. He hypothesized that interviewers, not respondents, are responsible for the data obtained for analysis because of their encoding characteristics. Thus, he reasoned that individual interviewers would have consistent preferences for the use of certain words, and therefore, would thus bias data collected, especially when open-end questions were used.

This hypothesis was tested across interviewers on a geographically dispersed sample of respondents, holding constant such variables as type of call (initial versus call-back), elapsed time interviewer had been working on the study, and sex of the respondent. Substantial idiosyncratic differences were found among interviewers; they did differ substantially with respect to the consistency of their word choices and in their tendency to be 'wordy'. Collins concluded that the open-end question should be used as sparingly as possible, that training sessions should include practice in recording, that interviewers should be made aware that their idiosyncrasies will contaminate the data and that verbatim transcriptions should be made wherever possible.[8]

Findings have been presented over the years as to the effect of the interviewer's class, race, age, sex, authority and deference on the interviewee and the necessity of minimizing these effects.[1,4,19] Little new work has been done; recent studies are mainly confined to elaboration of previous findings. Several writers have suggested that interviewers should 'play' the role which best suits the situation and, thus, be able to obtain rapport which will induce respondents to cooperate.[7,20] How such qualities can be identified in the selection process or incorporated into the interviewer training program is not known.

Weiss provides further insight into the ways in which low-income respondents perceive interviewers, stressing that one major difficulty is that words have different meanings for respondents than they do for interviewers. 'He [the lower class respondent] is used to talking about personal experiences only to listeners who share a great deal of experience and symbolism with him and with whom he can safely assume that words and gestures are assigned similar meanings. But in the interview, these assumptions break down.'[32]

Interviewer selection, training and control

The important areas of interviewer selection, training and control have recently been the subject of increased attention from at least a few researchers. Until very recently, the best study on the relation between interviewer characteristics and performance was done by Sheatsley in 1951. He found, in brief, that women were better interviewers than men, that married men were superior to single women, and that college majors in psychology, sociology and anthropology scored best in performance.[26]

In 1950, Guest and Nuckols reported that the Minnesota Clerical Test, the Guilford–Martin Test (which measures objectivity, agreeableness and cooperativeness), and the Auditory Number-Space Test (memory) had little predictive value for competency in interviewing.[14] Steinkamp has recently found that the more effective interviewers score significantly higher on dominance, reference evaluations regarding self-confidence and attention to detail, and have lower scores on needs associated with support required from others as measured by the Edwards Personal Preference Schedule.[27] The significance of these results is limited, however, by the study's small sample size. Hansen and Marks, working on the 1950 Census, found the Census Enumerator Selection Aid Test, which measured reading comprehension and ability to follow instructions, was effective in selecting interviewers who did well.[15] These results are still relevant.

Sudman has more recently reported on the results obtained from a study of interviewers employed by the National Opinion Center to determine what interviewer characteristics were most related to high quality and low cost performance. A special questionnaire was designed which sought data on those non-demographic personality characteristics and attitudes which were thought to be correlated with interviewing performance. The results obtained when this was used showed that:[30]

1. Performance increases and costs go down with increased education and intelligence.
2. High need achievement is the variable most strongly related to the quality of interviewing and to low interviewing costs.
3. High career orientation is related to high quality interviewing, but also to high costs.
4. Interviewers who have previously worked for other organizations are more likely to be high in cost.
5. Interviewers with heavy family commitments are less likely to be high cost interviewers and more likely to provide a better quality–cost ratio.
6. High efficiency in planning relates to lower interviewing costs.
7. Interviewers with high manipulative (Machiavellian) test scores are not high cost interviewers. Apparently, such interviewers tend to manipulate respondents and not the organization for which they work.

8. Such variables as happiness, financial need, membership in other organizations, religious behavior, perfectionism and size of place where reared do not appear to be related to quality of interviewing or to cost.

Sudman describes the system employed at NORC to evaluate the quality of the interviewer's work. Coders record the following types of interviewer error:

Type of error	Error weight
Answer missing	3
Irrelevant or circular answer	3
Lack of sufficient detail	2
'Don't know' – with no probe	2
Dangling probe	1
Multiple codes in error	1
Superfluous questions asked	1

The mean and the standard deviations of the error weight distribution for all studies are computed and a standard score for each interviewer is derived. Because studies vary in length as well as in complexity, standard scores are preferable to simple averages.[29]

Sudman also reports the results of an experiment designed to test the effectiveness of a formula pay method versus typical compensation by the hour. The formula method was derived from Bureau of the Census procedures which established standards for each part of the interviewer's job as determined from past experience. The formula method tested by Sudman held travel time constant between surveys, but varied the amount of time allotted for interviewing, editing, clerical operations and study, depending on the pretest results. All standards were worked out in minutes and used as a basis for payment. The advantages of the formula method versus the conventional method were reported to be that: (1) the amount of time required to check interviewer time sheets was reduced substantially; (2) each interviewer knew in advance how much she would earn on a given job; (3) total field costs were known in advance; and (4) efficient interviewers were rewarded and inefficient interviewers discouraged. Sudman says nothing about the effect of the formula method on quality with respect to his experiment, but reports that the Census Bureau found the introduction of similar standards reduced total interviewing costs by 10 per cent with no drop in quality.[28]

Collins suggests using idiosyncratic behavior as a way of detecting cheating. He argues that in fictitious interviews, one source of variance, the respondent, will be missing and that there will be too little variance around normative responses. He does not, however, go into detail about how to use this procedure.[8]

Summary and conclusions

Despite the obvious need for research in a large number of areas dealing with *interviewer bias,* the work reported in the literature since 1964 can only be described as sparse and of the type which adds little to existing knowledge. In fact, recent studies (Schyberger, Belson and Collins) show that the situation with regard to interviewer bias may be much worse than had previously been thought – even for relatively simple studies.

We find little that is new with respect to the not-at-home and refusal problem even though the earlier work by Dalenius, Politz and Simmons, and Ferber and Hauck offered the potential of considerable payouts if subjected to further research. Sudman's work with self-administered questionnaires, however, would seem to hold promise.

Belson raises important doubts about the use of a tape recorder, which has been thought by many to be the way of reducing errors. His research demonstrates that recorders may generate bias from upper-class respondents.

The last two or three decades have witnessed a stream of articles which document the potential biasing effect of the respondent's perception of the interviewer and vice versa – with respect to race, age, caste, class, sex and so on. Other than the insights provided by Weiss into the ways in which low-income respondents perceive interviewers, nothing new has been added in this area recently.

Relative to interviewer selection, training and control, Steinkamp has made a contribution by showing that the Edwards Personal Preference Schedule is helpful in selecting interviewers. Sudman has made a number of significant contributions on selection and control which should, over time, lead to an improvement in the quality–cost interviewing relationships.

The conclusion is unfortunately inescapable that, with but a few exceptions, notably the work by Sudman, the past several years have produced little that will improve field interviewing. It will do marketing little good to develop sophisticated and talented decision models if the input data contain large errors due to interviewer bias!

References

1. E. R. Athey, John E. Coleman, Audrey P. Reitmans and Jenny Long (Dec. 1960) 'Two experiments showing the effect of the interviewer's racial background in responses to questionnaires concerning racial issues'. *Journal of Applied Psychology,* **44,** 381–5.
2. William A. Belson (April 1965) 'Increasing the power of research to guide advertising decisions', *Journal of Marketing,* **29,** 35–42.
3. William A. Belson (Aug. 1967) 'Tape recording: its effects on accuracy of response in survey interview', *Journal of Marketing Research,* **4,** 253–60.
4. Mark Benney, David Reesman and Shirley A. Star (Sept. 1956) 'Age and sex in the interview', *The American Journal of Sociology,* **62,** 143–52.
5. Harper W. Boyd, Jr. and Ralph Westfall (April 1955) 'Interviewers as a source of errors in survey', *Journal of Marketing,* **19,** 311–24.

6. Harper W. Boyd, Jr. and Ralph Westfall (Feb. 1965) 'Interviewer bias revisited', *Journal of Marketing Research,* **2,** 58–63.

7. Charles F. Cannell and Floyd J. Fowler, Jr. (April 1964) 'A note on interviewer effect in self enumeration procedure', *American Sociological Review,* **29,** 270.

8. W. Andrew Collins, 'Idiosyncratic verbal behavior of interviewers', unpublished paper, Institute for Communication Research, Stanford University, 1968.

9. Tore Dalenius (Sept. 1961) 'Treatment of the non-response problem', *Journal of Advertising Research,* **1,** 3–5.

10. W. Edwards Deming (Dec. 1953) 'On a probability mechanism to attain an economic balance between the resultant error of response and the bias of non-response', *Journal of the American Statistical Association,* **48,** 743–72.

11. Barbara Snell Dohrenwend (Summer 1965) 'Some effects of open and closed questions on respondents' answers', *Human Organization,* **24,** 175–84.

12. J. Durbin and A. Stuart (1951) 'Differences in response rates of experienced interviewers', *Journal of the Royal Statistical Society,* **114,** Part II, 173.

13. Robert Ferber and Mathew Hauck (June 1964) 'A framework for dealing with response errors in consumer surveys', *Proceedings,* National Conference, American Marketing Association, 533–40.

14. Lester Guest and R. Nuckols (Fall 1950) 'A laboratory experiment in recording in public interviewing', *International Journal of Opinion and Attitude Research,* **4,** 346–52.

15. Robert H. Hansen and Eli S. Marks (Sept. 1958) 'Influence of the interviewer on the accuracy of survey results', *Journal of the American Statistical Association,* **53,** 635–55.

16. Herbert H. Hyman, William J. Cobb, Jacob J. Fildonan, Clyde W. Hart and Charles Herbert Stembler (1954) *Interviewing in Social Research.* Chicago: University of Chicago Press.

17. Clyde V. Kiser (Sept. 1964) 'Pitfalls in sampling for population study', *Journal of the American Statistical Association,* **59,** 251.

18. Leslie Kish and Irene Hess (June 1958) 'On non-coverage of sample dwellings', *Journal of the American Statistical Association,* **53,** 509–24.

19. Gerhard E. Lenski and John C. Leggett (March 1960) 'Caste, class and deference in the research interview', *The American Journal of Sociology,* **65,** 463–7.

20. Eleanor Maccoby and Nathan Maccoby (1954) 'The interview: a tool of social science', in Gardner Lindzey (ed.), *Handbook of Social Psychology,* **1,** Cambridge, Mass.: Addison-Wesley.

21. Charles S. Mayer (Nov. 1964) 'The interviewer and his environment', *Journal of Marketing Research,* **1,** 24–31.

22. Mildred B. Parten (1950) *Surveys, Polls and Samples,* N.Y.: Harper and Brothers.

23. Alfred Politz and W. Simmons (March 1949) 'An attempt to get the "not-at-homes" into the sample without callbacks', *Journal of the American Statistical Association,* **44,** 9–31.

24. Bo W:son Schyberger (Feb. 1967) 'A study of interviewer behavior', *Journal of Marketing Research,* **4,** 32.

25. Sam Shapiro and John C. Eberhardt (June 1947) 'Interviewer differences in an intensive interview situation', *International Journal of Opinion and Attitude Research,* **1,** 1–17.

26. Paul B. Sheatsley (Summer 1951) 'An analysis of interviewer characteristics and their relationship to performance, Part III', *International Journal of Opinion and Attitude Research,* **5,** 191–220.

27. Stanley W. Steinkamp (Dec. 1966) 'Some characteristics of effective interviewers', *Journal of Applied Psychology,* **50,** 487–92.

28. Seymour Sudman (Feb. 1966) 'New approaches to control of interviewing costs', *Journal of Marketing Research,* **3,** 56–61.

29. Seymour Sudman (Winter 1966) 'Quantifying interviewer quality', *Public Opinion Quarterly,* **30,** 664–7.

30. Seymour Sudman (1967) *Reducing the Cost of Surveys,* Chicago: Aldine Publishing Company.

31. Seymour Sudman, Andrew Greeley and Leonard Pinto (Aug. 1965) 'The effectiveness of self-administered questionnaires', *Journal of Marketing Research*, 2, 293–7.
32. Carol H. Weiss (Oct. 1966) 'Interviewing low-income respondents', *Welfare in Review*, 4, 3.

'How do you know if the informant is telling the truth ?'

John P. Dean and William Foote Whyte

Research workers who deal with interview data frequently are asked the question: 'How do you know if the informant is telling the truth?' If they are experienced research workers, they frequently push aside the question as one asked only by those unsophisticated in the ways of research. But the persistence with which it comes up suggests that we take it seriously and try to formulate it in respectable terms.

Those who ask the question seem bothered by the insight that people sometimes say things for public consumption that they would not say in private. And sometimes they behave in ways that seem to contradict or cast serious doubt on what they profess in open conversation. So the problem arises: Can you tell what a person *really* believes on the basis of a few questions put to him in an interview? Is this not a legitimate question?

The answer is, 'No' – not as stated. It assumes that there is invariably some basic underlying attitude or opinion that a person is firmly committed to, i.e. his *real* belief. And it implies that if we can just develop shrewd enough interviewing techniques, we can make him 'spill the beans' and reveal what this basic attitude really is.

To begin with, we must constantly bear in mind that the statements an informant makes to an interviewer can vary from purely *subjective* statements ('I feel terribly depressed after the accident') to almost completely *objective* statements ('The Buick swerved across the road into the other lane and hit the Ford head on'). Many statements, of course, fall somewhere in between: 'The driver of the Ford was driving badly because he had been drinking'; or 'It was the Ford driver's fault because he was drunk.'

In evaluating informants' statements we do try to distinguish the subjective and objective components. But no matter how objective an informant seems to be, the research point of view is: *The informant's statement represents merely the perception of the informant, filtered and modified by his cognitive and emotional reactions and reported through his personal verbal usages.* Thus we acknowledge initially that we are getting merely the informant's picture of the world as he sees it. And we are getting it only as he is willing to pass it on to us in *this particular interview situation*. Under other circumstances the moves he reveals to us may be much different.

Granted this, there are two questions that the research worker wants answered: (*a*) What light does the statement throw on the subjective sentiments of the informant? and (*b*) How much does the informant's report correspond in fact to 'objective reality'?

The informant's report of 'subjective data' (*a*)

The problem here is how to evaluate the informant's subjective report of what he feels or thinks about some subject under investigation. At the outset we must recognize that there are different kinds of subjective data that we may want the informant to report: (*a*) a *current emotional state* of the informant, such as anger, fear, anxiety or depression. Many informants have great difficulty in putting feelings of this sort into words. Even for the most articulate, the verbal expression of complex emotional states is a difficult thing; (*b*) *the informant's opinions*, that is, the cognitive formulation of his ideas on a subject; (*c*) *the informant's attitudes*, that is, his emotional reactions to the subjects under discussion; (*d*) *the informant's values*, that is, the organizing principles that underlie his opinions, attitudes and behavior; (*e*) *the informant's hypothetical reactions*, that is, his projection of what he would do, think or feel *if* certain circumstances prevailed; and (*f*) *the actual tendencies of the informant to behave or feel* when confronted with certain stimulus situations. Generally, of course, verbal reports are only part of the data on the basis of which we infer persons' tendencies to act. Equally important in making these inferences are past behavior and a variety of non-verbal cues that we may detect.

Each of these various kinds of subjective data are elicited by different kinds of questions put in different ways to the informant. The assumption that any one of these represents his 'real' feelings in the matter is, of course, unwarranted. For one thing, the informant may have conflicting opinions, values, attitudes or tendencies to act. In fact, the conflict among these various subjective data may be the most important subjective information we obtain. This approach puts in quite a different light the problem of using behavior as a way of validating attitudes. Take, for example, a young housewife who in an interview expresses herself as much in favor of careful budgeting of household finances. She indicates that she and her husband have carefully worked out how much they can afford to spend on various categories and have even gone so far as to make out envelopes in which they put the money allocated to these various purposes. Subsequent to the interview, however, she goes shopping with one of her close friends with whom she feels a good deal of social competition. Under the pressures of this situation she buys a dress which is out of line with her financial plan. It is not very meaningful to say that her behavior in buying the dress 'invalidates' her opinions in favor of budgeting. Nor does it make sense to ask what her 'real' attitudes toward budgeting are. But because we often expect reasonable behavior in the management of personal affairs and daily activities, we frequently try to get informants to give a rational and consistent picture of their sentiments and behavior when confronted with them in an interview situation. If this young housewife had been asked by the interviewer what she would do if she ran across an unusually attractive dress which was not within her budgetary planning, she might have said that she would refuse to buy it and would incorporate some budgeting plan for the future by which she might be able to purchase such a dress. But the sophisticated researcher does not expect informants to have consistent well-thought-out attitudes and values on the subjects he is inquiring about.

The difficulties in interpreting informants' reports of subjective data are seriously increased when the informant is reporting not his present feelings or attitudes but those he recollects from the past. This is because of the widespread tendency we all have to modify a recollection of past feelings in a selective way that fits them more comfortably into our current point of view.

But perhaps the major consideration that makes the evaluation of reports of subjective data difficult is the fact that they are so *highly situational*. If, for example, a Democrat is among some Republican friends whose opinions he values highly, he will hesitate to express sentiments that might antagonize or disconcert these friends. If, however, he is among his own intimate friends who think pretty much as he does, he will not hesitate to express a Democratic point of view and, if he is at a Democratic party meeting where there is considerable enthusiasm in support of party causes and he is swept up in this enthusiasm, he may express Democratic sentiments even more strongly than among his own friends. *The interview situation must be seen as just ONE of many situations in which an informant may reveal subjective data in different ways.*

The key question is this: *What factors can we expect to influence this informant's reporting of this situation under these interview circumstances?* The following factors are likely to be important:

1. Are there any ulterior *motives* which the informant has that might modify his reporting of the situation? While making a study among the foremen of a South American company, the researcher was approached one day by a foreman who expressed great interest in being interviewed. In the conversation which followed, he expressed himself with enthusiasm about every aspect of the company under discussion. When the interview closed, he said, 'I hope you will give me a good recommendation to the management.' His ulterior motives undoubtedly influenced his reporting.

2. Are there any *bars to spontaneity* which might inhibit free expression by the informant? For example, where an informant feels that the affairs of his organization or his own personal life should be put forward in a good light for public consumption, he will hesitate to bring up spontaneously the more negative aspects of the situation.
3. Does the informant have *desires to please* the interviewer so that his opinions will be well thought of? An interviewer known to be identified with better race relations might well find informants expressing opinions more favorable to minority groups than they would express among their own friends.
4. Are there any *idiosyncratic factors* that may cause the informant to express only one facet of his reactions to a subject? For example, in a follow-up interview, an informant was told that she had changed her attitude toward Jews. She then recalled that just before the initial interview a dealer had sent her a wrong couch and she implied that he had tried to cheat her. She recalled that he was Jewish and that she was still mad about this incident and reacted in terms of it to the question about Jews in the interview. A few days earlier or a few days later she would probably have expressed herself quite differently. Idiosyncratic factors such as mood, wording of the question, individual peculiarities in the connotations of specific words and extraneous factors such as the baby crying, the telephone ringing, etc. all may influence the way an informant articulates his reactions.

Unless they are taken into account, these various factors that influence the interview situation may cause serious problems and misinterpretation of the informant's statements. To minimize the problems of interpretation, the interview situation should be carefully structured and the interview itself should be carefully handled in the light of these influences. Outside influences should be avoided by arranging an appropriate time and place for interviewing that will eliminate them as much as possible.

The influence of ulterior motives can sometimes be quashed by pointing out that the researcher is in no position to influence the situation in any way. Bars to spontaneity can usually be reduced by assurances to the informant that his remarks are confidential and will be reported to no one else. The confidence that develops in a relationship over a period of time is perhaps the best guarantee of spontaneity, and informants who are important should be developed *over time* with care and understanding. Naturally the interviewer should not express or, indicate in any way, his disapproval of statements made by the informant or indicate any of his own values that might intrude in the situation. Idiosyncratic factors of connotation and meaning are difficult to account for, but it is certainly a good precaution to ask questions in many different ways so that the complex configuration that a person's sentiments represents can be more accurately understood.

While we never assume a one-to-one relationship between sentiments and overt behavior, the researcher is constantly relating the
sentiments expressed to the behavior he observes – or would expect to
observe – in the situation under discussion.

In one field situation, the informant was a restaurant supervisor. It
was already known that the restaurant owner was a graduate dietician
who placed a great deal of stress upon maintaining high professional
standards. Midway in the course of the interview, the supervisor
remarked in a casual manner – perhaps too casual – that she herself was
the only supervisor in the restaurant who was not a college graduate.
The supervisor did not elaborate on the point, *nor* did the interviewer
probe at this time. In a lull in the conversation a few minutes later, the
interviewer, using the opportunity to return to a topic previously
mentioned, said: 'I was interested in something you said earlier: that
you are the only supervisor here who is not a college graduate – '
Before another word was uttered, the supervisor burst into tears.
Clearly, the effect attached to the statement made earlier was repressed or concealed and became evident only as revealed in subsequent behavior when she cried.

In some cases the informant may be trying to tell himself – as well as
the interviewer – that he does not have a certain sentiment, and may
even have convinced himself. In the case of Joe Sloan, a gasoline plant
operator (see the article on 'Engineers and workers', *Human Organization,* **14**, No. 4, Winter, 1956) the interview took place shortly after
Sloan, a highly ambitious worker, had been demoted to a lower classification. He followed up this rebuff by talking with the plant manager
and personnel manager, and he reported calmly that they had not been
able to give him any encouragement about his future with the company. Since, even before this setback, Sloan had expressed strong
negative sentiments toward management – with apparent relish – one
might have expected him to be even more explosive, now that he had
this new provocation. The researcher was surprised and puzzled when
he said, 'I'm nonchalant now. Those things don't bother me anymore.'
Neither his gestures nor facial expression revealed any emotion.

A week later, Sloan suddenly walked off the job in response to a
condition that had recurred often in the past, with only mild expressions of dissatisfaction from Sloan and the other workers. Reflecting
on the incident later, we can see that we should have recognized
Sloan's 'nonchalant' statement as a danger signal. In the light of the
recent events that must have intensified his negative sentiments
toward management, he must have been making an effort to repress
these sentiments. Probably, being unable or unwilling to 'blow his top'
as before, he no longer had a safety valve and might have been
expected to take some rash and erratic action.

These cases suggest the importance of regarding any marked discrepancies between expressed sentiments and observed (or expected)
behavior as an open invitation to the researcher to focus his interviewing *and* observation in this problem area.

The informant's reporting of 'objective' data (*b*)

Frequently the research worker wants to determine from an interview what actually happened on some occasion pertinent to the research. Can we take what the informant reports at face value? In many instances the answer, of course, is 'No'.

Suppose an informant reports that a number of people are plotting against him. He may be revealing merely his own paranoid tendencies, in which case his statement must be seen as casting light primarily on his distorted perception of the world. But even though plots of this kind are rare in the world, it may just happen that, in this instance, people actually *are* trying to undermine the informant. It is therefore important for the researcher to know in what respects an informant's statement must be taken as a reflection of his own personality and perception and in which respects as a reasonably accurate record of actual events.

How much help any given report of an informant will be in reconstructive 'object reality' depends on how much distortion has been introduced into the report and how much we can correct for this distortion. The major sources of distortion in firsthand reports of informants are these:

1. The respondent just did not observe the details of what happened or cannot recollect what he *did* observe, and reports instead what he supposed happened. Data below the informant's observation or memory threshold cannot of course be reported.
2. The respondent reports as accurately as he can, but because his mental set has selectively perceived the situation, the data reported give a distorted impression of what occurred.
3. The informant unconsciously modifies his report of a situation because of his emotional needs to shape the situation to fit his own perspective. Awareness of the 'true' facts might be so uncomfortable that the informant wants to protect himself against this awareness.
4. The informant quite consciously modifies the facts as he perceives them in order to convey a distorted impression of what occurred.

Naturally, trained research workers are alert to detect distortion wherever it occurs. How can they do this? First of all, there is an important negative check: *implausibility*. If an account strongly strains our credulity and just does not seem at all plausible, then we are justified in suspecting distortion. For example, an informant, who lived a few miles away from the campus of a coeducational college, reported that one of the college girls had been raped in a classroom during hours of instruction by some of the men college students. She was quite vague as to the precise circumstances – for example, as to what the professor was doing at the time. (Did he, perhaps, rap the blackboard and say,

'May I have your attention, please?') This account was obviously lacking in plausibility. Things just do not happen that way. The account may, however, throw light on the informant's personal world. Through other reports we learned that a college girl had indeed been raped, but the offense had taken place at night, the girl was not on the college campus and the men were not college students. The woman who told this story was a devout member of a fundamentalist sect that was highly suspicious of the 'Godless university'. In this context, the story makes sense as a distortion the informant might unconsciously introduce in order to make the story conform to her perception of the university. The test of implausibility must be used with caution, of course, because sometimes the implausible *does* happen.

A second aid in detecting distortion is any knowledge we have of the *unreliability of the informant as* an accurate reporter. In the courtroom, the story of a witness is seriously undermined by any evidence that he has been inaccurate in reporting some important point. In first interviews we will generally have little evidence for judging an informant's reliability unless he happens to be reporting on some situation about which we have prior knowledge. But in repeated interviews, after what the informant has told us has been checked or corroborated by other reports, we can form some idea of how much we can rely on his account. Thus we learn to distinguish reliable from unreliable informants, although we must always be careful not to assume that, just because an informant has proven reliable in the past, we can continue to believe his accounts without further checking.

A third aid in detecting distortion is our *knowledge of an informant's mental set* and an understanding of how it might influence his perception and interpretation of events. Thus we would be on guard for distortion in a labor union leader's report of how management welched upon a promise it made in a closed meeting.

But the major way in which we detect distortion, and correct for it, is by *comparing an informant's account with the accounts given by other informants.* And here the situation resembles the courtroom setting, since we must weigh and balance the testimony of different witnesses, evaluate the validity of eyewitness data, compare the reliability of witnesses, take circumstantial evidence into account, appraise the motives of key persons and consider the admissibility of hearsay information. We may have little opportunity in field research for anything that resembles direct cross-examination, but we can certainly *cross-check* the accounts given us by different informants for discrepancies and try to clear these up by asking for further clarification.

Since we generally assure informants that what they say is confidential, we are not free to tell one informant what the other has told us. Even if the informant says, 'I don't care who knows it; tell anybody you want to', we find it wise to treat the interview as confidential. A researcher who goes around telling some informants what other informants have told him is likely to stir up anxiety and suspicion. Of course the researcher may be able to tell an informant what he has heard without revealing the source of his information. This may be perfectly appropriate where a story has wide currency so that an informant cannot infer the source of the information. But if an event is not widely known, the mere mention of it may reveal to one informant what another informant has said about the situation. How can the data be cross-checked in these circumstances?

An example from a field study of work teams at the Corning Glass Works illustrates this problem. Jack Carter, a gaffer (top man of the glass-making team), described a serious argument that had arisen between Al Lucido, the gaffer, and his servitor (his number 2 man) on another work team. Lucido and his servitor had been known as close friends. Since the relationship of the interpersonal relations on the team to morale and productivity were central to the study, it was important (1) to check this situation for distortion and (2) to develop the details.

First, the account Carter gave of the situation did not in any way seem implausible. Second, on the credibility of the witness, our experience indicated that Jack Carter was a reliable informant. Third, we had no reason to believe that Carter's mental set toward this other work team was so emotionally involved or biased as to give him an especially jaundiced view of the situation. Furthermore, some of the events he described he had actually witnessed and others he had heard about directly from men on the particular work team. Nevertheless, to check the story and to fill in the details regarding the development of the conflict, we wished to get an account from one of the men directly involved. So an appointment was scheduled with Lucido one day after work. Because it might be disturbing to Lucido and to the others if the research worker came right out and said, 'I hear you recently had an argument with Sammy, would you tell me about it?' the researcher sought to reach this point in the interview without revealing this purpose. Lucido was encouraged to talk about the nature of his work and about the problems that arose on his job, with the focus gradually moving toward problems of cooperation within the work team. After Lucido had discussed at length the importance of maintaining harmonious relationships within the work team, the research worker said, 'Yes, that certainly is important. You know I've been impressed with the harmonious relationships you have on your team. Since you and the servitor have to work closely together, I guess it's important that you and Sammy are such close friends. Still, I suppose that even the closest of friends can have disagreements. Has there ever been a time when there was any friction between you and Sammy?' Lucido remarked that indeed this had happened just recently. When the researcher expressed interest, he went on to give a detailed account of how the friction arose and how the problem between the two men had finally worked out. It was then possible to compare Lucido's account with that of Carter and to amplify the data on a number of points that Carter had not covered. The informant in this case probably never realized that the research worker had any prior knowledge of the argument he had with his servitor or that this matter was of any greater interest to the researcher than other things discussed in the interview. The main point is this: by the thoughtful use of the information revealed in the account of one informant, the researcher can guide other interviews toward data which will reveal any distortions incorporated in the initial account and usually will provide details which give a more complete understanding of what actually happened.

The problems of distortion are heavily compounded if the researcher is dealing with informants who are giving him secondhand reports. Here, the researcher has to deal, not only with the original distortion that the witness incorporated in the story he told to the informant, but also with any subsequent distortions that the informant introduced in passing it along to the researcher. Of course, an informant who has a shrewd understanding of the situations about which he is reporting secondhand may be able to take into account any distortions or bias in the reports he receives from those who talked to him. It *may* even be that the informant's lines of communications are more direct and intimate than the research worker can establish. In this case, the picture the informant gives may have validity beyond the picture the researcher might get directly from the eyewitnesses themselves.

This kind of situation is illustrated by the case of Doc, a street corner gang leader discussed in *Street Corner Society*. Doc was an extraordinarily valuable informant. Whenever the information he gave could be checked, his account seemed highly reliable. But he had an additional strength: he was also well-informed regarding what was happening in his own group and in other groups and organizations in his district. This was due to the position he occupied in the social structure of the community. Since he was the leader of his own group, the leaders of other groups naturally came to him first to tell him what they were doing and to consult him as to what they should do. His informal leadership position within his own group made him a connecting link between that group and other groups and organizations. Hence developments in the 'foreign relations' of the group were known by him before they reached the followers, and usually in more direct and accurate form.

Because of the wide variation in quality of informants, the researcher is always on the lookout for informants such as Doc who can give a reasonably accurate and perceptive account of events the research is interested in. These special informants are frequently found at key positions in the communication structure, often as formal or informal leaders in the organization. They have ability to weigh and balance the evidence themselves and correct for the distortions that may be incorporated from their sources of information. But it is important that they have no needs to withhold or distort the information they report to the researcher. Even so, wherever the researcher has to rest on secondhand reports he must be particularly cautious in his interpretation.

Conclusion

In conclusion, we should emphasize that the interviewer is not looking for *the true attitude or sentiment*. He should recognize that informants can and do hold conflicting sentiments at one time and they hold varying sentiments according to the situations in which they find themselves. As Roethlisberger and Dickson (*Management and the Worker*) long ago pointed out, the interview itself is a social situation, so the researcher must also consider how this situation may influence the expression of sentiments and the reporting of events.

With such considerations in mind, the researcher will not ask himself, 'How do I know if the informant is telling the truth?' Instead, the researcher will ask, 'What do the informant's statements reveal about his feelings and perceptions and what inferences can be made from them about the actual environment or events he has experienced?'

Human use of human subjects: the problem of deception in social psychological experiments

Herbert C. Kelman

In 1954, in the pages of the *American Psychologist,* Edgar Vinacke raised a series of questions about experiments – particularly in the area of small groups – in which 'the psychologist conceals the true purpose and conditions of the experiment, or positively misinforms the subjects, or exposes them to painful, embarrassing, or worse, experiences, without the subjects' knowledge of what is going on'. [p. 155] He summed up his concerns by asking, 'What . . . is the proper balance between the interests of science and the thoughtful treatment of the persons who, innocently, supply the data?'. [p. 155] Little effort has been made in the intervening years to seek answers to the questions he raised. During these same years, however, the problem of deception in social psychological experiments has taken on increasingly serious proportions.[1]

The problem is actually broader, extending beyond the walls of the laboratory. It arises, for example, in various field studies in which investigators enroll as members of a group that has special interest for them so that they can observe its operations from the inside. The pervasiveness of the problem becomes even more apparent when we consider that deception is built into most of our measurement devices, since it is important to keep the respondent unaware of the personality of attitude dimension that we wish to explore. For the present purposes, however, primarily the problem of deception in the context of the social psychological experiment will be discussed.

The use of deception has become more and more extensive, and it is now a commonplace and almost standard feature of social psychological experiments. Deception has been turned into a game, often played with great skill and virtuosity. A considerable amount of the creativity and ingenuity of social psychologists is invested in the development of increasingly elaborate deception situations. Within a single experiment, deception may be built upon deception in a delicately complex structure. The literature now contains a fair number of studies in which second- or even third-order deception was employed.

From *Psychological Bulletin,* 1967, **67,** 1–11.

One well-known experiment (Festinger & Carlsmith, 1959), for example, involved a whole progression of deceptions. After the subjects had gone through an experimental task, the investigator made it clear – through word and gesture – that the experiment was over and that he would now 'like to explain what this has been all about so you'll have some idea of why you were doing this'. [p. 205] This explanation was false, however, and was designed to serve as a basis for the true experimental manipulation. The manipulation itself involved asking subjects to serve as the experimenter's accomplices. The task of the 'accomplice' was to tell the next 'subject' that the experiment in which he had just participated (which was in fact a rather boring experience) had been interesting and enjoyable. He was also asked to be on call for unspecified future occasions on which his services as accomplice might be needed because 'the regular fellow couldn't make it and we had a subject scheduled'. [p. 205] These newly recruited 'accomplices', of course, were the true subjects, while the 'subjects' were the experimenter's true accomplices. For their presumed services as 'accomplices', the true subjects were paid in advance – half of them receiving $1, and half $20. When they completed their service, however, the investigators added injury to insult by asking them to return their hard-earned cash. Thus, in this one study, in addition to receiving the usual misinformation about the purpose of the experiment, the subject was given feedback that was really an experimental manipulation, was asked to be an accomplice who was really a subject and was given a $20 bill that was really a will-o'-the-wisp. One wonders how much further in this direction we can go. Where will it all end?

It is easy to view this problem with alarm, but it is much more difficult to formulate an unambiguous position on the problem. As a working experimental social psychologist, I cannot conceive the issue in absolutist terms. I am too well aware of the fact that there are good reasons for using deception in many experiments. There are many significant problems that probably cannot be investigated without the use of deception, at least not at the present level of development of our experimental methodology. Thus, we are always confronted with a conflict of values. If we regard the acquisition of scientific knowledge about human behavior as a positive value, and if an experiment using deception constitutes a significant contribution to such knowledge which could not very well be achieved by other means, then we cannot unequivocally rule out this experiment. The question for us is not simply whether it does or does not use deception, but whether the amount and type of deception are justified by the significance of the study and the unavailability of alternative (that is, deception-free) procedures.

I have expressed special concern about second-order deceptions, for example, the procedure of letting a person believe that he is acting as experimenter or as the experimenter's accomplice when he is in fact serving as the subject. Such a procedure undermines the relationship between experimenter and subject even further than simple misinformation about the purposes of the experiment; deception does not merely take place *within* the experiment, but encompasses the whole definition of the relationship between the parties involved. Deception that takes place while the person is within the role of subject for which he has contracted can, to some degree, be isolated, but deception about the very nature of the contract itself is more likely to suffuse the experimenter–subject relationship as a whole and to remove the possibility of mutual trust. Thus, I would be inclined to take a more absolutist stand with regard to such second-order deceptions – but even here the issue turns out to be more complicated. I am stopped short when I think, for example, of the ingenious studies on experimenter bias by Rosenthal and his associates (e.g. Rosenthal & Fode, 1963; Rosenthal, Persinger, Vikan-Kline, & Fode, 1963; Rosenthal, Persinger, Vikan-Kline, & Mulry, 1963). These experiments employed second-order deception in that subjects were led to believe that they were the experimenters. Since these were experiments about experiments, however, it is very hard to conceive of any alternative procedures that the investigators might have used. There is no question in my mind that these are significant studies; they provide fundamental inputs to present efforts at reexamining the social psychology of the experiment. These studies, then, help to underline even further the point that we are confronted with a conflict of values that cannot be resolved by fiat.

I hope it is clear from these remarks that my purpose in focusing on this problem is not to single out specific studies performed by some of my colleagues and to point a finger at them. Indeed, the finger points at me as well. I too have used deception, and have known the joys of applying my skills and ingenuity to the creation of elaborate experimental situations that the subjects would not be able to decode. I am now making active attempts to find alternatives to deception, but still I have not forsworn the use of deception under any and all circumstances. The questions I am raising, then, are addressed to myself as well as to my colleagues. They are questions with which all of us who are committed to social psychology must come to grips, lest we leave their resolution to others who have no understanding of what we are trying to accomplish.

What concerns me most is not so much that deception is used, but precisely that it is used without question. It has now become standard operating procedure in the social psychologist's laboratory. I sometimes feel that we are training a generation of students who do not know that there is any other way of doing experiments in our field – who feel that deception is as much de rigueur as significance at the 0.05 level. Too often deception is used not as a last resort, but as a matter of course. Our attitude seems to be that if you can deceive, why tell the truth? It is this unquestioning acceptance, this routinization of deception, that really concerns me.

I would like to turn now to a review of the bases for my concern with the problem of deception, and then suggest some possible approaches for dealing with it.

Implications of the use of deception in social psychological experiments

My concern about the use of deception is based on three considerations: the ethical implications of such procedures, their methodological implications, and their implications for the future of social psychology.

Ethical implications
Ethical problems of a rather obvious nature arise in the experiments in which deception has potentially harmful consequences for the subject. Take, for example, the brilliant experiment by Mulder and Stemerding (1963) on the effects of threat on attraction to the group and need for strong leadership. In this study – one of the very rare examples of an experiment conducted in a natural setting – independent food merchants in a number of Dutch towns were brought together for group meetings, in the course of which they were informed that a large organization was planning to open up a series of supermarkets in the Netherlands. In the High Threat condition, subjects were told that there was a high probability that their town would be selected as a site for such markets and that the advent of these markets would cause a considerable drop in their business. On the advice of the executives of the shopkeepers' organizations, who had helped to arrange the group meetings, the investigators did not reveal the experimental manipulations to their subjects. I have been worried about these Dutch merchants ever since I heard about this study for the first time. Did some of them go out of business in anticipation of the heavy competition? Do some of them have an anxiety reaction every time they see a bulldozer? Chances are that they soon forgot about this threat (unless, of course, supermarkets actually did move into town) and that it became just one of the many little moments of anxiety that must occur in every shopkeeper's life. Do we have a right, however, to add to life's little anxieties and to risk the possibility of more extensive anxiety purely for the purposes of our experiments, particularly since deception deprives the subject of the opportunity to choose whether or not he wishes to expose himself to the risks that might be entailed?

The studies by Bramel (1962, 1963) and Bergin (1962) provide examples of another type of potentially harmful effects arising from the use of deception. In the Bramel studies, male undergraduates were led to believe that they were homosexually aroused by photographs of men. In the Bergin study, subjects of both sexes were given discrepant information about their level of masculinity or femininity; in one experimental condition, this information was presumably based on an elaborate series of psychological tests in which the subjects had participated. In all of these studies, the deception was explained to the subject at the end of the experiment. One wonders, however, whether such explanation removes the possibility of harmful effects. For many persons in this age group, sexual identity is still a live and sensitive issue, and the self-doubts generated by the laboratory experience may take on a life of their own and linger on for some time to come.

Yet another illustration of potentially harmful effects of deception can be found in Milgram's (1963, 1965) studies of obedience. In these experiments, the subject was led to believe that he was participating in a learning study and was instructed to administer increasingly severe shocks to another person who after a while began to protest vehemently. In fact, of course, the victim was an accomplice of the experimenter and did not receive any shocks. Depending on the conditions, sizable proportions of the subjects obeyed the experimenter's instructions and continued to shock the other person up to the maximum level, which they believed to be extremely painful. Both obedient and defiant subjects exhibited a great deal of stress in this situation. The complexities of the issues surrounding the use of deception become quite apparent when one reads the exchange between Baumrind (1964) and Milgram (1964) about the ethical implications of the obedience research. There is clearly room for disagreement, among honorable people, about the evaluation of this research from an ethical point of view. Yet, there is good reason to believe that at least some of the obedient subjects came away from this experience with a lower self-esteem, having to live with the realization that they were willing to yield to destructive authority to the point of inflicting extreme pain on a fellow human being. The fact that this may have provided, in Milgram's (1964) words, 'an opportunity to learn something of importance about themselves, and more generally, about the conditions of human action' [p. 850] is beside the point. If this were a lesson from life, it would indeed constitute an instructive confrontation and provide a valuable insight. But do we, for the purpose of experimentation, have the right to provide such potentially disturbing insights to subjects who do not know that this is what they are coming for? A similar question can be raised about the Asch (1915) experiments on group pressure, although the stressfulness of the situation and the implications for the person's self-concept were less intense in that context.

While the present paper is specifically focused on social psychological experiments, the problem of deception and its possibly harmful effects arises in other areas of psychological experimentation as well. Dramatic illustrations are provided by two studies in which subjects were exposed, for experimental purposes, to extremely stressful conditions. In an experiment designed to study the establishment of a conditioned response in a situation that is traumatic but not painful,

Campbell, Sanderson, and Laverty (1964) induced – through the use of a drug – a temporary interruption of respiration in their subjects. 'This has no permanently harmful physical consequences but is nonetheless a severe stress which is not in itself painful . . . ' [p. 628]. The subjects' reports confirmed that this was a 'horrific' experience for them. 'All the subjects in the standard series said that they thought they were dying' [p. 631]. Of course the subjects, 'male alcoholic patients who volunteered for the experiment when they were told that it was connected with a possible therapy for alcoholism' [p. 629], were not warned in advance about the effect of the drug, since this information would have reduced the traumatic impact of the experience.[2] In a series of studies on the effects of psychological stress, Berkun, Bialek, Kern and Yagi (1962) devised a number of ingenious experimental situations designed to convince the subject that his life was actually in danger. In one situation, the subjects, a group of Army recruits, were actually 'passengers aboard an apparently stricken plane which was being forced to "ditch" or crash-land' [p. 4]. In another experiment, an isolated subject in a desolate area learned that a sudden emergency had arisen (accidental nuclear radiation in the area, or a sudden forest fire or misdirected artillery shells – depending on the experimental condition) and that he could be rescued only if he reported his position over his radio transmitter, 'which has quite suddenly failed' [p. 7]. In yet another situation, the subject was led to believe that he was responsible for an explosion that seriously injured another soldier. As the authors pointed out, reactions in these situations are more likely to approximate reactions to combat experiences or to naturally occurring disasters than are reactions to various laboratory stresses, but is the experimenter justified in exposing his subjects to such extreme threats?

So far, I have been speaking of experiments in which deception has potentially harmful consequences. I am equally concerned, however, about the less obvious cases, in which there is little danger of harmful effects, at least in the conventional sense of the term. Serious ethical issues are raised by deception per se and the kind of use of human beings that it implies. In our other interhuman relationships, most of us would never think of doing the kinds of things that we do to our subjects – exposing others to lies and tricks, deliberately misleading them about the purposes of the interaction or withholding pertinent information, making promises or giving assurances that we intend to disregard. We would view such behavior as a violation of the respect to which all fellow humans are entitled and of the whole basis of our relationship with them. Yet we seem to forget that the experimenter–subject relationship – whatever else it is – is a *real* interhuman relationship, in which we have responsibility toward the subject as another human being whose dignity we must preserve. The discontinuity between the experimenter's behavior in everyday life and his behavior in the laboratory is so marked that one wonders why there has been so little concern with this problem, and what mechanisms have allowed us to ignore it to such an extent. I am reminded, in this connection, of the intriguing phenomenon of the 'holiness of sin', which characterizes certain messianic movements as well as other movements of the true-believer variety. Behavior that would normally be unacceptable actually takes on an aura of virtue in such movements through a redefinition of the situation in which the behavior takes place and thus of the context for evaluating it. A similar mechanism seems to be involved in our attitude toward the psychological experiment. We tend to regard it as a situation that is not quite real, that can be isolated from the rest of life like a play performed on stage, and to which, therefore, the usual criteria for ethical interpersonal conduct become irrelevant. Behavior is judged entirely in the context of the experiment's scientific contribution and, in this context, deception – which is normally unacceptable – can indeed be seen as a positive good.

The broader ethical problem brought into play by the very use of deception becomes even more important when we view it in the light of present historical forces. We are living in an age of mass societies in which the transformation of man into an object to be manipulated at will occurs 'on a mass scale, in a systematic way, and under the aegis of specialized institutions deliberately assigned to this task' [Kelman, 1965]. In institutionalizing the use of deception in psychological experiments, we are, then, contributing to a historical trend that threatens values most of us cherish.

Methodological implications
A second source of my concern about the use of deception is my increasing doubt about its adequacy as a methodology for social psychology.

A basic assumption in the use of deception is that a subject's awareness of the conditions that we are trying to create and of the phenomena that we wish to study would affect his behavior in such a way that we could not draw valid conclusions from it. For example, if we are interested in studying the effects of failure on conformity, we must create a situation in which the subjects actually feel that they have failed, and in which they can be kept unaware of our interest in observing conformity. In short, it is important to keep our subjects naïve about the purposes of the experiment so that they can respond to the experimental inductions spontaneously.

How long, however, will it be possible for us to find naïve subjects? Among college students, it is already very difficult. They may not know the exact purpose of the particular experiment in which they are participating, but at least they know, typically, that it is *not* what the experimenter says it is. Orne (1962) pointed out that the use of deception 'on the part of psychologists is so widely known in the college population that even if a psychologist is honest with the subject, more often than not he will be distrusted'. As one subject pithily put it, ' "Psychologists always lie!".' Orne added that 'This bit of paranoia has some support in reality' [pp. 778–79]. There are, of course, other sources of human subjects that have not been tapped, and we could turn to them in our quest for naïveté. But even there it is only a matter of time. As word about psychological experiments gets around in whatever network we happen to be using, sophistication is bound to increase. I wonder, therefore, whether there is any future in the use of deception.

If the subject in a deception experiment knows what the experimenter is trying to conceal from him and what he is really after in the study, the value of the deception is obviously nullified. Generally, however, even the relatively sophisticated subject does not know the exact purpose of the experiment; he only has suspicions, which may approximate the true purpose of the experiment to a greater or lesser degree. Whether or not he knows the *true* purpose of the experiment, he is likely to make an effort to figure out its purpose, since he does not believe what the experimenter tells him, and therefore he is likely to operate in the situation in terms of his own hypothesis of what is involved. This may, in line with Orne's (1962) analysis, lead him to do what he thinks the experimenter wants him to do. Conversely, if he resents the experimenter's attempt to deceive him, he may try to throw a monkey wrench into the works; I would not be surprised if this kind of Schweikian game among subjects became a fairly well-established part of the culture of sophisticated campuses. Whichever course the subject uses, however, he is operating in terms of his own conception of the nature of the situation, rather than in terms of the conception that the experimenter is trying to induce. In short, the experimenter can no longer assume that the conditions that he is trying to create are the ones that actually define the situation for the subject. Thus, the use of deception, while it is designed to give the experimenter control over the subject's perceptions and motivations, may actually produce an unspecifiable mixture of intended and unintended stimuli that make it difficult to know just what the subject is responding to.

The tendency for subjects to react to unintended cues – to features of the situation that are not part of the experimenter's design – is by no means restricted to experiments that involve deception. This problem has concerned students of the interview situation for some time, and more recently it has been analyzed in detail in the writings and research of Riecken, Rosenthal, Orne and Mills. Subjects enter the experiment with their own aims, including attainment of certain rewards, divination of the experimenter's true purposes and favorable self-presentation (Riecken, 1962). They are therefore responsive to demand characteristics of the situation (Orne, 1962), to unintended communications of the experimenter's expectations (Rosenthal, 1963) and to the role of the experimenter within the social system that experimenter and subject jointly constitute (Mills, 1962). In any experiment, then, the subject goes beyond the description of the situation and the experimental manipulation introduced by the investigator, makes his own interpretation of the situation, and acts accordingly.

For several reasons, however, the use of deception especially encourages the subject to dismiss the stated purposes of the experiment and to search for alternative interpretations of his own. First, the continued use of deception establishes the reputation of psychologists as people who cannot be believed. Thus, the desire 'to penetrate the experimenter's inscrutability and discover the rationale of the experiment' [Riecken, 1962, p. 34] becomes especially strong. Generally, these efforts are motivated by the subject's desire to meet the expectations of the experimenter and of the situation. They may also be motivated, however, as I have already mentioned, by a desire to outwit the experimenter and to beat him at his own game, in a spirit of genuine hostility or playful one-upmanship. Second, a situation involving the use of deception is inevitably highly ambiguous since a great deal of information relevant to understanding the structure of the situation must be withheld from the subject. Thus, the subject is especially motivated to try to figure things out and likely to develop idiosyncratic interpretations. Third, the use of deception, by its very nature, causes the experimenter to transmit contradictory messages to the subject. In his verbal instructions and explanations he says one thing about the purposes of the experiment; but in the experimental situation that he has created, in the manipulations that he has introduced, and probably in covert cues that he emits, he says another thing. This again makes it imperative for the subject to seek his own interpretation of the situation.

I would argue, then, that deception increases the subject's tendency to operate in terms of his private definition of the situation, differing (in random or systematic fashion) from the definition that the experimenter is trying to impose; moreover, it makes it more difficult to evaluate or minimize the effects of this tendency. Whether or not I am right in this judgment, it can, at the very least, be said that the use of deception does not resolve or reduce the unintended effects of the experiment as a social situation in which the subject pursues his private aims. Since the assumptions that the subject is naïve and that he sees the situation as the experimenter wishes him to see it are unwarranted, the use of deception no longer has any special obvious advantages over other experimental approaches. I am not suggesting that there may not be occasions when deception may still be the most effective procedure to use from a methodological point of view. But since it raises at least as many methodological problems as any other type of procedure does, we have every reason to explore alternative approaches and to extend our methodological inquiries to the question of the effects of using deception.

Implications for the future of social psychology
My third concern about the use of deception is based on its long-run implications for our discipline and combines both the ethical and

methodological considerations that I have already raised. There is something disturbing about the idea of relying on massive deception as the basis for developing a field of inquiry. Can one really build a discipline on a foundation of such research?

From a long-range point of view, there is obviously something self-defeating about the use of deception. As we continue to carry out research of this kind, our potential subjects become more and more sophisticated, and we become less and less able to meet the conditions that our experimental procedures require. Moreover, as we continue to carry out research of this kind, our potential subjects become increasingly distrustful of us, and our future relations with them are likely to be undermined. Thus, we are confronted with the anomalous circumstance that the more research we do, the more difficult and questionable it becomes.

The use of deception also involves a contradiction between our experimental procedures and our long-range aims as scientists and teachers. In order to be able to carry out our experiments, we are concerned with maintaining the naïveté of the population from which we hope to draw our subjects. We are all familiar with the experimenter's anxious concern that the introductory course might cover the autokinetic phenomenon, need achievement, or the Asch situation before he has had a chance to complete his experimental runs. This perfectly understandable desire to keep procedures secret goes counter to the traditional desire of the scientist and teacher to inform and enlighten the public. To be sure, experimenters are interested only in temporary secrecy, but it is not inconceivable that at some time in the future they might be using certain procedures on a regular basis with large segments of the population and thus prefer to keep the public permanently naïve. It is perhaps not too fanciful to imagine, for the long run, the possible emergence of a special class, in possession of secret knowledge – a possibility that is clearly antagonistic to the principle of open communication to which we, as scientists and intellectuals, are so fervently committed.

Dealing with the problem of deception in social psychological experiments

If my concerns about the use of deception are justified, what are some of the ways in which we, as experimental social psychologists, can deal with them? I would like to suggest three steps that we can take: increase our active awareness of the problem, explore ways of counteracting and minimizing the negative effects of deception, and give careful attention to the development of new experimental techniques that dispense with the use of deception.

Active awareness of the problem

I have already stressed that I would not propose the complete elimination of deception under all circumstances, in view of the genuine conflict of values with which the experimenter is confronted. What is crucial, however, is that we always ask ourselves the question whether deception, in the given case, is necessary and justified. How we answer the question is less important than the fact that we ask it. What we must be wary of is the tendency to dismiss the question as irrelevant and to accept deception as a matter of course. Active awareness of the problem is thus in itself part of the solution, for it makes the use of deception a matter for discussion, deliberation, investigation and choice. Active awareness means that, in any given case, we will try to balance the value of an experiment that uses deception against its questionable or potentially harmful effects. If we engage in this process honestly, we are likely to find that there are many occasions when we or our students can forgo the use of deception – either because deception is not necessary (that is, alternative procedures that are equally good or better are available), because the importance of the study does not warrant the use of an ethically questionable procedure, or because the type of deception involved is too extreme (in terms of the possibility of harmful effects or of seriously undermining the experimenter-subject relationship).

Counteracting and minimizing the negative effects of deception
If we do use deception, it is essential that we find ways of counteracting and minimizing its negative effects. Sensitizing the apprentice researcher to this necessity is at least as fundamental as any other part of research training.

In those experiments in which deception carries the potential of harmful effects (in the more usual sense of the term), there is an obvious requirement to build protections into every phase of the process. Subjects must be selected in a way that will exclude individuals who are especially vulnerable; the potentially harmful manipulation (such as the induction of stress) must be kept at a moderate level of intensity; the experimenter must be sensitive to danger signals in the reactions of his subjects and be prepared to deal with crises when they arise; and, at the conclusion of the session, the experimenter must take time not only to reassure the subject, but also to help him work through his feelings about the experience to whatever degree may be required. In general, the principle that a subject ought not to leave the laboratory with greater anxiety or lower self-esteem than he came with is a good one to follow. I would go beyond it to argue that the subject should in some positive way be enriched by the experience, that is, he should come away from it with the feeling that he has learned something, understood something, or grown in some way. This, of course, adds special importance to the kind of feedback that is given to the subject at the end of the experimental session.

Postexperimental feedback is, of course, the primary way of counteracting negative effects in those experiments in which the issue is deception as such, rather than possible threats to the subject's well-being. If we do deceive the subject, then it is our obligation to give him a full and detailed explanation of what we have done and of our reasons for using this type of procedure. I do not want to be absolutist about this, but I would suggest this as a good rule of thumb to follow: Think very carefully before undertaking an experiment whose purposes you feel unable to reveal to the subjects even after they have completed the experimental session. It is, of course, not enough to give the subject a perfunctory feedback, just to do one's duty. Postexperimental explanations should be worked out with as much detail as other aspects of the procedure and, in general, some thought ought to be given to ways of making them meaningful and instructive for the subject and helpful for rebuilding his relationship with the experimenter. I feel very strongly that to accomplish these purposes, we must keep the feedback itself inviolate and under no circumstance give the subject false feedback or pretend to be giving him feedback while we are in fact introducing another experimental manipulation. If we hope to maintain any kind of trust in our relationship with potential subjects, there must be no ambiguity that the statement 'The experiment is over and I shall explain to you what it was all about' means precisely that and nothing else. If subjects have reason to suspect even that statement, then we have lost the whole basis for a decent human relationship with our subjects and all hope for future cooperation from them.

Development of new experimental techniques
My third and final suggestion is that we invest some of the creativity and ingenuity, now devoted to the construction of elaborate deceptions, in the search for alternative experimental techniques that do not rely on the use of deception. The kind of techniques that I have in mind would be based on the principle of eliciting the subject's positive motivations to contribute to the experimental enterprise. They would draw on the subject's active participation and involvement in the proceedings and encourage him to cooperate in making the experiment a success – not by giving the results he thinks the experimenter wants, but by conscientiously taking the roles and carrying out the tasks that the experimenter assigns to him. In short, the kind of techniques I have in mind would be designed to involve the subject as an active participant in a joint effort with the experimenter.

Perhaps the most promising source of alternative experimental approaches are procedures using some sort of role playing. I have been impressed, for example, with the role playing that I have observed in the context of the Inter-Nation Simulation (Guetzkow, Alger, Brody, Noel, & Snyder, 1963), a laboratory procedure involving a simulated world in which the subjects take the roles of decision-makers of various nations. This situation seems to create a high level of emotional involvement and to elicit motivations that have a real-life quality to them. Moreover, within this situation – which is highly complex and generally permits only gross experimental manipulations – it is possible to test specific theoretical hypotheses by using data based on repeated measurements as interaction between the simulated nations develops. Thus, a study carried out at the Western Behavioral Sciences Institute provided, as an extra, some interesting opportunities for testing hypotheses derived from balance theory, by the use of mutual ratings made by decision-makers of Nations A, B and C, before and after A shifted from an alliance with B to an alliance with C.

A completely different type of role playing was used effectively by Rosenberg and Abelson (1960) in their studies of cognitive dilemmas. In my own research program, we have been exploring different kinds of role-playing procedures with varying degrees of success. In one study, the major manipulation consisted in informing subjects that the experiment to which they had just committed themselves would require them (depending on the condition) either to receive shocks from a fellow subject, or to administer shocks to a fellow subject. We used a regular deception procedure, but with a difference: We told the subjects before the session started that what was to follow was make-believe, but that we wanted them to react as if they really found themselves in this situation. I might mention that some subjects, not surprisingly, did not accept as true the information that this was all make-believe and wanted to know when they should show up for the shock experiment to which they had committed themselves. I have some question about the effectiveness of this particular procedure. It did not do enough to create a high level of involvement, and it turned out to be very complex since it asked subjects to role-play subjects, not people. In this sense, it might have given us the worst of both worlds, but I still think it is worth some further exploration. In another experiment, we were interested in creating differently structured attitudes about an organization by feeding different kinds of information to two groups of subjects. These groups were then asked to take specific actions in support of the organization, and we measured attitude changes resulting from these actions. In the first part of the experiment, the subjects were clearly informed that the organization and the information that we were feeding to them were fictitious, and that we were simply trying to simulate the conditions under which attitudes about new organizations are typically formed. In the second part of the experiment, the subjects were told that we were interested in studying the effects of action in support of an organization on attitudes toward it, and they were asked (in groups of five) to role-play a strategy meeting of leaders of the fictitious organization. The results of this study were very encouraging. While there is obviously a great deal that we need to know about the meaning of this situation to the subjects, they did react differentially to the experimental manipulations and these reactions followed an orderly pattern, despite the fact that they knew it was all make-believe.

There are other types of procedures, in addition to role playing, that are worth exploring. For example, one might design field experiments in which, with the full cooperation of the subjects, specific experimental variations are introduced. The advantages of dealing with motivations at a real-life level of intensity might well outweigh the disadvantages of subjects' knowing the general purpose of the experiment. At the other extreme of ambitiousness, one might explore the effects of modifying standard experimental procedures slightly by informing the subject at the beginning of the experiment that he will not be receiving full information about what is going on, but asking him to suspend judgment until the experiment is over.

Whatever alternative approach we try, there is no doubt that it will have its own problems and complexities. Procedures effective for some purposes may be quite ineffective for others, and it may well turn out that for certain kinds of problems there is no adequate substitute for the use of deception. But there *are* alternative procedures that, for many purposes, may be as effective or even more effective than procedures built on deception. These approaches often involve a radically different set of assumptions about the role of the subject in the experiment: They require us to *use* the subject's motivation to cooperate rather than to bypass it; they may even call for increasing the sophistication of potential subjects, rather than maintaining their naïveté. My only plea is that we devote some of our energies to active exploration of these alternative approaches.

Notes

1. In focusing on deception in *social* psychological experiments, I do not wish to give the impression that there is no serious problem elsewhere. Deception is widely used in most studies involving human subjects and gives rise to issues similar to those discussed in this paper. Some examples of the use of deception in other areas of psychological experimentation will be presented later in this paper.
2. The authors reported, however, that some of their other subjects were physicians familiar with the drug; 'they did not suppose they were dying but, even though they knew in a general way what to expect, they too said that the experience was extremely harrowing' [p. 632]. Thus, conceivably, the purposes of the experiment might have been achieved even if the subjects had been told to expect the temporary interruption of breathing.

References

Asch, S. E. (1951) 'Effects of group pressure upon the modification and distortion of judgments', in H. Guetzkow (ed.), *Groups, Leadership, and Men*. Pittsburgh: Carnegie Press, pp. 177–90.
Baumrind, D. (1964) 'Some thoughts on ethics of research: after reading Milgram's "Behavioral Study of Obedience"', *American Psychologist*, **19**, 421–23.
Bergin, A. E. (1962) 'The effect of dissonant persuasive communications upon changes in a self-referring attitude', *Journal of Personality*, **30**, 423–38.
Berkun, M. M., Bialek, H. M., Kern, R. P. and Yagi, K. (1962) 'Experimental studies of psychological stress in man', *Psychological Monographs*, **76** (15, Whole No. 534).

Bramel, D. (1962) 'A dissonance theory approach to defensive projection', *Journal of Abnormal and Social Psychology,* **64,** 121–29.

Bramel, D. (1963) 'Selection of a target for defensive projection', *Journal of Abnormal and Social Psychology,* **66,** 318–24.

Campbell, D., Sanderson, R. E. and Laverty, S. G. (1964) 'Characteristics of a conditioned response in human subjects during extinction trials following a single traumatic conditioning trial', *Journal of Abnormal and Social Psychology,* **68,** 627–39.

Festinger, L. and Carlsmith, J. M. (1969) 'Cognitive consequences of forced compliance', *Journal of Abnormal and Social Psychology,* **58,** 203–10.

Guetzkow, H., Alger, C. F., Brody, R. A., Noel, R. C. and Snyder, R. C. (1963) *Simulation in international relations.* Englewood Cliffs, N.J.: Prentice-Hall.

Kelman, H. C. (1965) 'Manipulation of human behavior: an ethical dilemma for the social scientist', *Journal of Social Issues,* **21**(2), 31–46.

Milgram, S. (1963) 'Behavioral study of obedience', *Journal of Abnormal and Social Psychology,* **67,** 371–78.

Milgram, S. (1964) 'Issues in the study of obedience: A reply to Baumrind', *American Psychologist,* **19,** 848–52.

Milgram, S. (1965) 'Some conditions of obedience and disobedience to authority', *Human Relations,* **18,** 57–76.

Mills, T. M. (1962) 'A sleeper variable in small groups research: the experimenter', *Pacific Sociological Review,* **5,** 21–28.

Mulder, M. and Stemerding, A. (1963) 'Threat, attraction to group, and need for strong leadership', *Human Relations,* **16,** 317–34.

Orne, M. T. 'On the social psychology of the psychological experiment: with particular reference to demand characteristics and their implications', *American Psychologist,* **17,** 776–83.

Riecken, H. W. (1962) 'A program for research on experiments in social psychology', in N. F. Washburne (ed.), *Decisions, values and groups.* Vol. 2. New York: Pergamon Press, pp. 25–41.

Rosenberg, M. J. and Abelson, R. P. (1960) 'An analysis of cognitive balancing', in M. J. Rosenberg et al., *Attitude organization and change.* New Haven: Yale University Press, pp. 112–63.

Rosenthal, R. (1963) 'On the social psychology of the psychological experiment: The experimenter's hypothesis as unintended determinant of experimental results', *American Scientist,* **51,** 268–83.

Rosenthal, R. and Fode, K. L. (1963) 'Psychology of the scientist: V. Three experiments in experimenter bias', *Psychological Reports,* **12,** 491–511. (Monogr. Suppl. 3-V12.)

Rosenthal, R., Persinger, G. W., Vikan-Kline, L. and Fode, K. L. (1963) 'The effect of early data returns on data subsequently obtained by outcome-biased experimenters', *Sociometry,* **26,** 487–98.

Rosenthal, R., Persinger, G. W., Vikan-Kline, L. and Mulry, R. C. (1963) 'The role of the research assistant in the mediation of experimenter bias', *Journal of Personality,* **31,** 313–35.

Vinacke, W. E. (1954) 'Deceiving experimental subjects', *American Psychologist,* **9,** 155.

Measurement

Introduction

To be of any use to the researcher the raw data collected in the field has to be processed. When we process data we engage in the activity most basic to all science, measurement. At the simplest level we wish to classify observations/responses in terms of simple and meaningful categories. At the most sophisticated level we wish to construct a composite measuring instrument by means of which we can attempt to operationalize some important theoretical construct. The Readings in this section present the different facets of this process, and the central principles which underly them. We start with an extract from Oppenheim's book, *Questionnaire Design and Attitude Measurement*, in which he describes the basic procedures for coding survey data, including the different types of coding frame which can be employed. Vital to any such procedure is the issue of the reliability of the coded data (will one coder produce the same results as another?). Another central issue is the options open to the investigator about the particular categories he should use. These relate to the purposes of the investigation: What is the classification for? Inevitably in such a process there are underlying theoretical assumptions that the researcher is making and the success of his coding operation therefore comes down to a question of its *validity*.

    This concept is discussed in the next Reading by Cronbach and Meehl in which they set out their far-reaching theory of 'construct validity'. In the early part of this article, not reproduced here, they display the weaknesses of the traditional approaches to validity which depend on validating one particular measure by the strength of its relationships with other measures. In 'the logic of construct validation' they re-define validity in effect as the interpretability of observations/measurements in terms of the theory in which they play a part. In other words, it is just as important to collect evidence of no relation between one measure and another as it is to produce evidence of a relationship, depending on what the theory predicts. Though the references they use are taken from psychological literature, do not be put off by them. Their position has been adopted as a unifying principle by people working in all branches of social science, and has as much relevance for, say, the ethnographer as it does for the experimental psychologist.

Under-pinning the validity of any measurement is its reliability, and this topic provides the theme for a practical strategy developed by McKennell for the construction of attitude measures. McKennell approaches the principle of construct validity via the investigation of the dimensionality of attitude items culled from exploratory interviews; he then applies Cronbach's Alpha reliability coefficient as a criterion for the reliability of the composite measures obtained from sets of these items. Validation of these measures (in the construct sense) comes from an investigation of their relationships with other variables predicted from the theory in which they play a part. In such a strategy we see an excellent example of research techniques governed by sound methodological principles and grounded in the currency of everyday opinion.

The quantification of questionnaire data

A. N. Oppenheim

Coding frames

Each free-answer question, probe, sentence-completion item or other 'open' technique in our questionnaire will require its own classification scheme. Only rarely can we use a scheme devised for some other inquiry. Our first task will therefore be the design of all the classification schemes, usually known as 'codes' or 'coding frames', required for our particular study. Quite possibly we have already given this matter some thought during the pilot stages, and perhaps we have produced some tentative drafts for coding frames. However, the coding frames proposed during the pilot stage will have been based on the raw data obtained from pilot samples, and since the responses of such samples may differ markedly from those of the main sample, we must always construct our coding frame with the aid of responses from the main sample.

It is very tempting to start the design of our coding frames as soon as the first returns from the field work arrive back at the office. However, since these are likely to be unrepresentative, it is advisable to wait until all the returns or a substantial part of them are in. Otherwise, we run the risk that the coding frames will turn out to be a poor fit, so that they may have to be amended, perhaps several times, in the course of the coding operation. It is always undesirable to have to amend a coding frame in midstream, as it were, because amendments produce errors and are wasteful in that they require re-coding of questionnaires that have been coded already.

How do we set about designing a coding frame?

Probably the first step should be the examination of a representative sample of responses. In practice, we select a convenient number of questionnaires (say, fifty or sixty cases) on a representative basis and copy all the responses to a particular question onto sheets of paper. At the top of each sheet will be the text of the question as it appeared in

A. N. Oppenheim 'The quantification of questionnaire data', from *Questionnaire Design and Attitude Measurement*, London: Heinemann Educational Books, 1966, Ch. 9, pp. 227–48.

the questionnaire, and below that will be copied all the various answers given to that question by our subsample of fifty or sixty cases, each answer preceded by the case number. Where answers are few, for instance if the question applied to only part of the sample, more cases will be needed, until we have a sufficiently large and varied selection of answers. When we come to design the coding frame of the next free-answer question, we go through the entire batch of selected questionnaires again, copying all the responses to that particular question together, so that we can look at them.

From this point on we must bear in mind very clearly what it is that we are trying to do. By imposing a set of classificatory categories, perhaps eight or ten in number, on a very much larger and probably very varied set of responses, we are inevitably going to *lose information*. Bearing in mind the aims and hypotheses of the survey and the particular purpose of the question under consideration, we must so design the coding frame that this loss of information will occur where it matters least, enabling us to run our comparisons or test our hypotheses with the greatest accuracy. This means that our set of categories will not necessarily be designed simply 'to do justice to the responses'; other considerations may apply, and compromises often have to be made.

For a start, how many categories should we have? If there were no constraints, and we were anxious not to cause any distortion, we might like to have almost as many categories as there are responses, grouping under one heading only those responses that are identical. This is obviously not a practical proposition. Even if we could afford to follow so elaborate a coding scheme, we would probably find during the statistical analysis that each category contained only one case or a very few cases. Therefore, *the number of categories we can afford to have will in part be determined by the number of cases in the sample and the number of statistical breakdowns we shall use;* a category that will, in the final analysis and after subdivision of the sample, hold fewer than two or three dozen cases must usually be regarded as a luxury. However much it offends our semantic sensibilities or philosophical finesse, we must realize that it is pointless to retain a category that is used by too few people.

There is one exception to this argument. It sometimes happens that we have a hypothesis about a certain type of response being absent or very rare. In that case we might reserve a category for it in order to show just how rare it is. For instance, suppose we had asked people why they had changed from one brand of cigarettes to another, and suppose, further, that we wished to test the specific hypothesis that people very rarely admit to reasons of economy in answering such a question. In such a case we would make up a coding frame suitable to the distribution of the answers we get but, come what may, we should reserve one category for 'economic reasons', or something like that.

There are also purely technical considerations that are likely to reduce the number of categories. Most surveys will be analyzed by means of punch-card equipment. These cards consist, as we have seen, of 40, 60 or 80 columns, each containing twelve categories (running from 0 to 9, V and X), and a 'blank' position. It is technically feasible to run on into a second column if we wish to use more than twelve categories, or we can use two columns to make 99 or 144 categories (by using the first column for the tens, the second column for the units); we could continue in this way with three or more columns, or we could even multi-punch within the same column so as to produce dozens of different categories within one column – but such steps are not undertaken lightly, because they add to the complexity and reduce the speed of the analysis and often result in errors. Most survey practitioners try to keep their coding frames down to twelve categories for this reason, though they may go beyond this number occasionally. Since we will require categories for 'miscellaneous', 'don't know', and 'no answer', this would leave us effectively with nine possible categories. This number may, at first sight, seem impossibly small when the variety of responses is being considered yet it is surprising how often one starts off with a much more ambitious scheme only to find that eight or nine categories will suffice after all, with the added advantage of increased frequencies in each category.

These limitations may apply differently when we use a computer, especially one that has a punched-tape input; but card space is even more at a premium when we use edge-punched cards, which are sorted by hand or with a needle.

Thus we see how it has come about that the typical coding frame in many surveys will have fewer than a dozen categories. This means inevitably that the coding frame is relatively crude (entailing loss of information), and it becomes something of a challenge to devise a code that will do its job without too much sacrifice, within such limits.

What other considerations guide us in the composition of coding frames? Let us take, for example, a question asking for the respondent's favorite film star. Let us assume that we have copied the replies of five dozen people, and that we are now faced with the problem of classifying these responses. One approach might simply be by frequency. We allot, say, seven categories to the seven names occurring most often and lump the remaining names in one or two other categories. Or perhaps we wish to expand the frame; we could have dozens of categories, each with one film star's name, if we chose. Or we might decide to group the names under different labels, such as 'romantic', 'Western', 'musical', and so on, according to the type of role with which such film stars are associated. Then again, we may decide to have two coding frames, one for male and one for female film stars. Or we may wish to group together those stars who also appear on other mass media and those who do not. We may classify stars by their ages, or by their ethnic background, or by the number of divorces they have had. So we see that it is often not a simple matter to design a coding frame that will 'do justice to the data', and that, moreover, the type of coding frame we need will depend on what we wish to find out. Suppose, for instance, that we wish to examine the hypothesis that men will most often admire female film stars, whereas women will more often mention male film stars. In that case, all we need to do, strictly speaking, is to classify the responses by sex into just two categories, male stars and female stars. This would tell us all we needed to know – though it would not enable us to go very much further. On the other hand, suppose we had the hypothesis that a lot depends on the star's age in relation to one's own age, with younger respondents admiring a somewhat older and more mature person, while middle-aged respondents prefer a younger star. In that case we would need a fairly complex coding frame giving categories of age differentials, up or down from one's own age, and to do the coding we would need to know both the respondent's age and that of his most admired film star.

When we copy out the responses, it is helpful to group the respondents in terms of one or more variables of concern, such as sex, age, social mobility, and so on. This often suggests differences in content, flavor or expression between subgroups, and a coding frame can be designed to highlight these. For this reason, the copied responses must not merely be regarded as a try-out; they should be most carefully studied and perused.

Usually, the order of the categories is unimportant, and the categories are quite independent of one another. Sometimes, however, we may need a coding frame that is more like a rating scale. For instance, we may use some of our categories to indicate the degree of favorableness with which the respondent views a certain person or object; some responses would be classified as 'Highly favorable', others as 'Moderately favorable' or as 'Favorable with reservations', and so on. Sometimes the coding frame requires a logical structure; the classification of one's favorite subject at school might be an example. Here we would perhaps wish to use two linked frames, analogous to two punch-card columns: the first frame would have the broad categories, such as (1) 'languages', (2) 'numerical subjects', (3) 'natural history', and so forth, while the second frame would be different for each of the broader categories, and would contain the sub-categories, so that say, code 14 might be French, code 26 might be Trigonometry and code 36 could stand for Geology. When the question is somewhat more projective, we may require a frame-of-reference code. Suppose we had asked a sample of the general population the question: 'Why are caps worn?' and that our objective was to find out with what kind of role or group the wearing of caps was most readily associated. In that case our coding frame would not contain categories such as 'in order to command respect and obedience' or 'to protect the wearer's head'; but rather such categories as 'school', 'prison services', 'police and fire brigades', 'scout cubs and other youth groups', 'nurses and ambulance men', and so on. This means that the coder has to infer from the contents of the response what context was in the respondent's mind – if possible.

It should also be mentioned that for some questions, typically those used for classificatory purposes, there are probably some well-designed and elaborate coding frames available ready-made. A classification of occupational prestige might be one example. When using prepared coding frames one should follow the coding instructions most carefully, and, of course, the original question(s) should be the same, if comparability is desired with the results of other investigations using the same coding frame. Occasionally, too, we may have asked the same question in 'open' and in 'closed' form; in that case there may be something to be said for using at least some of the pre-codes of the 'closed' question as categories in the coding frame of the 'open' question.

Every coding frame is likely to need two or three categories that are standard, namely 'miscellaneous', 'don't know', and 'no answer' or 'not ascertained'. When we are pressed for space, the latter two categories are frequently grouped together. On the other hand, sometimes it is important to know how many respondents said that they did not know the answer, or which ones refused to commit themselves; these two categories may not be just 'waste categories'. Into 'miscellaneous' go all those responses that cannot readily be fitted into one of our prepared categories. In cases of doubt, it is better practice to classify a response as 'Miscellaneous' than to force it into another category. One reason for this is that it is best not to blur the limits of the categories. Another is that if such doubtful responses occur with unexpected frequency, then at some point they can be 'rescued', by making the decision to amend the coding frame and introducing a new category; in that case we merely have to look again at the responses coded 'Miscellaneous' with a view to reclassification, instead of having to recode every response category. Such a course of action should be seriously considered if the frequency of 'Miscellaneous' responses rises above, say, 15 per cent or so.

It should be realized that code categories can always be combined, putting together all the male film stars, or all the favorable plus moderately favorable responses, or all the respondents doing manual labor of any kind. This is sometimes necessary when we are dealing with small subanalyses, where the lack of cases is making itself felt.

Each category in a coding frame should be designated in the clearest possible way. It should be described in words, or given a label, and it is always helpful to give many illustrative examples taken from actual responses. Suppose we have asked people a question about the platform of a given political party and that we wish to classify the answers in terms of the amount of knowledge revealed by the respondents. In such a case it would not be enough to set up a coding frame with categories such as 'very good', 'adequate', 'poor' and so forth. Obviously, this would lead to inconsistencies among the coders and might not be clear to our readers. We have to set up definite criteria, such as: 'Very good: gives at least three different items of party policy correctly' together with some examples of actual responses. This is particularly important when numerous coders will be engaged on the same survey, in order to ensure consistency and reliability, but even where the investigator does all his own coding the categories should be as clear and as unambiguous as possible, for it is only too easy to change one's standards as one goes on. It is also necessary that the future reader know what is the precise meaning of each category; often verbal labels are ambiguous, but examples can make the meaning clear.

In the entire coding operation it is necessary to introduce frequent checks, both with others and with oneself, for statistics based on inconsistent coding can be very misleading. Some coding frames are relatively objective and merely require consistency and attention to detail on the part of the coder, for instance the coding of favorite school subjects. Other coding frames, however, require a certain amount of interpretation on the part of the coder, for instance coding the job dissatisfactions of teachers or the reasons people give for not saving more than they do. We then have to face the delicate problem of designing a coding frame that goes 'deep' enough, yet one that can be used consistently by the coding staff available, bearing in mind their training and experience. In some investigations it is necessary to check every coded response or to have two coders working independently on the same data and then discussing and resolving the differences between them. The primary aim must be consistency and the elimination of ambiguities; a coder who 'stretches' a category in order not to have to classify a response under 'Miscellaneous', or one who 'improves' a category from one day to the next, or who finds that he 'knows' what the respondent 'really meant', merely does the study a disservice. The better and clearer the coding frame, the fewer such occasions will arise.

We may now turn to some examples of coding frames.

Here, for a start, is a very simple code that enables us to classify a man's army service:

V   don't know, can't remember, etc.
X   no answer, not ascertained
0   no military service
1   private
2   noncommissioned ranks, below sergeant
3   noncommissioned ranks, sergeant and above
4   commissioned ranks up to and including captain
5   commissioned ranks, major and above
6   special service troops
7   Navy or air force, merchant navy
8   in service, rank not specified

Obviously this is a fairly crude code, designed for a particular purpose – chiefly, that of ascertaining the highest army rank attained by the respondent. Most of the categories are, therefore, prestige levels, and the categories are ordered, though this is not strictly necessary here. Note that, for special reasons, a separate category has been reserved for private. Also, that most of the other categories cover a range (from–to) of ranks, so that the highest and lowest rank have to be specified; thus, if we had worded category 2 as 'noncommissioned ranks up to sergeant', this would not have made it clear whether the rank of sergeant was or was not to be included in that category. Clearly, for other purposes one would code the material differently, in terms of home service versus various overseas theaters of war, or in terms of army, navy, air force or marines, and so on. For some purposes we can make use of what is known as an 'over-punch', say, for all those with any kind of overseas service; such a double code would enable us quickly to extract those respondents who had served abroad. Note, finally, that this is also an example of a logical code, which could largely have been anticipated except for the cut-off points for each category.

Next, we look at a somewhat similar example. Here is a coding frame for the answers to the question 'During the past seven days, how many hours have you spent reading newspapers?' in a student survey:

V   don't know, can't remember, etc.
X   no answer, not ascertained
0   none
1   less than 1 hour
2   1 hour to 2 hours 59 minutes
3   3 hours to 4 hours 59 minutes
4   5 hours to 6 hours 59 minutes
5   7 hours to 8 hours 59 minutes
6   9 hours to 10 hours 59 minutes
7   11 hours and over

Here we have another ordinal code, going up in regular steps of two hours. Obviously, the actual categories have been determined from a sample of responses; how else would we know that intervals of two hours would be the most appropriate or that very few students read newspapers for more than eleven hours a week? A 'miscellaneous' category is not, of course, required, but note that 'None' has been given a separate category on its own – to show which students had not read any newspapers at all.

In the same survey of student reading habits, some questions were asked about the most recent textbook that the student had read in the college library; one of the questions was 'What system did you follow in reading this book?' to which the following coding frame was applied:

V   don't know, no answer, not ascertained
X   miscellaneous
0   chapter headings
1   skim chapter by chapter, then make notes

2   read from cover to cover
3   skim and make notes
4   concentrate on one section only
5   use index, look up pages
6   read chapter summaries
7   just read conclusions
8   introduction only
9   read various sections thoroughly

We observe right away that the categories for 'don't know' and for 'no answer; not ascertained' have been grouped together in order to allow sufficient space for the other categories. We also notice that the categories are described in somewhat abbreviated style; this is liable to lead to misunderstandings. Likewise, it is not clear how categories 1 and 3 differ from each other; this kind of ambiguity should be avoided, and it should certainly be one of the points to be discussed with the coders before they start. The code is obviously based on the study of a sample of responses; it is neither ordinal nor logical, in our sense. To some extent, the makers of the frame were also guided by the knowledge of what the teaching staff regarded as good practice in getting the most out of one's time in the library. Last but not least important, this is a multiple-mention code: a student can obviously use two or more of these systems in reading a book, and we must so devise our code that we can cope with multiple answers (see below).

Also in the same study of student reading habits were questions about the most recent extracurricular book read. These books were coded as follows:

V   no answer, not ascertained, don't know
X   miscellaneous
0   biography, autobiography
1   travel and geography
2   crime, detection, Westerns, mysteries
3   poetry
4   essays and short stories
5   humor
6   plays
7   books about art, music, ballet, theater, etc.
8   theology, religious books
9   novels (see next column also)

Novels code
V   modern, romantic
X   modern, historical
0   modern, novel of ideas (social message)
1   modern, other
2   between wars, romantic
3   between wars, historical

4   between wars, novel of ideas (social message)
5   between wars, other
6   classical, romantic
7   classical, historical
8   classical, novel of ideas (social message)
9   classical, other

(N.B.: Classical meant that the book was published before 1914.)

This is an example of a double code and an example of a grouped code as well. To begin with, a relatively crude classification was made of the main types of books mentioned by students – a classification that cannot bear comparison to the elaborate system of classification employed by librarians but that sufficed for the purpose at hand. It then became evident from the study of a sample of responses that novels were by far the most popular type of extracurricular reading, and so it was decided to do a more detailed, but separate, classification of this kind of fiction. If a respondent mentioned a novel, he was given a 9 on the first coding frame, and coded once more on the second frame. In the second frame we have, first, three broad groupings (modern, between wars and classical [pre-1914]), and then, within each of these, four categories (romantic, historical, novel of ideas and other). This fits quite neatly within the confines of one punch-card column; if the student had not read a novel, this second column would remain blank. The relative crudeness of both these frames illustrates once again the inevitable compromise between the degree of refinement in which one can indulge, and the constraints of sample size, number of statistical breakdowns, quality of coders, punch-card space available and so on. Both frames also illustrate the need for examples; in the actual coding operation lists were kept of names of books that occurred frequently, together with their date of publication and agreed classification by content. Even so, there would obviously be much room for discussion and need for checking and cross-checking. In the end, if it seemed as if a particular book could fit into more than one category, it would be necessary to lay down a ruling, however arbitrary, in order to maintain consistency among the coders.

We now come to a more difficult kind of code. In an attitude study of teachers, the following question was put: 'In these days, what qualities in children do you think a teacher should encourage most?' This question is obviously very wide indeed, and the answers covered a considerable range. Here is the frame that was finally developed:

V   religion
X   ambition, striving
0   no answer, not ascertained, don't know
1   *self-development and happiness:* spontaneity, happiness, curiosity, creativity, self-reliance, active and open personality, originality

2 *rational use of energies for the attainment of educational and work goals:* industry, efficiency, perseverance

3 *active adjustment to social situations:* sociability, co-operativeness, comradeship

4 *inhibitory adjustment to social situations:* self-control, self-discipline, correct manners, cleanliness, orderliness

5 *inhibitory adjustment to authority figures:* respect for authority, deference to teachers and elders, obedience

6 *self-assertive adjustment to social situation:* competitiveness, toughness

7 *goodness, kindness, love, tolerance, generosity*

8 *adherence to enduring values, personal integrity:* truthfulness, honesty, sense of justice, sincerity, sense of honor, dignity, courage

9 other

This coding frame requires a good deal of interpretation of the responses, before they can be classified. The coders would have to think and discuss quite carefully; inevitably, coding this kind of material is slow. Note that often a broad verbal label has been given, followed by some examples. We observe that this, too, must be a multiple-mention code.

Finally, here is an example of a frame-of-reference code. The question asked was: 'Taking all things into account, what would be the most likely cause for another world war? I don't mean just the things that happen before a war, like Pearl Harbor, but the real cause.' Here is the coding frame:

V no answer; there will be no war

X don't know

0 military preparations as such

1 a specific nation or group of nations is mentioned as responsible

2 conflicting economic interests

3 power conflicts, tendencies for nations to want to expand, get more control

4 economic and social needs of underprivileged peoples

5 ideological conflicts, differences in political belief and systems

6 human nature in general, man's aggressive tendencies, reference to 'instincts', etc.

7 moral-ethical problems, breakdown of values, loss of religious influence

8 people's mistrust of each other, misunderstandings due to different social traditions and experiences, cultural differences

9 other

As we see, here we do not code the contents of the responses, but rather the framework within which the respondent seems to be thinking, his frame of reference. This kind of code places quite a heavy burden of interpretation on the coder and requires a special effort to ensure reliability. The results, however, can be quite revealing and may make the effort worthwhile.

It is worth mentioning that the analysis of sentence-completion items and other projective devices proceeds in much the same way as that outlined above.

For the content-analysis methods applied to written documents, radio broadcasts, case histories, propaganda, etc. the reader may be referred to Festinger & Katz.[1]

The coding and punching process

Perhaps the first thing we should do after designing all the coding frames is to draw a second small sample of completed questionnaires and try out the new codes. After making any necessary amendments the coding frames may now be finally typed or duplicated and, where necessary, assembled in a *code book* that is distributed to every coder, together with coding instructions. The coding instructions should lay down some general principles, such as the way to deal with queries, the case-numbering system, the method of coding multiple-answer questions, and even such details as the type and color of the pen or pencil to be used. In large survey organizations there may be a separate coding department dealing, perhaps, with several surveys at a time, and obviously some hierarchical arrangements have to be made in order to regulate the various responsibilities and the flow of work. In particular, there should be a standard procedure for keeping track of each questionnaire from the moment it comes into the coding section, for it is very easy for questionnaires to get lost, if they happen to become query cases, or part of a try-out sample, or if they get mixed up with a batch of questionnaires from another survey.

Usually, it is best to let each coder work right through each questionnaire, going from question to question and from code to code until he comes to the final page, because he gains an overall picture of the respondent and can check on any apparent inconsistencies. Sometimes, however, there may be a good reason for allotting one question or one batch of questions to one particular coder, who will code those questions and nothing else. This may happen, for instance, if a particularly elaborate socio-economic class code is used, in which case it saves time and reduces inconsistencies if one coder becomes thoroughly familiar with the coding frame and codes no other questions.

Suppose, now, that a coder has read a response, has studied the coding frame and has decided into which category the answer falls; how should he indicate that classification? There are, broadly speaking, only two possibilities, each with its variations: the coder will put the number indicating the classification either on the questionnaire itself or on a separate sheet of paper, usually known as a punch sheet. To decide which is most appropriate in a given survey, we must consider both the proportion of free-answer questions and the work of the punch operators who will put the data on tape, punch cards or edge-punched cards. The punch operators work fastest and with the least amount of error when they can work more or less automatically. Any disturbance, such as poorly written or illegible figures, entries left out, many pages to turn, and so on will break the smooth rhythm of their work and will cause delays and rising costs. From the punch operators' point of view, punch sheets are probably ideal: they never see the original questionnaires, there is no text to read, no pages to turn, just long rows of figures to punch, and an easy check at the end of each case. A punch sheet might consist of a sheet or a set of sheets of vertically and horizontally lined paper with the variables across the top and the case numbers down the side, as is illustrated by Table 17.1.

Table 17.1

Questions:	Q1	Q2a	Q2b	Q3	Q4	Q5i	Q5ii	Q5iii	
Col.	6	7	8	9	10	11	12/13	14	etc.

Case
numbers:
  62700
  62701
  62702
  62703
  etc.

Each question is given its own column or columns (in the case of analysis by punch-card machines) or its own variable number (in the case of analysis by computer), and the first few places are allocated to the case number. The job of the coder is to fill in all the entries for each case; the job of the punch girl is to punch each row (across the page) of the punch sheet onto cards or tape. If the questionnaire requires more than eighty columns, a second punch sheet is stated for each case, and so on. It is most important that no empty spaces be left on a punch sheet unless the 'blank' position has a specific meaning on that column; the punch sheet should not be passed on to the punch operators until all the queries have been resolved. Some survey organizations prefer punch sheets of a different design.

This procedure is, as we have remarked, ideal from the punch operators' point of view, but how does it affect the coders? This will depend largely on the number of closed or precoded questions in the survey. If the survey consists entirely of precoded questions then it is usually wasteful to have the responses copied specially onto punch sheets, and in any case, no coding will be required, so that after checking, the completed questionnaires are sent straight on to the punching section, and the punching takes place from the original questionnaires. If only a handful of free-answer questions have been asked, while the large majority are precoded, then most likely the coders will be instructed to put the coding entries directly onto the questionnaires, probably in the right-hand margin in line with the written answer. The punch operators will then punch the precoded questions as before and will insert the code entries where they arise. If there are large numbers of free-answer questions in the survey, then the decision whether or not to have punch sheets becomes more difficult, since their use involves the coder not merely in putting his code entries in the correct place on the punch sheet (instead of in the margin of the questionnaire) but also in the copying of all the precoded responses onto the punch sheets – a tedious operation, which can cause errors. If we decide not to use a punch sheet in these circumstances then it would be as well to take this into account in the layout of the questionnaire itself. Otherwise, the punchers will have to search through a maze of printed questions in order to 'pick up ' circled or checked precodes, interspersed with entries made by the coders. A well-planned layout, for instance by having all precodes down the right-hand side, can make this work easier, faster and, above all, more accurate; remember, for instance, that if a punch operator misses one figure all the remaining figures for that case will be one place 'out'. For this reason also it is important to check all questionnaires as they come in, especially if they have been filled in by respondents and not by interviewers, to make sure that no questions have been left out. Once in a while, usually when time presses, it may be best to have the questionnaires punched twice: once in order to punch only the pre-coded questions, and a second (later) time to punch only the free-answer (coded) questions, perhaps from a punch sheet; the two sets of data can be amalgamated by the machines subsequently, if that is desired, since both sets will carry the identifying case numbers.

We may remark in passing that use can be made of the identifying case numbers for classification purposes. Suppose, for instance, that we have a sample of children selected through their schools. We may, for example, decide to give each child a six-figure number: the first digit to indicate sex (1 or 2, meaning boy or girl); the second digit to indicate district or area (assuming there are not more than ten districts represented in our sample); the third digit will indicate the school that the child attends (assuming there are not more than ten schools in each district); the fourth digit might be used to indicate the grade or level within the particular school; and the last two digits will identify any given child within his or her class. Thus, case number 279513 would mean, to the initiated, a fifth-grade girl in school 9 in district 7, identifiable as No. 13 on the list of names for her class. Likewise, we can quickly bring together all the third graders, or all the children from district 4, or all the boys from school 81 (meaning school 1 in district 8), and so forth. There is no need to insist on numbering all cases consecutively; if there are only three school districts represented in the sample, then the remaining numbers in that column will remain unused.

In most coding operations, the first hundred or so cases will be the slowest and will give rise to the largest proportion of queries. The coders, though they have been carefully briefed and though the codes have been made as explicit as possible, will inevitably differ in their coding of certain responses, and there are also likely to be weaknesses in the coding frame. From the start, therefore, we must organize a procedure for dealing with queries, a procedure for regular discussion of difficult cases, a procedure for making amendments in the codes or the establishment of special rulings, and a checking procedure. In any but the smallest surveys there should be a coding supervisor, whose job it is to organize and implement these procedures, to do some of the check coding, and to decide whether or not a code will be amended. Earlier, when we discussed the 'miscellaneous' category, we saw that amending a code is something that is not to be done lightly, since it will involve recoding; by resisting the temptation to 'stretch' categories and by classifying all doubtful responses under 'miscellaneous', we can reduce the work of recording if, at a later stage, we should decide to make a new category for some of the cases hitherto classified as miscellaneous. In any case, it is always best to keep the meaning of each category as clear as possible; this will cause fewer doubts when we come to interpret the findings.

The life of the coder is greatly eased if, throughout the survey, we keep to certain consistencies in designing the coding frames. For instance, we may decide always to code 'miscellaneous' or 'other' as category 9, 'no answer' or 'not ascertained' as category 0, and so on. If we use gradings or ratings, we should try to make them all follow the same direction, from positive to negative.

One useful refinement in the coding process is the instruction 'record', in the case of certain questions. The instruction means that the coder is to copy out verbatim what the respondent or the interviewer has written, together with the identifying case number. For instance, in an election study we may ask our coders to 'record' any references to the Communist party, in order to study their particular flavor more closely. Sometimes, we may give this instruction because we wish to look more closely at certain selected cases or to use their answers as illustrative quotations in our report.

Multiple-mention codes

We have several times made reference to multiple-mention codes. This is one solution to the problem that arises when the respondent gives or is asked to give more than one answer to a question. Suppose we have asked: 'What do you mostly do in your spare time?' and let us assume that we have developed a broad set of nine categories. We can arbitrarily decide to allot, say, three punch-card columns to this question, one each for the first, second and third answer. We may even wish to assume that the order of the answers indicates the importance they have for the respondent, so that the first column will contain the most important answers – though many would question this assumption. We will also have to ignore all fourth and subsequent answers, while having to cope at the same time with the problem that not everyone has given three answers, or even two. Moreover, when it comes to the statistical analysis, we will have to treat each set of answers independently, and since the frequency distribution of the first answers may well be very different from that of the second and the third answers, how are we to interpret these results? In questions such as these it may be better to have a different wording, for instance: 'What are the three things you most enjoy doing in your spare time? Please put them in order of their importance to you.' Now that we have a reasonable assurance that most respondents will produce the same number of answers, we have done away with any possible fourth or fifth answers, and we can feel fairly sure that the first answer really is the most important one. Furthermore, if we find that the frequency distribution of this answer differs from that of the other two, then we can make use of their relative importance to say, for example, that photography usually rates first place among middle-class men, whereas working-class men only mention it as a second or third choice.

There is, however, another solution to this problem that can be applied when phrasing the question in the above way is not suitable or would 'force' the answers too much. Let us consider again the example given earlier from a student-readership survey, concerning the different systems used in reading a textbook in the college library. We saw then that many students might use more than one system while working from the same book. What would happen if we coded these responses all on the same column? Technically speaking, there would be no difficulty in the case of punch-card analysis, since it is possible to punch up to twelve holes in the same column, and since the machines can produce frequency distributions for each position on every column. The only difficulty that may arise is the sorting problem: if we wished to classify respondents into a dozen broad groups in accordance with their reading systems, how would we classify a respondent who has used more than one system? Perhaps we could first sort him in with those who have used his first system, and then re-sort him in with those who have used his second system, and so on, though this does become rather tedious. For this reason, multiple-mention codes are best avoided for questions that will be used to group respondents into subsamples. From the statistical point of view, we must find a way of coping with the problem of having more answers than we have respondents. There are no difficulties in tabulating such data and turning them into percentages, even though such percentages will add up to more than 100 per cent. Similarly, if we wish to study group differences we can compare such percentages – but the problem of assessing statistical significance presents a difficulty, because the data are not independent.

Let us take this problem a little further. Suppose that we had obtained, in the above example, the data contained in Table 17.2 for two hundred men and fifty women students:

Table 17.2

	Men (N=200)	Women (N=50)
V don't know, no answer	8%	8%
X miscellaneous	10	8
0 chapter headings	11	14
1 skim chapter by chapter, then make notes	18	16
2 read from cover to cover	10	36
3 skim and make notes, skim and make notes	25	30
4 concentrate on one section only	3	12
5 use index, look up pages	30	30
6 read chapter summaries	3	2
7 just read conclusions	36	34
8 introduction only	10	10
9 read various sections thoroughly	10	14

We might be tempted to raise the general question: Are reading systems related to the respondent's sex? However, this would require us to calculate a 12×2 chi-squared test of significance on the raw frequencies from which these percentages are derived, and this is not possible since chi-squared assumes that the entries in the cells are independent – an assumption that is not justified where more than one answer comes from the same individual. What we might do, however, is to test each category against all the others put together, in a series of 2×2 chi-squared tests. If we look again at these percentages we notice a substantial sex difference on category 2 ('read from cover to cover'): 10 per cent for men versus 36 per cent for the women (or, in raw frequencies: 20 out of 200 men and 18 out of 50 women). We can now test all those who responded in terms of category 2 against all those who did not (all non-2 responses), i.e. 180 men and 32 women, with the aid of an ordinary 2×2 chi-squared test. This reduces the problem of lack of independence. It allows the respondent to give as many answers as he likes, which can all be coded and used, and it makes no assumptions about their relative importance to the respondent. Note that we do the chi-squared tests on the total number of *cases* in each sample, not the total number of responses. This, then, is a way in which we can deal with the statistical analysis of multiple-mention codes.

Notes

1. Festinger, L. and Katz, D. eds. (1953) *Research Methods in the Behavioral Sciences.* New York, Dryden Press.

Construct validity in psychological tests

Lee J. Cronbach and Paul E. Meehl

The logic of construct validation

Construct validation takes place when an investigator believes that his instrument reflects a particular construct, to which are attached certain meanings. The proposed interpretation generates specific testable hypotheses, which are a means of confirming or disconfirming the claim. The philosophy of science which we believe does most justice to actual scientific practice will now be briefly and dogmatically set forth. Readers interested in further study of the philosophical underpinning are referred to the works by Braithwaite,[4] (esp. Ch. III), Carnap,[5,6] (pp. 56–69), Pap,[24] Sellars,[26,27] Feigl,[9,10] Beck,[2] Kneale,[19] (pp. 92–110), Hempel,[14,15] (Sec. 7).

The nomological net
The fundamental principles are these:

1. Scientifically speaking, to 'make clear what something *is*' means to set forth the laws in which it occurs. We shall refer to the interlocking system of laws which constitute a theory as a *nomological network*.
2. The laws in a nomological network may relate (*a*) observable properties or quantities to each other; or (*b*) theoretical constructs to observables; or (*c*) different theoretical constructs to one another. These 'laws' may be statistical or deterministic.
3. A necessary condition for a construct to be scientifically admissible is that it occur in a nomological net, at least *some* of whose laws involve observables. Admissible constructs may be remote from observation, i.e., a long derivation may intervene between the nomologicals which implicitly define the construct, and the (derived) nomologicals of type *a*. These latter propositions permit predictions about events. The construct is not 'reduced' to the observations, but only combined with other constructs in the net to make predictions about observables.

Extract from L. J. Cronbach and P. E. Meehl 'Construct validity in psychological tests', *Psychological Bulletin*, 1955, **52**, 281–302.

4. 'Learning more about' a theoretical construct is a matter of elaborating the nomological network in which it occurs, or of increasing the definiteness of the components. At least in the early history of a construct the network will be limited, and the construct will as yet have few connections.
5. An enrichment of the net such as adding a construct or a relation to theory is justified if it generates nomologicals that are confirmed by observation or if it reduces the number of nomologicals required to predict the same observations. When observations will not fit into the network as it stands, the scientist has a certain freedom in selecting where to modify the network. That is, there may be alternative constructs or ways of organizing the net which for the time being are equally defensible.
6. We can say that 'operations' which are qualitatively very different 'overlap' or 'measure the same thing' if their positions in the nomological net tie them to the same construct variable. Our confidence in this identification depends upon the amount of inductive support we have for the regions of the net involved. It is not necessary that a direct observational comparison of the two operations be made – we may be content with an intranetwork proof indicating that the two operations yield estimates of the same network-defined quantity. Thus, physicists are content to speak of the 'temperature' of the sun and the 'temperature' of a gas at room temperature even though the test operations are nonoverlapping because this identification makes theoretical sense.

With these statements of scientific methodology in mind, we return to the specific problem of construct validity as applied to psychological tests. The preceding guide rules should reassure the 'toughminded', who fear that allowing construct validation opens the door to nonconfirmable test claims. *The answer is that unless the network makes contact with observations, and exhibits explicit, public steps of inference, construct validation cannot be claimed.* An admissible psychological construct must be behavior-relevant[28] (p. 15). For most tests intended to measure constructs, adequate criteria do not exist. This being the case, many such tests have been left unvalidated, or a finespun network of rationalizations has been offered as if it were validation. Rationalization is not construct validation. One who claims that his test reflects a construct cannot maintain his claim in the face of recurrent negative results because these results show that his construct is too loosely defined to yield verifiable inferences.

A rigorous (though perhaps probabilistic) chain of inference is required to establish a test as a measure of a construct. To validate a claim that a test measures a construct, a nomological net surrounding the concept must exist. When a construct is fairly new, there may be few specifiable associations by which to pin down the concept. As research proceeds, the construct sends out roots in many directions, which attach it to more and more facts or other constructs. Thus the electron has more accepted properties than the neutrino; *numerical ability* has more than *the second space factor*.

'Acceptance', which was critical in criterion-oriented and content validities, has now appeared in construct validity. Unless substantially the same nomological net is accepted by the several users of the construct, public validation is impossible. If A uses *aggressiveness* to mean overt assault on others, and B's usage includes repressed hostile reactions, evidence which convinces B that a test measures *aggressiveness* convinces A that the test does not. Hence, the investigator who proposes to establish a test as a measure of a construct must specify his network of theory sufficiently clearly that others can accept or reject it[20] (cf. p. 406). A consumer of the test who rejects the author's theory cannot accept the author's validation. He must validate the test for himself, if he wishes to show that it represents the construct as *he* defines it.

Two general qualifications are in order with reference to the methodological principles 1–6 set forth at the beginning of this section. Both of them concern the amount of 'theory', in any high-level sense of that word, which enters into a construct-defining network of laws or lawlike statements. We do not wish to convey the impression that one always has a very elaborate theoretical network, rich in hypothetical processes or entities.

Constructs as inductive summaries. In the early stages of development of a construct or even at more advanced stages when our orientation is thoroughly practical, little or no theory in the usual sense of the word need be involved. In the extreme case the hypothesized laws are formulated entirely in terms of descriptive (observational) dimensions although not all of the relevant observations have actually been made.

The hypothesized network 'goes beyond the data' only in the limited sense that it purports to *characterize* the behavior facets which belong to an observable but as yet only partially sampled cluster; hence, it generates predictions about hitherto unsampled regions of the phenotypic space. Even though no unobservables or high-order theoretical constructs are introduced, an element of inductive extrapolation appears in the claim that a cluster including some elements not-yet-observed has been identified. Since, as in any sorting or abstracting task involving a finite set of complex elements, several non-equivalent bases of categorization are available, the investigator may choose a hypothesis which generates erroneous predictions. The failure of a supposed, hitherto untried, member of the cluster to behave in the manner said to be characteristic of the group, or the finding that a nonmember of the postulated cluster does behave in this manner, may modify greatly our tentative construct.

For example, one might build an intelligence test on the basis of his background notions of 'intellect', including vocabulary, arithmetic calculation, general information, similarities, two-point threshold, reaction time and line bisection as subtests. The first four of these correlate, and he extracts a huge first factor. This becomes a second approximation of the intelligence construct, described by its pattern of loadings on the four tests. The other three tests have negligible loading on any common factor. On this evidence the investigator reinterprets intelligence as 'manipulation of words'. Subsequently it is discovered that test-stupid people are rated as unable to express their ideas, are easily taken in by fallacious arguments and misread complex directions. These data support the 'linguistic' definition of intelligence and the test's claim of validity *for* that construct. But then a block design test with pantomime instructions is found to be strongly saturated with the first factor. Immediately the purely 'linguistic' interpretation of Factor I becomes suspect. This finding, taken together with our initial acceptance of the others as relevant to the background concept of intelligence, forces us to reinterpret the concept once again.

If we simply *list* the tests or traits which have been shown to be saturated with the 'factor' or which belong to the cluster, no construct is employed. As soon as we even *summarize the properties* of this group of indicators – we are already making some guesses. Intensional characterization of a domain is hazardous since it selects (abstracts) properties and implies that new tests sharing those properties will behave as do the known tests in the cluster, and that tests not sharing them will not.

The difficulties in merely 'characterizing the surface cluster' are strikingly exhibited by the use of certain special and extreme groups for purposes of construct validation. The P_d scale of MMPI [MinnesotaMulti-phasic Personality Inventory] was originally derived and cross-validated upon hospitalized patients diagnosed 'Psychopathic personality, asocial and amoral type'.[21] Further research shows the scale to have a limited degree of predictive and concurrent validity for 'delinquency' more broadly defined.[3,13] Several studies show associations between P_d and very special 'criterion' groups which it would be ludicrous to identify as *'the* criterion' in the traditional sense. If one lists these heterogeneous groups and tries to characterize them intensionally, he faces enormous conceptual difficulties. For example, a recent survey of hunting accidents in Minnesota showed that hunters who had 'carelessly' shot someone were significantly elevated on P_d when compared with other hunters.[23] This is in line with one's theoretical expectations; when you ask MMPI 'experts' to predict for such a group they invariably predict P_d or M_a or both. The finding seems therefore to lend some slight support to the construct validity of the P_d scale. But of course it would be nonsense to *define* the P_d component 'operationally' in terms of, say, accident proneness. We might try to subsume the original phenotype and the hunting-accident proneness under some broader category, such as 'Disposition to violate society's rules, whether legal, moral, or just *sensible*.' But now we have ceased to have a neat operational criterion, and are using instead a rather vague and wide-range class. Besides, there is worse to come. We want the class specification to cover a group trend that (nondelinquent) high school students judged by their peer group as least 'responsible' score over a full sigma higher on P_d than those judged most 'responsible'[11] (p. 75). Most of the behaviors contributing to such sociometric choices fall well within the range of socially permissible action; the proffered criterion specification is still too restrictive. Again, any clinician familiar with MMPI lore would predict an elevated P_d on a sample of (nondelinquent) professional actors. Chyatte's confirmation of this prediction[7] tends to support *both:* (*a*) the theory sketch of 'what the P_d factor is, psychologically'; and (*b*) the claim of the P_d scale to construct validity for this hypothetical factor. Let the reader try his hand at writing a brief phenotypic criterion specification that will cover both trigger-happy hunters and Broadway actors! And if he should be ingenious enough to achieve this, does his definition also encompass Hovey's report that high P_d predicts the judgments 'not shy' and 'unafraid of mental patients' made upon nurses by their supervisors[16] (p. 143)? And then we have Gough's report that *low* P_d is associated with ratings as 'good-natured'[12] (p. 40), Roessell's data showing that high P_d is predictive of 'dropping out of high school'.[25] The point is that all seven of these 'criterion' dispositions would be readily guessed by any clinician having even superficial familiarity with MMPI interpretation; but to mediate these inferences explicitly requires quite a few hypotheses about dynamics, constituting an admittedly sketchy (but far from vacuous) network defining the genotype *psychopathic deviate*.

Vagueness of present psychological laws. This line of thought leads directly to our second important qualification upon the network schema. The idealized picture is one of a tidy set of postulates which jointly entail the desired theorems; since some of the theorems are coordinated to the observation base, the system constitutes an implicit definition of the theoretical primitives and gives them an indirect empirical meaning. In practice, of course, even the most advanced physical sciences only approximate this ideal. Questions of 'categoricalness' and the like, such as logicians raise about pure calculi, are hardly even statable for empirical networks. (What, for example, would be the desiderata of a 'well-formed formula' in molar behavior theory?) Psychology works with crude, half-explicit formulations. We do not worry about such advanced formal questions as 'whether all molar-behavior statements are decidable by appeal to the postulates' because we know that no existing theoretical network suffices to predict even the *known* descriptive laws. Nevertheless, the sketch of a network is there; if it were not, we would not be saying *anything* intelligible about our constructs. We do not have the rigorous implicit definitions of formal calculi (which still, be it noted, usually permit of a multiplicity of interpretations). Yet the vague, avowedly incomplete network still gives the constructs whatever meaning they do have. When the network is very incomplete, having many strands missing entirely and some constructs tied in only by tenuous threads, then the 'implicit definition' of these constructs is disturbingly loose; one might say that the meaning of the constructs is underdetermined. *Since the meaning of theoretical constructs is set forth by stating the laws in which they occur, our incomplete knowledge of the laws of nature produces a vagueness in our constructs* (see Hempel,[15]; Kaplan,[17]; Pap,[24]). We will be able to say 'what anxiety is' when we know all of the laws involving it; meanwhile, since we are in the process of discovering these laws, we do not yet know precisely what anxiety is.

Conclusions regarding the network after experimentation

The proposition that x per cent of test variance is accounted for by the construct is inserted into the accepted network. The network then generates a testable prediction about the relation of the test scores to certain other variables, and the investigator gathers data. If prediction and result are in harmony, he can retain his belief that the test measures the construct. The construct is at best adopted, never demonstrated to be 'correct'.

We do not first 'prove' the theory, and then validate the test, nor conversely. In any probable inductive type of inference from a pattern of observations, we examine the relation between the total network of theory and observations. The system involves propositions relating test to construct, construct to other constructs, and finally relating some of these constructs to observables. In ongoing research the chain of inference is very complicated. Kelly and Fiske[18] (p. 124) give a complex diagram showing the numerous inferences required in validating a prediction from assessment techniques, where theories about the criterion situation are as integral a part of the prediction as are the test data. A predicted empirical relationship permits us to test all the propositions leading to that prediction. Traditionally the proposition claiming to interpret the test has been set apart as the hypothesis being tested, but actually the evidence is significant for all parts of the chain. If the prediction is not confirmed, any link in the chain may be wrong.

A theoretical network can be divided into subtheories used in making particular predictions. All the events successfully predicted through a subtheory are of course evidence in favor of that theory. Such a subtheory may be so well confirmed by voluminous and diverse evidence that we can reasonably view a particular experiment as relevant only to the test's validity. If the theory, combined with a proposed test interpretation, mispredicts in this case, it is the latter which must be abandoned. On the other hand, the accumulated evidence for a test's construct validity may be so strong that an instance of misprediction will force us to modify the subtheory employing the construct rather than deny the claim that the test measures the construct.

Most cases in psychology today lie somewhere between these extremes. Thus, suppose we fail to find a greater incidence of 'homosexual signs' in the Rorschach records of paranoid patients. Which is more strongly disconfirmed – the Rorschach signs or the orthodox theory of paranoia? The negative finding shows the bridge between the two to be undependable, but this is all we can say. The bridge cannot be used unless one end is placed on solider ground. The investigator must decide which end it is best to relocate.

Numerous successful predictions dealing with phenotypically diverse 'criteria' give greater weight to the claim of construct validity than do fewer predictions, or predictions involving very similar behaviors. In arriving at diverse predictions, the hypothesis of test validity is connected each time to a subnetwork largely independent of the portion previously used. Success of these derivations testifies to the inductive power of the test-validity statement, and renders it unlikely that an equally effective alternative can be offered.

Implications of negative evidence
The investigator whose prediction and data are discordant must make strategic decisions. His result can be interpreted in three ways:

1. The test does not measure the construct variable.
2. The theoretical network which generated the hypothesis is incorrect.
3. The experimental design failed to test the hypothesis properly. (Strictly speaking this may be analyzed as a special case of 2, but in practice the distinction is worth making.)

For further research. If a specific fault of procedure makes the third a reasonable possibility, his proper response is to perform an adequate study, meanwhile making no report. When faced with the other two alternatives, he may decide that his test does not measure the construct adequately. Following that decision, he will perhaps prepare and validate a new test. Any rescoring or new interpretative procedure for the original instrument, like a new test, requires validation *by means of a fresh body of data.*

The investigator may regard interpretation 2 as more likely to lead to eventual advances. It is legitimate for the investigator to call the network defining the construct into question, if he has confidence in the test. Should the investigator decide that some step in the network is unsound, he may be able to invent an alternative network. Perhaps he modifies the network by splitting a concept into two or more portions, e.g. by designating types of *anxiety*, or perhaps he specifies added conditions under which a generalization holds. When an investigator modifies the theory in such a manner, he is now required to *gather a fresh body of data* to test the altered hypotheses. This step should normally precede publication of the modified theory. If the new data are consistent with the modified network, he is free from the fear that his nomologicals were gerrymandered to fit the peculiarities of his first sample of observations. He can now trust his test to some extent, because his test results behave as predicted.

The choice among alternatives, like any strategic decision, is a gamble as to which course of action is the best investment of effort. Is it wise to modify the theory? That depends on how well the system is confirmed by prior data, and how well the modifications fit available observations. Is it worth while to modify the test in the hope that it will fit the construct? That depends on how much evidence there is – apart from this abortive experiment – to support the hope, and also on how much it is worth to the investigator's ego to salvage the test. The choice among alternatives is a matter of research planning.

For practical use of the test. The consumer can accept a test as a measure of a construct only when there is a strong positive fit between predictions and subsequent data. When the evidence from a proper investigation of a published test is essentially negative, it should be reported as a stop sign to discourage use of the test pending a reconciliation of test and construct, or final abandonment of the test. If the test has not been published, it should be restricted to research use until some degree of validity is established[1]. The consumer can await the results of the investigator's gamble with confidence that proper application of the scientific method will ultimately tell whether the test has value. Until the evidence is in, he has no justification for employing the test as a basis for terminal decisions. The test may serve, at best, only as a source of suggestions about individuals to be confirmed by other evidence[8,22].

There are two perspectives in test validation. From the viewpoint of the psychological practitioner, the burden of proof is on the test. A test should not be used to measure a trait until its proponent establishes that predictions made from such measures are consistent with the best available theory of the trait. In the view of the test developer, however, both the test and the theory are under scrutiny. He is free to say *to himself privately,* 'If my test disagrees with the theory, so much the worse for the theory.' This way lies delusion, unless he continues his research using a better theory.

Reporting of positive results

The test developer who finds positive correspondence between his proposed interpretation and data is expected to report the basis for his validity claim. Defending a claim of construct validity is a major task, not to be satisfied by a discourse without data. The *Technical Recom-*

mendations have little to say on reporting of construct validity. Indeed, the only detailed suggestions under that heading refer to correlations of the test with other measures, together with a cross reference to some other sections of the report. The two key principles, however, call for the most comprehensive type of reporting. The manual for any test 'should report all available information which will assist the user in determining what psychological attributes account for variance in test scores'[28] (p. 27). And, 'The manual for a test which is used primarily to assess postulated attributes of the individual should outline the theory on which the test is based and organize whatever partial validity data there are to show in what way they support the theory'[28] (p. 28). It is recognized, by a classification as 'very desirable' rather than 'essential', that the latter recommendaion goes beyond present practice of test authors.

The proper goals in reporting construct validation are to make clear (*a*) what interpretation is proposed, (*b*) how adequately the writer believes this interpretation is substantiated, and (*c*) what evidence and reasoning lead him to this belief. Without *a* the construct validity of the test is of no use to the consumer. Without *b* the consumer must carry the entire burden of evaluating the test research. Without *c* the consumer or reviewer is being asked to take *a* and *b* on faith. The test manual cannot always present an exhaustive statement on these points, but it should summarize and indicate where complete statements may be found.

To specify the interpretation, the writer must state what construct he has in mind, and what meaning he gives to that construct. For a construct which has a short history and has built up few connotations, it will be fairly easy to indicate the presumed properties of the construct, i.e. the nomologicals in which it appears. For a construct with a longer history, a summary of properties and references to previous theoretical discussions may be appropriate. It is especially critical to distinguish proposed interpretations from other meanings previously given the same construct. The validator faces no small task; he must somehow communicate a theory to his reader.

To evaluate his evidence calls for a statement like the conclusions from a program of research, noting what is well substantiated and what alternative interpretations have been considered and rejected. The writer must note what portions of his proposed interpretation are speculations, extrapolations, or conclusions from insufficient data. The author has an ethical responsibility to prevent unsubstantiated interpretations from appearing as truths. A claim is unsubstantiated unless the evidence for the claim is public, so that other scientists may review the evidence, criticize the conclusions and offer alternative interpretations.

The report of evidence in a test manual must be as complete as any research report, except where adequate public reports can be cited. Reference to something 'observed by the writer in many clinical cases' is worthless as evidence. Full case reports, on the other hand, may be a valuable source of evidence so long as these cases are representative and negative instances receive due attention. The report of evidence must be interpreted with reference to the theoretical network in such a manner that the reader sees why the author regards a particular correlation or experiment as confirming (or throwing doubt upon) the proposed interpretation. Evidence collected by others must be taken fairly into account.

Validation of a complex test 'as a whole'

Special questions must be considered when we are investigating the validity of a test which is aimed to provide information about several constructs. In one sense, it is naive to inquire 'Is this test valid?' One does not validate a test, but only a principle for making inferences. If a test yields many different types of inferences some of them can be valid and others invalid (cf. Technical Recommendation C2: 'The manual should report the validity of each type of inference for which a test is recommended'). From this point of view, every topic sentence in the typical book on Rorschach interpretation presents a hypothesis requiring validation, and one should validate inferences about each aspect of the personality separately and in turn, just as he would want information on the validity (concurrent or predictive) for each scale of MMPI.

There is, however, another defensible point of view. If a test is purely empirical, based strictly on observed connections between response to an item and some criterion, then of course the validity of one scoring key for the test does not make validation for its other scoring keys any less necessary. But a test may be developed on the basis of a theory which in itself provides a linkage between the various keys and the various criteria. Thus, while Strong's Vocational Interest Blank is developed empirically, it also rests on a 'theory' that a youth can be expected to be satisfied in an occupation if he has interests common to men now happy in the occupation. When Strong finds that those with high Engineering interest scores in college are preponderantly in engineering careers 19 years later, he has partly validated the proposed use of the Engineer score (predictive validity). Since the evidence is consistent with the theory on which all the test keys were built, this evidence alone increases the presumption that the *other* keys have predictive validity. How strong is this presumption? Not very, from the viewpoint of the traditional skepticism of science. Engineering interest may stabilize early, while interests in art or management or social work are still unstable. A claim cannot be made that the whole Strong approach is valid just because one score shows predictive validity. But if thirty interest scores were investigated longitudinally and all of them showed the type of validity predicted by Strong's theory, we would indeed be caviling to say that this evidence gives no confidence in the long-range validity of the thirty-first score.

Confidence in a theory is increased as more relevant evidence confirms it, but it is always possible that tomorrow's investigation will render the theory obsolete. The Technical Recommendations suggest a rule of reason, and ask for evidence for each *type* of inference for which a test is recommended. It is stated that no test developer can present predictive validities for all possible criteria; similarly, no developer can run all possible experimental tests of his proposed interpretation. But the recommendation is more subtle than advice that a lot of validation is better than a little.

Consider the Rorschach test. It is used for many inferences, made by means of nomological networks at several levels. At a low level are the simple unrationalized correspondences presumed to exist between certain signs and psychiatric diagnoses. Validating such a sign does nothing to substantiate Rorschach theory. For other Rorschach formulas an explicit a priori rationale exists (for instance, high $F\%$ interpreted as implying rigid control of impulses). Each time such a sign shows correspondence with criteria, its rationale is supported just a little. At a still higher level of abstraction, a considerable body of theory surrounds the general area of *outer control,* interlacing many different constructs. As evidence cumulates, one should be able to decide what specific inference-making chains within this system can be depended upon. One should also be able to conclude – or deny – that so much of the system has stood up under test that one has some confidence in even the untested lines in the network.

In addition to relatively delimited nomological networks surrounding *control* or *aspiration,* the Rorschach interpreter usually has an overriding theory of the test as a whole. This may be a psychoanalytic theory, a theory of perception and set, or a theory stated in terms of learned habit patterns. Whatever the theory of the interpreter, whenever he validates an inference from the system, he obtains some reason for added confidence in his overriding system. His total theory is not tested, however, by experiments dealing with only one limited set of constructs. The test developer must investigate far-separated, independent sections of the network. The more diversified the predictions the system is required to make, the greater confidence we can have that only minor parts of the system will later prove faulty. Here we begin to glimpse a logic to defend the judgment that the test and its whole interpretative system is valid at some level of confidence.

There are enthusiasts who would conclude from the foregoing paragraphs that since there is some evidence of correct, diverse predictions made from the Rorschach, the test as a whole can now be accepted as validated. This conclusion overlooks the negative evidence. Just one finding contrary to expectation, based on sound research, is sufficient to wash a whole theoretical structure away. Perhaps the remains can be salvaged to form a new structure. But this structure now must be exposed to fresh risks, and sound negative evidence will destroy it in turn. There is sufficient negative evidence to prevent acceptance of the Rorschach and its accompanying interpretative structures as a whole.

So long as any aspects of the overriding theory stated for the test have been disconfirmed, this structure must be rebuilt.

Talk of areas and structures may seem not to recognize those who would interpret the personality 'globally'. They may argue that a test is best validated in matching studies. Without going into detailed questions of matching methodology, we can ask whether such a study validates the nomological network 'as a whole'. The judge does employ some network in arriving at his conception of his subject, integrating specific inferences from specific data. Matching studies, if successful, demonstrate only that each judge's interpretative theory has some validity, that is not completely a fantasy. Very high consistency between judges is required to show that they are using the same network, and very high success in matching is required to show that the network is dependable.

If inference is less than perfectly dependable, we must know which aspects of the interpretative network are least dependable and which are most dependable. Thus, even if one has considerable confidence in a test 'as a whole' because of frequent successful inferences, one still returns as an ultimate aim to the request of the Technical Recommendation for separate evidence on the validity of each type of inference to be made.

Recapitulation

Construct validation was introduced in order to specify types of research required in developing tests for which the conventional views on validation are inappropriate. Personality tests, and some tests of ability, are interpreted in terms of attributes for which there is no adequate criterion. This paper indicates what sorts of evidence can substantiate such an interpretation, and how such evidence is to be interpreted. The following points made in the discussion are particularly significant.

1. A construct is defined implicitly by a network of associations or propositions in which it occurs. Constructs employed at different stages of research vary in definiteness.
2. Construct validation is possible only when some of the statements in the network lead to predicted relations among observables. While some observables may be regarded as 'criteria', the construct validity of the criteria themselves is regarded as under investigation.
3. The network defining the construct, and the derivation leading to the predicted observation, must be reasonably explicit so that validating evidence may be properly interpreted.
4. Many types of evidence are relevant to construct validity, including content validity, interitem correlations, interest correlations, test-'criterion' correlations, studies of stability over time and

stability under experimental intervention. High correlations and high stability may constitute either favorable or unfavorable evidence for the proposed interpretation, depending on the theory surrounding the construct.

5. When a predicted relation fails to occur, the fault may lie in the proposed interpretation of the test or in the network. Altering the network so that it can cope with the new observations is, in effect, redefining the construct. Any such new interpretation of the test must be validated by a fresh body of data before being advanced publicly. Great care is required to avoid substituting a posteriori rationalizations for proper validation.

6. Construct validity cannot generally be expressed in the form of a single simple coefficient. The data often permit one to establish upper and lower bounds for the proportion of test variance which can be attributed to the construct. The integration of diverse data into a proper interpretation cannot be an entirely quantitative process.

7. Constructs may vary in nature from those very close to 'pure description' (involving little more than extrapolation of relations among observation-variables) to highly theoretical constructs involving hypothesized entities and processes, or making identifications with constructs of other sciences.

8. The investigation of a test's construct validity is not essentially different from the general scientific procedures for developing and confirming theories.

Without in the least *advocating* construct validity as preferable to the other three kinds (concurrent, predictive, content), we do believe it imperative that psychologists make a place for it in their methodological thinking, so that its rationale, its scientific legitimacy and its dangers may be explicit and familiar. This would be preferable to the widespread current tendency to engage in what actually amounts to construct validation research and use of constructs in practical testing, while talking an 'operational' methodology which, if adopted, would force research into a mold it does not fit.

References

1. American Psychological Association (1953) *Ethical Standards of Psychologists.* Washington, D.C.: American Psychological Association, Inc.
2. Beck, L. W. (1950) 'Constructions and inferred entities', *Phil. Sci.,* **17.** Reprinted in H. Feigl and M. Brodbeck (eds) (1953) *Readings in the Philosophy of Science.* New York: Appleton-Century-Crofts, pp. 368–81.
3. Blair, W. R. N. (1950) 'A comparative study of disciplinary offenders and non-offenders in the Canadian Army', *Canad. J. Psychol.,* **4,** 49–62.
4. Braithwaite, R. B. (1953) *Scientific Explanation.* Cambridge: Cambridge University Press.

5. Carnap, R. (1953a) 'Empiricism, semantics, and ontology', *Rev. int. de Phil.*, 1950, II, 20–40. Reprinted in P. P. Wiener (ed.), *Readings in Philosophy of Science*, New York: Scribner's, pp. 509–21.
6. Carnap, R. (1953b) *Foundations of Logic and Mathematics. International Encyclopedia of Unified Science*, I, No. 3. Pages 56–69 reprinted as 'The interpretation of physics', in H. Fiegl and M. Brodbeck (eds), *Readings in the Philosophy of Science*. New York: Appleton-Century-Crofts, pp. 309–18.
7. Chyatte, C. (1949) 'Psychological characteristics of a group of professional actors', *Occupations*, **27**, 245–50.
8. Cronbach, L. J. (1955) 'The counselor's problems from the perspective of communication theory', in Vivian H. Hewer (ed.), *New Perspectives in Counseling*. Minneapolis: University of Minnesota Press.
9. Feigl, H. (1950) 'Existential hypotheses', *Phil. Sci.*, **17**, 35–62.
10. Feigl, H. (1953) 'Confirmability and confirmation', *Rev. int. de Phil.*, 1951, **5**, 1–12. Reprinted in P. P. Wiener (ed.), *Readings in Philosophy of Science*. New York: Scribner's, pp. 522–30.
11. Gough, H. G., McClosky, H. and Meehl, P. E. (1952) 'A personality scale for social responsibility', *J. abnorm. soc. Psychol.*, **47**, 73–80.
12. Gough, H. G., McKee, M. G. and Yandell, R. J. (1953) 'Adjective check list analyses of a number of selected psychometric and assessment variables'. Unpublished manuscript. Berkeley: IPAR.
13. Hathaway, S. R. and Monachesi, E. D. (1953) *Analyzing and Predicting Juvenile Delinquency with the MMPI*. Minneapolis: University of Minnesota Press.
14. Hempel, C. G. (1952) 'Problems and changes in the empiricist criterion of meaning', *Rev. int. de Phil.*, 1950, **4**, 41–63. Reprinted in L. Linsky, *Semantics and the Philosophy of Language*. Urbana: University of Illinois Press, pp. 163–85.
15. Hempel, C. G. (1952) *Fundamentals of Concept Formation in Empirical Science*. Chicago: University of Chicago Press.
16. Hovey, H. B. (1953) 'MMPI profiles and personality characteristics', *J. consult. Psychol.*, **17**, 142–46.
17. Kaplan, A. (1946) 'Definition and specification of meaning', *J. Phil.*, **43**, 281–88.
18. Kelly, E. L. and Fiske, D. W. (1951) *The Prediction of Performance in Clinical Psychology*. Ann Arbor: University of Michigan Press.
19. Kneale, W. (1953) *Probability and Induction*. Oxford: Clarendon Press, 1949. Pages 92–110 reprinted as 'Induction, explanation, and transcendent hypotheses', in H. Feigl and M. Brodbeck (eds), *Readings in the Philosophy of Science*. New York: Appleton-Century-Crofts, pp. 353–67.
20. Macfarlane, J. W. (1942) 'Problems of validation inherent in projective methods', *Amer. J. Orthopsychiat.*, **12**, 405–10.
21. McKinley, J. C. and Hathaway, S. R. (1944) 'The MMPI: V. Hysteria, hypomania, and psychopathic deviate', *J. appl. Psychol.*, **28**, 153–74.
22. Meehl, P. E. and Rosen, A. (1955) 'Antecedent probability and the efficiency of psychometric signs, patterns or cutting scores', *Psychol. Bull.*, **52**, 194–216.
23. *Minnesota Hunter Casualty Study*. (1954) St Paul: Jacob Schmidt Brewing Company.
24. Pap, A. (1953) 'Reduction-sentences and open concepts', *Methodos*, **5**, 3–30.
25. Roessel, F. P. (1954) 'MMPI results for high school drop-outs and graduates'. Unpublished doctor's dissertation, University of Minnesota.
26. Sellars, W. S. (1948) 'Concepts as involving laws and inconceivable without them', *Phil. Sci.*, **15**, 287–315.
27. Sellars, W. S. (1954) 'Some reflections on language games', *Phil. Sci.*, **21**, 204–28.
28. 'Technical recommendations for psychological tests and diagnostic techniques', *Psychol. Bull. Supplement*, 1954, **51**, 2, Part 2, 1–38.

Attitude measurement: use of coefficient alpha with cluster or factor analysis

Aubrey McKennell

(puit AS)

Introduction

Attitudes occupy an interdisciplinary position, and in assessing them sociologists have long utilized scaling techniques – Thurstone, Likert, Guttman – designed primarily by psychologists. Yet for exploratory surveys of the general population these techniques have definite limitations.[1] This paper describes a new approach. Originally designed as an adaptation of psychological test theory to meet the requirements of this special research situation,[2] it should have applications to scale construction in other contexts.

In exploring the structure of attitudes in a given topic area it is good practice to try out a representative[3] set of opinion statements (items) in a pilot or scale-development study, and to be prepared to use many more items at this stage than need be retained eventually. The aim is first to explore and discover the main dimensions along which individuals vary. Each dimension can then be represented economically in the survey proper using fewer items. Economy is necessary since sociologists rarely, if ever, carry out a survey solely in order to operationalize a concept.[4] Scale construction is undertaken to provide more refined and reliable variables than do the answers to the individual items, but only as a step in preparation for further analysis. Short scales are therefore at a premium in the main survey. Apart from problems of rapport in the interview situation, questionnaire space and interview time must be reserved for enquiry into the demographic, sociological and behavioural variables with which the attitude data will ultimately be related.[5]

The problem is how to achieve both economy and representativeness in attitude measurement without forfeiting the requirements of reliability and homogeneity inherent in scaling. For economy, two opposing principles in scale construction have to be reconciled: the more items on which a scale is based the higher its reliability, yet as scales become too long they require a disproportionate amount of

From *Sociology*, 1970, **4**, 227–45.

questionnaire space. For representativeness, techniques are needed which will search out the true dimensionality of the data, without unduly favouring the hypothesis that the area is undimensional.[5] The quest for representativeness, it will also be argued, entails, in addition, a 'construct validity' approach to the relation between concept and measure.

The simplest technique for finding the main dimensions underlying an item set is cluster analysis, in which items are assigned to subsets so that the level of intercorrelation of items within a subset is high and that between subsets is low. The same objective is implied in constructing homogeneous tests by means of factor analysis.[6] Both factor and cluster analysis are fairly well known techniques, but neither provides information on the reliability of measurement, or on the cost in reliability when a reduced set of items is carried forward from pilot to main survey.

A quantitative expression for the trade-off between scale length and reliability is given in one version of the formula for the alpha coefficient, discussed below. It is shown how this formula can be used to derive rapid reliability estimates from the intercorrelations between the defining items of a cluster or factor, or some selection of these items. The method is rapid because in a factor or cluster analysis the item intercorrelations are already available and, given these, approximate values of alpha can be looked up in a table. As well as aiding judgements about test length, the alpha formula also leads to an item analysis procedure. Finally the formula clarifies the distinction and shows the relation between homogeneity and reliability, allowing the scale constructor to take both aspects into account in the final scale. Altogether, the use of alpha in conjunction with factor or cluster analysis provides a total approach to scale construction which compares favourably with other techniques. These claims are illustrated with an example below. But first it is necessary to give an account of some of the properties of the alpha coefficient.

Alpha as a coefficient of reliability

'Alpha' is the label given by Cronbach (1951) to a particular type of coefficient which measures the reliability of a test, or item battery, in the special sense of its internal consistency. This coefficient is at the centre of modern psychometric thinking on the subject of reliability, of which only a brief and necessarily oversimplified account is given here.[7]

A test is perfectly reliable if individuals obtain exactly the same score on it on two separate occasions. The degree of reliability can, in principle, be measured by testing a sample of individuals twice and finding the correlation between the two sets of scores. This correlation (or actually its square) is then the coefficient of reliability, varying between zero and unity. This test-retest method of estimating reliability is seldom practical in the survey context since it requires a second approach to the same informants. Moreover it has theoretical difficulties. The informants may remember their previous replies giving a coefficient that is spuriously high, or if the time between testings is too great there may have been a genuine change in the function being measured, resulting in a coefficient that is spuriously low.

For these reasons a split-half method of estimating reliability is often used. The series of items constituting the test is divided into two halves, and treated as two tests. The correlation between the scores on the two half-tests is then found and corrected for the effects of halving.[8] Alpha is directly related to this split-half method of estimating reliability. Several split-half coefficients can be obtained from the same testing, and these will vary somewhat, depending on which items are allocated to one or the other half-tests. It can be shown (Cronbach, 1951) that alpha is the mean of all possible split-half coefficients.

The case for knowing the reliability of measuring instruments should be self-evident. A variable measured with zero or near-zero reliability would show no correlation with any other variable whatsoever. The researcher might then conclude that it was unimportant. In fact, it could be a very important variable, and the correct conclusion would be that he had failed to measure it. In general, the maximum correlation any variable can have with another is limited by the reliability with which it is measured. Two variables may be perfectly correlated in reality, but the obtained correlation will be low if the reliability of the measuring instruments is low. From a knowledge of the reliability coefficient, however, it is possible to calculate what the true correlation would be if one had a perfect measuring instrument.[9]

These are important uses of the reliability coefficient which make a knowledge of the alpha value for a test important in its own right. In this paper, however, we are concerned less with these applications than with the way a special version of the formula for alpha can be adapted for test construction purposes along with factor or cluster analysis.

The 'short-cut' formula for coefficient alpha

The entire test construction procedure in this paper is based on the properties of the following formula:

$$\text{Alpha} = \frac{n\bar{r}_{ij}}{1 + (n-1)\,\bar{r}_{ij}} \tag{1}$$

where n = the number of separate items in the test
$\bar{r}_{ij}$ = the average of all the inter-item correlations

and alpha is the reliability of the total score obtained by summing the score on the separate items.

This is not the usual form of the formula for coefficient alpha which appears in the textbooks (e.g. Baggaley, 1964; Guilford, 1954). It is an approximate form.[10] The approximation to the correct value will be very close, however, under the conditions of application recommended in this paper – namely when applied to the items in a relatively homogeneous cluster. The virtue of using this particular formula is the short-cut it provides to the estimation of alpha whenever the intercorrelations between items are available, as they are in cluster or factor analysis. It is then a simple matter to take any subset of items and compute the average of all their intercorrelations. This value, $\bar{r}_{ij}$, may then be entered into the above formula together with the value of n, the number of items. The value of alpha, so obtained, is an estimate of the reliability of the n items used as a test battery. It is not necessary to solve the formula directly each time, if use is made of Table 19.1. This gives the values for alpha corresponding to different combinations and n and $\bar{r}_{ij}$.

Table 19.1 Alpha Values by Approximate Formula*

$\bar{r}_{ij}$ Average inter-item correlation	Number of items in the test (n)											
	2	3	4	5	7	10	15	20	25	30	40	50
0.05	0.10	0.14	0.17	0.21	0.27	0.34	0.44	0.51	0.57	0.61	0.68	0.72
0.10	0.18	0.25	0.31	0.36	0.44	0.53	0.63	0.69	0.74	0.77	0.82	0.85
0.15	0.26	0.35	0.41	0.47	0.55	0.64	0.73	0.78	0.81	0.84	0.88	0.90
0.20	0.33	0.43	0.50	0.56	0.64	0.71	0.79	0.83	0.86	0.88	0.91	0.93
0.25	0.40	0.50	0.57	0.63	0.70	0.77	0.83	0.87	0.89	0.91	0.93	0.94
0.30	0.46	0.56	0.63	0.68	0.75	0.81	0.87	0.90	0.91	0.92	0.94	0.96
0.35	0.52	0.62	0.68	0.73	0.79	0.84	0.89	0.92	0.93	0.94	0.96	0.96
0.40	0.57	0.67	0.73	0.77	0.82	0.87	0.91	0.93	0.94	0.95	0.96	0.97
0.45	0.62	0.71	0.77	0.80	0.85	0.89	0.92	0.94	0.95	0.96	0.97	0.98
0.50	0.67	0.75	0.80	0.83	0.88	0.91	0.94	0.95	0.96	0.97	0.98	0.98
0.55	0.71	0.79	0.83	0.86	0.90	0.92	0.95	0.96	0.97	0.97	0.98	0.98
0.60	0.75	0.82	0.86	0.88	0.91	0.94	0.96	0.97	0.97	0.98	0.98	0.99
0.65	0.79	0.85	0.88	0.90	0.93	0.95	0.97	0.97	0.98	0.98	0.99	0.99
0.70	0.82	0.88	0.90	0.92	0.94	0.96	0.97	0.98	0.98	0.99	0.99	0.99
0.75	0.86	0.90	0.92	0.94	0.95	0.97	0.98	0.98	0.99	0.99	0.99	0.99
0.80	0.89	0.92	0.94	0.95	0.97	0.98	0.98	0.98	0.99	0.99	0.99	1.00

*Approximate formula: $\dfrac{n\bar{r}_{ij}}{1 + (n-1)\bar{r}_{ij}}$

Another virtue of the above formula is that it brings out very well how the reliability of a test depends on its internal consistency or homogeneity ($\bar{r}_{ij}$) and its length (n). This can be seen on common sense grounds. With perfectly reliable items all measuring the same thing, any one of the items would be all that was necessary to measure the particular dimension with perfect reliability. For such items the value of $\bar{r}_{ij}$, and the value of alpha, would be unity. In practice, however, when an informant responds to a single item his reply may be haphazard or, what comes to the same thing statistically, may be determined by some idiosyncratic interpretation of the item.[11] As a result of these response 'errors' even items which appear from their content to tap the same dimension hardly ever intercorrelate perfectly. Values of $\bar{r}_{ij}$ vary widely with the topic area under investigation, but seldom exceed 0.5. Unreliability at the item level is of course the main justification for scaling. Since the errors on particular items are random they tend to cancel out; and the total score obtained by adding the scores on successive items tends increasingly to be determined by the common factor running through the items. Cronbach (1951) shows in fact that alpha will be an estimate of the first factor variance in a test unless it contains distinct clusters of items. A test will not of course contain distinct clusters if it consists of items which themselves define a single cluster or factor, as recommended in this paper.

Use of alpha with factor and cluster analysis

The use of alpha in attitude scale construction will be illustrated with some data selected from a survey on smoking habits and attitudes (McKennell and Thomas, 1967). Table 19.2 shows the matrix of intercorrelations between twelve statements of opinion about smoking. Opinions concerning the health effects of smoking were studied in another matrix leading to a separate scale (actually scales) concerned with the health aspect. The objective in Table 19.2 was to construct a scale to measure in general terms, without reference to specific reasons, the degree of approval or disapproval of smoking. On analysis, the correlations between the items in this putative scale revealed two distinct clusters, as reflected in Table 19.2.

Table 19.2 is a clustered correlation matrix. That is, the original correlations among the items have been rearranged so that the correlation matrix itself reveals the clusters and the relation between clusters. This is achieved by renumbering the items in the study so those that cluster together are in sequence along the borders of the correlation matrix. This has the effect of throwing on to the main diagonal of the matrix the triangular submatrices of relatively high correlations corresponding to each cluster. The off-diagonal boxes then contain the correlations at a lower level between the items in different clusters. Only a two-cluster matrix is being considered for simplicity, but the principle is the same when several distinct clusters are found in the initial matrix. The relations between m clusters will be shown in $m(m-1)/2$ off-diagonal boxes in the clustered correlation matrix. Once a correlation matrix has been clustered and sectioned in this way it presents a meaningfully organized and readily inspectable set of data replacing what may initially have appeared as a chaotic mass of numbers.

Table 19.2 Intercorrelations* between 12 opinion statements on smoking

Item no.													
1. Smoking costs more than the pleasure's worth	x												
2. I hope(d) my own children never smoked	27	x											
3. Children should be discouraged from smoking	23	39	x										
4. Smoking is a nuisance	33	40	33	x	cluster A								
5. Smoking is like drug taking	37	36	26	50	x								
6. People who don't smoke shouldn't start	29	43	36	34	45	x							
7. Smoking does more good than harm (disagree)	25	30	19	31	25	26	x						
8. Young people smoke to feel grown up	12	15	16	24	21	14	23	x	cluster B				
9. Smoking is a dirty habit	24	35	21	46	44	36	27	18	x				
10. Smoking is pleasurable (disagree)	28	21	16	35	25	13	33	03	30	x			
11. Smoking can help people relax (disagree)	22	15	09	24	14	13	24	05	22	50	x		
12. Smoking can help nervousness (disagree)	16	09	08	18	11	05	16	00	20	37	64	x	
	1	2	3	4	5	6	7	8	9	10	11	12	
							Item No.						

*Decimal point omitted.

Before this useful arrangement can be secured it is necessary to specify some assignment rule for allocating items to clusters. McQuitty's (1957) Elementary Linkage Analysis can be used to locate clusters of items even in very large matrices in a matter of minutes. The method is only approximate however since its speed depends on assigning each item to the cluster with which it has the highest single correlation. This will usually but not always be the cluster with which it has the highest *average* correlation. Item 7 in Table 19.2, for example, belongs to the first cluster on the latter assignment rule, but would be placed in the second on the McQuitty rule. Occasional large discrepancies can arise between the results of the two assignment rules, especially where the largest single correlation for an item is a chance result of sampling variability. Assignment on the basis of the highest average correlation on the other hand will tend to optimize $\bar{r}_{ij}$ and hence alpha for the cluster, and is therefore to be preferred on reliability theory.

An exact clustering on the latter basis can be achieved using Holtzinger and Harman's (Harman, 1967) B-coefficient, but the method is laborious. The same end results can be achieved much more quickly by clustering and sectioning a matrix using the McQuitty method as a first approximation. Any gross errors of assignment are detectable by the appearance of runs of high correlations in the rows or columns of an off-diagonal box. An offending item can then be reallocated to the cluster with which it has the highest average correlation.

If a computer is used to obtain the correlation matrix, and the relevant program is available, it can be as easy as not to factor the matrix in the same computer run. The results of the factor analysis can then be used to cluster the correlation matrix. For example, Table 19.3 shows the Varimax factors obtained from rotating the first two principal components extracted from Table 19.2. The important thing to note is that although the items load on more than one factor, the items

Table 19.3 Factor Loadings, $\bar{r}_{ij}^*$ and r_{it} Values for the Items in Table 19.2‡

Item no.	Principal components		Varimax factor loadings		$\bar{r}_{ij}^*$		
	(I)	(II)	(A)	(B)	(A)	(B)	r_{it}
1.	56	02	49	− 27	26	22	55
2.	62	27	68	− 08	33	15	60
3.	50	28	58	− 01	27	11	45
4.	72	11	68	− 27	36	26	69
5.	67	26	71	− 12	40	17	63
6.	60	35	70	00	33	10	53
7.	55	03	45	− 31	26	24	54
8.	32	25	40	05	18	03	27
9.	65	07	59	− 26	31	24	64
10.	57	− 48	24	− 70	22	57	60
11.	50	− 70	06	− 86	16	42	52
12.	40	⁻71	02	− 82	11	49	43

‡ (Decimal points omitted.)

$\bar{r}_{ij}^*$ Average of the correlations of each item with items in cluster A or cluster B.

r_{it} Correlation of each item with the total score summated over the twelve items.

which have the highest loading on a Varimax factor are also the defining items for a cluster. By assigning each item to the factor on which it has the highest loading, therefore, we can achieve a cluster analysis with the desired property of maximum $\bar{r}_{ij}$ values within clusters. However, this neat result cannot always be relied upon to occur, even for matrices that show pronounced clusters. It depends on rotating as many factors as there are clusters. For example when three principal components were extracted from Table 19.2 and rotated, it was found that the first cluster was broken up, with items 7 and 8 falling on a separate factor. When four components were rotated, the remaining items in cluster A split further, with items 2, 3 and 6 falling on one factor and items 1, 4, 5 and 9 on another. Since there is no way of knowing how many components to rotate in advance, the results of a factor analysis will sometimes disagree with a cluster analysis of the same matrix. Nevertheless in using factor analysis to construct homogeneous tests it is desirable to have factors that correspond with clusters. That is to say, the items of a group identifying a factor should have substantially higher intercorrelations than with the other items in the total set. In this sense, and for this purpose, cluster analysis is not only the simpler technique, it is more basic. Factor analysis of the matrix is not necessary, but if factors are obtained they can serve as the starting point for a cluster analysis which in turn can serve as a check on the factor analysis. Where the cluster solution obtained from factoring turns out to be only approximate it can be corrected in the same way as one obtained from a McQuitty analysis, as described earlier.

Having completed the cluster analysis the next step is to consider the properties of the scales which can be constructed from each subset of items. The method of clustering will have ensured that the maximum attainable homogeneity has been achieved. The reliability of measurement can be ascertained by entering Table 19.1 with the values of n and $\bar{r}_{ij}$ to find alpha for the cluster. Thus the nine-item cluster in Table 19.2 has an $\bar{r}_{ij}$ of 0.30 yielding an alpha of 0.79; the three-item cluster with $\bar{r}_{ij} = 0.50$ has an alpha of 0.75. (The adequacy of these alpha values and the problem of test length and item selection will be discussed further below.) Table 19.2, however, offers a third possibility for scale construction. If item 8 is disregarded, all the remaining items are positively correlated. This is sufficient to show that running through the matrix is a general factor, which could be measured using a battery of items for both clusters.[12] The $\bar{r}_{ij}$ and alpha values for the entire matrix (excluding item 8) are 0.27 and 0.79, respectively. Homogeneity is lowered by seeking to measure what is common to both clusters, but this is compensated for in the reliability of measurement by the inclusion of more items.

Reliability and 'construct validity'

Should the common factor in Table 19.2 be measured? Are the group factors corresponding to the clusters worth measuring on their own? These questions cannot be answered by reference solely to homogeneity and reliability, and show that these properties, while necessary, are not a sufficient condition for a useful scale. Items could cluster and exhibit high internal consistency because they tapped a narrow range of content, being slight rewordings of the same statement, for example,[13] or because they elicited some kind of common response set independent of content,[14] or because of some statistical artefact effecting the size of the correlation coefficients.[15]

Suspicion of spurious internal consistency may often be removed (or confirmed) simply by accepting the apparent meaning of the items which cluster; but at times inspection of the item content may be insufficient for a correct interpretation of the dimension which can be measured by the items. The precise way in which the meaning of items 10, 11 and 12 in Table 19.2 differs from that of the remaining items may not be immediately obvious, for example. It can be argued that the soundest procedure is to give an obtained cluster the benefit of any doubt, use the clustered items (or a selection of them) as a scale and base the judgement of the utility of the scale, and the interpretation of its meaning, on its pattern of correlation with other variables in the study.

In the case of scales derived from cluster A and B in Table 19.2, for example, it was found for both in the main study that non-smokers showed more negative attitudes than smokers. This is consistent with the existence of an underlying general factor. The difference between smokers and non-smokers was much greater, however, on scale B than scale A. Scale B, but not scale A, was found to correlate with independent measures of the need to smoke. Scale A on the other hand was linked to specific negative attitudes to smoking (belief in the health risk and favourable opinions about anti-smoking campaigns) to a much greater extent than scale B. The pattern of correlations so far supported an interpretation of scale A as measuring general evaluation (like–dislike) of smoking, and scale B as measuring belief in the extent to which smoking serves a definite function for the smoker. This interpretation was strengthened on examining the characteristics of a subgroup of smokers whose attitudes were decidedly negative on scale A but positive on scale B. These turned out to be heavy, addicted smokers, who would like to give up and had made frequent unsuccessful attempts to do so. Both scales were necessary to record the fact that these smokers' attitudes were ambivalent, in that they acknowledged yet resented the hold their habit had over them. In this instance, the decision to carry forward the group factors found in the pilot and work with them in the main study was justified by the results.

The entire process of elaborating and verifying the meaning of scales, after their construction, in terms of a whole network of relationships with other variables in the survey, is akin to what Cronbach (1955) has described as 'construct validation'. It seems a sound procedure to follow when the aim is to explore and leave room for real discoveries about the structure of attitudes in the population. The investigator is protected during the process of scale construction from the consequences of his, possible faulty, preconceptions about the number and nature of important attitude dimensions in the area under study. This information is allowed to emerge as far as possible from the responses of the informants themselves.

Reliability and homogeneity are essential preconditions for establishing the construct validity of a scale: without reliability there would be no correlation with any external variable; without homogeneity, measurement of one thing at a time, the meaning of any obtained correlations would be uninterpretable.

Use of alpha in decisions on test length

As long as the scale construction work contains a genuine element of exploration the possibility exists of discovering clusters that are under-represented in the item sample as well as other clusters that are larger than necessary for reliable measurement. If, as is desirable, the scaling work has been done prior to the main study, decisions will be required on how many (and which) items to discard from the large clusters, and whether to derive further items to build up small clusters. There can of course be no standard of length relevant to all attitude measures since, by formula (1), the number of items necessary to reach a given reliability level varies with the homogeneity of the item battery. As noted earlier, cluster A ($\bar{r}_{ij} = 0.30$) has an alpha of 0.79, cluster B ($\bar{r}_{ij} = 0.50$) an alpha of 0.75. We can measure almost as reliably with the three items as with the entire set of nine items available for the first cluster. The consequences for reliability of selecting a subset of items to represent cluster A can easily be determined from formula (1). The detailed item selection procedure is discussed in the next section. But we may note that four items – 2, 4, 5 and 6 – taken alone, have an $\bar{r}_{ij}$ of 0.41 and hence an alpha of 0.73. The rise in homogeneity (0.30 to 0.41) has not quite compensated for the drop from nine to four items for cluster A, but the saving in questionnaire space was here judged well worth the marginal loss in reliability (0.79 to 0.73). In the case of cluster B it was judged that although only three items were available, the level of reliability reached was not so low as to warrant a further cycle of scale development work to obtain more items.

Obviously, the length of scale deemed adequate in any situation depends in its turn on the level of reliability we are prepared to accept as adequate. What value should be aimed at? The answer must vary with the nature of the research. The formula for alpha shows that no matter how low the intercorrelations ($\bar{r}_{ij}$) between items (as long as all values of $\bar{r}_{ij}$ are positive) we can always make the total score more reliable by increasing n, the number of items that enter into it. In testing personality and intelligence, for example, psychologists aim at reliabilities of 0.90 or above, though the $\bar{r}_{ij}$ values in these fields tend to be lower even than those for attitude measurement. As a consequence psychological tests tend to be extremely long. The subjects for these tests are usually drawn from 'captive' populations – schoolchildren, students, job applicants, members of the armed forces, mental patients and so on – who can be subjected to test batteries of the enormous length necessary to reach the required standards of reliability. Such a solution for attaining high reliability is rarely open to the sample survey practitioner.

Fortunately the surveys for which measures reliable at the 0.90 level are essential are also rare. Reliability at this level is required for discriminating between individuals when a great deal hinges on the accurate placement of a single individual. In the survey situation, however, we are never called upon to interpret the score of a single individual. Our measuring instruments usually need only be reliable enough to distinguish between very broad groups of informants. Lazarsfeld's (1955) classical discussion of the problems of multivariate analysis in sociology, for example, is couched entirely in terms of dichotomized variables. Galtung (1967) even argues that variables with more than three values should be avoided in exploratory research. Moreover, in analysing relationships between variables in such broad categories, interest has traditionally been in establishing the direction and statistical significance of an association rather than in estimating its absolute size. It should be possible to achieve statistical significance[16] without insisting on scales whose reliabilities are exactingly high providing they are not too low. Higher levels of reliability will be required where conclusions rest on comparisons between the size of coefficients of association. With increasing access to computers this style of analysis of survey data is likely to become more common (McKennell 1965). Developments like Blalock's (1964) causal path analysis also depend on knowledge of exact values for correlation coefficients. The pace-makers in the latter field are finding that they need to give careful attention to the problem of reliability and measurement error (Siegel and Hodge, 1968). Any attempt to specify not just the correlation but the exact form of the relationship between variables would call for still higher reliability levels. Such attempts are rare in survey research but an instance is the author's study of community reactions to aircraft noise (McKennell, 1969). In seeking the multiple regression relationship between annoyance and various noise exposure measures it was clear that reliable measurement was no less important on the subjective than the physical side of the equation. The scale used to measure aircraft noise annoyance had an alpha of 0.90. Quite a lengthy scale would have been employed to reach this level had it proved necessary. In the event, because of the high homogeneity of annoyance reactions ($\bar{r}_{ij} = 0.60$), just six items were sufficient. Other attitudes occupying a less key position in the analysis were measured at a lower level of reliability. Alpha coefficients were calculated for some 20 scales in the aircraft noise survey and the smoking survey (McKennell and Thomas, 1967) from which the example in Table 19.2 was taken. While there is an occasional alpha as low as 0.50 the majority are above 0.60, and where special care was taken in the construction of the scale, above 0.70. A five-item scale measuring degree of belief in the lung cancer hazard, for example, had an alpha of 0.74.

More comparative data would be desirable, but further guidelines on acceptable levels of reliability can be gleaned by considering the effect of measurement error on the size of obtained correlations. Such estimates can be derived from the formula for 'correction for attenuation'.[9] Variables perfectly correlated in reality will produce obtained correlations no higher than the reliability with which they are measured. That is, if the true correlation was unity and both reliabilities 0.50, the obtained correlation would be 0.50. Actual correlations less than unity are reduced by a factor equal to the reliability coefficient. For example, a true correlation of 0.60 would yield a correlation of only 0.30 (0.60 × 0.50) if the reliability of the measures correlated was 0.50. Where both actual correlation and measurement reliability are small, the obtained correlation could be reduced to the point where it appeared statistically insignificant. With an actual correlation of 0.30 and reliabilities of 0.50, for example, the obtained correlation would be 0.15. Such examples suggest that we ought to be seriously concerned when the reliability of our measuring instruments sink below a level of, say, 0.6 to 0.7. Certainly we ought to be aware of the fact. One wonders how much of the low level of correlation so typical of social research, and ascribed to the complexity of the phenomena, really arises from unrecognized measurement error. Suspicion of measurement error should be particularly acute where weak associations are found using single opinion items selected without benefit of scaling.

At the present time it is not possible to offer more than these broad guidelines to acceptable levels of reliability in survey research. The use of alpha, however, does place the researcher in a position to balance the number of scale items required against the level of reliability he is prepared to accept or wants to attain. The procedure still leaves a great deal to the researcher's good judgement, more perhaps than might be thought desirable, but seems a considerable advance over the usual situation where no such information is available to aid this kind of decision.

Use of alpha in item selection

Once it is decided to use only a subset of the items in a cluster, a technique is required for selecting the best items from the pool. By formula (1), for a given number of items, n, reliability will be greatest when $\bar{r}_{ij}$ is a maximum. Each item will contribute to $\bar{r}_{ij}$ according to its average correlation with the other items in the cluster. It is a simple matter to compute this value which we shall term $\bar{r}_{ij}*$ (to distinguish it from $\bar{r}_{ij}$, the average for all the items in the cluster). If the items are ordered in terms of $\bar{r}_{ij}$, this gives the order in which they should be discarded in order to preserve the maximum possible $\bar{r}_{ij}$ and alpha values for the remaining item.[17] Table 19.4 shows the items in cluster A, in our example, ordered by their $\bar{r}_{ij}*$ values (taken from Table 19.3).

Table 19.4 Reliability after discarding successive items

	Item no.								
	8	7	3	1	9	6	2	4	5
n	9	8	7	6	5	4	3	2	–
$\bar{r}_{ij}*$	0.18	0.26	0.27	0.26	0.31	0.33	0.33	0.36	0.40
$\bar{r}_{ij}$	0.30	0.33	0.35	0.37	0.40	0.41	0.42	0.50	–
Alpha	0.79	0.79	0.79	0.76	0.77	0.73	0.69	0.67	–

n = number of items remaining in the scale after item on the left discarded.
$\bar{r}_{ij}*$ = initial correlation of each item with the other eight items.
$\bar{r}_{ij}$ = average intercorrelation of the n items.
Alpha = reliability value for the n items.

The second row of the table gives the alpha value for the remaining items after each item has been discarded. The scale constructor thus has precise knowledge of the effect on reliability of discarding successive items. The final decision on the subset of items to be carried forward for measurement purposes can be made accordingly.

As Table 19.4 illustrates, alpha values can remain high on this approach even as the scale is shortened, since convergence is towards items with high internal consistency, representing the core, as it were, of the factor being measured. The procedure is automatic enough to be programmed for a computer. But since the calculations are not onerous it is as well to do them by hand. One can then watch that the increment in homogeneity is not being brought about by a convergence towards items which are exceptionally highly intercorrelated only because they are worded almost identically. In this case the last few retained items would be tending to measure a 'wording factor', specific to them, and different from the common factor underlying the cluster. (For this reason, too, items with very similar wording should be omitted from the sample of items used in the field work.) Also, since small differences in $\bar{r}_{ij}*$ do not greatly effect the ultimate alpha value, one need not be completely inflexible at the item selection stage. Between two items, the one with a slightly smaller $\bar{r}_{ij}*$ value might still be retained, say, if its content looked more 'interesting' to informants, and would help rapport in the interview situation.

Scoring and combining items

Once a subset of items has been selected to form a scale, an informant's scale score is obtained by simply adding the scores on the separate items. As in Likert scaling, all the items carry equal weight. It can be shown (Richardson, 1941) that with nominal weights of unity, each item carries an effective weight (in the total score variance) proportional to its $\bar{r}_{ij}*$ value. This fact was allowed for in the choice of items for the final subset. While each item in the final subset could be weighted by its $\bar{r}_{ij}*$ value, there is little to be gained by introducing fractional weights. Where the range of weights is small and the items positively correlated, the correlation between the composite scores obtained with any two sets of (positive) weights is very high. This has been shown theoretically by Richardson (1941) and demonstrated empirically by Likert (1932), amongst others. By the same token, where cluster-directed factors are concerned, the use of rigorously derived weights for estimating factor scores (Harman, 1967) is not worth the trouble. Simply scoring the defining items of the factor as unity and the rest zero would yield scores which were highly correlated. This has been shown empirically (Horn, 1965). Where factors correspond with clusters, therefore, the same method of simple, unweighted summation can be employed to obtain scale scores.

Similar considerations lead to a rejection of the notion of using standardized scores rather than raw scores for the items. Standardizing would be the equivalent of using a fractional weight for each item inversely proportional to the standard deviation of its raw scores. Of course one should take steps to equalize any gross inequality in the range of scores if, say, a two-point response scale had been used for some items and seven-point scales for others. It is neater if all the item response scales have a standard form. The conventional five-point Likert scales (with categories ranging from, Strongly Agree to Strongly Disagree) will probably give as good results as any other. But there is reason for thinking that the number of scale points is a technical detail the importance of which has been over rated. The work of Peabody (1962) and also Komorita and Graham (1965) indicates that when scores are obtained by summing the ratings on a battery of bipolar scales (including the Likert type), the number of points on the individual scales makes little difference to the reliability of the total score.

Relationship of the alpha approach to other techniques

Although complex psychometric issues arise under this head, there are some outstanding points that can be made briefly.

(a) There is a direct relationship between item selection procedures on the alpha approach and the Likert technique. The latter selects items which have the highest value for the correlation, $\bar{r}_{ij}$, between the score on the item and the total score on the set of items. This approach maximizes internal consistency, as defined by $\bar{r}_{ij}$, the average of all such correlations.

It can be shown (Nunnally, 1967) that

$$\bar{r}_{ij} = \bar{r}_{it}^2 \tag{2}$$

when all item intercorrelations are equal, a condition which is approximated for single cluster of items. The selection of items which maximizes $\bar{r}_{ij}$ on the alpha approach, and $\bar{r}_{it}$ on the Likert technique, would therefore tend to be the same. Substituting (2) in (1) an alternative formula for alpha is obtained which could be used with the Likert technique. It is not so convenient as the $\bar{r}_{ij}$ formula for monitoring the effects of item selection on reliability, since each time an item is discarded it is necessary to return to the raw data to find the $\bar{r}_{it}$ values for computing the revised alpha estimates.

The principal difference between the alpha and Likert procedures is the inability of the latter to detect when more than one dimension is represented in the item set. Consider the $\bar{r}_{it}$ values[18] in the last column of Table 19.3, for example. These give no indication that the item set divides into two distinct clusters. Described by Green (1954) as a single common factor model for attitude measurement, the Likert technique at best will lead to a scale which measures what is most general to an item set. As a tool for exploring and representing the structure of attitudes in a population it therefore has limitations. Distinct attitudes of importance to substantial numbers of informants may well be missed in the process of imposing a hypothesis of undimensionality on the data. Usually the separate clusters in a matrix will overlap, as in Table 19.2, so that the hypothesis would be not so much false as oversimple. The technique however contains no safeguard against the inadvertent scaling together of clusters of items which are independent. The composite score for such an item combination would be a confounding of the different dimensions present and hence uninterpretable.

(b) The value of $\bar{r}_{ij}$ is closely related to the coefficient of reproducibility in Guttman or cumulative scaling (White and Saltz, 1957; Cronbach, 1951; Scott, 1960). A perfect Guttman scale would also be a perfectly reliable scale in terms of alpha. Perfect or even near-perfect scales hardly ever occur in practice. Both item unreliability and the presence of more than one dimension can lead to low reproducibility, but the Guttman technique does not allow these quite different sources of 'error' to be distinguished. It is a technique therefore for testing a hypothesis of undimensionality rather than for exploring the number of dimensions present. Items covering two independent dimensions would not Guttman scale, but items covering two distinct but *related* dimensions might. A cumulative scale with a coefficient of reproducibility of 0.91 can in fact be constructed from items 3, 4, 7, 9, 10, 11, 12 (which is the cumulative order) in Table 19.2. Like the Likert procedure, Guttman scaling focuses on what is most general in the item set at the risk of missing important secondary dimensions. But Guttman scaling, even when applied to the items in a single cluster, does not afford a criterion for assessing how far a lengthening of the scale by adding items will improve its efficiency as a measuring instrument. Nor does it provide clear-cut criteria for the selection of items. Certainly, the Guttman model makes fewer assumptions about the data, in that only relations at an ordinal level of measurement are assumed. But any advantage here may be thought dearly bought at the expense of the practical limitations just noted. The issue of measurement levels is discussed more generally below.

(c) The present alpha approach, being based on the values of r_{ij}, is easily combined with factor and cluster analysis techniques. So combined there is a ready safeguard against false inferences of unidimensionality, and an additional gain in the information obtained about reliability in relation to test length.

Guttman scaling, the Likert technique and factor and cluster analysis are all internal consistency approaches to the problem of scale construction. The researcher who uses any of these techniques will be protected against using ostensible measures that are actually of zero or near zero reliability. Factor and cluster analysis in addition provide information on the number of separate dimensions in the item pool. But the alpha approach, especially when combined with factor or cluster analysis, does all these things, and in addition provides a simultaneous criterion on reliability in relation to test length, as well as providing a criterion for item selection.

Levels of measurement

The alpha approach, stemming from psychological test theory, entails manipulations of the data which assume interval scale properties even at the item level.[19] The calculation and interpretation of $\bar{r}_{ij}$ as a product moment correlation, which the theory requires, for example, involves this assumption (amongst others). The approach therefore runs counter to the convention that has grown up in both psychology and sociology (stronger perhaps in the latter) that statistics appropriate for interval measures are inadmissable with ordinal data. Here the standpoint adopted by this author is pragmatic.[20] Measurement conventions are not immutable. This particular one, though venerable, has never been universally accepted, and there is currently some reaction against it.[21] By taking a stronger view of the data access is gained to the world of measurement of the psychometrician. More powerful analytical techniques become available. The burden of this paper has been that these psychometric techniques, when suitably adapted, are extremely useful for scale construction in the sample survey context. At the present stage of social science, it can be argued, fruitfulness in applied research is as good a guide to the choice of a measurement model as the views taken by rival theorists[21] about its axiomatic properties.

Notes

1. See the discussion on Likert and Guttman scaling towards the end of the article. The Thurstone technique, not discussed in the paper, works on an entirely different algorithm. It can hardly be regarded as an exploratory tool. Even more than the former methods it imposes *a priori* notions of unidimensionality. Items are scaled by the direct assessment of a group of judges operating on this belief.
2. The technique was initially developed for use with Government Social Survey work (McKennell, 1968).
3. Psychometricians theorize about sampling 'a domain of items' or a 'universe of content', but there are no agreed, rigorous procedures for drawing such a sample. The author favours preliminary unstructured interviews and group discussions, with individuals typical of the population to be surveyed, as a means of gathering representative opinion statements.
4. This point has been made forcefully by Glock (1967), who draws the distinction between 'time-bound' associations used for scale construction and 'time-ordered' associations used in analysis.
5. The scheme for analysing such mixed variables would accord with what Galtung (1967, p. 23) has termed the 'intervening variable model'.

6. Other more formally acceptable 'non-metric' models for multidimensional scaling certainly exist (Lazarsfeld, 1950; Coleman, 1957; Coombs 1964) and are still being developed (Guttman 1968). But as Scott (1968) notes in his recent review, these models have not yet found wide application. They have so far remained scaling theories rather than routinely applicable techniques. This appears to be so for areas in addition to attitude assessment. Levy and Pugh (1969), for example, despite their attention to formal models of measurement, nevertheless felt thrown back on the traditional factor analytic approach when faced with a practical problem of multidimensional scaling.

7. The main reference here is still Cronbach's classical (1951) paper. The article by Tryon (1957) has been influential in the account it gives of the relationship between various formulae. Tryon's treatment largely supersedes that by Guilford (1954).

8. The Spearman–Brown formula for estimating the reliability of the full-length test from the correlation of halves is $2r_n/(1 + r_n)$ where r_n is the correlation between halves.

9. The true correlation between variables x and y is $r_{xy}/\sqrt{r_{xx}r_{yy}}$ known as the 'correction for attenuation' where r_{xy} is the obtained correlation, and r_{xx} and r_{yy} are the reliability coefficients for x and y.

10. An easy way of seeing the derivation of this form of the alpha coefficient is by way of the Spearman–Brown formula mentioned in note 8. For the general case this is

$$r_{nn} = \frac{nr_{ii}}{1 + (n - 1)r_{ii}}$$

where r_{ii} is the reliability of the test of unit length and r_{nn} is the reliability of a test n times as long.

If r_{ii} is set equal to r_{ij} (i.e. the reliability of an element or item in the test) then r_{nn} is the reliability of the total test. This is the form of the alpha formula used in this paper. The derivation here assumes all items have equal reliabilities, equal intercorrelations and equal frequency of endorsement. These assumptions are involved in the Spearman–Brown formula. The necessity of these theoretical assumptions has been questioned by Tryon (1957) amongst others.

Note that an alternative name for alpha is Kuder-Richardson Formula 20, after the psychometricians who originally developed the formula for the case of dichotomous items. Cronbach's term 'alpha', is now more widely used and covers the case of multi-category items.

11. If a proportion of informants share the same idiosyncratic point of view, or if several factors are important in the response, we have a multifactorial situation. I have left this out of account in order to simplify the essence of the argument.

12. This statement is confirmed by the occurrence of a first principal component (Table 19.3) which accounts for a substantial proportion of the variance in the matrix. When a general factor is present in the matrix it is usually possible as well as desirable to choose in advance (but also permissible to fix afterwards) the direction of scoring of each item which yields consistently positive correlations in the matrix. For the items in Table 19.2, for example, responses unfavourable to smoking were consistently scored high.

13. This was one of the early criticisms made against the high internal consistency (high reproducibility) required by Guttman scaling (Festinger 1947).

14. There is a vast literature on response sets. For a brief overview see Scott (1968). There is a suggestion of an acquiescent response set in Table 19.2, since items which call for disagreement tend to cluster. However, the work of construct validation, described later, shows that informants were reacting to the content of the items.

15. Product moment correlation coefficients should be used for computing alpha (in the case of dichotomous items there will be phi coefficients, $\sqrt{\chi^2/N}$). This coefficient can be at its maximum value between two items only when they both have similar response distributions. There is a considerable literature on the ramifications of this peculiarity of the coefficient. Its seriousness as a source of spurious 'difficulty factors' is still a matter of dispute (e.g. Dingman, 1958; Borgatta, 1965). It is

possible to correct alpha for the effect of disparate item distributions, but Cronbach (1951) argues that at the level of $\bar{r}_{ij}$ normally encountered, the correction makes not enough difference to be worthwhile. It is characteristic of the psychometric tradition to make strong assumptions about the data (e.g. variables normally distributed on interval scales) in order to use classical statistical theory, and then test the effects of departure from these assumptions. See also note 21.

16. It should not be forgotten, however, that with the large samples customary in survey work, the presence of measurement error is likely to be more important than sampling error as a source of the within-group variability (standard errors) on which significance tests and confidence limits are calculated.

17. Strictly new values of $\bar{r}_{ij}^*$ should be calculated after each item is discarded. It is doubtful if such an iterative procedure is worthwhile. Important discrepancies in $\bar{r}_{ij}^*$ values would tend to remain, while minor reversal would be unimportant.

18. No correction has been made for the inclusion of the item itself in the total score. Such a correction, however, would not effect the point being made.

19. The total or summated score would not have inbuilt the properties of an interval scale; but by the argument which follows we would be willing to treat it as such if it were analytically convenient to do so.

20. For a fuller expression of the pragmatic approach to measurement see Levy and Pugh (1969).

21. In psychology the strictures of, say, Stevens (1946) or Siegel (1956) about levels of measurement and appropriate statistics can be countered by the arguments of writers such as Nunnally (1967) and Adams *et al.* (1965), and by such empirical work as that of Baker *et al.* (1966). In sociology the purist position of, say, Galtung (1967, page 341) on ordinal measures can be matched against the vigorous productivity of the Blalock and Blalock (1968) school. The latter's use of regression and correlation coefficients implies interval scale assumptions. Borgatta (1969) explicitly states the view that sociologists' attraction to 'non-parametric' approaches is a 'fad' which is passing in favour of the classical statistical procedures that historically have been neglected in the discipline.

References

Adams, E. W., Fagot, R. F. and Robinson, R. E. (1965) 'A theory of appropriate statistics', *Psychometrika,* **30,** 99–128.

Baggaley, A. P. (1964) *Intermediate Correlation Methods.*

Baker, B. V., Hardyck, C. D. and Petrinovich, L. F. (1966) 'Weak measurements versus strong statistics', *Educ. and Psychol. Measmt.,* XXVI, 291–309.

Blalock, H. M. and Blalock, A. B. (eds) (1968) *Methodology in Social Research.* London: McGraw-Hill.

Blalock, H. M. (1964) *Casual Interferences in Nonexperimental Research.* Chapel Hill, N.C.: University of North Carolina Press.

Borgatta, E. F. (ed.) (1969) 'Prologue: the current status of methodology in sociology', in E. F. Borgatta (ed.), *Sociological Methodology.* San Francisco: Jossey Bass.

Borgatta, E. F. (1965) 'Difficulty factors and the use of r_{phi}', *J. Gen. Psychol.,* **73,** 321–37.

Coleman, James S. (1957) 'Multidimensional scale analysis', *American Journal of Sociology,* **63,** 253–63.

Coombs, C. H. (1964) *A Theory of Data.* New York: Wiley.

Cronbach, L. J. (1951) 'Coefficient alpha and the internal structure of tests', *Psychometrika,* **16,** 297–334.

Cronbach, L. J. and Meehl (1955) 'Construct validity in psychological tests', *Psychol. Bull.,* **52,** 177–93.

Dingman, H. F. (1958) 'The relation between coefficients of correlation and difficulty factors', *Brit. J. Stats. Psychol.,* **11,** 13–17.

Festinger, L. (1947) 'The treatment of qualitative data by "scale analysis"', *Psychol. Bull.*, **44**, 149–61.

Galtung, J. (1967) *Theory and Methods of Social Research*. London: George Allen and Unwin.

Glock, C. Y. (1967) 'Survey design and analysis in sociology', in C. Y. Glock (ed.) *Survey Research in the Social Sciences*, New York: Russel Sage Foundation.

Green, B. F. (1954) 'Attitude measurement', in G. Lindzey (ed), Handbook of Social Psychology. Reading, Mass.: Addison-Wesley.

Guilford, J. P. (1954) *Psychometric Methods* (2nd edn). New York: McGraw-Hill.

Guttman, L. (1968) 'A general nonmetric technique for finding the smallest coordinate space for a configuration of points', *Psychometrika*, **33**, 469–506.

Harman, H. H. (1967) *Modern Factor Analysis* (2nd edn). Chicago: University of Chicago Press.

Horn, J. L. (1965) 'An empirical comparison of various methods for estimating common factor scores', *Educ. and Psychol. Measmt.*, **25**, 313–22.

Komorita, S. S. and Graham, W. K. (1965) 'Number of scale points and the reliability of scales', *Educ. and Psychol. Measmt*, **25**, 987–95.

Lazarsfeld, P. F. (1950) 'The logical and mathematical foundation of latent structure analysis, in *Measurement and Prediction*. S. A. Stouffer *et al.*, Princeton University Press.

Lazarsfeld, P. F. (1955) 'The interpretation of statistical relations as a research operation', in P. F. Lazarsfeld and M. Rosenberg (eds), *The Language of Social Research*. New York Free Press.

Levy, P. and Pugh, D. (1969) 'Scaling and multivariate analysis in the study of organizational variables', *Sociology*, **3**, 193–213.

Likert, R. (1932) 'A technique for the measurement of attitudes', *Archives of Psychology, N.Y.* No. 140.

McKennell, A. C. (1965) 'Correlational analysis of social survey data', *Sociological Review*, **13**, 157–81.

McKennell, A. C. (1969) 'Methodological problems in a survey of aircraft noise annoyance', *The Statistician*, **19**.

McKennell, A. C. and Thomas, R. K. (1967) *Smoking Habits and Attitudes of Adolescents and Adults*. H.M.S.O. Government Social Survey Report. SS353/B.

McKennell, A. C. (1968) *Use of Coefficient Alpha in Constructing Attitude and Similar Scales*. Government Social Survey Methodological Paper No. 139.

McQuitty, L. L. (1957) 'Elementary linkage analysis', *Educ. and Psychol. Measmt.*, **17**, 207–29.

Nunnally, J. C. (1967) *Psychometric Theory*. McGraw-Hill.

Peabody, D. (1962) 'Two components in bi-polar scales: direction and extremeness', *Psychol. Rev.*, **69**, 65–73.

Richardson, M. W. (1941) 'The combination of measures', in P. Horst (ed.), *The Prediction of Personal Adjustment*. N.Y. Social Science Research Council.

Scott, W. A. (1960) 'Measures of test homogeneity', *Educ. and Psychol. Measmt.*, **20**, 751–57.

Scott, W. A. (1968) 'Attitude measurement', in Vol. 2, G. Lindzey and E. Aronson. *The Handbook of Social Psychology*. Second edition. London: Addison-Wesley.

Siegel, P. M. and Hodge, R. W. (1968) 'A causal approach to the study of measurement error', in H. M. and A. B. Blalock, *Methodology in Social Research*. London: McGraw-Hill.

Siegel, S. (1956) *Nonparametric Statistics*. London: McGraw-Hill.

Stevens, S. S. (1946) 'On the theory of scales of measurement', *Science*, **103**, 677–80.

Tryon, R. C. (1957) 'Reliability and behaviour domain validity: reformulation and historical critique', *Psychol. Bull.* LIV, 9–17.

White, W. B. and Saltz, E. (1957) 'Measurement of reproducibility', *Psychol. Bull.*, **54**, 81–99.

Section 5

Data analysis and report

Introduction

Data analysis in social research is concerned primarily with the unravelling of relationships between variables. In the case of the experiment, the relationship is in principle a fairly straightforward one. A hypothesis is formulated that a dependent variable (representing a phenomenon of interest) is directly influenced by one or more independent variables (the causes of the phenomenon) and the experiment is designed in such a way that these relations can be tested empirically, uncontaminated by the effects of other variables. In a survey such controls are possible only to a limited degree, and much of the analysis consists of looking for patterns in data collected over a number of variables which may lend support to certain kinds of hypothesis.

Both surveys and experiments entail collection of a set of observations on a sample of individuals; in ethnographic research the need for completeness of data gives way to the collection of relevant data on particular individuals; the process is more like one of putting together the inter-locking pieces of a jigsaw to build up a picture of what a miniature social system is really like.

Experiments and surveys are characterized generally by quantitative data analysis in which statistical tests are applied, whereas in ethnographic studies the main emphasis is usually on qualitative analysis, i.e. the interpretation of social actions, in which no attempt is made to assess the magnitude of influences or whether the relationships through which they are manifested could have arisen by chance. As some of the Readings that follow show, and as we have already seen in a reading by Kish in Section 2, slavish and often inappropriate reliance on the use of statistical tests in surveys and experiments often gets in the way of the development of sound theory to which all data analysis in social science is directed. On the other hand, rejection of quantitative methods on the part of ethnographers can greatly weaken the plausibility of their theoretical assertions. In this sense both schools have a lot to learn from each other. Experimenters and survey researchers need not feel guilty about using imaginative insights in the exploration of the data they have collected alongside the testing of specific hypotheses; and ethnographers should be continually on the look out for points in the research process where hypotheses need to be put to a rigorous test and to collect such data as may enable this to be done.

Finally analysis is only the technical means by which research conclusions are drawn. Whether they gain acceptance in the wider community and the effects such an acceptance is likely to have on policy making and theory is crucially dependent on the way the results are presented. In social science one of the most difficult issues is what can be said and cannot be said legitimately about the subjects of a social enquiry. This ethical dimension which operates at all levels of the research process becomes of vital significance in the research report. Here the chickens veritably come home to roost, both in relation to the various errors that have occurred as the consequences of particular decisions that have been taken earlier on in the research process and ethical dilemmas that may have occurred in the process of collecting data and in drawing conclusions from them.

In the readings in this section all these various aspects of data analysis occur. The first, by Rosenberg, deals with the cornerstone of the logic of survey analysis, the control of extraneous variables, which may account for the simple two variable relationships on which much weight is so often placed. He points out the common fallacy in referring to such relationships as spurious. It is the interpretation of the relationship which is spurious, and only through the elaboration of tabulated data through the control of 'test' factors can appropriate causal inferences be legitimately drawn. Rosenberg's article is concerned with a basic analytic strategy; in the article that follows it by Selvin and Stuart some important but frequently overlooked cautions are made regarding the use of statistical tests especially in the analysis of survey data. Selvin and Stuart's useful distinction between 'snooping', 'fishing' and 'hunting' draws attention to the statistical fallacies inherent in much of current survey analysis practice. Implicit in much of what Selvin and Stuart have to say is the need for theory, which statistics may then be used as a legitimate tool to test. This point comes out again in the reading by Ahlgren and Walberg, who, in a more technical article, present regression analysis as a comprehensive data analytic strategy for surveys and experiments. They emphasize the origins of both regression analysis and analysis of variance in the mathematical theory of 'the general linear model', and discuss some of the assumptions, of crucial importance to the researcher, on which the model depends.

A quite different strategy for analysis is described by Becker. He shows how the participant observer can sharpen and refine his research hypotheses through the different stages of fieldwork, and finally in the research report itself, in which the underlying principle, analytic induction, gives him the logical guidelines that he needs. Finally, another article by Becker on the ethical problems in publishing field reports completes the Reader. Though Becker's concerns are again with the problems of writing up participant observation where issues of maintaining anonymity for informants may become of paramount importance, many of his comments have just as much relevance for experimental and survey research.

Extraneous variables

Morris Rosenberg

The reason why sociology tends to focus on asymmetrical relationships and, in particular, on the relationship between properties and dispositions or behavior is rooted in the nature of its subject matter. The sociologist is characteristically interested in the relationship of social experience to individual mental processes and acts. He thus tends to select as his independent variable certain groups, collectivities or social categories and chooses as his dependent variable socially relevant opinions, attitudes, values or actions. Thus he may ask: Are workers more alienated than middle-class people? Do Catholics vote Democratic more than Protestants? Are older people more prejudiced than younger people? Are small town youngsters less likely to go on to college than city dwellers? And so on.

Given proper sample and research design, the analyst may be able to provide correct answers to these questions. But these results are essentially descriptive. They may show that Catholics vote Democratic more than Protestants do, but they do not indicate *why* this is so. While it is valuable to explain such a relationship on the basis of informed speculation, it is still more valuable to subject this speculation to systematic test. The most important systematic way of examining the relationship between two variables is to introduce a third variable, called a test factor, into the analysis. This is what is meant by the process of *elaboration*.

The test factor, it should be stressed, is introduced solely for the purpose of increasing one's understanding of the original two-variable relationship. The aim of the analysis is to determine whether the relationship between X (the independent variable) and Y (the dependent variable) is due to Z (the test factor).

But what is meant by saying that the relationship is 'due to' Z, or that Z is 'responsible for' or the 'determinant of' the relationship between X and Y? In the present discussion, these terms have a rather definite meaning. To say that the relationship between X and Y is due to Z is to

---

Morris Rosenberg, 'Extraneous variables', from *The Logic of Survey Analysis*, New York: Basic Books Inc., 1968, Ch. 2, pp. 23–40 and 52–3.

mean that *were it not for Z*, there would be *no* relationship between X and Y. The statement, 'Catholics have lower suicide rates because they are more integrated', must be translated as, 'Were Catholics not more integrated, they would not have lower suicide rates.' Similarly, 'Lower-class people have higher rates of schizophrenia because they are more socially isolated', is translated as, 'Were lower class people not more socially isolated, they would not have higher rates of schizophrenia.'

The procedural aspect of the key phrase 'were it not for' is to *control on,* or *hold constant,* the test factor, thereby eliminating its influence on the relationship. Let us consider how one 'holds constant' a test factor by means of the technique of *subgroup classification.*[1]

Assume we begin with the finding that older people are more likely than younger people to listen to religious programs on the radio[2] (Table 20.1). In considering why this may be so, we suggest that perhaps this is due to the factor of education. Translated: were older people not more poorly educated, then they would not be more likely to listen to religious programs.

Table 20.1 Age and listening to religious programs*

Listen to religious programs	Young listeners	Old listeners
Yes	17%	26%
No	83	74
Total per cent	100	100

*Paul F. Lazarsfeld and Morris Rosenberg (eds) (1955) *The Language of Social Research.* Glencoe, Ill.: The Free Press, p. 117, Table 4 (abridged and adapted). (Reprinted with permission of The Macmillan Company. Copyright 1955 by The Free Press, A Corporation.)

The task, then, is to eliminate the influence of education. This can be done simply by comparing older and younger people of *equal education.* Thus, one compares the listening habits of *well-educated* and *poorly educated* old and young people. Table 20.2 shows the results.

We see that among the well-educated, older people are hardly more likely to listen to religious programs, and the same is true among poorly educated people. Thus, were it not for education, there would be almost no relationship between age and listening. These data thus point to the following conclusion: older people are more likely to listen to religious programs because older people are generally more poorly educated and poorly-educated people are more likely to listen to religious programs.

This analytic process may be expressed more generally by means of technical terminology. Typically one begins with a relationship between an independent variable (age) and a dependent variable (religi-

Table 20.2 Age and listening to religious programs, by education*

Listen to religious programs	High education		Low education	
	Young	Old	Young	Old
Yes	9%	11%	29%	32%
No	91	89	71	68
Total per cent	100	100	100	100

*Paul F. Lazarsfeld and Morris Rosenberg, *op. cit.*, p. 117, Table 4 (abridged and adapted). (Reprinted with permission of The Macmillan Company. Copyright 1955 by The Free Press, A Corporation.)

ous program listening). One then seeks to explain this relationship by introducing an explanatory variable, called a test factor (education). The method used is to *stratify* on the test factor and to examine the contingent associations. 'Stratification' means that we have broken the test factor into its component categories. In this case it is highly educated and poorly educated; in other cases it might be men and women, or Catholics, Protestants and Jews, or upper, middle and lower classes, etc.

The process of stratification creates 'contingent associations'. In Table 20.2, two contingent associations appear. The first is the association between age and program listening among the well-educated; the second is the association between age and listening among the poorly-educated. If the test factor has more categories (say, grammar school education, high school education, college education and postgraduate education) then there will be more contingent associations – one for each category. If the relationship between age and listening disappears within each contingent association, then we can say that the relationship is due to the test factor (education).

In order to understand the relationship between two variables, then, it is necessary to introduce additional variables into the analysis. But which variables should these be? In order to answer this question, it is necessary to digress momentarily to discuss a peculiar but decisive characteristic of sociological variables, namely, the fact that they are 'block-booked'.

The concept of block-booking is drawn from the field of mass communications research. At an earlier period in the history of the film industry, it was customary for film producers to rent films to exhibitors en masse; for example, in blocks of five. Thus an exhibitor had the option of renting or not renting a block of five films, but could not choose among them. If the block contained, say, one highly desirable film, one fairly desirable film and three undesirable films, the exhibitor was compelled to take the undesirable films in order to obtain the desirable ones.

Human beings (or other sociological units) are similarly 'block-booked'. Each man (or group, or region) may be characterized in terms of a number of dimensions. When we describe a man in terms of certain characteristics, we are at the same time describing him in terms of other characteristics.

Let us say that we find that blue-collar workers are more alienated than white-collar workers. But blue-collar workers differ from white-collar workers in many ways other than in the type of work they do. They tend to be more poorly educated; they are more likely to be Catholic; they are more likely to be liberal on economic issues and illiberal on social issues; they are less likely to engage in abstract modes of thought; they are less likely to have high IQs; they are more likely to come from large families; and so on.

'Blue-collar', then, means a great many things. When we try to explain why blue-collar workers are more alienated, then, we do so by giving consideration to these other factors associated with the status of blue-collar workers. It is these 'block-booked', or associated, characteristics which enable us to understand why blue-collar workers are more alienated. The aim of the analysis is to ascertain *what there is* about being a blue-collar worker which accounts for the relationship with alienation.

Block-booking is the central fact of survey analysis. One cannot properly understand the relationship between an independent and a dependent variable without taking account of the fact that other variables are associated with them. These associated variables become the 'test factors'.

But not all test factors have the same meaning, serve the same theoretical purpose or have the same statistical properties. At least six types of test factors may be distinguished: extraneous variables, component variables, intervening variables, antecedent variables, suppressor variables and distorter variables. The purpose of this discussion is to suggest how these types of test factors enable one to achieve sounder, more precise and more meaningful interpretations of two-variable relationships.

Extraneous variables

When a research investigator discovers a relationship between two variables, the first question he implicitly asks is: 'Is it real?' Knowing that sociological variables are 'block-booked', he is concerned to know whether there is an *inherent link* between the independent and dependent variables or whether it is based on an accidental connection with some associated variable. In short, he must guard against what are called 'spurious relationships'.

Strictly speaking, there is no such thing as a spurious relationship; there are only spurious interpretations. It is customary to use the term 'spurious relationship', however, to refer to a case in which there is no meaningful or inherent link between the two variables; the relationship is due solely to the fact that each of the variables happens accidentally to be associated with some other variable. It is a relationship which, on the surface, appears to be *asymmetrical* but which, on closer analysis, turns out to be *symmetrical* (for example, two indicators of the same concept, two consequences of the same cause, two elements of a functional unity, two manifestations of a joint complex or two factors fortuitously associated).

The point is obvious when one considers gross examples. A common favorite is the finding that in Sweden there is a relationship between the number of storks in an area and the number of children born in the area.[3] One calls this relationship spurious, even though there is nothing spurious about the relationship; what is spurious is the *interpretation* that the storks bring the babies.

Or one finds that the death rate among people in hospitals is higher than that among people of comparable age outside of hospitals. This hardly justifies the conclusion that hospitals are inimical to health and length of life. Again, one finds that there is a positive association between the number of firemen at a fire and the amount of damage done. But this does not mean that the firemen did the damage.

In the above examples, the reason for the original relationship is always some associated third variable. The reason for the relationship between number of storks and number of babies is rural–urban location. Most storks are found in rural areas and the rural birth rate is higher than the urban birth rate. Similarly, the reason for the relationship between the number of firemen and the amount of the damage is the size of the fire. Large fires call forth more firemen and also cause more damage.

Unless one guards against such accidental associations, one is in danger of reaching erroneous and misleading conclusions. The significance of this point for sociological theory is apparent. Much ingenious and suggestive speculation, leading to important theoretical conclusions, may be advanced to explain certain empirical relationships, when the truth of the matter lies in the fact that an accidental link binds the independent and dependent variables. Without such a check, there may enter into the body of sociological theory ideas which are erroneous but which may exert a wide influence in the field.

No one, of course, will be deceived by the examples cited above. But let us consider some more serious illustrations. In each case we start with a relationship between two variables, we speculate on the meaning of this relationship and we find that our interpretations are erroneous and misleading by virtue of our failure to take account of extraneous variables.[4]

Example A
A striking example of the theoretical importance of considering control variables appears in a study by Goldhamer and Marshall. In their

book, *Psychosis and Civilization,*[5] they undertook to examine the widely held assumption that rates of psychosis had increased over the last century. And, in fact, the data did show a striking and consistent rise. It would not be difficult to suggest some of the changing conditions of life which created intensified stress and which might be responsible for mental breakdown: the increased mobility aspirations which were largely frustrated; the shift from the farm to the city, substituting the isolation and anonymity of urban living for the social integration of rural life; the breakdown in the stabilizing force of religion; the heightened competitiveness of economic life; the development of urban slums; the increased anomie of a swiftly changing and socially mobile society; the breakdown of the stability of the family expressed in increased rates of divorce, etc. All these factors represented theoretical bases for accounting for the observed rise in the rate of psychosis.

Goldhamer and Marshall noted that the increased rates of hospitalization for psychosis between 1845 and 1945, however, failed to take account of the factor of *age*. If one examined the rates of psychosis within each age category, one found (with the exception of those over 50) that *there was virtually no change over the century-long period*. The relationship was largely a spurious one.

How did age produce this misleading interpretation? The most common psychosis of advanced age is senile dementia; this is primarily an organic (rather than a functional) psychosis and is more often due to physiological degeneration than to psychological stress. Now, the advances in medicine during the period 1845–1945 had produced an increase in average length of life of the population. Hence, the proportion of old people in the population was much greater in the later period, thus producing a very large *number* of people with senile dementia. There has also been 'an increased tendency to hospitalize persons suffering from the mental diseases of the senium'.[6] Hence, the higher total rate of psychosis in 1945 was largely a reflection of the changing age distribution of the population and a tendency to hospitalize older people, not a reflection of increased societal stress (except perhaps among older people).

This is a striking illustration of how an elaborate and sophisticated theoretical structure might have been constructed to account for a relationship which was, in fact, completely misleading by virtue of the failure to take account of an extraneous variable.

Example B

Assume that a research study finds that older people read fewer books than younger people. What accounts for this relationship? One might reason that increasing age is often associated with a degeneration of eyesight and that these visual difficulties discourage reading among the elderly. One might further speculate that increasing age tends to produce a boredom with fiction and a general flagging of intellectual interests, thus producing a disinclination to read. These reasons appear to make sense and the data may be interpreted as supporting certain assumptions about the effects of aging.

There would thus appear to be an 'inherent link' between age and book readership. In fact, however, it may be an 'accidental link'. When people who are now older were growing up, advanced education was much less widespread. It may thus be that the reason older people now read less is that, as a group, they are less well educated and that people with poorer education are less interested in books. In this case, age in itself would have no effect on book reading. The relationship would be entirely due to the fact that both age and book reading happen to be associated with education.

Example C
In a well-known study of the relationship between occupational structure and child-rearing practices, Miller and Swanson[7] suggested that location in the economic system would create a family integration setting which would influence the choice of child-rearing practices. The hypothesis was that the *entrepreneurial* families would emphasize self-control and an active and independent approach to the world, whereas *bureaucratic* families would stress an accommodating and adjustive way of life. This hypothesis was clearly supported by the data.

This significant theoretical contribution was, however, questioned by Lawrence Haber.[8] Haber noted that in the 1930s child-care advice, guided by the theory of behaviorism, stressed restriction and control, whereas in the 1940s, under the influence of Dewey and others, more permissive practices were the vogue. This raised the possibility that the differences in child-rearing practices in bureaucratic and entrepreneurial families were not an outcome of occupational and technological imperatives but were a reflection of the patterns current at different times.

In the Miller and Swanson study, respondents were classified as entrepreneurial if the husband was self-employed, if most of his income came from profits, fees or commissions, if he worked in an organization with few levels of supervision, and if he (or his wife) was born on a farm or outside the United States. Others were classified as bureaucratic. But, argued Haber, these groups also tended to differ in *age*. 'In the United States, foreign-born adults are as a group older than native-born adults; self-employed men are on the average older than salaried men; managers, owners and proprietors tend to be older than professionals.'[9] In other words, the entrepreneurial group tends to be older than the bureaucratic group, a fact confirmed by Miller and Swanson's data. Haber thus concluded:

Given the age differences between the middle-class entrepreneurial mothers, a larger proportion of the entrepreneurial mothers than of the bureaucratic mothers would have reared their children during the early 1930s. Based on a median age of 23 years at the time of the birth of the first child, the proportion of women actively engaged in child care by 1937 is greater among entrepreneurial mothers than bureaucratic mothers. Under the influence of the advice and child care practices available as parental role models, proportionately more of the entrepreneurial group would have adopted the type of child-rearing current at the time. We would expect that the children of the entrepreneurial families have been raised in a substantially different climate of opinion from the bureaucratic families, who were proportionately more exposed to the advice and practices of the 1940s.

One would expect that the older, entrepreneurial population would be more likely than the younger, more recent parents in the bureaucratic group to have engaged in scheduled feeding, early control over elimination and masturbation and to have demanded more independence and self-control.[10]

The failure to take account of the extraneous variable of age may thus create a radically misleading theoretical interpretation. The profound significance of such test factors for theoretical understanding is thus evident.

To summarize: whenever we find a relationship between two variables, we attempt to make sense of it by suggesting how the independent variable exercises some influence on the dependent variable. The danger always lurks, however, that we are being misled. There may, in fact, be no 'inherent link' between the two variables but simply a common association with a third variable. In other words, a relationship which appears to be asymmetrical may, in fact, be symmetrical.

The method of determining whether one has made a misleading interpretation is to control on the test factor. If, when the influence of the extraneous test factor is held constant, one finds that the relationship disappears, then it may be concluded that the relationship is due to the extraneous variable. If one is to avoid drawing erroneous or misleading conclusions from data, therefore, it is essential to guard against such accidental links.

Support of an interpretation

Just as test factors may be introduced to show that highly plausible interpretations are actually misleading, so may they provide evidence that highly dubious interpretations are actually sound. An investigation of the relationship between parental interest and adolescent self-esteem[11] affords a case in point.

In this study, adolescents were requested to think back to the period when they were about 10 or 11 years old and were asked, 'During this period (age 10 or 11) did your mother know who most of your friends

Table 20.3 Reports of mother's knowledge of child's friends and subject's self-esteem*

Respondent's self-esteem	'During this period (age 10 or 11) did your mother know who most of your friends were?'		
	All or most	Some or none	Don't know or can't remember
High	46%	32%	27%
Medium	23	25	38
Low	30	43	35
Total per cent	100	100	100
Number	(1407)	(133)	(26)

*Morris Rosenberg, 'Parental interest and children's self-conceptions', *Sociometry*, XXVI (March 1963), p. 38, Table 1 (adapted). (Reprinted with permission of the American Sociological Association.)

were?' Table 20.3 shows that the more friends known by the mother, according to the the respondent's report, the larger the proportion with high self-esteem.

However, one is immediately suspicious of such a finding. It is entirely possible that the child who dislikes, or gets on poorly with, his mother will 'remember' her as showing little interest in, or knowledge of, people who were important to him at an earlier age. In this case, the relationship might simply reflect the fact that adolescents with unfavorable attitudes toward their mothers say that their mothers did not know their friends, and these people also tend to have low self-esteem. The task, then, is to control an unfavorable attitude toward mothers in order to see whether the relationship then vanishes.

One question which partly reflects the student's present attitude toward his mother is, 'When your parents disagree, whose side are you usually on – your mother's or your father's?' Table 20.4 shows that whether the adolescent says he is usually on his mother's side or usually on his father's side, or identifies with both equally, those who say that their mothers knew few of their friends are less likely to have high self-esteem than those who say she knew many. It is thus questionable whether the original relationship is due to the respondents' dislike of their mothers, since the difference obtains among those who do or do not identify with their mothers in this situation.

But perhaps it is not the respondent's *present* identification with the mother, but his past reactions to her, which are crucial. In other words, the adolescent may remember disliking his mother when he was 10 or 11 and may thus assume that she knew nothing of his friends at that time. In order to examine this point, respondents were asked, 'When you were about 10 or 11 years old, to whom were you most likely to talk about personal things?' Table 20.5 shows that whether the child said he confided mostly in his mother, in some other person, or in no

Table 20.4 Reports of mother's knowledge of child's friends and subject's self-esteem, by identification with parents*

Respondent's self-esteem	Student currently identifies chiefly with . . .					
	Mother		Father		Both equally	
	Mother knew friends . . .					
	All or most	Some or none	All or most	Some or none	All or most	Some or none
High	43%	32%	39%	27%	52%	39%
Medium	23	22	29	33	22	29
Low	34	45	32	40	26	32
Total per cent	100	100	100	100	100	100
Number	(381)	(40)	(185)	(15)	(407	(31)

*Morris Rosenberg, *op. cit.*, p. 40, Table 3. (Reprinted with permission of the American Sociological Association.)

one, those who said their mothers knew most of their friends tended to have higher self-esteem than those who said their mothers knew few of their friends. The result is thus not due to a negative attitude toward the mother during this earlier period under consideration.

But a third possibility must also be considered. It may not be the child's attitude toward his mother in general, but his recollection of how she behaved toward his *friends* in particular, that colors his recollection of whether she knew his friends. If he recalls her as being unpleasant toward his friends, he might assume that she took little interest in knowing who they were. After the adolescents indicated whether their mothers knew most of their friends, they were asked, 'How did she usually act toward them?' Table 20.6 shows that *irrespective of whether the students said their mothers were friendly or not friendly,* those who said their mothers knew most of their friends had higher self-esteem than those who said their mothers knew few of their friends. Their recollection of whether their mothers knew their friends is, then, not simply a reflection of their favorable or unfavorable memories of their mothers' behavior toward their friends.

We thus see that irrespective of whether the adolescent says he did or did not chiefly confide in his mother at an earlier time; irrespective of whether he identifies with her, with his father, or with both equally at the present time; and irrespective of whether he says she was friendly or unfriendly to his mates, the student who reports that his mother knew most of his friends tends to have higher self-esteem than the one who reports that she knew few. It is likely, then, that the reported differential knowledge of friends does not simply reflect the student's biased perception of, or attitudes toward, the mother.

Table 20.5 Reports of mother's knowledge of child's friends and subject's self-esteem, by tendency to confide in others*

Respondent's self-esteem	Most likely to talk about personal things to . . .					
	Mother		Other person		No one or can't remember	
	Mother knew friends . . .					
	All or most	Some or none	All or most	Some or none	All or most	Some or none
High	51%	39%	41%	35%	46%	29%
Medium	23	32	26	20	21	30
Low	26	29	33	45	34	41
Total per cent	100	100	100	100	100	100
Number	(540)	(41)	(537)	(55)	(195)	(27)

*Morris Rosenberg, *op. cit.,* p. 39, Table 2. (Reprinted with permission of the American Sociological Association.)

Table 20.6 Reports of mother's knowledge of child's friends and subject's self-esteem, by mother's behaviour towards friends*

Respondent's self-esteem	How mother acted toward child's friends . . .					
	Very friendly		Fairly friendly		Not friendly	
	Mother knew child's friends . . .					
	All or most	Some or none	All or most	Some or none	All or most	Some or none
High	48%	34%	45%	33%	32%	21%
Medium	23	24	26	28	29	26
Low	29	41	29	39	40	53
Total per cent	100	100	100	100	100	100
Number	(1091)	(58)	(259)	(51)	(38)	(19)

*Morris Rosenberg, *op. cit.,* p. 40, Table 4. (Reprinted with permission of the American Sociological Association.)

These three controls, of course, do not firmly establish that the report of mother's knowledge of friends is not contaminated with an associated variable, but they add to one's confidence in the measure. There is now stronger reason to believe that the answers reflect mothers' knowledge rather than the biased perception of the respondent.

Sometimes a very simple control may afford decisive support for a theory. For example, it was Durkheim's contention that in periods of national crisis, the collective sentiments were stimulated, the collective passions excited and the level of social integration enhanced, thus leading to a reduction in suicide.[12] As an illustration of national crises, he considered great national wars. He showed that in various European countries the outbreak of war was very consistently followed by an appreciable decline in the suicide rate. But, Durkheim suggested, the relationship between war and suicide might be misleading because it was so difficult to keep track of suicides in the field of battle. How could this be checked? Very simply. Durkheim examined the suicide rates for *women* and found that these rates also declined during the war crises.[13] In effect, Durkheim examined the relationship of war crises to suicide controlling on sex. Since the relationship still obtained, confidence in his interpretation was enhanced.

We thus see that one special virtue of introducing test factors is to *increase* one's confidence that the observed relationship is a true one. This is of particular value when the relationship deals with obviously and grossly contaminated variables. Without the crucial test, a broad shadow of doubt may continue to hang over the interpretation.

Limitations on controls

The introduction of controls thus has a positive role to play in interpretation by increasing one's confidence that there is a meaningful and inherent link between the two variables. But how much confidence can one have? After all, one may establish that the relationship is not due to a particular extraneous variable, but this does not mean that it may not be due to a different extraneous variable. The procedure, then, is to control on these other relevant extraneous variables and see whether the relationship continues to obtain. Each time that one controls on a relevant variable and finds that the relationship remains, one's confidence that the relationship is real increases and the danger of misleading interpretations decreases.

It is never possible, however, to be absolutely certain that the relationship is not misleading. Each variable is block-booked with so many others that there is no foolproof assurance that some extraneous factor which has not been considered may not actually be responsible for the relationship. One can only be certain that the relationship is real if one has controlled on all extraneous variables, which is obviously impossible.

The problem is a serious one, but some of the implicit solutions adopted to deal with it are indefensible. One erroneous solution is to reason that if one cannot have complete confidence that the relationship is real, however many controls one introduces, then there is no point in introducing controls at all. But this argument overlooks the fact that much of science – particularly social science – is built upon degrees of confidence rather than certainty regarding one's conclusions. If one result may occur 1 in 10 times by statistical chance and another 1 in 1,000 times, we do not simply dismiss both findings on the grounds that they may be attributable to sampling variation. On the contrary, we have greater confidence that the latter result is not a reflection of sampling accident. Similarly (other things equal), we have greater confidence that a relationship is real if we have controlled on relevant variables than if we have not.

The second erroneous solution is to suggest that since one can never be certain that one's interpretation is not faulty by virtue of failure to consider an extraneous variable, then it is best not to interpret the relationship at all. One may be satisfied simply to report the descriptive result. To those who wish to understand social phenomena rather than simply to describe them, however, such a solution is totally unsatisfactory. It involves the abandonment of any hope for the development of a theoretically-based empirical social science.

A third erroneous procedure sometimes adopted by research workers is to introduce certain control variables routinely. They may automatically control on social class, sex, age, and perhaps one or two other variables. Such a rote procedure affords little confidence that one has not overlooked some essential variable.

On what bases, then, are decisions to introduce controls made? The first point is that one must consider whether the control variable is *relevant* or is otherwise implicated in the result. This is a logical, not a statistical, operation. If, for example, one finds a relationship between social class and size of income-tax payments, this relationship is obviously not due to child-rearing practices, recreational patterns or speech mannerisms. It is logically senseless to control on these variables since they obviously cannot explain the relationship.

In cases of this sort, however, what is logically senseless to one man may not be so to another. In doubtful cases – where it is not perfectly apparent that the potential test factor is not implicated, or where positive empirical evidence that it is not is available – the cautious procedure is to introduce the controls. Nevertheless, this logical procedure will effectively eliminate the need to introduce a large number of control variables.

An equally important consideration is this: before one introduces a control variable, one must have some idea of the relationship of the test factor to the independent and dependent variables. This point is frequently overlooked by those who routinely or automatically introduce standard controls. If the test factor is not associated statistically *both* with the independent *and* the dependent variables, then it cannot be responsible for the relationship.

Assume, for example, that the research worker finds a relationship between social class and mental illness. He then considers whether this relationship may be misleading. His reflection might proceed as follows: 'I know that Protestants are more likely to be middle or upper class and Catholics are more likely to be working class. Perhaps it is not "lower classness" that is responsible for the mental illness but the fact that lower class people are more likely to be Catholic and that something about Catholicism is conducive to mental illness. I will therefore control on religion to see if the relationship between social class and mental illness disappears.' But this researcher may know that Catholics do *not* have higher rates of mental illness. Therefore, the higher working-class rates cannot be due to the fact that they are more likely to be Catholics. *There is thus no need to control on religion.* In this case the test factor (religion) is related to the independent variable (class) but is not related to the dependent variable (mental illness). One cannot say that lower-class people have higher rates of mental illness because they are more likely to be Catholic if one knows that Catholics do not have higher mental illness rates.

The same consideration applies to the connection between the test factor and the independent variable. Assume we find that Democrats are more strongly opposed to the legal desegregation of private clubs. One might then reason: 'Perhaps Democrats are more authoritarian and authoritarians are more likely to oppose desegregation. I can check this hypothesis by controlling on authoritarianism.' But if one has positive evidence that Democrats are *not* more authoritarian, then this cannot be the explanation. There is no need to control on this variable.

In sum, if the purpose is to guard against a misleading interpretation, then the test factor is introduced only if (1) there is a theoretical or empirically based reason for assuming that it accounts for the relationship, and (2) there is no evidence indicating that it is *not* related both to the independent and dependent variables. These considerations mitigate the problem of having to 'control on everything'.

From the foregoing discussion, it is plain that consideration of extraneous variables may have important theoretical consequences. If, for example, one attempts to interpret a relationship between an independent and a dependent variable without introducing test factors, one's explanation is often in the realm of 'plausibility' and the confidence that can be placed in it is dependent upon the analyst's intellectual acuity, theoretical sophistication and knowledge of the field. If, however, one introduces a test factor, then one is in a position to select from between alternative kinds of interpretation, depending upon whether the relationship does or does not vanish. One is then guided not solely by one's reasoning, but one's reasoning is forced in the direction dictated by the pattern of the data. Other things equal, speculation which is disciplined and guided by the pattern of the data will tend to be more compelling.

A central theoretical contribution of taking account of extraneous variables is that it guards against the erroneous or misleading interpretation. While essentially a 'cautious' contribution, and thus not very striking, it may be just as important for the total field that erroneous generalizations are abandoned, that blind alleys are avoided, as that more positive contributions are made. Especially in sociology, where post-factum explanations are all too easily available to account for findings, this contribution is especially valuable.

Notes

1. The techniques of standardization and partial correlation may also be employed to hold constant a test factor. For a simple method of computing standardizations, see Morris Rosenberg, 'Test factor standardization as a method of interpretation', *Social Forces*, XLI (Oct. 1962), 53–61. Partial correlation is a very powerful statistical procedure, but unfortunately is not suitable for many kinds of sociological data. Given appropriate data, any of the three procedures may be employed; the logic remains unchanged. While examples using standardization and partial correlation will be used on occasion in our discussion, most of the examples will be based on subgroup classification, since this method requires no knowledge of statistics, reveals conditional relationships and demonstrates the logical principles most sharply.
2. Paul F. Lazarsfeld (1955) 'Interpretation of statistical relations as a research operation', in Paul F. Lazarsfeld and Morris Rosenberg (eds), *The Language of Social Research*. Glencoe, Ill.: The Free Press, p. 117.
3. Herbert Hyman (1955) *Survey Design and Analysis*. Glencoe, Ill.: The Free Press, p. 285.
4. The terms 'antecedent variable' [Patricia Kendall and Paul F. Lazarsfeld (1950) 'Problems of survey analysis', in R. K. Merton and P. F. Lazarsfeld (eds), *Continuities in Social Research: Studies in the Scope and Method of 'The American Soldier'*. Glencoe, Ill.: The Free Press, pp. 156–7] and 'invalidating factor' (Hyman, *op. cit.*, p. 247) have also been applied to this concept. Subsequent discussion will make clear why the term 'extraneous variable' is preferred.
5. Herbert Goldhamer and Andrew W. Marshall (1949) *Psychosis and Civilization*. Glencoe, Ill.: The Free Press.
6. *Ibid.*, p. 91.
7. Daniel R. Miller and Guy E. Swanson (1958) *The Changing American Parent*. New York: John Wiley & Sons, Inc.
8. Lawrence D. Haber, 'Age and integration setting: a re-appraisal of *The Changing American Parent*', *American Sociological Review*, XXVII (Oct. 1962), 682–89.
9. *Ibid.*, p. 686.
10. *Ibid.*, p. 687. (Reprinted by permission of the American Sociological Association.)
11. Morris Rosenberg, 'Parental interest and children's self-conceptions', *Sociometry*, XXVI (March 1963), 35–49.
12. Emile Durkheim, *Suicide*, trans. John A. Spaulding and George Simpson. Glencoe, Ill.: The Free Press, 1951, p. 205.
13. *Ibid.*

Data-dredging procedures in survey analysis

Hanan C. Selvin and Alan Stuart

Introduction and summary

It is a commonplace of the statistical design of experiments that the hypotheses to be tested should be formulated before examining the data that are to be used to test them. Even in experimental situations, this is sometimes not possible, and in the last decade or so some progress has been made toward the development of more flexible testing procedures which allow the data to be dredged for hypotheses in certain ways. In survey analysis, which is commonly exploratory, it is rare for precise hypotheses to be formulable independently of the data. It follows that normally no precise probabilistic interpretations can validly be given to relationships found among the survey variables. In practice, this has not prevented survey practitioners from reporting probability levels as if they were precisely meaningful. Most investigators are so accustomed to making probability statements that a survey report looks naked without them, but we fear that many survey reports are wearing the Emperor's clothes. This paper offers a classification of data-dredging procedures and some comments on their use.

Survey analysis

The survey analyses we consider here are *explanatory* or *theoretical*; such a survey aims, not primarily to describe some population by estimating one or more of its parameters (although this may be one of its aims) but, by invoking more general substantive propositions, to explain why certain phenomena in that population behave as they do. One may want to learn how people make up their minds in an election, why the rates of mental illness vary from one social class to another, or how new farm practices diffuse through a rural community. Even when the problem derives from practical concerns, the theoretically-oriented survey always involves such nonstatistical tasks as the 'operationalization' of the variables (what does it mean to say that an instructor at an American university was 'frightened' by the investigations of the McCarthy era?) and the interpretation of the statistical findings, often by reference to variables on which data were not gathered (to what extent is the observed relation between social class and arrests for juvenile delinquency a manifestation of differential treatment by the police?).

Most surveys of this kind are based on long questionnaires and large samples. A typical academic survey may ask 100 questions of 1,000 people, and market surveys, if they usually ask fewer questions, may have 10,000 cases or more. Gathering and processing the data take a long time – several months in most cases – and analysing the data for their theoretical implications may take even longer. With such a long and expensive procedure, the survey analyst wants to maximize the intellectual returns on his investment. Rarely, if ever, does he undertake a study with a single specific hypothesis in mind. He usually has many diffuse and ill-formulated hypotheses in mind; and the marginal cost of an additional question is so low that many different problems can be investigated in the same survey without raising its cost very much. Indeed, the vein of data in most surveys is so rich and the amount of information extracted by the original analyst so little that libraries of survey data have been established to facilitate 'secondary analysis', the re-study of surveys for purposes that may not have been intended by the original investigator.

In the sense that relatively few of the possible and meaningful hypotheses are specified in advance of gathering the data, the typical survey is exploratory, and the analyst alternates between examining the data and formulating hypotheses. In an experiment the form of the analysis is specified in the design, but the form of survey analysis typically evolves as the data are examined. In the present state of the art there is seldom only a single viable path at any stage of the analysis, so that the analyst has a great deal of freedom, regardless of the configurations of the data.

To make the survey analyst's problem more vivid, we may liken him to a hunter stalking an unknown quarry through an unfamiliar landscape with an arsenal of complex weapons. This metaphor suggests the names we have given to some practices of survey analysts: snooping, fishing and hunting.

Ordered and unordered observations: snooping

The effect of knowledge of the data upon the performance of statistical tests has long been known. Perhaps its best-known manifestation is in the case when a single random sample of $n(>2)$ observations is available from a known distribution, say the normal with zero mean, unit variance for convenience. The difference between any predesignated pair of observations (say, the 4th and 17th in order of drawing) is itself normal, with zero mean, variance two; so is the difference between any pair of observations chosen at random. But if the pair to be compared is chosen in any way related to the values observed, their difference is not normally distributed. In particular, if we choose the *largest* observed difference between pairs (which is, of course, the sample range) its distribution depends critically on n and is never normal.

We may put the point more generally, without reference to normality: the set of n observations on a variable y may either be labelled y_1, $y_2, \ldots, y_n$ where the subscript refers to the order of drawing, or $y_{(1)}$, $y_{(2)}, \ldots y_{(n)}$ where $y_{(1)} \leqslant y_{(2)} \leqslant \ldots \leqslant y_{(n-1)} \leqslant y_{(n)}$ are the ordered sample values. The distribution of the differences between any pair of y's defined by their places in the ordering, $y_{(r)} - y_{(s)}$, is obtainable if r and s are fixed. Thus, we can calculate the distribution of the range (the case $r=n$, $s=1$) for any n; we can also calculate the distribution of the difference between any other *predesignated* pair of ordered observations.

Similarly, so long as we follow a precisely predesignated procedure, we can use test procedures involving a sequence of pairwise comparisons. Such are the *multiple comparisons* tests in the analysis of variance. In the extreme case, we may even be able to predesignate an infinite class of comparisons to be made on the data – this is what is equivalently done in the 'all contrasts' procedures of Tukey and Scheffé (see Scheffé, 1959), where every linear function (with coefficients summing to zero) of a set of variables may validly be tested simultaneously with a known probability level. In conformity with the term 'data-snooping', which has sometimes been used in connection with these procedures, we define the first category in our classification of data-dredging procedures: SNOOPING is the process of testing from the data all of a *predesignated* (though possibly infinite) set of hypotheses. It will be seen from the discussion above that snooping is a rigorous and valid statistical procedure. It is, however, rather limited in scope because of the difficulty of solving the mathematical problems involved when large numbers of correlated tests are to be made. We believe that the two applications we have mentioned (range and all-contrasts procedures) are the only important snooping procedures in practice.

Searching for a model: fishing

Snooping procedures, or at least such as have so far been developed, are of little practical use to the survey practitioner as opposed to the experimentalist. Pre-data hypotheses are commonly imprecise or even non-existent, and often one of the principal motives for undertaking a survey is to provide material from which some rather precise hypothesis may be dredged. One may, for example, wish to decide which independent variables to include in a relationship explaining one or more other variables.

In studies with a single important dependent variable – for example, of voting behavior – analysts frequently examine all possible two-variable relations between the dependent variable and independent variables, but only a few of these relations will appear in the published report, the others not being considered 'useful'. A more elaborate form of fishing appears in many computer programs for regression, in which the independent variables are screened by the program to see if they account for a worthwhile (possibly predetermined) proportion of the variation in the dependent variable; those that fail to meet this test do not appear in the final regression equation.

We therefore define our second category: FISHING is the process of using the data to choose which of a number of candidate variables to include in an explanatory model.

Here we come upon another aspect of the conditioning of statistical tests by knowledge of the data. If we decide, on the basis of the data, to discard one or more variables from an explanatory relation, we cannot validly apply standard statistical procedures to the retained variables in the relation as though nothing had happened. In the nature of the case, the retained variables have had to pass some kind of preliminary test (possibly an imprecise intuitive one) that the discarded variables failed. In our picturesque terminology the fish which don't fall through the net are bound to be bigger than those which do, and it is quite fruitless to test whether they are of average size. Not only will this alter the performance of all subsequent tests on the retained explanatory model – it may destroy unbiasedness and alter mean-square-error in estimation (see Larson and Bancroft, 1963, a, b and their references). Some of these fishing effects have been investigated for regression models with predesignated candidate variables, and for a number of preliminary tests leading to pooling procedures in the analysis of variance and elsewhere. Box and Cox (1964) consider general methods of fishing for the appropriate scale on which to analyze experimental data.

Although the results of these investigations throw light on the nature of the conditioning imposed by preliminary search procedures, this conditioning is not of a simple or clearcut kind, and many of the important questions for survey analysts have not yet been examined. In general, we can only say that any preliminary search of data for a model, even when the alternatives are predesignated, affects the probability levels of all subsequent tests based on that model on the same data, and in no very simple way, and also affects the characteristics of subsequent estimation procedures. The only valid course for the survey analyst is to use different data for testing the model he has dredged from his first set of data. This need not involve a new sample since the initial sample may be divided (by carefully randomized methods which take account of all the complexities of the sample structure) into two parts for just this purpose.

But even if such segregation is not carried out (because the sample is too small or for other reasons), we do not suggest that fishing is a reprehensible procedure – indeed it is often the only way to produce the food needed for the survey analyst's thought. We are arguing only that the survey analyst should admit that he *has* been fishing, rather than pretend that the model fell upon him as manna from heaven, and take the consequences, which are that the apparent probability levels of tests may have little relation to their true probability levels, and that the properties of estimates may be radically different from what is supposed.

Computers make it possible for fishing trips to be completely systematic. Thus Morgan and Sonquist (1963 a, b; see also Sonquist and Morgan, 1964) have developed a program that fishes for the most important independent variables and the most important successive dichotomizations of these variables. In other words, it isolates the successive splits of the sample that account for as large a proportion of the variation in the dependent variable as possible, with a specified minimum level of variation, usually 0.5 per cent, for each split. They write (1963a, p. 433):

Most statistical estimates carry with them procedures for estimating their sampling variability. Sampling stability with the proposed program would mean that using a different sample, one would end up with the same complex groups segregated. No simple quantitative measure of similarity seems possible, nor any way of deriving its sampling properties. The only practical solution would seem to be to try the program out on some properly designed half-samples, taking account of the original sample stratification and controls, and to describe the extent of similarity of the pedigrees of the groups so isolated. Since the program 'tries' an almost unlimited number of things, no significance tests are appropriate, and in any case the concern is with discovering a limited number of 'indexes' or complex constructs which will explain more than other possible sets.

Fishing for the variables to go into a model, though often a complex procedure, is essentially a variant of the ordering of observations discussed on p. 280: the candidate variables are ordered into two classes, 'useful' and 'not useful'. To ignore this fact in subsequent analysis is the same kind of error as to ignore the fact that the range of a normal sample is not normally distributed. Its effects on a survey analysis may be devastating.

Non-predesignated parameters: hunting and the chi-square test

Whereas snooping predesignates all tests to be made, and fishing uses a predesignated set of candidate variables, HUNTING involves no predesignation: the data are simply dredged for information in the area of interest. Hunting is distinguished from snooping and fishing in that it is impossible, *in principle*, for rigorous statistical tests to be devised to cover the procedure, since the procedure itself is necessarily ill-defined and consequently impossible to express in the precise language of a computer program. It has an analog, often not recognized as such, in general statistical practice. Consider the ordinary 'curve-fitting' procedure – we have a sample distribution of observations in k groups and fit a theoretical distribution (with p parameters estimated quite properly by efficient methods from the grouped data) which we then test by chi-square with $k—p—1$ degrees of freedom. But how was the *form* of the theoretical distribution chosen? In most cases known to us, it is hunted for by eye-examination of the histogram. This imposes an unknown (but presumably large) number of constraints[1] upon the agreement between observed and theoretical distributions, and destroys the probability level of the subsequent chi-square test, which is only valid if the form of the theoretical distribution is given by pre-data knowledge. It is a somewhat startling fact that most P-values reported in routine curve-fitting chi-square tests are meaningless, but it underlines our main point in this section, that hunting, by its very nature, precludes subsequent probability statements.

Hunting can take many forms. As defined here, it involves searching through a body of data and examining many relations in order to find some worth testing. Or one may examine a single hypothesis in several different bodies of data – as in parapsychology experiments, when the probability of a run of successful guesses is computed only after a subject gets 'hot'. Sterling (1959) has pointed out that fallacious test results may appear when different investigators examine the same false hypothesis. Here the failure to replicate published studies and the practice of publishing only 'significant' results mean that a procedure intended to guard against the acceptance of 'chance' outcomes actually promotes their acceptance. Tullock (1959) has remarked that this is even more likely to happen when a single investigator does a series of studies and reports only those hypotheses that turn out to be 'significant'.

Because hunting offers maximum scope for the data-dredger, since there are no rules at all, it must always be acknowledged, at the cost of subsequent probability statements. What is more, there is no possibility that hunting can ever be made to lead to precise probability statements. Hunting is essential to many survey analysts. As with fishing, the only criticism to be made is of the delusion that one has to pay no price for the sport.

It is worth remarking that in general hunting cannot be made probabilistically respectable by splitting the sample in advance. When one is fishing for a single model, or carrying out a single chi-square test, one essentially wishes to test a single hypothesis, and segregation of one part of the data for this purpose will make this possible as indicated above. But hunting typically throws up a group of interrelated hypotheses, and we do not know in advance how many these will be, so there is no possibility of separating off a part of the data for each hypothesis to be tested independently. (It would be pleasant to imagine the survey analyst with a large stock of reserve sub-samples to test the hypotheses he hunts up, but this is unrealistic.)[2] If hunting on one sub-sample produces a number of related hypotheses, the results of the tests of them carried out on a second sub-sample will be correlated in unknown ways unless we follow a strictly predesignated testing procedure whose statistical properties are known. Nevertheless it must presumably be better in general to use a reserve sub-sample for this purpose than to have no such sub-sample at all.

Notes

1. Moreover, these constraints are not linear functions of the group frequencies, so there is no possible way of adjusting degrees of freedom from them.
2. For a discussion of ways in which libraries of survey data might be used to test hypotheses derived from hunting, see Selvin (1965).

References

Box, G. E. P. and Cox, E. R. (1964) 'An analysis of transformations', *Journal of the Royal Statistical Society,* B, **26,** 211–52.

Larson, H. J. and Bancroft, T. A. (1963a) 'Sequential model building for prediction in regression analysis I', *Annals of Mathematical Statistics,* 462–79.

Larson, H. J. and Bancroft, T. A. (1963b) 'Biases in prediction by regression for certain incompletely specified models', *Biometrika,* **50,** 391–402.

Morgan, J. N. and Sonquist, J. A. (1963a) 'Problems in the analysis of survey data – and a proposal', *JASA,* **58,** 415–34.

Morgan, J. N. and Sonquist, J. A. (1963b) 'Some results of a non-symmetrical branching process that looks for interaction effects', *Proceedings of the Social Statistics Section, American Statistical Association, 1963,* 40–53.

Scheffé, H. (1959) *The Analysis of Variance.* New York: John Wiley and Sons.

Selvin, H. C. (1965) 'Durkheim's *Suicide*: further thoughts on a methodological classic', in Robert A. Nisbet (ed.), *Emile Durkheim.* Englewood Cliffs, N.J.: Prentice-Hall, pp. 113–36.

Sonquist, J. A. and Morgan, J. N. (1964) *The Detection of Interaction Effects.* Ann Arbor: Survey Research Center, The University of Michigan.

Sterling, T. D. (1959) 'Publication decisions and their possible effects on inferences drawn from tests of significance – or vice-versa', *JASA,* **54,** 30–4.

Tullock, G. (1959) 'Publication decisions and tests of significance – a comment', *JASA,* **54,** 593.

Generalized regression analysis

Andrew Ahlgren and Herbert J. Walberg

Behavioral research workers often conceive of regression in the limited sense of the linear, additive model in which the independent variables have a straight-line relation to the dependent variable and do not interact. In the first part of this chapter, *Regression Models*, the simplistic conception of regression analysis is enlarged to include some curvature and interaction. In the second part, *Regression versus Analysis of Variance*, regression is compared to and contrasted with analysis of variance. [. . .] Throughout, our discussion will be almost entirely concerned with regression concepts, strategies, and interpretations, with little attention to mathematical derivations and computation. [. . .]

Some stylistic decisions have been made for the sake of clarity. Independent variables will often be called 'predictors', and dependent variables will sometimes be called 'criteria'. We recognize that there is usually no real prediction done and, moreover, that the assignment to independent or dependent status is often subjective; but the informal terms 'predictor' and 'criterion' are more readily understood than the technical terms, and the term 'independent' is needed to express unrelatedness. Similarly, the technical convention is to write coefficients as subscripted bs (b_1, b_2, b_3, etc.), but in many places we have used just a, b, c, etc. because equations are easier to read without all those subscripts. (Nonetheless, these arbitrary symbols will eventually be referred to generically as 'b weights'.)

Regression models

Simple regression
In ordinary two-variable regression, a straight line is found that best fits a swarm of data points that represent scores of two variables Y and

Extract from Andrew Ahlgren and Herbert J. Walberg, 'Generalized regression analysis', from Daniel J. Amick and Herbert J. Walberg (eds), *Introductory Multivariate Analysis*. Berkeley: McCutchan Publishing Corporation, 1975, Ch. 2, pp. 8–52.

X (Fig. 22.1). The criterion for 'best fit' is that the data points deviate less from that line than from any other. More precisely, the line that best expresses the 'regression of Y on X' is the line for which the average squared deviation of Y values from the line is a minimum. The line therefore indicates the best guesses for estimating subjects' Y scores when their X scores are known. The estimated values for Y are written $\hat{Y}$, and the line can be described by an equation:

$$\hat{Y} = bX + constant$$

(See Fig. 22.2.)

Coefficient b describes the slope of the line: how rapidly $\hat{Y}$ changes as X changes. The constant term describes how high the line is where $X = 0$. (When a value of 0 has no meaning for the variable, such as for IQ, the constant term is just a mathematical artifact that raises or lowers the whole regression line.)

If both the Y and X scores were expressed as deviations from their means, $y = Y - \bar{Y}$ and $x = X - \bar{X}$, then the same relationship could be written without the constant term:

$$\hat{y} = bx$$

(See Fig. 22.3.)

If, further, both the Y and X scores are rescaled (by their standard deviations s_x and s_y) to have the same standard deviation (1.0) as well as the same mean (0),

$$z_x = \frac{x}{s_x} \quad \text{and} \quad z_y = \frac{y}{s_y}$$

the relationship can be written as:

$$\hat{z}_y = \beta z_x$$

(See Fig. 22.4.)

Here the Greek letter β (beta) is the 'standardized regression coefficient', and has a simple relationship to the 'raw regression coefficient' b:

$$\beta = b \left(\frac{s_x}{s_y} \right)$$

The β does not mean quite the same thing as the b. The raw-score coefficient b indicates the amount of change in Y that accompanies a certain change in X, and so depends on the scale of the two scores. Because the z_x and z_y scores have the same total variation, the standard-score coefficient β indicates the proportion of total variation in Y that can be 'accounted for' by variation in X. (More precisely, the proportion of variance accounted for by X is equal to β^2.)

The β coefficient is identical to the familiar Pearson product-moment correlation coefficient r. For example, if the correlation between IQ and Authoritarianism in a sample is 0.40, the proportion of variance in Authoritarianism 'explainable' by IQ is equal to $(0.40)^2 =$

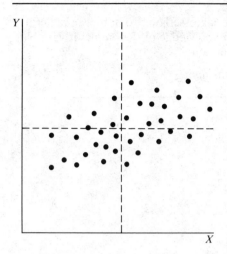

Fig. 22.1

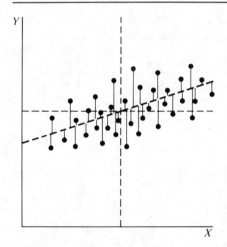

Fig. 22.2

0.16; that is, IQ can 'explain' 16 per cent of the total variance in Authoritarianism (in that sample). [. . .]

The significance of the regression in a sample of size N can be tested with an F ratio:

$$F = \frac{r^2}{1 - r^2} \, (N - 2).$$

where the degrees of freedom for F are 1 and $N - 2$.

Multiple regression

Criterion Y scores can also be regressed on two or more predictors. Values of Y are estimated from knowledge of the predictor variables X_1, X_2, etc. by a regression equation:

$$\hat{Y} = b_1X_1 + b_2X_2 + \ldots + constant$$

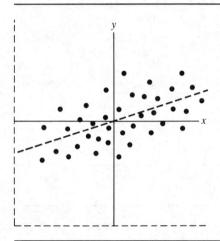

Fig. 22.3

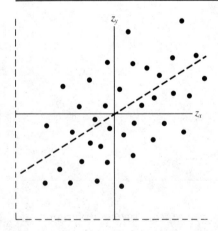

Fig. 22.4

The coefficients b_1, b_2, etc. are given values (by computer program) that will minimize the differences between the actual values of Y and the estimates $\hat{Y}$. (Again, it is the average squared deviation of Y from $\hat{Y}$ that is minimized.)

The relationship between Y and the predictors is expressed by a multiple correlation R, and the proportion of variance in Y accounted for by the predictors together is equal to R^2. (It is important to realize that R is always positive; the direction of the relationship is inferred from the signs of the b coefficients.) The overall significance of the regression using n predictors in a sample of size N can be tested with an F ratio:

$$F = \frac{R^2}{1 - R^2} \left(\frac{N - n - 1}{n} \right)$$

where the degrees of freedom for F are n and $N - n - 1$. (Note that when $n = 1$ this equation for F becomes the same as in simple r.)

As for simple regression, the multiple regression can be expressed in 'deviation' form by rescaling all the variables to a mean of 0:

$$\hat{y} = b_1 x_1 + b_2 x_2 + \ldots$$

or in 'standardized' form by further rescaling all the variables to the same variance:

$$\hat{z}_y = \beta_1 z_{x1} + \beta_2 z_{x2} + \ldots$$

Each standardized regression coefficient β_i is related to the corresponding raw regression coefficient b_i as described above for simple regression, but the βs are no longer identical to the simple r correlations between the predictors and Y. The βs depend not only on the relation between each predictor and Y, but also depend on the relationships *among the predictors*. (In the unusual case that the predictors are completely uncorrelated with each other, the βs do become equal to the simple r correlations.)

As a result of this interdependence of coefficients, the interpretation of how much each predictor 'contributes' to the prediction model is a tricky business, and can involve looking back and forth between bs, βs, Rs, Fs, rs, and even more! A partial escape from the ambiguities of interpreting multiple regression analysis is afforded by the 'planned stepwise' approach.

Stepwise multiple regression

In stepwise regression, a series of regression models is tried, each model including a different set of variables. There are many varieties of stepwise, some adding one variable at a time, some deleting one variable at a time, and most of them let the computer program make the decisions of which variable to add or drop on each step – usually on the basis of which new variable will make the most significant change in prediction. These different varieties do not necessarily end up with the same 'best' model, and they take maximum advantage of sampling and measurement error.

We recommend here a stepwise procedure in which the researcher decides in advance what the order of entry of terms will be, based on a conceptual view of the relationships among the variables. For each step there will be an overall significance test for R (as given above); there will also be a significance test for *improvement* in R achieved by that step:

$$F = \frac{R^2\,new - R^2\,old}{1 - R^2\,new}(N - n - 1)$$

where n is the 'new' number of predictors and the degrees of freedom for F are 1 and $N - n - 1$.

Each step of a stepwise multiple regression results in a sets of bs, a corresponding set of βs, an overall F test for the significance of the model and an F test for the significance of the improvement on that step. Depending on which computer program is used, each step may also generate F tests for each term already in the model – testing the significance of its contribution to prediction beyond that possible with all the other variables already in the model. Another possible output for each step is a 'preview' of what might be contributed by each of the variables *not* yet in the model – in the form of F tests for entry or partial correlations with Y (or both).

There is no way to write a readable account of how to orchestrate all this information; it is an art that one develops through practice (or so we hope). [. . .] We will concentrate almost entirely on the overall significance of R and the significance of the increase in R on each step. Since R^2 is easier to interpret (as 'per cent of variance accounted for'), the discussion will usually refer to R^2 rather than to R.

Curvature

It would surely be expected in the behavioral sciences that relationships among some variables would show accelerations or decelerations of effect (Figs. 22.5 and 22.6) and even an occasional optimal or minimal effect (Figs. 22.7 and 22.8). Such apparently simple curvature can be approximated fairly well by some portion of a parabola (Figs. 22.9–22.12). A parabola is described by an equation of the form $Y = aX^2 + bX + constant$. The coefficients a, b, and the constant term shift the parabola around and change its shape. By proper choice of coefficients, any part of any shape parabola can be used to fit a scatterplot of data. Thus, by including an X^2 term as well as the X term, a multiple regression can fit a regression curve to a great variety of accelerated or optimal relationships – the regression program will determine the best values for a, b, and the constant.

A $+$ or $-$ weight for the X term by itself indicates a rising or falling straight line, and a $+$ or $-$ weight for the X^2 term implies a curving upward or downward from what that straight line would be. Figures 22.9 and 22.12 correspond to a $+$ weight for X^2, while Figs. 22.10 and 22.11 correspond to a $-X^2$ term.

The value of R^2 obtained with the X term alone indicates how well the relationship can be approximated by a section of a straight line, and

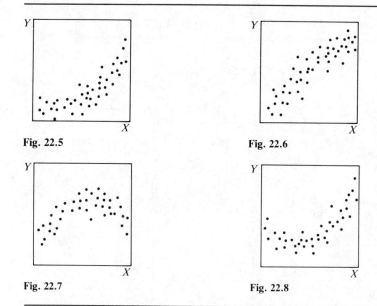

Fig. 22.5

Fig. 22.6

Fig. 22.7

Fig. 22.8

the R^2 obtained when both X and X^2 terms are included indicates how well the relationship can be approximated by a section of a parabola. (Most statistical packages for regression analysis allow manipulation of the input variables before analysis – so a new variable X^2 can be computed internally by squaring X and used subsequently in variable lists.)

The *increase* in R^2 resulting from adding the X^2 term is related to the amount of curvature in the relationship. However, the regression coefficients must be interpreted with considerable caution. The relative sizes of the X and X^2 weights depend on where the zero is on the X scale. The zero-point for any scales besides a ratio scale (a rarity in behavioral science) is more or less arbitrary, and thus so too are the X and X^2 weights.

For example, in Fig. 22.8, the upward curvature means that there must be a $+X^2$ term, but gives no clue as to whether an X term will also be necessary. If the zero for the X scale were in the middle of the data range – as would be the case for a deviation score – the curve would be a parabola with turning point at $X = 0$ and could be described simply as $Y = aX^2 + c$: the weight for the X term would be zero. (Figure 22.13 shows how there is no X term; the curve bends up from a horizontal line.) If, on the other hand, the zero of the X scale were at the left extreme of the data range – as would be the case for most raw test scores – then the turning point of the parabola would be far from $X = 0$ and a large – weight on the X term would be needed to represent the curve properly. (Figure 22.14 shows how the curve bends up from a steeply descending straight line.)

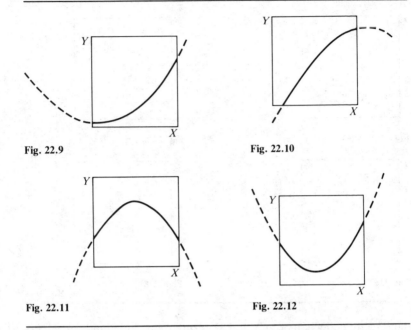

Fig. 22.9   Fig. 22.10

Fig. 22.11   Fig. 22.12

It is not uncommon to find that the X term makes a significant contribution only when X^2 is entered too. This would clearly be the case for Fig. 22.7, for example (if the zero for the X scale were at the left edge of the plot), for neither a straight line nor a parabola with origin at $X = 0$ would fit the data at all. On the other hand, an initially significant X term might vanish when X^2 is entered too. This would likely be the case for Fig. 22.5 (if the zero were at the left edge), since the X^2 term could account for the data well by itself. If both X and X^2 terms are necessary to fit the data well, the overall relation should be considered 'quadratic', and not (e.g. in Fig. 22.14) as a 'negative linear effect and positive square effect'.

The least ambiguous way to assess the nature of the relationship is to draw the regression curve. The raw regression weights can be used to sketch the regression line by choosing several values for X in the range of actual data and plugging them into the regression equation to get estimated values of Y. These 'predicted' values may be plotted on a graph of Y versus X, and a smooth curve drawn through them.

The importance of curving the regression line is inferred from the increase in R^2 afforded by including the X^2 term – or by the statistical *significance* of that increase, depending on what you mean by 'important'. The curve-fitting method by itself says nothing about whether Y has a 'truly' curvilinear relation to X or whether X is just scaled inappropriately (and should therefore be transformed to a new scale X' that would have a linear relationship to Y. This issue can be resolved

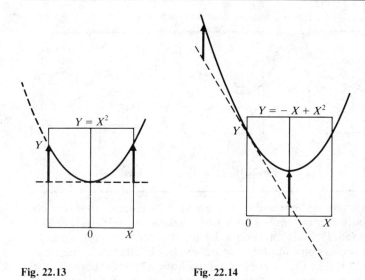

Fig. 22.13   **Fig. 22.14**

only on the basis of other knowledge about the meaningfulness of X and Y — that is, their relationships to other variables. Thus if Y were found to have similar curvilinear relationships to a variety of variables besides X, one might conclude that Y itself was inappropriately scaled and would therefore benefit from transformation. (When, on the other hand, a clear maximum or minimum appears in the data range, then there is something inherently nonlinear about the relationship that no monotonic transformation can remove.)

What about higher power terms? Adding an X^3 or even an X^4 term might improve the fit by subtly changing the curvature, although there will also be the danger of decreased significance for the overall regression (because of the decreased degrees of freedom for error) and general inconvenience. One may reasonably doubt that the precision of behavioral data allows much advantage to extensive polynomial fitting of a relationship, particularly for unreliable measures and small samples. Yet there are some distinct types of patterns in data distributions that can be matched only by including third- or fourth-power terms.

Just as a description of a single maximum or minimum requires at least an X^2 term, a plateau (Fig. 22.15) or a maximum–minimum pair (Fig. 22.16) requires at least an X^3 term. As before, the weights assigned to the X, X^2 and X^3 terms are highly sensitive to the zero-point chosen for the X scale, and the contribution of the X^3 term is best judged from the increase in R^2 when it is added.

Going one step further, a double maximum (Fig. 22.17) or double minimum would require an X^4 term for its description. Such a bimodal

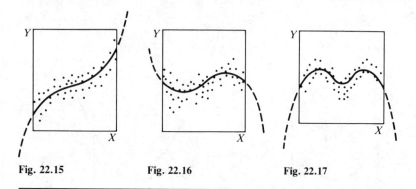

Fig. 22.15   **Fig. 22.16**   **Fig. 22.17**

distribution might be found in the behavioral sciences, but it is doubtful that any more complicated set of maxima and minima would be encountered. Power terms above X^4 might contribute significantly to multiple regressions, but few researchers would attempt a qualitative interpretation. To the extent that terms above X^2 merely make statistically significant minor adjustments on the slope of the regression curve, it would be doubtful whether those refinements would transfer to other samples. Indeed, for behavioral data, even the X^2 term seldom improves prediction much after the X term is entered.

There is another constraint on the utility of higher power terms that arises when the predictor variable has discrete levels rather than a continuous distribution. As will be explained more extensively later in *Regression versus Analysis of Variance*, a variable with k levels is fitted as completely as possible by terms up to the $k-1$ power. Thus, for example, regression on a three-level predictor is achieved by X and X^2 terms – no higher power terms could possibly contribute more.

In all of this polynomial fitting, there has been no serious meaning attached to the power terms – inclusion of X^2 or X^3 has been advocated only to make the regression curve fit the data better. The statistical significance of adding an X^2 term, for example, has not been taken to mean that there is some way in which X 'has a square effect' on Y, only that there is some diminishing-returns character to the relationship (Fig. 22.6) or that there is an optimal middle value for X (Fig. 22.7). [. . .] It goes without saying, we hope, that there is no ground for extrapolating the relationship beyond the range of data in the sample. For example, a significant $-X^2$ term for Fig. 22.6 would not imply that new data further to the right would reach maximum Y and then descend.

Multiple predictors: without interaction

When we consider the relationship of Y to two variables X_1 and X_2, the curvilinear discussion of the last section needs very little extension. If the effect of X_1 on Y is independent of the effect of X_2 on Y, and vice versa, then the foregoing discussion can be applied directly to X_1 and X_2 separately. If no interaction were expected, one could choose to enter the terms in a stepwise regression either in the order

$X_1, X_2, ..., X_1^2, X_2^2, ...$

or in the order

$X_1, X_1^2, ..., X_2, X_2^2, ...$

The first order has the conceptual advantage of trying the simplest (i.e. linear) model first, while the second order has the advantage of trying one variable at a time. In either case, the final step would produce the same equation for estimating values of Y:

$$\hat{Y} = a_1X_1 + b_1X_2 + ... + a_2X_1^2 + b_2X_2^2 + ... + constant$$

This full equation would be used, of course, only if all the terms made significant contributions to increasing R^2; otherwise the equation from the last significant step would be used. For the sake of parsimony, the more complex terms are dropped unless they account for a noticeable amount of additional variance.

When there are two predictor variables it is possible to sketch the regression surface (rather than a line). The drawing is more difficult, and will be worth while only if one or both of the square terms make significant contributions. Figure 22.18 shows a plane regression surface corresponding to $+X_1$ and $+X_2$ terms.

Figure 22.19 shows a regression surface for which the regression weights (both $+$) would fall mainly on X_2 and X_1^2. The effect of a second-power term is to curve the surface away from a plane – up for a $+$ weight and down for a $-$ weight. Since in the example only X_1 has a substantial second-power term, the regression plane is curved up only in the X_1 direction. Anywhere on this surface, the surface *rises steadily* with increases in X_2, and *rises acceleratedly* with increases in X_1.

Several other examples are given in Figs. 22.20, 22.21 and 22.22. Note that for all these surfaces the X_1 and X_2 effects are independent – the slope of the surface in the X_1 direction is the same across all values of X_2, and the slope of the surface in the X_2 direction is the same across all values of X_1.

A simpler graphic representation can be made by drawing, say, three regression lines for Y on X_1, one for each of three levels of X_2. If X_2 is actually a three-level variable rather than continuous, this sketch becomes the familiar plot used to display effects in a two-way analysis of variance. In effect, the diagram presses three slices of the surface flat.

Figure 22.23 shows how the surface of Fig. 22.18 would appear in the simpler representation. This form of diagram makes it easier to 'type' regression relationships – either for interpretation of polynomial terms or for planning a priori inclusion of such terms. Figure 22.24 displays typical diagrams that would correspond to independent

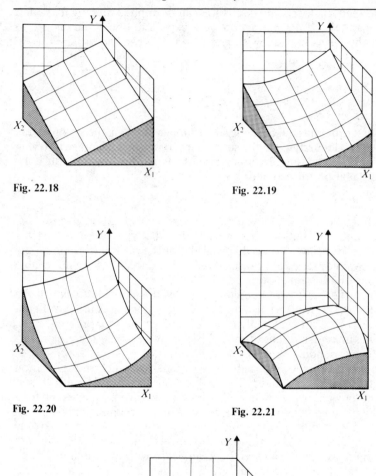

Fig. 22.18

Fig. 22.19

Fig. 22.20

Fig. 22.21

Fig. 22.22

effects of first- and second-order terms for two predictors X_1 and X_2. It is important to realize that the choice of which is to be X_1 and which X_2 is arbitrary, and need have nothing to do with the order of entry into

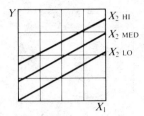

Fig. 22.23

the multiple regression. For example, Figs. 22.24(f) and 22.24(h) display the same set of relationships; one would choose whichever form of diagram was easier to interpret or to explain a proposition.

The diagrams will be fairly self-evident on inspection, but note that:

(1) X_1 effects appear as *slopes* of the lines;
(2) X_2 effects appear as *separations* of the lines;
(3) X_1^2 effects appear as *uneven* slopes–i.e., as curvature of the lines;
(4) X_2^2 effects appear as *uneven* separations of the lines.

Whatever the shapes and separations, however, the lines are always parallel, implying that the effect of X_1 on Y is the same no matter what the level of X_2 is. This is the necessary result of our having insisted that the X_1 and X_2 effects are independent of one another. If we wish to allow for possible interaction of X_1 and X_2 in their effects on Y, then we must include new terms in the regression.

Multiple predictors: with interaction
It can be shown (with a little calculus) that in a two-predictor model the value of X_2 cannot affect the slope of $\hat{Y}$ versus X_1 unless there are terms in the equation that are products of X_1 and X_2. (In a calculus context, the first X_1= derivative of the function $\hat{Y} = f(X_1)$ must depend on X_2.) The simplest such term is just X_1X_2. (Product terms can be generated internally by most statistical packages for multiple regression.) Thus the simplest regression model allowing for interaction would be:

$$\hat{Y} = aX_1 + bX_2 + cX_1X_2 + constant$$

The terms would be entered in stepwise order X_1, X_2, and then X_1X_2; if a significant increase in R^2 is obtained by adding the X_1X_2 term, then there is a significant linear interaction of X_1 and X_2 in their effect on Y – the effect of X_1 on Y is different for different values of X_2, and vice versa.

Similar to the case of interpreting the regression weights for X and X^2 terms, the weights for X_1, X_2, and X_1X_2 depend in part on where the zeros are chosen for the X_1 and X_2 scales. Thus it is possible that the X_1 term will not appear significant on its initial entry into the model, but

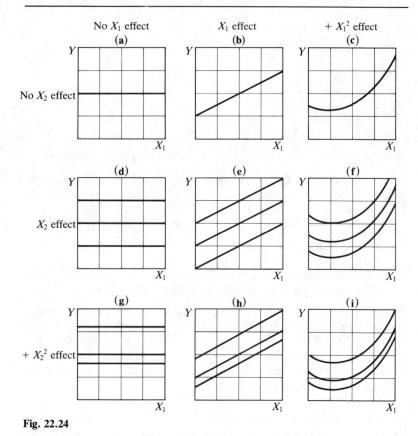

Fig. 22.24

that it will *become* significant when the X_1X_2 term (also significant) is entered.

The best idea of the relationship is obtained by graphing the equation over the range of actual data. This is done by using the raw regression weights to plot $\hat{Y}$ versus X_1 for each of several levels of X_2 (say, a high level, a mean level and a low level). Two points are enough to describe a straight line, of course, and 5 or 6 will do for almost any curve you are likely to find. A $+X_1X_2$ term implies a surface curving up from whatever plane is established by X_1 and X_2 independently, and a $-X_1X_2$ term implies a curving down. (The surface still consists of straight lines in the X_1 and X_2 directions, and the curvature appears only along the direction of the diagonal between X_1 and X_2.)

Figure 22.18 shows positive linear X_1 and X_2 effects with no interaction; Fig. 22.25 shows the effect of adding a $-X_1X_2$ interaction term. The result is a depressing of the high$-X_1$ high$-X_2$ corner of the plot.

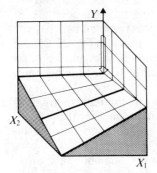

Fig. 22.25

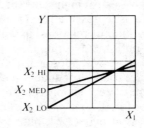

Fig. 22.26

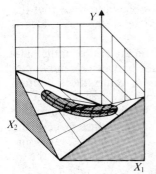

Fig. 22.27

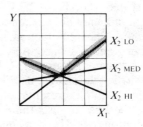

Fig. 22.28

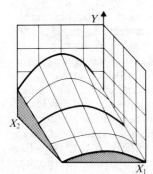

Fig. 22.29

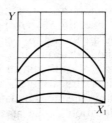

Fig. 22.30

(A $+X_1X_2$ term would elevate this corner.) The surface is twisted – Y might increase with X_1 at low values of X_2, but not change at all (or even decrease) with X_1 at high values of X_2. This twist can best be seen when the surface is represented by a few slices as it is in Fig. 22.26. An example of this kind of relationship would be the dependence of an easy test score on IQ and testing time – if either IQ or time becomes very large, the score will approach 100 per cent correct. Hence the regression surface rounds off under a 'ceiling', no matter how great IQ or times becomes. Very simply a significant product term produces different slopes for the $\hat{Y}$ versus X_1 lines; the contour lines are no longer parallel as in Fig. 22.24, but converge or diverge.

If the lines have different slopes but always lie one above the other (in the major part of the data range), the interaction is called 'ordinal'; sometimes such an interaction can be removed by suitable transformations of one scale or the other. If, however, the lines cross, indicating that the X_1 effect is clearly reversed for different levels for X_2, the interaction is called 'disordinal': and one is obliged to infer that the significant interaction term is not just an artifact of the way the variables are scaled. (See Fig. 22.28.)

Although there are no maxima or minima on the entire mathematical surface for a linear interaction, a correlation between X_1 and X_2 can lead to there being a maximum or minimum value for the actual distribution of data. Figure 22.27 shows a surface with a large $-X_1X_2$ weight, on which the shaded distribution of data has a minimum; Fig. 22.28 shows a flat representation of the same surface, where the shading of the line suggests the density of observations. Thus some data distributions could be 'accounted for' about equally well by the set of terms X_1, X_2, $X_1 X_2$ or the set of terms X_1, X_2, X_1^2, X_2^2. (The reasonableness of this can be seen in the extreme that X_1 and X_2 are highly correlated, in which case X_1X_2 would be virtually the same as either X_1^2 or X_2^2; and both equations would reduce to X_1 and X_1^2 – a parabola in a single Y versus X_1 plane.) The moral is that highly correlated predictors either ought not both be used in multiple regression or ought to be summed into a single composite score. If highly correlated predictors are used, to get whatever tiny increment of prediction that one affords beyond the other, then no great unique meaning can be attributed to second-order or product terms.

When X_1^2 and X_2^2 terms are added as well as X_1X_2, the curved contour lines are, as for the linear interaction case, seen to diverge or converge. In cases with strong X_1^2 weights which produce a maximum or minimum within the range of data, a significant X_1X_2 term will mean a shift in the location of the maximum for different X_2 levels. For example, the optimal value of anxiety for taking a test might be greater for subjects with higher levels of risk taking. [. . .]

The sequence of entering all the 'quadratic' terms of X_1 and X_2 into a stepwise regression should probably be X_1, X_1^2, X_2, X_2^2, X_1X_2, which builds from simple to complex in attempting to account for variance in

Y. The early entry of the second-order terms, reflecting the low assurance with which most behavioral variables can be taken as properly scaled, allows some curvature of relationship with one variable to possibly preclude the need for a second variable, and allows some curvature of relationship with both variables to possibly preclude the need for an interaction between them.

As usual, the exact weights assigned by the regression program are sensitive to the choice of zero-points for the X_1 and X_2 scales, and the importance of each term can best be judged by the increase it produces in R^2. Because similar effects on the regression surface can be realized by squared and product terms, statements about relative contributions to the complete regression equation are probably less important than qualitative description of the surface or contour plots.

Table 22.1 displays a possible order of entry for a multiple regression with two predictors, and some testable hypotheses about their contributions. The adequacy of X_1 in general to account for *Y* is judged by the R^2 when all terms in X_1 alone are included. The additional independent contribution of X_2 is judged by the increase in R^2 realized after all X_2 terms are entered, and the contribution of an interaction between X_1 and X_2 is judged by the increase in R^2 realized by adding product terms after all X_1 and X_2 terms. The contribution of X_2 beyond

Table 22.1 Tests of significance in a two-predictor stepwise multiple regression

Term added to regression	Set for which increase in R tested	Contribution inferred on entry*
X_1	*	Linear relation to X_1
X_1^2	*	Curvature of relation to X_1
(Possible higher-order terms of X_1)	*———————	Overall effect of X_1 alone
X_2	*	Additional linear contribution by X_2
X_2^2	*	Curvature of additional contribution by X_2
(Possible higher-order terms of X_2)	*————|————	Overall additional (independent) contribution of X_2
X_1X_2	*	Interaction of X_1 and X_2, beyond their independent effects
(Possible higher-order interaction terms for X_1 and X_2)	*———	Overall contribution by X_2 beyond what is possible with X_1 alone.

*Terms entered early may be seen to make a significant contribution only after later terms have also been entered, or initially significant terms may vanish. Contributions of single terms to the final regression equation are often difficult to characterize and a drawing of the regression surface or contours may be more valuable than belaboring algebraic terms.

what can be realized by X_1 terms alone is judged by the significance of adding the set of all terms containing X_2 – including any product terms.

The F for adding a set of predictors can easily be calculated by hand, provided that the computer program prints out the 'regression sum of squares' (SSR) and the 'residual [error] sum of squares' (SSE) for each step. If, after inclusion of n terms, inclusion of an additional set of m terms raises the regression sum of squares from SSR_{old} to SSR_{new}, then the F ratio for testing the significance of adding that set is

$$F = \frac{SSR_{new} - SSR_{old}}{SSE_{new}} \left(\frac{N - n - m - 1}{m} \right)$$

where the degrees of freedom for F are m and $N - n - m - 1$. This equation reduces to that for adding one term (when $m = 1$), or to that for the overall model (when $n = 0$).

All this advice on order and grouping is predicated on there being some rationale for the effects of X_1 and X_2, and for why one might be expected to have a more fundamental effect and therefore be entered before the other. In the absence of such a rationale, the investigator finds himself in the forest of interpretive strategems into which one is led by shotgun approaches to research; the reader is referred to the paper by Darlington (1968) as a guide to the forest.

It is conceivable that more complicated interactions might occur, e.g. of the form $X_1^2 X_2$. This would be the proper characterization if X_2 had strongest effect on Y when X_1 had a middle value, with weaker effects at both high and low extremes of X_1. Indeed, such a model has been recently presented by Clifford (1972), who found that improvement in performance is most strongly related to task difficulty at middle levels of motivation. Figures 22.29 and 22.30 display such an interaction in both surface and contour formats. In effect, the $X_1 X_2$ term can shift the position of the $\hat{Y}$ versus X_1 parabola around for different values of X_2; but the $X_1^2 X_2$ term allows the *shape* of the parabola to change for different values of X_2. (In the calculus context, the second X_1 = derivative of $\hat{Y} = f(X_1)$ depends on X_2.) We doubt that anything beyond a $X_1^2 X_2$ term would lend itself to interpretation.

A natural limitation to the number of possible terms occurs when the predictors have only a few levels rather than continuous distributions. If one predictor has k_1 levels and a second predictor has k_2 levels, then the total number of terms necessary to completely specify the regression possibilities is $k_1 \times k_2$. For example, if predictor A has three levels and predictor B has four levels, there would be a maximum of twelve terms:

$A, A^2, B, B^2, B^3, AB, AB^2, AB^3, A^2B, A^2B^2, A^2B^3, constant$

This principle corresponds to the number of degrees of freedom familiar in analysis of variance and will be discussed further in the second part of this chapter.

When more than two predictors are used, however, characterizing the relationships can be very difficult. With three predictors it would still be practical to draw contour plots between two of them for each of several levels of the third, but with four or more predictors the investigator is almost surely reduced to numerical descriptions of contribution. The number of possible terms, even if all variables were arbitrarily restricted to square terms, is tremendous. For example, there would be 91 such terms for four variables. Even though 82 of the terms could be grouped into 'interaction' and tested as a single set, the convenience that makes regression analysis so attractive begins to fade with the necessity of even specifying the calculation of 82 new variables. Fortunately, when using many predictors the researcher is usually not as concerned with explanatory mechanisms as he is with the significance of contribution for a novel last variable entered, or with the 'unexplained' residuals left after all available predictors have been entered.

Regression versus analysis of variance

Because many researchers are more familiar with the analysis of variance (ANOVA) approach, and because in many situations regression analysis offers some advantages over ANOVA, we will discuss the underlying equivalence of the two approaches and certain differences in conceptualization and convenience.

Categorial variables

Consider a simple experiment in which response units (students or classes) are assigned randomly to two 'treatments' such as instructional methods. In ANOVA this experiment would yield one principal result: the contrast of criterion means for the two treatments, which would be tested for statistical significance by an F ratio. The experiment can be analyzed in an entirely equivalent way by regression. Each response unit is assigned a value on a dichotomous 'dummy' variable that represents the treatment effect, coding one treatment as '1' and the other as '0'. (Any two numbers would serve, but 1 and 0 nicely suggest the presence or absence of a treatment or trait. More sophisticated codes can give the resulting regression coefficients some convenient properties, but the advantage is slight against the inconvenience of figuring out the precise code.)

The criterion Y is then regressed on the dummy treatment variable X in the usual model $\hat{Y} = aX + constant$. The regression coefficient R will represent the magnitude of relationship between treatment and criterion (in this special case R is the Pearson r and is identical to the 'point-biserial' r), and the F test for the significance of R will represent the significance of the treatment difference. The grand mean and the treatment means are easily computed with other simple statistical routines (usually available on the same computer run in a statistical package). The significance arrived at in this way will be identical to that found from the ANOVA F ratio (Draper and Smith, 1966). (The ANOVA of which we write is fixed-effects ANOVA, and, if no attempt is made to equalize cell sizes, technically a weighted-means analysis.)

If there are more than two treatment levels, additional dummy variables can be used to represent the additional contrasts. If there are k groups, then $k - 1$ dummy variables are required. For example, if there were three treatments the first dummy variable X_1 would be coded '1' for treatment 1 and '0' for the other two treatments, and the second dummy variable X_2 would be coded '1' for treatment 2 and '0' for the other two treatments. The regression model would be $\hat{Y} = aX_1 + bX_1 + constant$. A third dummy would be redundant, since treatment 3 is already represented – by having a '0' for both X_1 and X_2. The treatment 'main effect' on Y would correspond to the multiple R for the inclusion of both X_1 and X_2 terms, and the F test for R would be equivalent to the F test for the main effect.

If there are two factors (either classifications of response units or dimensions of treatment), another set of dummy variables is required. For example, in a study of three treatment groups for both sexes there would have to be a pair of dummy variables for treatment (X_1 and X_2 as before), and another dummy variable X_3 for sex – say, $X_3 = 1$ for males and $X_3 = 2$ for females. That is:

Coding

Variable

$$\text{Treatment} \begin{cases} X_1\text{: method 1} = 1; \text{ methods 2 and 3} = 0 \\ X_2\text{: method 2} = 1; \text{ methods 1 and 3} = 0 \end{cases}$$

Sex X_3: male = 1; female = 2

The regression model would be:

$$\hat{Y} = aX_1 + bX_2 + cX_3 + dX_3X_1 + eX_3X_2 + constant.$$

In this example, the first two terms on the right side of the equation together represent the treatment main effect, the next term represents the sex main effect and the next two terms together represent the interaction effect between sex and treatment. The total number of terms (including the constant) corresponds to the number of cells in the ANOVA design: $2 \times 3 = 6$. The number of terms for each effect corresponds to the degrees of freedom for that effect in ANOVA, and the constant term corresponds to the 1 df for the grand mean. The df for error is the number of units less the number of terms (including the constant), corresponding exactly to the df for error in ANOVA – the

Table 22.2 Multiple regression as analysis of variance

Term entered	df for step	Corresponding ANOVA interpretation*
X_1	1	⎫
X_2	1	⎬ 2 _ _ _ _ _ _ _ _ Treatment 'main effect'
X_3	1	_ _ _ _ _ _ _ _ Sex 'main effect'
X_3X_1	1	⎫
X_3X_2	1	⎬ 2 _ _ _ _ _ _ _ _ Treatment – sex 'interaction effect'
Constant	1	'Grand mean'
Total	6	
Error	N – 6	Error

*With the convenient coding scheme of 0 and 1, the regression coefficients are not numerically identical to the ANOVA contrasts (as they would be with more sophisticated coding schemes), but tests of significance are equivalent. The interaction variance may be grouped with the error as is sometimes done in ANOVA by simply omitting the X_3X_1 and X_3X_2 terms from the regression model.

number of units less the number of cells. Table 22.2 displays these relationships.

Note that in a nonorthogonal design (unequal or nonproportional cell sizes), the sex term should really be entered first, so that the treatment effect will be 'adjusted' for possible differences in sex among the treatment groups. In orthogonal design, the order makes no difference.

If a sequence of multiple regressions is run stepwise, testing the significance of increase in R from one step to the next corresponds to testing sequentially the significance of the ANOVA effects. The value of R^2 represents the proportion of total variance accounted for by the model, and so corresponds to the intraclass correlation coefficient or, more generally, ω^2 (Hays 1963, pp. 512–13). (It is not common in ANOVA, however, for calculations of ω^2 to be made at all, much less made for the successive contributions of factors.) The F ratios for the increase in R^2 obtained by adding each successive set of terms to the regression are equivalent to the F ratios that would have been found in the corresponding ANOVA (Cohen, 1968).

If the predictors were ordinal, with some claim to being equally spaced, then a preferred alternative to the generation of dummy scores would be to use X, X^2, X^3, etc. As mentioned earlier, a k-category variable would require $k - 1$ such terms (X, X^2, ..., X^{k-1}) to account for the relationship completely. Significant power terms might be interpreted step by step as representing curvature or even maxima or minima, similar to trend analysis in ANOVA. This alternative has the advantage that the first term or two may possibly account for most of the accountable variance – in which case higher-order terms that make little additional contribution may be deleted from the model for conceptual parsimony. If a predictor is ordinal, then an ordinary ANOVA has low power for detecting a trend; trend analysis, on the other hand, is an advanced technique. The multiple regression approach offers an equivalent to trend analysis in a more familiar and convenient form.

If the predictors were of questionably equal spacing or were plainly only categorial, the power terms could still be used *collectively* to represent the main effects. For a three-category predictor, for example, a regression equation would have to fit three group means; since *any* three points can be fitted by a parabola, the combination of an X and X^2 term would suffice to completely specify the model. The categories could be coded 1, 2, 3, in any order. No special meaning would attach to the weights for the X and X^2 terms; the *combined* contribution of X and X^2 would simulate the 'main effect'. This alternative to the dummy variables has the advantage of using data cards as they are normally punched, without having to regroup or repunch cards or give program instructions for generating the dummy variables.

Continuous variables

Consider now a learning experiment with a two-factor design employing two continuous variables, say mental ability A and duration of treatment B. In ANOVA design, an investigator might trichotomize A and cut B into four levels; then he would test the main effects and interaction in a 3×4 design with $df = 12$. A more elegant alternative in ANOVA would be to test, instead of simple A and B main effects, 'linear and quadratic trends' of A and 'linear, quadratic, and cubic trends' of B – plus the six interactions of trends, again with $df = 12$. (Such a 3×4 example appears in Winer, 1971, p. 388.)

Either the main-effects or the trend analyses could be performed in a regression model on the subdivided A and B scores, entering the twelve terms A, A^2, B, B^2, B^3, AB, AB^2, AB^3, A^2B, A^2B^2, A^2B^3, and the *constant,* and would yield results equivalent to the ANOVA. The order of entry of the terms would be the same whether the model was simply main-effects or the more elaborate trend version, but in the main-effects case the F tests would be grouped (e.g. B, B^2, and B^3 together would represent the B main effect and all the product terms of A and B would together represent the interaction effect).

In regression analysis, however, it is possible to use A and B as the original continuous variables, without collapsing them into levels. Beyond the procedural economy, this use of continuous variables allows full use of the information in the scores. An example of this advantage is Cronbach's (1968) reanalysis by multiple regression of two-predictor data (intelligence and creativity) previously run on ANOVA. By using the continuous values of intelligence and creativity scores rather than dichotomizing them at the median (and thereby avoiding an immediate loss of about 36 per cent in the amount of information), regression analyses on only the linear and linear interaction terms were shown to be more powerful and more parsimonious than the 2×2 ANOVAs.

The use of continuous variables in regression analysis can be viewed as equivalent to analysis of covariance. Consider again a two-predictor model where a criterion Y is to be related to predictors A and B; limiting our model to just the linear and linear interaction terms, we have

$$\hat{Y} = aA + bB + cAB + constant$$

If we entered these terms in order in a stepwise multiple regression, the first step by itself would yield simply the correlation of Y and A – that is, to use the example above, the predictability of the criterion from intelligence. Adding the B term on the next step would show an increase in R, representing an additional predictability of Y from B *after Y is regressed on A* – that is, the effect of creativity on the criterion after the effects of intelligence are 'controlled' or 'statistically removed'. This amounts to an analysis of covariance for creativity, with intelligence being the 'adjusting' covariate. (The analogy becomes an equivalence if the B variable is subdivided into levels rather than is continuous.) Should the AB term prove to be significant, then the effect of B is different for different levels of A – say, creativity has a stronger relation to performance for dull children than it does for bright children. Under linear assumptions, a test of this product term is formally equivalent to the test for homogeneity of regression so often overlooked in analysis of covariance (Ahlgren and Walberg, 1969).

A use of regression analysis related to the covariance idea is the case of repeated measures. For example, suppose that pretest, posttest and delayed posttest data have been collected for a sample. The posttest could be used as the criterion and the pretest entered first in a multiple regression, before any hypothesized treatment variables. Significant increases in R realized by entering a subsequent treatment term would indicate prediction of the posttest beyond what was predictable from the pretest – that is, a treatment effect on pre-test gain. (The interpretation might be easier if residuals $(Y-\hat{Y})$ are calculated from the regression of posttest or pretest, and these residuals then entered as criteria in a multiple regression on treatment variables.) A second multiple regression, using the delayed posttest as criterion and entering first both pretest and posttest, would allow inferences about the contribution of treatment to 'decay' of pre-post changes. (Again one might use a two-stage process of first calculating residuals and then entering them as criteria in a subsequent regression.) In both cases, product terms between treatment and pretest would represent interaction – differential treatment effects for different kinds of subjects.

Confounding

A final correspondence between ANOVA and regression is the problem of nonorthogonality, represented in ANOVA by unequal cell sizes and in regression by correlated (co-linear) predictor variables. In both troublesome cases, the effects of predictors are confounded, and usually those variables entering either model later in a series of tests are less likely to be found significant.

With a priori ideas about the nature of predictor effects, it is possible to order entry into the model logically and thus capitalize on the collinearity rather than suffer from it. If, for example, the predictors were SES and level of education, the case might reasonably be made that the effects of SES are prior in time to the effects of education (even if some of the effects of SES are mediated by education), and hence the SES effect should be tested first. (This example takes us close to 'path analysis', the elaborate study of direct and indirect influences.) Or, in any design where a novel variable is being hypothesized, either as a trait or a treatment, the putative predictor should be entered *last,* after better-established variables. In the absence of at least speculation on causal relations, however, the investigator will find himself in the interpretive forest mentioned earlier.

Historically, experimentalists have tended to use orthogonal ANOVA by assigning response units to cells equally (or, in a pinch, proportionally) or by the expedient of throwing extra cases out – or both. Analogously, economists, psychometrists and sociologists using regression analysis have usually struggled to find (or construct) predictors with low intercorrelations.

It is always possible to eliminate colinearity in regression by assigning or throwing out to 'uncorrelate' artificially the predictor variables; in this way regression analysis can always be made equivalent to orthogonal ANOVA. The 'uncorrelating' procedure is hampered by limitations of the natural pool of response units, the magnitude of the intercorrelations and the spacing of selection boundaries. One method is to transform the predictors into intrinsically orthogonal 'factors' – this approach is discussed at length in the chapter on canonical analysis. Whether one spends one's time in uncorrelating predictors or in dissecting correlated contributions will depend in part on how compelling the predictors are as real and important descriptions of behavior.

The issue of how response units are distributed on the variables is relevant to regression analysis in another way, even if there is only one predictor variable. Suppose, for example, that American students of Oriental background were found to perform significantly better on achievement tests, through an ANOVA on two equal, randomly selected samples. If 'ethnicity' (Oriental versus others) were used as a predictor in a general national sample of the student population, the contribution of race would nonetheless be found to be very small – corresponding to the fact that very little of the variability in achievement among American students could be attributed to being Oriental. The ethnic effect might be real, but not very important in a population with so few Orientals. The regression could be made exactly equivalent to the ANOVA by using equal samples, but that necessity may not occur to the researcher as readily when a computer run can be set up without attending at all to the proportions in the population.

Some advantages of regression analysis
Generalized regression has at least three advantages over ANOVA:

(1) the use of continuous variables, (2) less data processing time, and (3) direct, comprehensive estimates of the magnitude and significance of the independent variable effects. The advantage of continuous variables should not be argued too strongly. Feldt (1958) has shown that the loss of precision in grouping scores is trivial when at least five levels are used. However, when the number of subjects is small, or when the number of factors is large, or both, it is usually difficult to maintain adequate cell sizes. Regression of ungrouped scores not only analyzes all the accountable variance, but saves the investigator the bothersome task of establishing suitable cutting points.

The second advantage, that of shorter processing time, arises because traditional and currently popular procedures of ANOVA were designed before modern computers. The student and the researcher must often learn special 'time-saving' computational methods that can be obstacles to the conceptual problems of the analysis. Therefore, despite the complexity of behavioral problems, many investigators limit their research to simple textbook designs. This propensity has influenced computer program designs wastefully: generally programs are often limited to orthogonal designs with only a few factors and one dependent variable; many programs have been written for only one restricted analysis; and few make use of the computer's speed at matrix operations. Ten-way orthogonal ANOVA programs are available at a few institutions, but almost any university computation center has a flexible 100-variable regression program.

A related consideration is the setup time for an analysis, a mundane but crucial problem when time or resources are limited. Generally ANOVA programs require sorting cards into cells and getting counts or punching a cell designation for each response unit. In most regression programs, the investigator simply reads in all his data with a format card. (In some programs, an additional header card giving the number of response units is necessary.) If several different models are to be tried, either initially or after inspection of the results, most ANOVA programs would require repunching or resorting of data cards. The regression analyst can simply use a control card to select multiple sets of predictors and criteria (and transformations thereof) on the same computer run. This flexibility of regression programs is particularly convenient in exploratory research. The Coleman Report (1966) exemplifies capitalizing on the ease with which alternative models may be tried.

As a third advantage, the generalized regression model in practice provides comprehensive and useful estimates of magnitudes of effects as well as their significance. The most obvious instance is the multiple regression coefficient: when squared (R^2) it indicates directly how much variance in the dependent variable is associated with (or accounted for by) the independent variables; when tested for significance, it indicates the probability of overall association between all the independent variables and the dependent variable. In ANOVA, ω^2s (estimates of accountable variance) ordinarily are not summed or otherwise combined to indicate or test the total variance accounted for by all effects. For example, in a five-way factorial design, one of the five main effects or ten interaction effects could easily appear significant by chance alone, and variance analysts rarely use a comprehensive test of this possibility.

A particularly useful aspect of the estimating advantage in regression is the examination of increments in the variance accounted for (i.e. in R^2) found with the ordered, stepwise inclusion of independent variables. Examination of the variance accounted for may often be more useful and valid than determining probabilities of null hypotheses in educational research. For example, a correlation of $r = 0.10$ is significant at the $p < 0.05$ level with a sample of 500 cases – yet it implies that only 1 per cent of the variance is accounted for ($0.10^2 = 0.01$).

The significance of successive incremental contributions of confounded independent variables may be estimated in nonorthogonal ANOVA by entering the factor in question after the other factors (Bock and Haggard, 1968) or by analysis of covariance. However, these analyses do not estimate the magnitude of relationship – i.e. they do not directly yield the additional variance accounted for by the factor in question. Regression is more useful in this situation since the step on which the factor in question is added to all the 'covariables' gives directly the increment in criterion variance accounted for.

Of course, neither regression nor any other statistical technique can substitute for a careful conceptual formulation of the research problem and adequate experimental designs prior to data collection. Survey research and quasi experiments may yield clues about powerful sources of variance, but they do not permit statistical tests of causal hypotheses. Still, limited resources make it likely that these kinds of work will continue; and regression can make a good contribution to sorting out the most potent independent variables to be pursued further by true experiments.

In this brief comparative review of regression and ANOVA, a number of important theoretical issues and assumptions have not been brought out, and the interested reader is referred to Anderson (1958), Bock (1963, 1967), Bock and Haggard (1968), Cohen (1965, 1968), Darlington (1968), Draper and Smith (1966), and Tatsuoka and Tiedeman (1963). Efficient computer algorithms for univariate and multivariate regression have been outlined by Bock (1963), and some existing programs are referenced by Bock and Haggard (1968). Cohen's (1965, 1968) discussions of the assumptions of regression and ANOVA are readable and valuable; he shows that regression is just as robust as ANOVA with regard to violation of the normality and homogeneity assumptions of the dependent variable and argues that regression may be effectively applied to 'random' as well as 'fixed' variables with negligible practical effects on the validity of the generalization.

References

Anderson, T. W. (1958) *An Introduction to Multivariate Analysis.* New York: Wiley.

Ahlgren, A. and Walberg, H. J. (1969) 'Homogeneity of regression tests: Assumptions, limitations, alternatives', *Am. Educ. Res. J.,* **6**, 696–700.

Bock, R. D. (1963) 'Programming univariate and multivariate analysis of variance', *Technometrics,* **5**, 95–117.

Bock, R. D. (1967) 'Contributions of multivariate experimental designs to educational research', in Raymond B. Cattel (ed.), *Handbook of Multivariate Experimental Psychology.* Chicago: Rand McNally.

Bock, R. D. and Haggard, E. A. (1968) 'The use of multivariate analysis in behavioral research', in Dean K. Whitla (ed.), *Handbook of Measurement and Assessment in the Behavioral Sciences.* Reading, Mass.: Addison-Wesley.

Clifford, M. M. (1972) 'Effects of competition as a motivational technique in the classroom', *Am. Educ. Res. J.,* **9**, 123–37.

Cohen, J. (1968) 'Multiple regression as a general data-analytic system', *Psychological Bulletin,* **70**, 426–43.

Cohen, J. (1965) 'Some statistical issues in psychological research', in Benjamin B. Wolman (ed.), *Handbook of Clinical Psychology.* New York: McGraw-Hill.

Coleman, J. S., *et al.* (1966) *Equality of Educational Opportunity.* Washington, D.C.: US Government Printing Office.

Cronbach, L. J. (1968) 'Intelligence? Creativity? A parsimonious reinterpretation of the Wallach–Kogan data', *Am. Educ. Res. J.,* **5**, 491–511.

Darlington, R. B. (1968) 'Multiple regression in psychological research and practice', *Psychological Bulletin,* **69**, 161–82.

Draper, N. R. and Smith, H. H. (1966) *Applied Regression Analysis.* New York: Wiley.

Feldt, L. S. (1958) 'A comparison of the precision of three experimental designs employing a concomitant variable', *Psychometrika,* **23**, 335–53.

Hays, W. L. (1963) *Statistics.* New York: Holt, Rinehart and Winston.

Tatsuoka, M. M. and Tiedeman, D. V. (1963) 'Statistics as an aspect of scientific method in research on teaching', in N. L. Gage (ed.), *Handbook of Research on Teaching.* Chicago: Rand McNally.

Winer, B. J. (1971) *Statistical Principles in Experimental Design.* New York: McGraw-Hill.

Problems of inference and proof in participant observation

Howard S. Becker

The participant observer gathers data by participating in the daily life of the group or organization he studies.[1] He watches the people he is studying to see what situations they ordinarily meet and how they behave in them. He enters into conversation with some or all of the participants in these situations and discovers their interpretations of the events he has observed.

Let me describe, as one specific instance of observational technique, what my colleagues and I have done in studying a medical school. We went to lectures with students taking their first two years of basic science and frequented the laboratories in which they spend most of their time, watching them and engaging in casual conversation as they dissected cadavers or examined pathology specimens. We followed these students to their fraternity houses and sat around while they discussed their school experiences. We accompanied students in the clinical years on rounds with attending physicians, watched them examine patients on the wards and in the clinics, sat in on discussion groups and oral exams. We ate with the students and took night call with them. We pursued interns and residents through their crowded schedules of teaching and medical work. We stayed with one small group of students on each service for periods ranging from a week to two months, spending many full days with them. The observational situations allowed time for conversation and we took advantage of this to interview students about things that had happened and were about to happen, and about their own backgrounds and aspirations.

Sociologists usually use this method when they are especially interested in understanding a particular organization or substantive problem rather than demonstrating relations between abstractly defined variables. They attempt to make their research theoretically meaningful, but they assume that they do not know enough about the organization *a priori* to identify relevant problems and hypotheses and that they must discover these in the course of the research. Though

From *American Sociological Review*, 1958, **23**, 652–60.

participant observation can be used to test *a priori* hypotheses, and therefore need not be as unstructured as the example I have given above, this is typically not the case. My discussion refers to the kind of participant observation study which seeks to discover hypotheses as well as to test them.

Observational research produces an immense amount of detailed description; our files contain approximately five thousand single-spaced pages of such material. Faced with such a quantity of 'rich' but varied data, the researcher faces the problem of how to analyze it systematically and then to present his conclusions so as to convince other scientists of their validity. Participant observation (indeed, qualitative analysis generally) has not done well with this problem, and the full weight of evidence for conclusions and the processes by which they were reached are usually not presented, so that the reader finds it difficult to make his own assessment of them and must rely on his faith in the researcher.

In what follows I try to pull out and describe *the basic analytic operations carried on in participant observation,* for three reasons: to make these operations clear to those unfamiliar with the method; by attempting a more explicit and systematic description, to aid those working with the method in organizing their own research; and, most importantly, in order to propose some changes in analytic procedures and particularly in reporting results which will make the processes by which conclusions are reached and substantiated more accessible to the reader.

The first thing we note about participant observation research is that analysis is carried on *sequentially*,[2] important parts of the analysis being made while the researcher is still gathering his data. This has two obvious consequences: further data gathering takes its direction from provisional analyses; and the amount and kind of provisional analysis carried on is limited by the exigencies of the field work situation, so that final comprehensive analyses may not be possible until the field work is completed.

We can distinguish three distinct stages of analysis conducted in the field itself, and a fourth stage, carried on after completion of the field work. These stages are differentiated, first, by their logical sequence: each succeeding stage depends on some analysis in the preceding stage. They are further differentiated by the fact that different kinds of conclusions are arrived at in each stage and that these conclusions are put to different uses in the continuing research. Finally, they are differentiated by the different criteria that are used to assess evidence and to reach conclusions in each stage. The three stages of field analysis are: the selection and definition of problems, concepts, and indices; the check on the frequency and distribution of phenomena; and the incorporation of individual findings into a model of the organization under study.[3] The fourth stage of final analysis involves problems of presentation of evidence and proof.

Selection and definition of problems, concepts and indices

In this stage, the observer looks for problems and concepts that give promise of yielding the greatest understanding of the organization he is studying, and for items which may serve as useful indicators of facts which are harder to observe. The typical conclusion that his data yield is the simple one that a given phenomenon exists, that a certain event occurred once, or that two phenomena were observed to be related in one instance: the conclusion says nothing about the frequency or distribution of the observed phenomenon.

By placing such an observation in the context of a sociological theory, the observer selects concepts and defines problems for further investigation. He constructs a theoretical model to account for that one case, intending to refine it in the light of subsequent findings. For instance, he might find the following: 'Medical student X referred to one of his patients as a "crock" today.'[4] He may then connect this finding with a sociological theory suggesting that occupants of one social category in an institution classify members of other categories by criteria derived from the kinds of problems these other persons raise in the relationship. This combination of observed fact and theory directs him to look for the problems in student–patient interaction indicated by the term 'crock'. By discovering specifically what students have in mind in using the term, through questioning and continued observation, he may develop specific hypotheses about the nature of these interactional problems.

Conclusions about a single event also lead the observer to decide on specific items which might be used as indicators[5] of less easily observed phenomena. Noting that in at least one instance a given item is closely related to something less easily observable, the researcher discovers possible shortcuts easily enabling him to observe abstractly defined variables. For example, he may decide to investigate the hypothesis that medical freshmen feel they have more work to do than can possibly be managed in the time allowed them. One student, in discussing this problem, says he faces so much work that, in contrast to his undergraduate days, he is forced to study many hours over the weekend and finds that even this is insufficient. The observer decides, on the basis of this one instance, that he may be able to use complaints about weekend work as an indicator of student perspectives on the amount of work they have to do. The selection of indicators for more abstract variables occurs in two ways: the observer may become aware of some very specific phenomenon first and later see that it may be used as an indicator of some larger class of phenomena; or he may have the larger problem in mind and search for specific indicators to use in studying it.

Whether he is defining problems or selecting concepts and indicators, the researcher at this stage is using his data only to speculate about possibilities. Further operations at later stages may force him to discard most of the provisional hypotheses. Nevertheless, problems of evidence arise even at this point, for the researcher must assess the individual items on which his speculations are based in order not to waste time tracking down false leads. We shall eventually need a systematic statement of canons to be applied to individual items of evidence. Lacking such a statement, let us consider some commonly used tests. (The observer typically applies these tests as seems reasonable to him during this and the succeeding stage in the field. In the final stage, they are used more systematically in an overall assessment of the total evidence for a given conclusion.)

The credibility of informants
Many items of evidence consist of statements by members of the group under study about some event which has occurred or is in process. Thus, medical students make statements about faculty behavior which form part of the basis for conclusions about faculty–student relations. These cannot be taken at face value; nor can they be dismissed as valueless. In the first place, the observer can use the statement as evidence *about the event,* if he takes care to evaluate it by the criteria an historian uses in examining a personal document.[6] Does the informant have reason to lie or conceal some of what he sees as the truth? Does vanity or expediency lead him to mis-state his own role in an event or his attitude toward it? Did he actually have an opportunity to witness the occurrence he describes or is hearsay the source of his knowledge? Do his feelings about the issues or persons under discussion lead him to alter his story in some way?

Secondly, even when a statement examined in this way proves to be seriously defective as an accurate report of an event, it may still provide useful evidence for a different kind of conclusion. Accepting the sociological proposition that an individual's statements and descriptions of events are made from a perspective which is a function of his position in the group, the observer can interpret such statements and descriptions as indications of the individual's perspective on the point involved.

Volunteered or directed statements
Many items of evidence consist of informants' remarks to the observer about themselves or others or about something which has happened to them; these statements range from those which are a part of the running casual conversation of the group to those arising in a long intimate tête-à-tête between observer and informant. The researcher assesses the evidential value of such statements quite differently, depending on whether they have been made independently of the observer (volunteered) or have been directed by a question from the observer. A freshman medical student might remark to the observer or to another student that he has more material to study than he has time

to master; or the observer might ask, 'Do you think you are being given more work than you can handle?', and receive an affirmative answer.

This raises an important question: to what degree is the informant's statement the same one he might give, either spontaneously or in answer to a question, in the absence of the observer? The volunteered statement seems likely to reflect the observer's preoccupations and possible biases less than one which is made in response to some action of the observer, for the observer's very question may direct the informant into giving an answer which might never occur to him otherwise. Thus, in the example above, we are more sure that the students are concerned about the amount of work given them when they mention this of their own accord than we are when the idea may have been stimulated by the observer asking the question.

The observer—informant—group equation

Let us take two extremes to set the problem. A person may say or do something when alone with the observer or when other members of the group are also present. The evidential value of an observation of this behavior depends on the observer's judgment as to whether the behavior is equally likely to occur in both situations. On the one hand, an informant may say and do things when alone with the observer that accurately reflect his perspective but which would be inhibited by the presence of the group. On the other hand, the presence of others may call forth behavior which reveals more accurately the person's perspective but would not be enacted in the presence of the observer alone. Thus, students in their clinical years may express deeply 'idealistic' sentiments about medicine when alone with the observer, but behave and talk in a very 'cynical' way when surrounded by fellow students. An alternative to judging one or the other of these situations as more reliable is to view each datum as valuable in itself, but with respect to different conclusions. In the example above, we might conclude that students have 'idealistic' sentiments but that group norms may not sanction their expression.[7]

In assessing the value of items of evidence, we must also take into account the observer's role in the group; for the way the subjects of his study define that role affects what they will tell him or let him see. If the observer carries on his research incognito, participating as a full-fledged member of the group, he will be privy to knowledge that would normally be shared by such a member and might be hidden from an outsider. He could properly interpret his own experience as that of a hypothetical 'typical' group member. On the other hand, if he is known to be a researcher, he must learn how group members define him and in particular whether or not they believe that certain kinds of information and events should be kept hidden from him. He can interpret evidence more accurately when the answers to these questions are known.

Checking the frequency and distribution of phenomena

The observer, possessing many provisional problems, concepts and indicators, now wishes to know which of these are worth pursuing as major foci of his study. He does this, in part, by discovering if the events that prompted their development are typical and widespread, and by seeing how these events are distributed among categories of people and organizational sub-units. He reaches conclusions that are essentially quantitative, using them to describe the organization he is studying.

Participant observations have occasionally been gathered in standardized form capable of being transformed into legitimate statistical data.[8] But the exigencies of the field usually prevent the collection of data in such a form as to meet the assumptions of statistical tests, so that the observer deals in what have been called 'quasi-statistics'.[9] His conclusions, while implicitly numerical, do not require precise quantification. For instance, he may conclude that members of freshmen medical fraternities typically sit together during lectures while other students sit in less stable smaller groupings. His observations may indicate such a wide disparity between the two groups in this respect that the inference is warranted without a standardized counting operation. Occasionally, the field situation may permit him to make similar observations or ask similar questions of many people, systematically searching for quasi-statistical support for a conclusion about frequency or distribution.

In assessing the evidence for such a conclusion the observer takes a cue from his statistical colleagues. Instead of arguing that a conclusion is either totally true or false, he decides, if possible, how *likely* it is that his conclusion about the frequency or distribution of some phenomenon is an accurate quasi-statistic, just as the statistician decides, on the basis of the varying values of a correlation coefficient or a significance figure, that his conclusion is more or less likely to be accurate. The kind of evidence may vary considerably and the degree of the observer's confidence in the conclusion will vary accordingly. In arriving at this assessment, he makes use of some of the criteria described above, as well as those adopted from quantitative techniques.

Suppose, for example, that the observer concludes that medical students share the perspective that their school should provide them with the clinical experience and the practice in techniques necessary for a general practitioner. His confidence in the conclusion would vary according to the nature of the evidence, which might take any of the following forms:

1. Every member of the group said, *in response to a direct question,* that this was the way he looked at the matter.
2. *Every* member of the group *volunteered* to an observer that this was how he viewed the matter.

3. *Some given proportion* of the group's members either *answered* a direct question or *volunteered* the information that he shared this perspective, but none of the others was asked or volunteered information on the subject.
4. Every member of the group was asked or volunteered information, but *some given proportion said* they viewed the matter from the differing perspective of a prospective specialist.
5. No one was asked questions or volunteered information on the subject, but *all members were observed to engage in behavior* or to make other statements from which the analyst *inferred* that the general practitioner perspective was being used by them as a basic, though unstated, premise. For example, all students might have been observed to complain that the University Hospital received too many cases of rare diseases that general practitioners rarely see.
6. *Some given proportion* of the group *was observed* using the general practitioner perspective as a basic premise in their activities, but *the rest of the group* was not observed engaging in such activities.
7. *Some proportion* of the group *was observed* engaged in activities implying the general practitioner perspective while *the remainder* of the group was observed engaged in activities implying the perspective of the prospective specialist.

The researcher also takes account of the possibility that his observations may give him evidence of different kinds on the point under consideration. Just as he is more convinced if he has many items of evidence than if he has a few, so he is more convinced of a conclusion's validity if he has *many kinds* of evidence.[10] For instance, he may be especially persuaded that a particular norm exists and affects group behavior if the norm is not only described by group members but also if he observes events in which the norm can be 'seen' to operate – if, for example, students tell him that they are thinking of becoming general practitioners and he also observes their complaints about the lack of cases of common diseases in University Hospital.

The conclusiveness which comes from the convergence of several kinds of evidence reflects the fact that separate varieties of evidence can be reconceptualized as deductions from a basic proposition which have now been verified in the field. In the above case, the observer might have deduced the desire to have experience with cases like those the general practitioner treats from the desire to practice that style of medicine. Even though the deduction is made after the fact, confirmation of it buttresses the argument that the general practitioner perspective is a group norm.

It should be remembered that these operations, when carried out in the field, may be so interrupted because of imperatives of the field situation that they are not carried on as systematically as they might be. Where this is the case, the overall assessment can be postponed until the final stage of postfield work analysis.

Construction of social system models

The final stage of analysis in the field consists of incorporating individual findings into a generalized model of the social system or organization under study or some part of that organization.[11] The concept of social system is a basic intellectual tool of modern sociology. The kind of participant observation discussed here is related directly to this concept, explaining particular social facts by explicit reference to their involvement in a complex of interconnected variables that the observer constructs as a theoretical model of the organization. In this final stage, the observer designs a descriptive model which best explains the data he has assembled.

The typical conclusion of this stage of the research is a statement about a set of complicated interrelations among many variables. Although some progress is being made in formalizing this operation through use of factor analysis and the relational analysis of survey data,[12] observers usually view currently available statistical techniques as inadequate to express their conceptions and find it necessary to use words. The most common kinds of conclusions at this level include:

1. Complex statements of the necessary and sufficient conditions for the existence of some phenomenon. The observer may conclude, for example, that medical students develop consensus about limiting the amount of work they will do because (a) they are faced with a large amount of work, (b) they engage in activities which create communication channels between all members of the class, and (c) they face immediate dangers in the form of examinations set by the faculty.
2. Statements that some phenomenon is an 'important' or 'basic' element in the organization. Such conclusions, when elaborated, usually point to the fact that this phenomenon exercises a persistent and continuing influence on diverse events. The observer might conclude that the ambition to become a general practitioner is 'important' in the medical school under study, meaning that many particular judgments and choices are made by students in terms of this ambition and many features of the school's organization are arranged to take account of it.
3. Statements identifying a situation as an instance of some process or phenomenon described more abstractly in sociological theory. Theories posit relations between many abstractly defined phenomena, and conclusions of this kind imply that relationships posited in generalized form hold in this particular instance. The observer, for example, may state that a cultural norm of the medical students is to express a desire to become a general practitioner; in so doing, he in effect asserts that the sociological theory about the functions of norms and the processes by which they are maintained which he holds to be true in general is true in this case.

In reaching such types of conclusions, the observer characteristically begins by constructing models of parts of the organization as he comes in contact with them, discovers concepts and problems, and the frequency and distribution of the phenomena these call to his attention. After constructing a model specifying the relationships among various elements of this part of the organization, the observer seeks greater accuracy by successively refining the model to take account of evidence which does not fit his previous formulation;[13] by searching for negative cases (items of evidence which run counter to the relationships hypothesized in the model) which might force such revision; and by searching intensively for the interconnections *in vivo* of the various elements he has conceptualized from his data. While a provisional model may be shown to be defective by a negative instance which crops up unexpectedly in the course of the field work, the observer may infer what kinds of evidence would be likely to support or to refute his model and may make an intensive search for such evidence.[14]

After the observer has accumulated several partial-models of this kind, he seeks connections between them and thus begins to construct an overall model of the entire organization. An example from our study shows how this operation is carried on during the period of field work. (The reader will note, in this example, how use is made of findings typical of earlier states of analysis.)

When we first heard medical students apply the term 'crock' to patients we made an effort to learn precisely what they meant by it. We found, through interviewing students about cases both they and the observer had seen, that the term referred in a derogatory way to patients with many subjective symptoms but no discernible physical pathology. Subsequent observations indicated that this usage was a regular feature of student behavior and thus that we should attempt to incorporate this fact into our model of student–patient behavior. The derogatory character of the term suggested in particular that we investigate the reasons students disliked these patients. We found that this dislike was related to what we discovered to be the students' perspective on medical school: the view that they were in school to get experience in recognizing and treating those common diseases most likely to be encountered in general practice. 'Crocks', presumably having no disease, could furnish no such experience. We were thus led to specify connections between the student–patient relationship and the student's view of the purpose of his professional education. Questions concerning the genesis of this perspective led to discoveries about the organization of the student body and communication among students, phenomena which we had been assigning to another part-model. Since 'crocks' were also disliked because they gave the student no opportunity to assume medical responsibility, we were able to connect this aspect to the student–patient relationship with still another tentative model of the value system and hierarchical organization of the school, in which medical responsibility plays an important role.

Again, it should be noted that analysis of this kind is carried on in the field as time permits. Since the construction of a model is the analytic operation most closely related to the observer's techniques and interests he usually spends a great deal of time thinking about these problems. But he is usually unable to be as systematic as he would like until he reaches the final stage of analysis.

Final analysis and the presentation of results

The final systematic analysis, carried on after the field work is completed, consists of rechecking and rebuilding models as carefully and with as many safeguards as the data will allow. For instance, in checking the accuracy of statements about the frequency and distribution of events, the researcher can index and arrange his material so that every item of information is accessible and taken account of in assessing the accuracy of any given conclusion. He can profit from the observation of Lazarsfeld and Barton that the 'analysis of "quasi-statistical data" can probably be made more systematic than it has been in the past, if the logical structure of quantitative research at least is kept in mind to give general warnings and directions to the qualitative observer'.[15]

An additional criterion for the assessment of this kind of evidence is the state of the observer's conceptualization of the problem at the time the item of evidence was gathered. The observer may have his problem well worked out and be actively looking for evidence to test an hypothesis, or he may not be as yet aware of the problem. The evidential value of items in his field notes will vary accordingly, the basis of consideration being the likelihood of discovering negative cases of the proposition he eventually uses the material to establish. The best evidence may be that gathered in the most unthinking fashion, when the observer has simply recorded the item although it has no place in the system of concepts and hypotheses he is working with at the time, for there might be less bias produced by the wish to substantiate or repudiate a particular idea. On the other hand, a well-formulated hypothesis makes possible a deliberate search for negative cases, particularly when other knowledge suggests likely areas in which to look for such evidence. This kind of search requires advanced conceptualization of the problem, and evidence gathered in this way might carry greater weight for certain kinds of conclusions. Both procedures are relevant at different stages of the research.

In the post field work stage of analysis, the observer carries on the model building operation more systematically. He considers the character of his conclusions and decides on the kind of evidence that might cause their rejection, deriving further tests by deducing logical consequences and ascertaining whether or not the data support the deductions. He considers reasonable alternative hypotheses and whether or not the evidence refutes them.[16] Finally, he completes the job of establishing interconnections between partial models so as to achieve an overall synthesis incorporating all conclusions.

After completing the analysis, the observer faces the knotty problem of how to present his conclusions and the evidence for them. Readers of qualitative research reports commonly and justifiably complain that they are told little or nothing about the evidence for conclusions or the operations by which the evidence has been assessed. A more adequate presentation of the data, of the research operations, and of the researcher's inferences may help to meet this problem.

But qualitative data and analytic procedures, in contrast to quantitative ones, are difficult to present adequately. Statistical data can be summarized in tables, and descriptive measures of various kinds and the methods by which they are handled can often be accurately reported in the space required to print a formula. This is so in part because the methods have been systematized so that they can be referred to in this shorthand fashion and in part because the data have been collected for a fixed, usually small, number of categories – the presentation of data need be nothing more than a report of the number of cases to be found in each category.

The data of participant observation do not lend themselves to such ready summary. They frequently consist of many different kinds of observations which cannot be simply categorized and counted without losing some of their value as evidence – for, as we have seen, many points need to be taken into account in putting each datum to use. Yet it is clearly out of the question to publish all the evidence. Nor is it any solution, as Kluckhohn has suggested for the similar problem of presenting life history materials,[17] to publish a short version and to make available the entire set of materials on microfilm or in some other inexpensive way; this ignores the problem of how to present *proof.*

In working over the material on the medical school study a possible solution to this problem, with which we are experimenting, is a description of the natural history of our conclusions, presenting the evidence as it came to the attention of the observer during the successive stages of his conceptualization of the problem. The term 'natural history' implies not the presentation of every datum, but only the characteristic forms data took at each stage of the research. This involves description of the form that data took and any significant exceptions, taking account of the canons discussed above, in presenting the various statements of findings and the inferences and conclusions drawn from them. In this way, evidence is assessed as the substantive analysis is presented. The reader would be able, if this method were used, to follow the details of the analysis and to see how and on what basis any conclusion was reached. This would give the reader, as do present modes of statistical presentation, opportunity to make his own judgment as to the adequacy of the proof and the degree of confidence to be assigned the conclusion.

Conclusion

I have tried to describe the analytic field work characteristic of participant observation, first, in order to bring out the fact that the technique consists of something more than merely immersing oneself in data and 'having insights'. The discussion may also serve to stimulate those who work with this and similar techniques to attempt greater formalization and systematization of the various operations they use, in order that qualitative research may become more a 'scientific' and less an 'artistic' kind of endeavor. Finally, I have proposed that new modes of reporting results be introduced, so that the reader is given greater access to the data and procedures on which conclusions are based.

Notes and References

1. This paper grew out of my experience in the research reported in Howard S. Becker, Blanche Geer, Everett C. Hughes, and Anselm L. Strauss (1961) *Boys in White: Student Culture in Medical School.* Chicago: University of Chicago Press. I worked out the basic approach in partnership with Blanche Geer and we then applied it in writing up our study of medical education and in the research reported in Becker, Geer and Hughes (1968) *Making the Grade: The Academic Side of College Life.* New York: John Wiley and Sons. Our own experience has been largely with the role Gold terms 'participant as observer', but the methods discussed here should be relevant to other field situations. Cf. Raymond L. Gold. 'Roles in sociological field observations', *Social Forces,* **36** (March 1958), 217–23.

2. In this respect, the analytic methods I discuss bear a family resemblance to the technique of *analytic induction.* Cf. Alfred Lindesmith (1947) *Opiate Addiction.* Bloomington: Principia Press, especially pp. 5–20, and the subsequent literature cited in Ralph H. Turner, 'The quest for universals in sociological research', *American Sociological Review,* **18** (Dec. 1953), 604–11.

3. My discussion of these stages is abstract and simplified and does not attempt to deal with practical and technical problems of participant observation study. The reader should keep in mind that in practice the research will involve all these operations simultaneously with reference to different particular problems.

4. The examples of which our hypothetical observer makes use are drawn from *Boys in White.*

5. The problem of indicators is discussed by Paul F. Lazarsfeld and Allen Barton (1951) 'Qualitative measurement in the social sciences: classification, typologies and indices', in Daniel Lerner and Harold D. Lasswell (eds), *The Policy Sciences: Recent Developments in Scope and Method.* Stanford: Stanford University Press, pp. 155–92; 'Some functions of qualitative analysis in sociological research', *Sociologica,* **1** (1955), 324–61 [this important paper parallels the present discussion in many places]; and Patricia L. Kendall and Paul F. Lazarsfeld (1950) 'Problems of survey analysis', in R. K. Merton and P. F. Lazarsfeld (eds) *Continuities in Social Research,* Glencoe: Free Press, pp. 183–86.

6. Cf. Louis Gottschalk, Clyde Kluckhohn, and Robert Angell (1945) *The Use of Personal Documents in History, Anthropology, and Sociology.* New York: Social Science Research Council, pp. 15–17, 38–47.

7. See further, Howard S. Becker, 'Interviewing medical students', *American Journal of Sociology,* **62** (Sept. 1956), 199–201.

8. See Peter M. Blau, 'Co-operation and competition in a bureaucracy', *American Journal of Sociology,* **59** (May 1954), pp. 530–5.

9. See the discussion of quasi-statistics in Lazarsfeld and Barton, 'Some functions of qualitative analysis . . .'. *op. cit.,* pp. 346–8.

10. See Alvin W. Gouldner (1954) *Patterns of Industrial Bureaucracy,* Glencoe, Ill.: Free Press, pp. 247–69.

11. The relation between theories based on the concept of social system and participant observation was pointed out to me by Alvin W. Gouldner. See his 'Some observations on systematic theory, 1945–55', in Hans L. Zetterberg (ed.), *Sociology in the United States of America.* Paris: UNESCO, 1956, pp. 34–42; and 'Theoretical requirements of the applied social sciences', *American Sociological Review,* **22,** (Feb. 1957), pp. 92–102.

12. See Alvin W. Gouldner 'Cosmopolitans and locals: toward an analysis of latent social roles', *Administrative Science Quarterly,* **2** (Dec. 1957), 281–306, and **3** (March 1958), 444–80; and James Coleman, 'Relational analysis: the study of social structure with survey methods', *Human Organization,* **17,** 28–36.

13. Note again the resemblance to analytic induction.

14. See Alfred Lindesmith's discussion of this principle in 'Comment on W. S. Robinson's "The Logical Structure of Analytic Induction"', *American Sociological Review,* **17** (Aug. 1952), 492–3.

15. 'Some functions of qualitative analysis . . .', *op. cit.,* p. 348.

16. One method of doing this, particularly adapted to testing discrete hypotheses about change in individuals or small social units (though not in principle limited to this application), is 'The technique of discerning', described by Mirra Komarovsky in Paul F. Lazarsfeld and Morris Rosenberg (eds), *The Language of Social Research.* Glencoe, Ill.: Free Press, 1955, pp. 449–57. See also the careful discussion of alternative hypotheses and the use of deduced consequences as further proof in Lindesmith, *Opiate Addiction, passim.*

17. Gottschalt et al., *op. cit.,* pp. 150–6.

Problems in the publication of field studies

Howard S. Becker

The problem

Publication of field research findings often poses ethical problems. The social scientist learns things about the people he studies that may harm them, if made public, either in fact or in their belief. In what form and under what conditions can he properly publish his findings? What can he do about the possible harm his report may do?

Although many social scientists have faced the problem, it seldom receives any public discussion. We find warnings that one must not violate confidences or bring harm to the people one studies, but seldom a detailed consideration of the circumstances under which harm may be done or of the norms that might guide publication practices.

Let us make our discussion more concrete by referring to a few cases that have been discussed publicly. Most thoroughly discussed, perhaps, is the 'Springdale' case, which was the subject of controversy in several successive issues of *Human Organization*.[1] Arthur Vidich and Joseph Bensman published a book – *Small Town in Mass Society* – based on Vidich's observations and interviews in a small, upstate New York village. The findings reported in that book were said to be offensive to some of the residents of Springdale; for instance, there were references to individuals who, though their names were disguised, were recognizable by virtue of their positions in the town's social structure. Some townspeople, it is alleged, also found the 'tone' of the book offensive. For instance, the authors used the phrase 'invisible government' to refer to people who held no official position in the town government but influenced the decisions made by elected officials. The implication of illegitimate usurpation of power may have offended those involved.

Some social scientists felt the authors had gone too far, and had damaged the town's image of itself and betrayed the research bargain

Howard S. Becker, 'Problems in the publication of field studies', from A. J. Vidich, J. Bensman and M. R. Stein (eds), *Reflections on Community Studies*. New York: John Wiley and Sons Inc. (1964), pp. 267–84.

other social scientists had made with the townspeople. The authors, on the other hand, felt they were dealing with problems that required discussing the facts they did discuss. They made every effort to disguise people but, when that was impossible to do effectively, felt it necessary to present the material as they did.

In another case John F. Lofland and Robert A. Lejeune[2] had students attend open meetings of Alcoholics Anonymous, posing as alcoholic newcomers to the group. The 'agents' dressed in different social-class styles and made various measurements designed to assess the effect of the relation between the social class of the group and that of the newcomer on his initial acceptance in the group. Fred Davis[3] criticized the authors for, among other things, failing to take into account the effect of publication of the article on the attitudes of A.A. toward social science in view of its possible consequences on the A.A. program. (A.A. groups might have refused to cooperate in further studies had the authors reported, for instance, that A.A. groups discriminate on the basis of social class. That their finding led to no such conclusion does not negate Davis' criticism.)

Lofland[4] suggested in reply that the results of the study were in fact not unfavorable to A.A., that it was published in a place where A.A. members would be unlikely to see it, and, therefore, that no harm was actually done. Julius Roth,[5] commenting on this exchange, noted that the problem is not unique. In a certain sense all social science research is secret, just as the fact that observers were present at A.A. meetings was kept secret from the members. He argued that we decide to study some things only after we have been in the field a while and after the initial agreements with people involved have already been negotiated. Thus, even though it is known that the scientist is making a study, the people under observation do not know what he is studying and would perhaps (in many cases certainly would) object and refuse to countenance the research if they knew what it was about.

When one is doing research on a well-defined organization such as a factory, a hospital or a school, as opposed to some looser organization such as a community or a voluntary association, the problem may arise in slightly different form. The 'top management' of the organization will often be given the right to review the social scientist's manuscript prior to publication. William Foote Whyte describes the kinds of difficulties that may arise.

I encountered such a situation in my research project which led finally to the publication of Human Relations in the Restaurant Industry. *When members of the sponsoring committee of the National Restaurant Association read the first draft of the proposed book, some of them had strong reservations. In fact, one member wrote that he had understood that one of the purposes of establishing an educational and research program at the University of Chicago was to raise the status of the restaurant industry. This book, he claimed, would have the opposite effect, and therefore he recommended that it should not be published. In this case, the Committee on Human Relations in Industry of that university had a contract guaranteeing the right to publish, and I, as author, was to have the final say in the matter. However, I hoped to make the study useful to the industry, and I undertook to see what changes I could make while at the same time retaining what seemed to me, from a scientific standpoint, the heart of the study. . . . The chief problem seemed to be that I had found the workers not having as high a regard for the industry as the sponsoring committee would have liked. Since this seemed to me an important part of the human relations problem, I could hardly cut it out of the book. I was, however, prepared to go as far as I thought possible to change offensive words and phrases in my own text without altering what seemed to me the essential meaning.*[6]

It should be kept in mind that these few published accounts must stand for a considerably larger number of incidents in which the rights of the people studied, from some points of view, have been infringed. The vast majority of such incidents are never reported in print, but are circulated in private conversations and documents. In discussing the problem of publication I am, somewhat ironically, often prevented from being as concrete as I would like to be because I am bound by the fact that many of the cases I know about have been told me in confidence.

Not much is lost by this omission, however. Whether the institution studied is a school for retarded children, an upper-class preparatory school, a college, a mental hospital or a business establishment, the story is much the same. The scientist does a study with the cooperation of the people he studies and writes a report that angers at least some of them. He has then to face the problem of whether to change the report or, if he decides not to, whether to ignore or somehow attempt to deal with their anger.

Conditions affecting publication

Fichter and Kolb have presented the most systematic consideration of ethical problems in reporting.[7] They begin by suggesting that several conditions, which vary from situation to situation, will affect the problem of reporting. First, the social scientist has multiple loyalties: to those who have allowed or sponsored the study, to the source from which research funds were obtained, to the publisher of the research report, to other social scientists, to the society itself and to the community or group studied and its individual members. These loyalties and obligations often conflict. Second, the group under study may or may not be in a position to be affected by the published report. A historical study, describing the way of life of a people who never will have access to the research report, poses few problems, whereas the description of a contemporary community or institution poses many. Third, problems arise when the report analyzes behavior related to traditional and sacred values, such as religion and sex, and also when the report deals with private rather than public facts. Fourth, when data are presented in a statistical form, the problem of identifying an individual does not arise as it does when the mode of analysis is more anthropological.

Fichter and Kolb distinguish three kinds of harm that can be done by a sociological research report. It may reveal secrets, violate privacy or destroy or harm someone's reputation.

Finally, Fichter and Kolb discuss four variables that will affect the social scientist's decision to publish or not to publish. First, his conception of science will affect his action. If he regards social science simply as a game, he must protect the people he has studied at any cost, for his conception of science gives him no warrant or justification for doing anything that might harm them. He will feel a greater urgency if he believes that science can be used to create a better life for people.

The social scientist's decision to publish will also be affected by his determination of the degree of harm that will actually be done to a person or group by the publication of data about them. Fichter and Kolb note that there is a difference between imaginary and real harm and that the subjects of studies may fear harm where none is likely. On the other hand, it may be necessary to cause some harm. People, even those studied by social scientists, must take responsibility for their actions; a false sentimentality must not cause the scientist to cover up that responsibility in his report.

Fichter and Kolb further argue that the scientist's decision to publish will be conditioned by the degree to which he regards the people he has studied as fellow members of his own moral community. If a group (they use the examples of Hitler, Stalin, Murder Incorporated and the Ku Klux Klan) has placed itself outside the moral community, the social scientist can feel free to publish whatever he wants about them without worrying about the harm that may be done. They caution, however, that one should not be too quick to judge another group as being outside the moral community; it is too easy to make the judgment when the group is a disreputable one: homosexuals, drug addicts, unpopular political groups and so on.

Fichter and Kolb conclude by suggesting that the urgency of society's need for the research will also condition the scientist's decision to publish. Where he believes the information absolutely necessary for the determination of public policy, he may decide that it is a lesser evil to harm some of the people he has studied.

Although the statement of Fichter and Kolb is an admirable attempt to deal with the problem of publication, it does not do justice to the complexities involved. In the remainder of this paper I will first consider the possibility that the relationship between the social scientist and those he studies contains elements of irreducible conflict. I will then discuss the reasons why some reports of social science research do not contain conflict-provoking findings. Finally, I will suggest some possible ways of dealing with the problem.

Before embarking on the main line of my argument, I would like to make clear the limits of the area to which my discussion is meant to apply. I assume that the scientist is not engaged in willful and malicious defamation of character, that his published report has some reasonable scientific purpose, and therefore do not consider those cases in which a scientist might attempt, out of malice, ideological or personal, to destroy the reputation of persons or institutions. I further assume that the scientist is subject to no external constraint, other than that imposed by his relationship to those he has studied, which would hinder him in reporting his results fully and freely. In many cases this assumption is not tenable. Vidich and Bensman argue[8] that a researcher who does his work in the setting of a bureaucratic research organization of necessity must be unable to report his results freely; he will have too many obligations to the organization to do anything that would harm its interests in the research situation and thus cannot make the kind of report required by the ethic of scientific inquiry. Although I do not share their belief that bureaucratic research organizations necessarily and inevitably restrict scientific freedom, this result certainly occurs frequently. (One should remember, however, that the implied corollary of their proposition – that the individual researcher will be bound only by the ethic of scientific inquiry – is also often untrue. Individual researchers on many occasions have shown themselves to be so bound by organizational or ideological commitments as to be unable to report their results freely.) In any case my argument deals with the researcher who is encumbered only by his own conscience.

The irreducible conflict

Fichter and Kolb seem to assume that, except for Hitler, Stalin and others who are not members of our moral community, there is no irreconcilable conflict between the researcher and those he studies. In some cases he will clearly harm people and will refrain from publication; in others no harm will be done and publication is not problematic. The vast majority of cases will fall between and, as men of good will, the researcher and those he studies will be able to find some common ground for decision.

But this analysis can be true only when there is some consensus about norms and some community of interest between the two parties. In my view that consensus and community of interest do not exist for the sociologist and those he studies.

The impossibility of achieving consensus, and hence the necessity of conflict, stems in part from the difference between the characteristic approach of the social scientist and that of the layman to the analysis of social life. Everett Hughes has often pointed out that the sociological view of the world – abstract, relativistic and generalizing – necessarily deflates people's view of themselves and their organizations. Sociological analysis has this effect whether it consists of a detailed description of informal behavior or an abstract discussion of theoretical categories. The members of a church, for instance, may be no happier to learn that their behavior exhibits the influence of 'pattern variables' than to read a description of their everyday behavior which shows that it differs radically from what they profess on Sunday morning in church. In either case something precious to them is treated as merely an instance of a class.

Consensus cannot be achieved also because organizations and communities are internally differentiated and the interests of subgroups differ. The scientific report that pleases one faction and serves its interests will offend another faction by attacking its interests. Even to say that factions exist may upset the faction in control. What upsets management may be welcomed by the lower ranks, who hope the report will improve their position. Since one cannot achieve consensus with all factions simultaneously, the problem is not to avoid harming people but rather to decide which people to harm.

Trouble occurs primarily, however, because what the social scientist reports is what the people studied would prefer not to know, no matter how obvious or easy it is to discover. Typically, the social scientist offends those he studies by describing deviations, either from some formal or informal rule, or from a strongly held ideal. The deviations reported are things that, according to the ideals of the people under study, should be punished and corrected, but about which, for various reasons that seem compelling to them, nothing can be done. In other words the research report reveals that things are not as they ought to be and that nothing is being done about it. By making his report the social scientist makes the deviation public and may thereby force people to enforce a rule they have allowed to lapse. He blows the whistle both on those who are deviating but not being punished for it and on those who are allowing the deviation to go unpunished.[9] Just as the federal government, by making public the list of persons to whom it has sold a gambling-tax stamp, forces local law-enforcement officials to take action against gamblers whose existence they have always known of, so the social scientist, by calling attention to deviations, forces those in power to take action about things they know to exist but about which they do not want to do anything.

Certain typical forms of blowing the whistle recur in many studies. A study of a therapeutic organization – a mental hospital, a general hospital, a rehabilitation center – may show that many institutional practices are essentially custodial and may in fact be antitherapeutic. A study of a school reveals that the curriculum does not have the intended effect on students, and that many students turn out to be quite different from what the members of the faculty would like them to be. A study of a factory or office discloses that many customary practices are, far from being rational and businesslike, irrational and wasteful. Another typical situation has already been mentioned: a study reveals that members of the lower ranks of an organization dislike their subordinate position.

Nor is this phenomenon peculiar to studies that depend largely on the techniques of anthropological field work, though it is probably most common among them. Any kind of social science research may evoke a hostile reaction when it is published. Official statistics put out by communities or organizations can do this. For example, remember the indignation when the 1960 Census revealed that many major cities had lost population, the demands for recounts by Chambers of Commerce, and so on. By simply enumerating the number of inhabitants in a city, and reporting that number publicly, the Bureau of the Census deflated many public-relations dreams and caused a hostile reaction. The statistics on admissions and discharges to hospitals, on salaries and similar matters kept by hospitals and other institutions can similarly be analyzed to reveal great discrepancies, and the revelation can cause much hostile criticism. The results of survey research similarly can cause trouble, as for instance, when a survey of students reveals that they have reactionary political or cultural attitudes. A program of testing can produce the same result by showing that an organization does not recruit people of as high a caliber as it claims, or that a school does not have the effect on its students it supposes it has. Any kind of research, in short, can expose a disparity between reality and some rule or ideal and cause trouble.

That the sociologist, by publishing his findings, blows the whistle on deviance whose existence is not publicly acknowledged may explain why the poor, powerless and disreputable seldom complain about the studies published about them. They seldom complain, of course, because they are seldom organized enough to do so. Yet I think further reasons for their silence can be found. The deviance of homosexuals or drug addicts is no secret. They have nothing to lose by a further exposure and may believe that an honest account of their lives will counter the stereotypes that have grown up about them. My own studies of dance musicians and marihuana users bear this out.[10] Marihuana users, particularly, urged me to finish my study quickly and publish it so that people could 'know the truth' about them.

It may be thought that social science research exposes deviation only when the scientist has an ax to grind, when he is particularly interested in exposing evil. This is not the case. As Vidich and Bensman note:

One of the principal ideas of our book is that the public atmosphere of an organization or a community tends to be optimistic, positive, and geared to the public relations image of the community or the organization. The public mentality veils the dynamics and functional determin-

ants of the group being studied. Any attempt in social analysis at presenting other than public relations rends the veil and must necessarily cause resentment. Moreover, any organization tends to represent a balance of divergent interests held in some kind of equilibrium by the power status of the parties involved. A simple description of these factors, no matter how stated, will offend some of the groups in question.[11]

Unless the scientist deliberately restricts himself to research on the ideologies and beliefs of the people studied and does not touch on the behavior of the members of the community or organization, he must in some way deal with the disparity between reality and ideal, with the discrepancy between the number of crimes committed and the number of criminals apprehended. A study that purports to deal with social structure thus inevitably will reveal that the organization or community is not all it claims to be, not all it would like to be able to feel itself to be. A good study, therefore, will make somebody angry.

Self-censorship: a danger

I have just argued that a good study of a community or organization must reflect the irreconcilable conflict between the interests of science and the interests of those studied, and thereby provoke a hostile reaction. Yet many studies conducted by competent scientists do not have this consequence. Under what circumstances will the report of a study fail to provoke conflict? Can such a failure be justified?

In the simplest case, the social scientist may be taken in by those he studies and be kept from seeing the things that would cause conflict were he to report them. Melville Dalton states the problem for studies of industry.

In no case did I make a formal approach to the top management of any of the firms to get approval or support for the research. Several times I have seen other researchers do this and have watched higher managers set the scene and limit the inquiry to specific areas — outside management proper — as though the problem existed in a vacuum. The findings in some cases were then regarded as 'controlled experiments', which in final form made impressive reading. But the smiles and delighted manipulation of researchers by guarded personnel, the assessments made of researchers and their findings, and the frequently trivial areas to which alerted and fearful officers guided the inquiry — all raised questions about who controlled the experiments.[12]

This is probably an uncommon occurrence. Few people social scientists study are sophisticated enough to anticipate or control what the researcher will see. More frequently, the social scientist takes himself in, 'goes native', becomes identified with the ideology of the dominant faction in the organization or community and frames the question to which his research provides answers so that no one will be hurt. He does not do this deliberately or with the intent to suppress scientific knowledge. Rather, he unwittingly chooses problems that are not likely to cause trouble or inconvenience to those he has found to be such pleasant associates. Herbert Butterfield, the British historian, puts the point well in his discussion of the dangers of 'official history'. He talks of the problems that arise when a government allows historians access to secret documents.

A Foreign Secretary once complained that, while he, for his part, was only trying to be helpful, Professor Temperley (as one of the editors of the British Documents [On the Origins of the War of 1914]) *persisted in treating him as though he were a hostile Power. Certainly it is possible for the historian to be unnecessarily militant, and even a little ungracious in his militancy; but what a satisfaction it is to the student if he can be sure that his interests have been guarded with the unremitting jealousy! And if we employ a watchdog (which is the function the independent historian would be expected to perform on our behalf), what an assurance it is to be able to feel that we are served by one whom we know to be vigilant and unsleeping! The ideal, in this respect, would certainly not be represented by the picture of a Professor Temperley and a Foreign Secretary as thick as thieves, each merely thinking the other a jolly good fellow; for this historian who is collecting evidence — and particularly the historian who pretends as an independent authority to certify the documents or verify the claims of the government department — must be as jealous and importunate as the cad of a detective who has to find the murderer amongst a party of his friends. One of the widest of the general causes of historical error has been the disposition of a Macaulay to recognize in the case of Tory witnesses a need for historical criticism which it did not occur to him to have in the same way for the witnesses on his own side. Nothing in the whole of historiography is more subtly dangerous than the natural disposition to withhold criticism because John Smith belongs to one's own circle or because he is a nice man, so that it seems ungracious to try to press him on a point too far, or because it does not occur to one that something more could be extracted from him by importunate endeavor. In this sense all is not lost if our historian-detective even makes himself locally unpopular; for (to take an imaginary case) if he communicates to us his judgment that the Foreign Office does not burn important papers, the point is not without its interest; but we could only attach weight to the judgment if he had gone into the matter with all the alertness of an hostile enquirer and with the keenly critical view concerning the kind of evidence which could possibly authorise a detective to come to such a conclusion. And if an historian were to say: 'This particular group of documents ought not to be published, because it would expose the officials concerned to serious misunderstandings', then we must answer that he has already thrown in his lot with officialdom — already he is thinking of their interests rather than ours; for since these documents, by definition, carry us outside the framework of stories somebody wants to impose on us, they are the very ones that the independent historian must most desire. To be sure, no documents can be published without laying many people open to griev-ous misunderstanding. In this connection an uncommon significance must attach therefore to the choice of the people who are to be spared. The only way to reduce misunderstanding is to keep up the clamour for more and more of the strategic kinds of evidence. . . .*[13]

It is essential for everybody to be aware that the whole problem of 'censorship' to-day has been transformed into the phenomenon of 'auto-censorship' — a matter to be borne in mind even when the people involved are only indirectly the servants of government, or are attached by no further tie than the enjoyment of privileges that might be taken away. It is even true that where all are 'pals' there is no need for censorship, no point where it is necessary to imagine that one man is being overruled by another. And in any case it is possible to conceive of a State in which members of different organizations could control or prevent a revelation with nothing more than a hint or a wink as they casually pass one another amidst the crowd at some tea-party.[14]

Although Butterfield is speaking of the relations of the social scientist to a national government, it takes no great leap of imagination to see the relevance of his discussion to the problem of the sociologist who has studied a community or organization.

Finally, even if he is not deceived in either of the ways so far suggested, the social scientist may deliberately decide to suppress conflict-provoking findings. He may suppress his findings because publication will violate a bargain he has made with those studied. If, for example, he has given the subjects of his study the right to excise offensive portions of his manuscript prior to publication in return for the privilege of making the study, he will feel bound to honor that agreement. Because of the far-reaching consequences such an agree-ment could have, most social scientists take care to specify, when reaching an agreement with an organization they want to study, that they have the final say as to what will be published, though they often grant representatives of the organization the right to review the manu-script and suggest changes.

The social scientist may also suppress his findings because of an ideological commitment to the maintenance of society as it is now constituted. Shils makes the following case.

Good arguments can be made against continuous publicity about public institutions. It could be claimed that extreme publicity not only breaks the confidentiality which enhances the imaginativeness and reflective-ness necessary for the effective working of institutions but also destroys the respect in which they should, at least tentatively, be held by the citizenry.[15]

He believes that the first of these considerations is probably correct and thus constitutes a legitimate restriction on scientific inquiry, whereas the second, although not entirely groundless ethically, is so unlikely to occur as not to constitute a clear danger.

It is only in the case of deliberate suppression that an argument can be made, for in the other two cases the scientist presumably reports all his findings, the difficulty arising from his failure to make them in the first place. I will discuss the problem of the research bargain in the next section, in the context of possible solutions to the problem of publication. It remains only to consider Shils' argument before concluding that there is no reasonable basis for avoiding conflict over publication by failing to include the items that will provoke conflict.

Shils rests his case on the possibility that the publicity generated by research may interfere with the 'effective working of institutions'. When this occurs the scientist should restrict his inquiry. We can accept this argument only if we agree that the effective working of institutions as they are presently constituted is an overriding good. Shils, in his disdain for the 'populistic' frame of mind that has informed much of American sociology (his way of characterizing the 'easy-going irreverence toward authority' and the consequent tendency to social criticism among social scientists), is probably more ready to accept such a proposition than the majority of working social scientists. Furthermore, and I do not know that he would carry his argument so far, the right of public institutions to delude themselves about the character of their actions and the consequences of those actions does not seem to me easily defended.

Possible solutions

An apparently easy solution to the dilemma of publishing findings and interpretations that may harm those studied is to decide that if a proper bargain has been struck at the beginning of a research relationship no one has any right to complain. If the researcher has agreed to allow those studied to censor his report, he cannot complain when they do. If the people studied have been properly warned, in sufficient and graphic detail, of the consequences of a report about them and have still agreed to have a study done, then they cannot complain if the report is not what they would prefer. But the solution, from the point of view of either party, ignores the real problems.

From the scientist's point of view, the problem is only pushed back a step. Instead of asking what findings he should be prepared to publish, we ask what bargain he should be prepared to strike. Considering only his own scientific interests, he should clearly drive the hardest bargain, demanding complete freedom, and should settle for less only when he must in order to gain access to a theoretically important class of institutions that would otherwise be closed to him.

When we look at the problem from the side of those studied, reaching a firm bargain is also only an apparent solution. As Roth pointed out,[16] the people who agree to have a social scientist study them have not had the experience before and do not know what to expect; nor are they aware of the experience of others social scientists have studied. Even if the social scientist has pointed out the possible consequences of a report, the person whose organization or community is to be studied is unlikely to think it will happen to him; he cannot believe this fine fellow, the social scientist with whom he now sees eye to eye, would actually do something to harm him. He thinks the social scientist, being a fine fellow, will abide by the ethics of the group under study, not realizing the force and scope of the scientist's impersonal ethic and, particularly, of the scientific obligation to report findings fully and frankly. He may feel easy, having been assured that no specific item of behavior will be attributed to any particular person, but will he think of the 'tone' of the report, said to be offensive to the inhabitants of Springdale?

Making a proper research bargain, then, is no solution to the problem of publication. Indeed, with respect to the question of *what to publish*, I think there is no general solution except as one may be dictated by the individual's conscience. But there are other questions and it is possible to take constructive action on them without prejudicing one's right to publish. The social scientist can warn those studied of the effect of publication and help them prepare for it. When his report is written he can help those concerned to assimilate what it says and adjust to the consequences of being reported on publicly.

It is probably true that the first sociological report on a given kind of institution sits least well, and that succeeding studies are less of a shock to those studied, creating fewer problems both for the researcher and those he studies. The personnel of the first mental hospital or prison studied by sociologists probably took it harder than those of similar institutions studied later. Once the deviations characteristic of a whole class of institutions have been exposed they are no longer secrets peculiar to one. Subsequent reports have less impact. They only affirm that the deviations found in one place also exist elsewhere. Those whose institutions are the subject of later reports can only suffer from having it shown that they have the same faults, a lesser crime than being the only place where such deviations occur. The difference between 'In this mental hospital attendants beat patients' and 'In this mental hospital *also*, attendants beat patients' may seem small, but the consequences of the difference are large and important.

By having those he studies read earlier reports on their kind of institution or community, the social scientist can lead them to understand that what he reports about them is not unique. By making available to them other studies, which describe similar deviations in other kinds of institutions and communities, he can teach them that the deviations whose exposure they fear are in fact characteristic features of all human organizations and societies. Thus a carefully thought out educational program may help those reported on come to terms with what the scientist reports, and spare both parties unnecessary difficulties.

The program might take the form of a series of seminars or conversations, in which the discussion would move from a consideration of social science in general to studies of similar institutions, culminating in a close analysis of the about-to-be-published report. In analyzing the report the social scientist can point out the two contexts in which publication will have meaning for those it describes.

First, it can affect their relations with other groups outside the institution: the press, the public, national professional organizations, members of other professions, clients, citizens' watchdog groups, and so on. By describing facts about the organization that may be interpreted as deviations by outside groups, the social scientist may endanger the institution's position with them. Second, the publication of descriptions of deviation may add fuel to internal political fires.[17] The social scientist, by discussing the report with those it describes, can help them to face these problems openly and warn them against one-sided interpretations of his data and analyses. For instance, he can help them to see the kinds of interpretations that may be made of his report by outside groups, aid them in assessing the possibility of serious damage (which they are likely to overestimate), and let them test on him possible answers they might make to adverse reaction.

If he confers with institutional personnel, he will no doubt be present when various people attempt to make use of his work in a selective or distorted way for internal political advantage, when they cite fragments of his conclusions in support of a position they have taken on some institutional or community issue. He can then, at the moment it takes place, correct the distortion or selective citation and force those involved to see the issue in more complete perspective.

In conferring with representatives of the institution or community, the social scientist should keep two things in mind. First, although he should be sensitive to the damage his report might do, he should not simply take complaints and make revisions so that the complaints will cease. Even with his best efforts, the complaints may remain, because an integral part of his analysis has touched on some chronic sore point in the organization; if this is the case, he must publish his report without changing the offending portions. Second, his conferences with representatives of the organization should not simply be attempts to softsoap them into believing that no damage will occur when, in fact, it may. He must keep this possibility alive for them and make them take it seriously; unless he does, he is only postponing the complaints and difficulties to a later time when reactions to the report, within and outside the organization, will bring them out in full strength. In this connection it is useful to make clear to those studied that the preliminary report, if that is what they are given, is slated for publication in some form, even though it may be substantially revised; this fact is sometimes forgotten and many criticisms that would be made if it were clear that the document was intended for publication are not made, with the result that the process must be gone through again when the final version is prepared.

People whose organizations have been studied by social scientists often complain that the report made about them is 'pessimistic' or 'impractical', and their complaint points to another reason for their anger. Insofar as the report gives the impression that the facts and situations it describes are irremediable, it puts them in the position of being chronic offenders for whom there is no hope. Although some social science reports have such a pessimistic tone, it is more often the case that the report makes clear that there are no easy solutions to the organization's problems. There are solutions, but they are solutions that call for major changes in organizational practice, and for this reason they are likely to be considered impractical. The social scientist can explain that there are no panaceas, no small shifts in practice that will do away with the 'evils' his report describes without in any way upsetting existing arrangements, and thus educate those he has studied to the unpleasant truth that they cannot change the things they want to change without causing repercussions in other parts of the organization.[18] By the same token, however, he can point to the directions in which change is possible, even though difficult, and thus relieve them of the oppressive feeling that they have no way out.

A regime of conferring with and educating those studied may seem like an additional and unwelcome job for the social scientist to take on. Is it not difficult enough to do the field work, analyze the data and prepare a report, without taking on further obligations? Why not finish the work and leave, letting someone else bear the burden of educating the subjects of the study? Although flight may often seem the most attractive alternative, the social scientist should remember that, in the course of working over his report with those it describes, he may get some extremely useful data. For instance, in the course of discussions about the possible effect of the report on various audiences, it is possible to discover new sources of constraint on the actors involved that had not turned up in the original study. One may be told about sources of inhibition of change that are so pervasive as to never have been mentioned until a discussion of change, occasioned by the report, brings them to light. The desire for further data, coupled with simple altruism and the desire to avoid trouble, may prove sufficiently strong motive for an educational effort.

Conclusion

In discussing the several facets of the problem, I have avoided stating any ethical canons. I have relied on those canons implicit in the scientific enterprise in suggesting that the scientist must strive for the freest possible conditions of reporting. Beyond that I have said only that it is a matter of individual conscience. In so restricting my remarks and in discussing the problem largely in technical terms, I have not meant to indicate that one need have no conscience at all, but only that it must remain a matter of individual judgment.

I ought properly, therefore, to express my own judgment. Briefly, it is that one should refrain from publishing items of fact or conclusions that are not necessary to one's argument or that would cause suffering out of proportion to the scientific gain of making them public. This judgment is of course ambiguous. When is something 'necessary' to an argument? What is 'suffering'? When is an amount of suffering 'out of proportion'? Even though the statement as it stands cannot determine a clear line of action for any given situation, I think it does suggest a viable vantage point, an appropriate mood, from which decisions can be approached. In particular, it suggests on the one hand that the scientist must be able to give himself good reasons for including potentially harmful material, rather than including it simply because it is 'interesting'. On the other hand, it guards him against either an overly formal or an overly sentimental view of the harm those he studies may suffer, requiring that it be serious and substantial enough to warrant calling it 'suffering'. Finally, it insists that he know enough about the situation he has studied to know whether the suffering will in any sense be proportional to gains science may expect from publication of his findings.

The judgment I have expressed is clearly not very original. Nor is it likely that any judgment expressed by a working social scientist would be strikingly original. All the reasonable positions have been stated long ago. The intent of this paper has been to show that a sociological understanding of what we do when we publish potentially harmful materials may help us make the ethical decision that we must, inevitably, make alone.

Notes and References

1. The discussion of the Springdale case began with an editorial, 'Freedom and responsibility in research: the "Springdale case"', in *Human Organization,* **17** (Summer 1958), 1–2. This editorial provoked comments by Arthur Vidich and Joseph Bensman, Robert Risley, Raymond E. Ries and Howard S. Becker, *ibid.,* **17** (Winter 1958–59), 2–7, and by Earl H. Bell and Ure Bronfenbrenner, *ibid.,* **18** (Summer 1959), 49–52. A final statement by Vidich appeared in *ibid.,* **19** (Spring 1960), 3–4. The book whose effects are discussed is Arthur Vidich and Joseph Bensman (1958) *Small Town in Mass Society.* Princeton, N.J.: Princeton University Press, 1958.
2. John F. Lofland and Robert A. Lejeune, 'Initial interaction of newcomers in Alcoholics Anonymous: a field experiment in class symbols and socialization', *Social Problems,* **8,** (Fall 1960), 102–11.

3. Fred Davis, 'Comment', *Social Problems,* **8** (Spring 1961), 364–5.
4. John F. Lofland, 'Reply to Davis', *ibid.,* 365–7.
5. Julius A. Roth, 'Comments on secret observation', *Social Problems,* **9** (Winter 1962), 283–4.
6. William Foote Whyte (1959), *Man and Organization: Three Problems in Human Relations in Industry.* Homewood, Ill.: Irwin, pp. 96–7.
7. Joseph H. Fichter and William L. Kolb, 'Ethical limitations on sociological reporting', *American Sociological Review,* **18** (Oct. 1953), pp. 96–7.
8. Arthur Vidich and Joseph Bensman (1964) 'The Springdale case: academic bureaucrats and sensitive townspeople', in Arthur J. Vidich *et al., Reflections on Community Studies.* New York: Wiley, pp. 345–8.
9. I have discussed the role of the person who makes deviation public, the rule enforcer, at some length in *Outsiders: Studies in the Sociology of Deviance.* New York: Free Press of Glencoe, 1963, pp. 155–63.
10. The studies are reported in Becker, *Outsiders, op. cit.,* pp. 41–9.
11. Vidich and Bensman, (1959) 'Comment', *op. cit.*
12. Melville Dalton (1959) *Men Who Manage: Fusions of Feeling and Theory in Administration.* New York: Wiley, p. 275.
13. Herbert Butterfield (1951) 'Official history: its pitfalls and criteria', in his *History and Human Relations.* London: Collins, pp. 194–5.
14. *Ibid.,* pp. 197–8.
15. Edward A. Shils (1959) 'Social inquiry and the autonomy of the individual', in Danier Lerner (ed.), *Meaning of the Social Sciences.* New York: Meridian Books, p. 137. I am indebted to William Kornhauser for calling this article to my attention.
16. Roth, *op. cit.*
17. The danger of exposure to external publics is most salient in studies of institutions; the danger of exposure of deviation within the group studied is most important in studies of communities.
18. See the discussion of panaceas in Howard S. Becker and Blanche Geer (1963) 'Medical education', in Howard E. Freeman, Leo G. Reeder, and Sol Levine (eds), *Handbook of Medical Sociology.* Englewood Cliffs, N.J.: Prentice-Hall, pp. 180–4.

Index